AN INTRODUCTION
TO RHETORICAL
COMMUNICATION

EIGHTH EDITION

AN INTRODUCTION TO RHETORICAL COMMUNICATION

JAMES C. McCROSKEY

West Virginia University

Allyn and Bacon

Boston • London • Toronto • Sydney • Tokyo • Singapore

iii

Series Editor: *Karon Bowers*
Editor-in-chief, social sciences: *Karen Hanson*
Series editorial assistant: *Jennifer Becker*
Marketing manager: *Jackie Aaron*
Composition and prepress buyer: *Linda Cox*
Manufacturing buyer: *Julie McNeill*
Cover administrator: *Jenny Hart*
Editorial-production service: *Shepherd, Inc.*
Text designer: *Shepherd, Inc.*
Electronic composition: *Shepherd, Inc.*

Library of Congress Cataloging-in-Publication Data

McCroskey, James C.
    An introduction to rhetorical communication / James C. McCroskey.—8th ed.
    p. cm.
    Includes bibliographical references and indexes.
    ISBN 0-205-31722-7
    1. Oral communication.   I. Title.

PN4121.M24 2000
302.2'242—dc20   00-022630
                                                             CIP

Printed in the United States of America
10 9 8 7 6 5 4 3 2 1 05 04 03 02 01 00

Photo Credits
p.4, Corbis/Bettman; p. 32, Tony Freeman, Photo Edit; p. 44, Will Faller; p. 68, Robert Harbison; p. 84, Robert Harbison; p. 130, John Coletti; p. 170, Will Hart; p. 185, John Coletti; p. 195, Robert Harbison; p. 218, Peter Southwick, Stock/Boston; p. 234, Library of Congress; p. 252, Brian Smith; p. 279, Will Faller; p. 299, Richard Drew, Wide World Photos.

CONTENTS

■ ■ ■ ■ ■

CHAPTER EIGHT
Diversity and Culture   142

PART III   MESSAGE PREPARATION
AND PRESENTATION   161

CHAPTER NINE
Message Preparation:
Preliminary Considerations   163

CHAPTER TEN

Informative Messages   175

CHAPTER ELEVEN

Message Preparation: Invention   188

CHAPTER TWELVE
Message Preparation: Disposition   214

CHAPTER THIRTEEN
Message Preparation: Style   232

CHAPTER FOURTEEN
Introducing and Concluding Messages in Rhetorical Communication   251

CHAPTER FIFTEEN
Message Presentation: Oral Delivery   269

PREFACE

The eighth edition of *An Introduction to Rhetorical Communication* appears as the world enters a new millennium. The study of communication is entering its sixth millennium. The study of rhetorical communication is well into its third millennium. When we reference anything in terms of millennia, we are considering time on such a massive scale it is difficult to bring it into the context of our own brief existence. And yet, maybe this is the appropriate context for understanding the place of communication in the history of human existence. The study of communication is among the most ancient of human concerns.

When the first edition of this book was written, my purpose was to draw on both classical rhetorical theory and contemporary social science to provide a coherent introduction to the study of rhetorical communication. That remains the purpose of the eighth edition. However, the eighth edition is born into a world that has changed dramatically from the world of the first edition. We now live in a world society. The days of the insular national society have past. The monocultural existence lived by most people in both the developed and underdeveloped worlds of the 1960s has given way to the multinational, multicultural existence most people experience today. These changes have not changed the core nature of rhetorical communication. However, they have made effective rhetoric even more difficult. With the major advances of opportunity experienced by minorities and women, the expansion of the internet, the World Wide Web, the development of dominant multinational corporations in most aspects of the world economy, and the free flow of international travel, there are many, many more rhetorical communicators than ever before. And the diversity of both sources and receivers of rhetorical communication makes classical theory's injunction to "analyze and adapt to your audience" a much more profound, and difficult, demand than ever before. This book is designed to assist you in developing your abilities to meet that demand.

The book is organized in four sections. The first section is devoted to getting started. Chapter 1 traces the long and distinguished history of rhetorical theory. Chapter 2 provides an overview of the elements inherent in rhetorical communication. Chapter 3 focuses on the most serious problem many students face when attempting to learn to be effective speakers: stage fright. I have attempted to synthesize the latest thoughts generated from work on self-perception of communication competence, willingness to communicate, and communication apprehension with both the older and the newest work in the area of stage fright, including the new communibiological approach. I believe it is the most thorough and up-to-date explanation of the problem available. Understanding stage fright will not magically make it go away, but such understanding is a vital step in controlling this problem.

The second section is devoted to basic theory about rhetorical communication. The concern of this section is the traditional concern of scholars in rhetorical communication: the audience (Chapter 4); the speaker (Chapter 5); and the message, both verbal (Chapter 6) and nonverbal (Chapter 7). In keeping with the times, an important chapter has been added to this section, a chapter on Diversity and Culture (Chapter 8). These chapters form the foundation upon which the remainder of the book is based.

The third section of the book focuses specifically on rhetorical communication in one-to-many contexts. The section opens with a discussion of the basic steps in developing a message (Chapter 9). This is followed by a chapter on informative messages (Chapter 10). The remainder of the section is directed toward four of the five classical rhetorical cannons— invention (Chapter 11), disposition (Chapter 12), style (Chapter 13), and delivery (15)—and to the problems of introducing and concluding messages (Chapter 14).

The final chapter (16) is the only one included in Section 4. It has remained virtually unchanged through all eight editions. It focuses on "Ethics and Rhetorical Communication." Its purpose in this edition, as it has been for each previous edition, is to provoke discussion of the important ethical choices facing people as rhetorical communicators. While many will prefer to read this chapter last, it is written purposefully so that it does not require reading the previous chapters for full understanding. Hence, you are encouraged to read it earlier and use it to help you evaluate the other aspects of rhetorical communication. Some readers have been enthusiastic in their praise for the views expressed in this chapter. Others have been equally enthusiastic in their condemnation of these same views. It is clear that the chapter accomplishes the purpose for which it was written.

Appendix A contains six examples of verbal messages employed in rhetorical communication. The first five speeches, all of which have appeared in previous editions, provide a wide variety of speaking styles and topics. The "newcomer" to this edition is a timely speech by actor and outspoken leader of the National Rifle Association, Charlton Heston. This speech was addressed to college students, but caused quite a stir in many political camps. The topic, "Winning the Cultural War," is particularly relevant to the cultural stress felt on many college and university campuses today.

I want to express my appreciation to several individuals:

To David A. Frank, Glenn Kuper, and James Vickrey for providing particularly useful pre-revision reviews of IRC's seventh edition.

To Robert Stephen Reid for catching an error printed in all previous editions. Hermagoras now has his rightful place in Chapter 12.

And, to Karon Bowers for being one the best editors with whom I have had the pleasure of working over the past 35 years of book-writing.

Thank you all for making this edition the best one yet.

James C. McCroskey
Morgantown, W. V.

PART **I**

GETTING STARTED

■ ■ ■ ■ ■ ▬▬▬▬▬▬▬▬▬▬▬▬▬▬▬▬▬▬▬▬▬▬▬▬▬▬▬▬

CHAPTER 1

A RHETORICAL TRADITION

In theory and in practice, rhetorical communication has a long and distinguished history. Since this book has evolved from that tradition, it is important to become familiar with some of that history to better understand how we got to where we are today. It is not possible to present a complete survey of that history within the limited space available here. Such a survey would necessitate not several chapters in a book, but several volumes. This survey, therefore, must be sketchy and selective, restricted to introducing some of the key figures and some of the significant developments in the long history of rhetorical communication. It does not include the great orators of history, although their contribution to the theory of rhetorical communication has certainly been important. Rather, attention focuses primarily on the authors whose works have influenced the development of rhetorical theory. In some cases, the influence has been positive; in others, negative. The purpose here is merely to indicate some of the highlights of the history of rhetorical communication in order to provide a better base from which to evaluate and understand the theory discussed throughout this book.

Before exploring the specifics of this historical view, it is important to place this book into perspective. There is much concern in contemporary higher education with a diversity of cultural views. The rhetorical communication perspective, while evolving from a variety of cultures, is not a multicultural one. It represents one primary cultural view of human communication. The cultural view within which the history of rhetorical communication has evolved is best described as a Greco-Roman, Judeo-Christian world view. Its primary influences have come from the Middle East, Europe, and Northern Africa. It has had its most profound impact in areas now dominated by English-speaking peoples, although it is not without influence in other parts of the world.

Manifestations of this approach to human communication are apparent in, and have a major impact on, the legal, political, and economic structures of many countries, probably most notably the United States. Thus, if one is to understand these structures, one must understand the nature of rhetorical communication within these cultures. This world view sees communication as an instrumental activity. That is, communication is seen as the way people get things done. It flourishes in environments that view freedom, liberty, justice, equality, individual responsibility, and the importance of the individual as primary values. It should be recognized from the outset, then, that the rhetorical communication perspective is not the only way significant numbers of people in the world come to view communication. It is, however, the only view that will be explored in this book.

EARLIEST WRITINGS

The importance of rhetorical communication has been recognized for thousands of years. The oldest essay ever discovered, written about 3000 B.C., consists of advice on how to speak effectively. This essay was inscribed on a fragment of parchment addressed to Kagemni, the eldest son of the pharaoh Huni. Similarly, the oldest extant book is a treatise on effective communication. Known as the *Precepts,* this book was composed in Egypt about 2675 B.C. by Ptah-Hotep. It was written for the guidance of the pharaoh's son. These works are significant because they establish the historical fact that interest in rhetorical communication is nearly five thousand years old, the actual contribution they made to subsequent rhetorical theory was minimal. It is very doubtful that rhetorical theorists for several thousand years afterward were even aware that these works had been written.

THE GREEK PERIOD

Most scholars agree that the history of rhetorical communication as we know it today begins some twenty-five hundred years after Kagemni's early

writing, during the fifth century B.C., at Syracuse, in Sicily. Although isolated bits of information concerning communication were found in Homer's works, the formulation of the first works on rhetorical communication in Greece is generally attributed to Corax and Tisias. When a democratic regime was established in Syracuse after the overthrow of Thrasybulus, the citizens flooded the courts to recover property that had been confiscated during the reign of this tyrant. The "art of rhetoric" that Corax developed was intended to help ordinary people prove their claims in court. Although Corax and his pupil Tisias are usually credited with the authorship of a manual on public speaking, the work is no longer extant. We are not certain of its contents, but scholars have suggested that it included two items significant for the later development of rhetorical theory. The first was a theory of how arguments should be developed from probabilities, a theory that was to be much more fully developed by Aristotle a century later. Corax and Tisias are also generally credited with developing the first concept of organization of a message. They suggested that a message should have at least three parts: a proem, a narration or demonstration, and an epilogue. These three parts are roughly equivalent to the three parts we say should be included in a message today: an introduction, a body, and a conclusion.

The term *sophistry* is generally thought of today as referring to deceitful reasoning. As originally used, the term *sophist* referred to anyone who was a teacher. In Athens, during the fifth century B.C., a comparatively large number of itinerant teachers lectured on literature, science, philosophy, and, particularly, rhetoric. These sophists set up small schools and charged their students fees for tutoring. The schools proved to be so rewarding financially that a number of rather unscrupulous people were drawn into the profession. These were the individuals who eventually brought the sophists an unsavory reputation. It is most incorrect, however, to attribute to all the sophists the deplorable characteristics of these unscrupulous individuals. In fact, many of the sophists were highly moral people who made major contributions to the theory of rhetorical communication.

Protagoras of Abdara, sometimes called the father of debate, was one of the first and most important sophists. In his teaching he contended that there were two sides to every proposition and that speakers ought to be able to argue either side. This view, which is still commonly accepted by teachers of argumentation, debate, and law, was one of Protagoras's three main contributions to rhetorical thought. Protagoras also introduced the concept of *commonplaces,* that is, segments of speeches constructed in such a way that they had no reference to any particular occasion but could be used whenever a person was called upon to speak in public. Protagoras is also generally credited with being the founder of our system of grammar. He classified and distinguished the parts of speech, the tenses, and the moods.

Contemporary with Protagoras was Gorgias of Leontini. Gorgias is recognized as one of the first rhetoricians to perceive the importance of exciting the emotions in persuasion. The Platonic dialogue that bears Gorgias' name portrays him as an individual not concerned with the ethics of his means of persuasion. In addition, Gorgias placed great emphasis on style, particularly on the figures of speech, such as antithesis and parallelism. Later rhetoricians who concentrated on the cultivation of a highly literary style of address may be thought of as following the tradition started by Gorgias.

The most influential of the Greek sophists was clearly Isocrates. Indeed, his influence probably was even greater during the Greek period than that of Aristotle. Isocrates also represents the best of the sophists in another context: He was a highly ethical man with noble ideas and unimpeachable standards of intellectual integrity. Just where he received his education is not clear, but it is believed that he studied under Tisias and that he also may have studied under Gorgias and Socrates. There is no question, however, about his impact as a teacher. When he set up a school of oratory, he soon had more students than any other sophist, even though he charged unusually high tuition fees. In fact, he managed to acquire considerable wealth as a result of his teaching.

A reticent man with a weak voice, Isocrates was never himself an orator. However, he wrote many fine orations for other people to deliver. Although many discourses by Isocrates are extant, his *Art of Rhetoric* has been lost. Two of his works, *Antidosis* and *Against the Sophists,* provide us with some insight into his thinking.

Isocrates made two major contributions to the theory of rhetoric. One was his development of rhetorical style. He took the artificial and exaggerated style of Gorgias and refined it into an appropriate vehicle for both spoken and written communication. Probably Isocrates' most important contribution was his view of the proper education of the ideal orator. He believed that the whole person must be brought to bear upon the process of communication. Therefore, the orator should be trained in the liberal arts and, above all else, be a good person. This view had a major influence upon both Cicero and Quintilian.

Although we refer to the teachers of rhetoric during the early Greek period as the sophists, we should take care to avoid thinking of the individual sophists as being all alike. They were as diverse as teachers are today. Although some were exhibitionists and unscrupulous practitioners, others were highly moral and significant theorists. From this group sprang both ideas that were to become basic tenets of solid rhetorical theory and ideas that were to lead to the decay, and almost the demise, of rhetorical theory. The sophists' contributions to their society were major, and their contributions to our society's view of communication are only slightly smaller.

Plato is generally credited with two major contributions to the development of rhetorical theory. Clearly one of his most important contributions, which he presented in his dialogue the *Gorgias,* was his stinging criticism of the rhetoric practiced in his day. He likened it to cookery and cosmetics and suggested that it was merely a form of flattery. It is important to emphasize that this was the sophists' rhetoric of excess, not the kind of rhetoric that developed after Plato. Plato's more important contribution was the foundation for an art of rhetoric laid down in the *Phaedrus*, which involved the composition of three speeches on love. There he gave his thoughts on what would be necessary in order to establish a truly good theory of rhetoric. Plato is sometimes credited with a third contribution: that he served as a catalytic agent for his pupil Aristotle. Some people consider Aristotle's *Rhetoric* as an answer to the criticism of rhetoric made by his teacher. It is not known whether this is true but the *Rhetoric* clearly does provide answers applicable to Plato's criticism, and his views certainly cannot be considered extensions of Plato's.

Most rhetorical scholars agree that Aristotle was the greatest theorist ever to write on rhetorical communication, and his *Rhetoric* is the most influential work ever composed on the subject. The *Rhetoric*, which he wrote about 330 B.C., consists of three books. They have been called the books of the speaker, of the audience, and of the speech.

Book I discusses the distinction between rhetorical communication and dialectical communication (the process of inquiry). Aristotle takes his contemporaries to task for dwelling upon irrelevant matters in their rhetorical theory rather than concentrating on proofs, particularly enthymemes (arguments from probabilities). Rhetoric is defined in this book as "the faculty of discovering in a particular case what are the available means of persuasion." This faculty, Aristotle suggests, is the distinguishing element of rhetoric and belongs to no other art. To Aristotle, the means of persuasion are primarily *ethos* (the nature of the source), *pathos* (the emotion of the audience), and *logos* (the nature of the message presented by the source to the audience). In Book I, the author dwells upon the nature of rhetorical thought and particularly upon the concept of invention. His main guide to the invention of argument for persuasion is the use of *topoi*, or "lines of argument." Aristotle also distinguishes three different kinds of speaking: *deliberative* (speaking in the legislature), *forensic* (speaking in the law court), and *epideictic* (speaking in a ceremonial situation). Given the nature of the culture of Greece during his time, these were seen as the only kinds of speaking that were of importance to study.

Book II concerns the nature of the audience. Much discussion is directed to the question of how the emotions of the audience members are evoked by the communicator's message. Aristotle also considers such things as the wealth and the age of the listeners as factors in determining how they will perceive the message. After treating the nature of the audience in considerable depth, Aristotle returns to his discussion of *topoi* and how they may be used to generate argument.

Books I and II of the *Rhetoric* concern primarily what we may call the invention process. Aristotle's rhetorical theory is usually referred to as "invention centered," and accurately so. There is some reason to believe that the *Rhetoric* was not intended to be a complete rhetoric but only the theory of rhetorical invention. Books I and II concern the philosophy of rhetoric and describe in some detail the essential nature of rhetoric and the process of invention, whereas Book III (which was written some time later) is devoted to the nature of the speech and its presentation to an audience.

The main emphasis in Book III is on style. Aristotle's discussion of style, however, is quite different from that of the sophists. Rather than talking about the requisites of good style, Aristotle stresses clarity. He also suggests that propriety and liveliness are desirable. Aristotle barely mentions delivery; obviously he was not enthusiastic about this element in rhetoric. He suggests that we must pay attention to it only because of the "sorry nature of the audience." On what we should do for effective delivery, Aristotle provides very little guidance. The final part of Book III is devoted to disposition. It suggests that there are only two parts necessary in a speech: the statement of the point, and the proof. There is some discussion, however, of means of developing all three of the parts that are normally found in a message: the introduction, the body, and the conclusion.

The *Rhetoric* is more a philosophy of rhetoric than a theory of rhetoric. Of the five classical canons of rhetoric—*invention, disposition, style, memory,* and *delivery*—only invention receives full treatment by Aristotle. His treatment of disposition and style are adequate. He gives only passing mention to delivery and makes no mention at all of memory. There is reason to wonder if we indeed have a complete theory of rhetoric as propounded by Aristotle. For many centuries Aristotle's works were lost. We know of two that have never been recovered. One of them, *Theodectea,* reportedly dealt in great depth with the subject matter of Book III of the *Rhetoric.* The other, *Gryllus,* was a history of rhetoric. Aristotle may well have written other books for the *Rhetoric,* as well as other complete works. For many years the anonymous work *Rhetorica ad Alexandrum* was believed to be one of his works, but modern scholars have concluded that it was not. Whoever wrote it, it was never an influential work in the history of rhetoric. Whether Aristotle wrote more on the theory of rhetoric than we now have from his hand will remain an open question.

Reviewing Aristotle's overall theory of rhetoric, we find in it three essential elements. The first is that all arguments must be based on *probabilities.* Aristotle held that absolute verifiable truth is unobtainable in most cases. Therefore, persuasion must be based on what an audience believes to be true. While Plato found this factor in rhetoric a defect, Aristotle perceived it as a necessity. The second essential element is his conception of the basic problem in rhetorical communication as one of *audience adaptation.* Aristotle believed that you could not persuade a person unless you knew what was likely to persuade that person. That is, he believed that a knowledge of what we call psychology was essential to the art of rhetorical communication. These two essential elements in Aristotle's rhetorical theory produce the third: its basic *amorality.* Aristotle suggested that his theory could be used by anyone: by a good person or a bad person, by a person seeking worthy ends or unworthy ends. At the same time, he suggested that rhetoric was a self-regulating art. By that he meant that a person who is unethical, or who advocates evil, is less likely to be successful than a moral person who advocates goodness. As his justification, Aristotle claimed that good and right, by their very nature, are more powerful persuasive tools than their opposites.

Aristotle's influence upon rhetorical theory, ever since his own day, has been monumental—the most significant contribution in all its history. Theories of rhetoric taught by such writers as Cicero, Quintilian, and George Campbell, as well as by most modern writers, are essentially Aristotelian. In a very real sense, the writers since Aristotle have simply refined his original theories, extending them only in rare cases. Theories set forth in the *Rhetoric* appear in all respectable textbooks on rhetorical communication today.

One other work from the Greek period deserves mention, although its author and its exact date are unknown. It was written some time around the first century B.C. or the first century A.D. and has come to be called *On Style.* This work deals entirely with style and is noteworthy mainly for one reason: Most later rhetoricians discussed the three styles for messages that the author suggested—the elevated, or high, style; the elegant, or middle, style; and the plain, or low, style. The author also suggested a fourth, the forcible style. *On Style,* the final noteworthy work on rhetoric in the Greek period, appeared approximately at the beginning of the Roman period in rhetorical theory.

THE ROMAN PERIOD

Rhetorica ad Herennium, written about 82 B.C. is the earliest extant Latin work on rhetoric. Its author remains unknown, although it has been variously attributed to Cicero and Confucius. It is a plainly written book that resembles a student's notebook. It contains the earliest extant discussion of the canon of memory and also one of the earliest treatments of the canon of style. Delivery is also considered in some depth. Little attention is accorded invention and disposition, though on the subject of disposition the author does suggest that there are six parts to a rhetorical message: introduction, statement of facts (narration), division, proof, refutation, and conclusion. Although this work made virtually no impact when it was written, it was widely used in the later Middle Ages and during the Renaissance. In fact, with the revival of rhetoric during the Tudor period, this book was the basic elementary text in the English grammar school curriculum. Unlike Aristotle's *Rhetoric,* it was not a philosophy of rhetoric; rather, *Rhetorica ad Herennium* is a "how-to" book, simple and direct. While this is probably the reason that the work was so widely used later on, it is also the work's main weakness: It is overly simple.

Although Cicero was probably not the author of *Rhetorica ad Herennium,* he definitely was the author of several other writings on rhetoric. Most significant are his *de Inventione, de Oratore, Orator, Partitiones Oratoriae, Brutus, de Optimo Genere Oratorum,* and *Topica.* Cicero added little to rhetorical theory; his main function was to clarify and refine Greek rhetorical theories. His chief influence during his own time was the part he played in mediating the controversy between the exponents of the florid style (Asiatics) and the exponents of the plain style (Atticists). His appeal to later generations emerged as a result of his extension of the scope of rhetoric. Aristotle had held that rhetoric had no proper subject matter, but Cicero's ideal orator was knowledgeable in all areas of learning. Cicero felt the orator must have this extensive knowledge in order to develop good arguments. Therefore, Cicero's training of the orator contained a broad liberal-arts approach. This widening of the scope of rhetoric was consistent with the thinking of the individuals who revived rhetoric during the Renaissance. Consequently, Cicero's influence during that period was much stronger than Aristotle's.

M. Fabius Quintilianus (Quintilian), a Spaniard who migrated to Rome, was second only to Cicero in his influence on later generations of rhetorical theorists and practitioners. Quintilian was the first teacher of rhetoric to be hired by the Roman government. He had become such a successful pleader in the law courts that the emperor Vespasian established a position for him in Rome, the prestige of which made Quintilian the supreme authority on rhetoric. After he retired from teaching he produced a massive work on the training of the orator, the *Institutio Oratoria,* composed of twelve books, his only extant writing. Book I discusses the education necessary for the study of rhetoric. Book II defines the nature and scope of rhetoric. Books III through VII deal with rhetoric itself, with emphasis on invention and disposition. Books VIII through X concern style, while Book XI treats memory and delivery. Finally, Book XII sets forth Quintilian's view of the requirements for the perfect orator. One of the most often quoted passages from Quintilian's work is his definition of the orator as "the good man speaking well." Although Quintilian observed that the ethos of an orator was determined by how the orator was perceived by the audience, his thorough description of what a "good man" should be has often been interpreted as setting the requisites for a source to be perceived as highly credible. This misinterpretation has led to a distorted view of the concept of ethos that has prevailed up to modern times and is still presented in many textbooks concerned with rhetorical communication.

Quintilian's main contribution to the history of rhetorical communication is not so much theoretical as it is practical: the teacher's concern with the student. Quintilian's *Institutio Oratoria* presents a total program for the education of the student of rhetoric. He makes it clear that, to be a truly effective communicator, the student needs to learn not only the canons of rhetoric but also such varied things as geometry and gymnastics. This broad liberal-arts approach to the training of the communicator had a major effect upon the training of later generations.

Another work that appeared during the Roman period deserves mention. Entitled *On the Sublime*, it is generally attributed to a writer named Longinus, about whom nothing further is known. *On the Sublime* was the first major work on rhetorical and literary criticisms. It did not develop a total theory of criticism, however, the author was concerned strictly with style.

THIRD CENTURY A.D. TO THE RENAISSANCE

If we think of rhetoric in Aristotelian terms, we may say that there is little history of rhetoric during the Middle Ages. However, them was much that was called rhetoric. During this period a new group of sophists developed. These teachers of rhetoric had great prestige but used their position to amaze the audience rather than to persuade it. They employed flashy and elaborate style and delivery and were highly entertaining. The schools of rhetoric of that time had two types of curriculum: the sophistic and the political. The latter dealt with the practical application of the art of rhetoric but was so overshadowed by the former that eventually the practical rhetoric ceased.

Little is known about the development of rhetorical theory during this period. The only major name in the period was that of Augustine, who was a teacher of rhetoric before his conversion to Christianity. In his *Confessions* he tells of turning away from the sophistic rhetoric taught to him in his youth. Book IV of his *de Doctrina Christiana* may be the best work on preaching that ever has been written. During a time when there was almost no practical rhetoric, Augustine emphasized that the preacher should be concerned with rhetoric as a means of persuading people rather than as a means of exhibitionism.

With the notable exception of Augustine, the rhetoricians of this period made little or no contribution to the advancement of rhetorical theory. Bede, Alcuin, Cassiodorus, Isidore, and John of Salisbury were all noteworthy rhetoricians of this period. Their function, however, was primarily translating or paraphrasing earlier works rather than developing theories of their own. Indeed, it may be said that throughout the Middle Ages rhetoric stood still, if it did not move backward. Not until the Renaissance did any further advances in rhetorical theory come about.

THE RENAISSANCE

The rebirth of rhetorical theory during the Renaissance was not an auspicious occurrence. Although rhetorical works representing the Aristotelian tradition existed during this period, they were not the dominant rhetorical works. The dominant ones viewed rhetoric as the study of style and delivery. Worthy of notice in this context is the thinking of Petrus Ramus, who saw logic and rhetoric as separate disciplines. To logic, Ramus assigned invention and disposition; to rhetoric, only style and delivery. Some works representing this faulty view of rhetoric were Richard Sherry's *A Treatise of Schemes and Tropes Gathered out of the Best Grammarians and Orators*, Henry Peacham's *Garden of Eloquence*, and Dudley Fenner's *Artes of Logike and Rhetorike*. Two works in England were Leonard Cox's *The Arte or Crafte of Rhetoryke* and Thomas Wilson's *Arte of Rhetorique*. Cox's brief work was the first book on rhetoric published in the English language. Both of these writings conserved the classic tradition of rhetoric.

Early in the seventeenth century Sir Francis Bacon produced two works that included references to rhetoric: *The Advancement of Learning* (1605) and *De Augmentis Scientiarum* (1623). Because Bacon's theories of rhetoric were not condensed into one treatise but were spread through these two works unsystematically, it is reasonable to believe that he did not make a major impact upon his contemporaries' views of the process of rhetoric.

Bacon compartmentalized the mind into faculties: understanding, reason, imagination, memory, appetite, and will. He then suggested that rhetoric is the function of applying reason to imagination for the better moving of the will. This type of faculty psychology carried over through many years, and to this day it is not completely extinct.

Bacon did not limit rhetoric to speech making, as had the Greek and Roman writers; he also included writing that was designed for utilitarian purposes. His treatment of invention included discussion of commonplaces and *topoi* as aids to generating argument. He discussed at length the errors that people made through faulty inferences. Bacon also included an ethical basis for his rhetoric, contending that the furtherance of good is the function of a true rhetoric. Although his influence upon his contemporaries was somewhat limited, his influence upon later writers was a major one, particularly because of his faculty psychology.

THE COLONIAL PERIOD

Most of the influential theorists during the colonial period were British. However, the first one considered here is a French rhetorician named Fenelon, who thought of rhetoric as a social instrument. Although rhetoric in the early colonial period was generally characterized by ornate style, Fenelon contended, as had Aristotle before him, that matter was more important than manner.

Fenelon did not agree with the Ramistic approach to rhetoric, which separated logic and rhetoric, but, on the contrary, emphasized the close relationship between the two. He also advocated naturalness in rhetoric, particularly in style and delivery. For Fenelon, the main goal in style was clarity. He held that delivery should be unaffected and natural rather than artificial and mechanical.

Representing the antithesis of Fenelon's naturalness was a group of theorists that constituted what is known as the *elocutionary* movement. The movement's founders were Thomas Sheridan (*Lectures on Elocution*, 1756), Joshua Steele (*Prosodia Rationalis*, 1775), John Walker (*Elements of Elocution*, 1781), and James Burg (*The Art of Speaking*, 1761). These men also believed in naturalness, but of a different kind. They developed their bodies of theory in response to the "new science." The elocutionists believed that humans were controlled by natural laws and that these controlling laws were systematic and not to be disregarded. Thus, they proceeded to reduce speaking to a scientific system. Their scientific method was to observe speakers' voices and manners and to codify what kinds of responses various types of vocal manipulation and physical gesticulation produced.

Unfortunately, although the elocutionists desired to develop a natural system of delivery, they produced highly artificial systems. The group was influential for over a hundred years, however, and today there are isolated elocution schools in major cities of the United States.

Although the elocutionists were the primary rhetoricians of the late eighteenth and early nineteenth centuries, three contemporary theorists developed theories significantly different from theirs. These variant theories were based on the classical rhetoric and primarily restated, clarified, and extended the classical theories. The three British theorists were George Campbell, Hugh Blair, and Richard Whateley.

Campbell's *Philosophy of Rhetoric* is precisely what its name suggests: a philosophical treatment of rhetoric. It is not a systematic treatment, as was Aristotle's, but rather a probing of various areas of learning for ideas relevant to rhetoric. The *Philosophy of Rhetoric* does not treat the classical canons of rhetoric directly, but discusses them in the course of considering other topics, including the sources of knowledge, evidence, and human passions; the source of communication; the analysis of audiences; wit, humor, and ridicule; and the purity, clarity, and vividness of language. Campbell defines eloquence (rhetoric) as the "art or talent by which the discourse is adapted to its end." He further suggests that rhetoric may have any one of four purposes: to enlighten the understanding, to please the imagination, to move the passions, or to influence the will. These purposes, though based upon the now discredited faculty psychology, are not unlike some that are suggested in modern textbooks. Although it never received attention from rhetoricians to the extent the elocutionists' writing did, Campbell's *Philosophy of Rhetoric* was regularly studied in American colleges until after the Civil War.

Clearly the most popular and influential work to come from this period was Blair's *Lectures on Rhetoric and Belles Lettres* (1783). Ten of its forty-seven lectures concern public speaking. Two present the history of rhetoric. Three examine rhetoric in various settings: the assembly, the court, and the pulpit. One lecture is devoted to the sermon. Two lectures discuss the parts of the speech, and two are devoted to delivery.

Blair does not consider invention but does direct his attention to the other canons of rhetoric. His best known, but most questionable, contribution was his concept of taste. To Blair, effective rhetoric was not that which produced a response in a receiver but rather that which met Blair's standards of taste. This view led to criticism of oratory on the basis of its aesthetic qualities—that is, the degree to which it met the high standards of taste—rather than on its utilitarian merit.

Blair's book was by far the most popular work on rhetoric in both Britain and the United States during this period, but it was to lead to the demise of classical rhetoric in America. Because of his concentration on style and taste, Blair's theories could be applied to written as well as oral discourse. In the nineteenth century, rhetoric in the United States came to deal primarily with written communication. The causes of this were varied, but it probably came about as a reaction to the excesses of the elocutionists. If the oral aspects of rhetoric were ignored, it was possible to disassociate oneself from the elocutionary rhetoric. Therefore, it is not clear whether this switch to written communication was a natural outgrowth of the increase in the written form of communication at that time or a response to the excesses of the oral form.

The last of the three great atypical British writers of the colonial period was Whateley, whose *Elements of Rhetoric* (1828) was heavily influenced by Aristotle. Like Aristotle, Whateley considered rhetoric an offshoot of logic, but his rhetorical theory was somewhat different from Aristotle's. Whateley defined rhetoric as "argumentative composition, generally and exclusively." The *Elements of Rhetoric* has four sections. The first section is devoted to invention and disposition, the second primarily concerns the use of ethos and pathos, and the other two are devoted to style and delivery.

This work is noteworthy for its development of such Aristotelian concepts as probability; the distinction between argument and example, and argument and analogy; and the concepts of presumption and burden of proof. Whateley's conception of ethos also was unique. Not since Aristotle had a writer clearly indicated that the ethos of the source could be determined only on the basis of the audience's perception.

The last writer worthy of note in the colonial period was John Quincy Adams. As holder of the chair of rhetoric at Harvard University, Adams presented a series of lectures on rhetoric, which set forth in America for the first time a thoroughly classical view of the subject. Although the lectures were published and were used at Harvard for a time, they were replaced by Blair's work. Adams nevertheless had the distinction of being the first American rhetorician in the classical tradition, though he did not contribute anything to the historical development of rhetorical theory. He did, however, serve as President of the United States.

THE TWENTIETH CENTURY

James A. Winans, an American speech teacher and one of the founders of what has come to be known as the National Communication Association, was one of the first Americans to make a significant contribution to rhetorical theory. In his book *Public Speaking* (1915), he introduced the psychology of attention as the basis for a system of public address. Winans defined persuasion as gaining and maintaining fair, favorable, and undivided attention. He made another major contribution through his distinction between conversational style and conversational quality. His discussion of delivery is probably the finest treatment of this canon of rhetoric in the English language. Modern students will profit greatly from reading Winans's excellent treatise.

During the early part of the twentieth century, several other Americans made contributions worthy of attention. Charles Henry Woolbert was the first to approach rhetoric as a behavioral science. Herbert A. Wichelns was the first to make a clear distinction between rhetorical criticism and literary criticism. I. A. Richards and Kenneth A. Burke are frequently credited with beginning a new rhetoric. Richards's influence on rhetoric stems primarily from *The Meaning of Meaning*, a book on semantics that he wrote with C. K. Ogden, and from his book *The Philosophy of Rhetoric*. Richards preferred not to restrict himself to the persuasive aspect of language but was concerned, rather, with how language in any kind of discourse works to produce understanding in an audience. We may say that Richards was the first major communication theorist in the modern sense. Burke's primary contribution to the theory of rhetoric was his concept of identification. He suggested that, for people to persuade other people, they must identify themselves with the audience, or become "consubstantial" with the audience. Other concepts that he advanced which had a significant impact on twentieth-century scholars were a dramatistic metaphor and his theory of form, both of which are relevant to public speaking performances. Burke's major work on rhetoric was *A Rhetoric of Motives*.

Contemporary works on rhetoric and communication are more numerous and varied than those of any other time in the history of the theory of rhetorical communication. Several hundred works devoted to this subject, in whole or in part, are currently in print. In many cases, the differences among these works outweigh their similarities.

The most important influence in the late twentieth century has come from scholars with a social science orientation. Social science perspectives were introduced in the early twentieth century by Woolbert and others, but it was not until the 1960s that this approach flowered and became a substantial influence, one that has been felt in all editions of this book. Other books with a rhetorical orientation influenced by the social science movement have appeared as works on interpersonal communication, organizational communication, political communication, instructional communication, mass communication, health communication, and intercultural communication. These works represent the efforts of whole new subfields within the broader field of communication. The lasting importance of these contributions and their authors can best be judged by future generations of scholars.

During the last quarter of the twentieth century two other groups rose to prominence. These groups came to have a variety of labels, but the two most common were the "post-modernists" and the "Marxist-Feminists." Some writers were identified with both of these groups. Both were highly critical of the predominant Western culture and political processes of the late twentieth century. Many of these writers viewed the rhetoric of the time, principally neo-Aristotelian approaches, to be racist, sexist, and paternalistic. Similarly, many of these writers expressed extremely negative views towards science and rejected virtually all scientific findings because they believed they were inherently racist and sexist, because science itself, in their view, represented a masculine, paternalistic view of the world. Not all of these writers took such extreme positions, however. Some saw traditional rhetoric (stripped of its racist and paternalistic assumptions) to be of considerable value.[1] We may better understand these extreme responses if we put the history of traditional rhetoric in perspective.

HISTORY IN PERSPECTIVE

The discussion of twenty-five hundred years of scholar's contributions to rhetorical communication is not meant to be overwhelming.[2] Only the person planning to specialize in the history of rhetoric will probably ever need to know most of the specific information included here. What we hope you have been able to glean from all of this is that we who are living in the twenty-first century are far from the first to try to come to grips with how human communication works and how we can make it work better. This concern has drawn the attention of the greatest Western scholars over the ages. The study of rhetorical communication has been central to liberal education for most of recorded history. To a major extent, the degree to which you are able to master intellectually the process of communicating with other human beings will be the degree to which you expand your potential to succeed as a citizen of a Western society.

Although the work of the scholars through history is of value to us today, we need to recognize that our world is greatly different than it was even fifty years ago. Throughout most of the past two and a half millennia, the concepts of freedom, liberty, equality, and other aspects of the world view common to Western societies have meant very different things than we mean when we use them today. Recognize that the people who were able to participate in the rhetoric of Athenian society of around 300 B.C. (or most anywhere else in Europe, Africa, or the Middle East) were a very small proportion of the people in the society. They were virtually all male, nonslaves who owned considerable property, and were fairly well educated. Much of the population consisted of slaves, and of course over half of the nonslaves were women, people who had virtually no rights at all. The theories of rhetoric, then, were designed for the elite few males who could participate in the government and economic systems of the culture.

This same basic pattern survived in the Judeo-Christian, Greco-Roman cultures of Western societies, including the United States, until very recently. Slavery was not abolished until the nineteenth century in the United States. But even after that, neither former slaves nor their descendents were allowed to vote or to participate fully in most aspects of everyday economic or political life. Although women were finally given the right to vote in the 1920s, neither women nor the descendents of former slaves were granted the legal status of equality until the 1960s in the United States, and they still do not have that status in many other countries. It should not be surprising, therefore, that few nonwhite scholars have had an opportunity to make meaningful contributions to the study of rhetorical communication.[3]

At about the time the first edition of this book was written (the early to middle 1960s), education (particularly higher education) began going through enormous change in the United States. Women, minorities, and white males of the middle and lower classes flowed into schools in enormous numbers. The interests of these individuals were not fully consistent with those of the former occupants of higher education, those representing the economic and cultural elite. This led to a revolution in the study of human communication that drew increasing attention to the communication that exists outside the infrastructure dominated by the cultural elite. The study of rhetorical communication became open to those who had never had an opportunity to study it, and the questions these new scholars asked often were very different than the ones asked by those who went before them. What this revolution has or will produce will be best interpreted by future scholars, but it will certainly be different. Most likely the new theories and applications will be most valuable if they are informed by the work of the past so that previous mistakes are not made again. The following chapters are designed to provide that informational starting point.

The following chapters outline the basic elements of rhetorical communication as developed over the centuries. While the primary concern is rhetorical communication in the person-to-group context, these foundational elements may be applied with equal force in the many other contexts in which human communication occurs. Chapters 2–5 focus primarily on information and orientations brought to the study of rhetoric from the social scientific study of communication. While some integration with concepts from classical rhetoric occurs in these chapters, an even greater degree of integration occurs in the chapters in Section 3 of this book.

DISCUSSION QUESTIONS

1. Of what use is knowledge of the history of the theories of rhetorical communication to the modern student of that art?

2. Why did such a strong interest in rhetoric develop in the fifth century B.C. in Sicily? Why did it not develop sooner? Why did rhetoric decline during the Middle Ages?

3. What do you think of the claim that democracy and rhetoric are inseparable?

4. To what extent is it true that psychology is an offshoot of rhetoric?

5. Are there any elements of sophistry or of elocution in contemporary high school or college speech contests?

6. Why has our history of the theories of rhetorical communication failed to refer more often to parts of the world other than Western Europe and North America?

7. Are Confucianism and rhetoric compatible?

8. Is there a place for a female or a member of a minority in a field of scholarship that has been dominated by an elite few European males for 2500 years? If so, what is it? If not, then what are the alternatives for females and members of minorities?

NOTES

1. See, for example, M. C. Nussbaum, "Aristotle, Feminism, and Needs for Functioning," *Texas Law Review* 70 (1992): 1119–1928.

2. Those wanting a much more thorough review should see, G. A. Kennedy, *Classical Rhetoric and Its Christian and Secular Tradition from Ancient to Modern Times,* 2nd, rev. and enl. ed. (Chapel Hill: University of North Carolina Press, 1999), and G. A. Kennedy, *Comparative Rhetoric: An Historical and Cross-Cultural Introduction* (New York: Oxford University Press, 1998).

3. It is important to recognize that Western rhetoric is not the only rhetorical tradition. See X. Lu, *Rhetoric in Ancient China Fifth to Third Century B.C.: A Comparison with Classical Greek Rhetoric,* Studies in Rhetoric/Communication (Columbia: University of South Carolina Press, 1998).

CHAPTER 2

THE NATURE OF RHETORICAL COMMUNICATION

Communication is a central fact of human existence. The extent to which we find life pleasing and rewarding depends in large measure upon the extent to which we are successful in influencing and controlling our environment. We can control some factors in our environment by our own physical actions; for example, we may grow some of our own food. But, by ourselves, we can neither control nor influence many other important factors affecting us. We must act in concert with other people. The most common means of securing cooperation from other people is rhetorical communication. Rhetorical communication is the primary tool with which we influence and control the thoughts and actions of other people, as well as the environment in which we live. It must be emphasized that the terms *influence* and *control* are not used here in a derogatory sense. People must exert influence and control in order to survive. This we have in common with lower forms of life. Many people argue that the primary characteristic distinguishing humans from these life forms is our ability to use the tool of rhetorical communication.

Rhetorical communication is arguably the most important and valuable skill a person can possess. As Daniel Webster once put it, "If all of my possessions and powers were to be taken from me with one exception, I would choose to keep the power of speech, for by it I could soon recover all the rest." (*Speech* as used by Webster, is synonymous with *rhetorical communication*.) Webster might have been able to regain "all the rest" with his power of speech, but unfortunately not everyone is so skilled in the practice of rhetorical communication.

Skill in rhetorical communication depends upon three factors: *desire, understanding,* and *experience.* That you have chosen to read this book suggests that you already have the desire to develop your skill. This book is devoted to presenting the information necessary to gain an understanding of the process of rhetorical communication. In your class you may have an opportunity to obtain some experience in this art, but the bulk of your experience will come after you finish the class in which you are currently enrolled. It is up to you to study the material presented in the following chapters and to put your understanding of rhetorical communication into practice in later life. You may never become as skilled as Daniel Webster. But if you really desire to be more effective in rhetorical communication, if you study the material in the following chapters, and if you employ your understanding of rhetorical communication in later life, you will find your life far more pleasant and rewarding. Furthermore, the society in which you live will be enhanced because you will be able to make your maximum contribution to your own well-being and to that of your fellow human beings.

THE MEANING OF RHETORICAL COMMUNICATION

Communication has become one of the most commonly used words in the English language. Like many other words, it means different things to different people. We have communications satellites. We study the communication of dolphins. We worry that we cannot communicate with another country. We hear people claim that parents and teenagers just cannot communicate with one another any more.

Actually, thousands of jobs in the contemporary world deal with communication. The internet, telephone, telegraph, radio, and television industries are communication industries, as are the newspaper, magazine, and book industries. Communication is the heart of the professions of teaching, ministry, and law. More and more, as automation progresses, employment in industries producing everything from automobiles to popcorn boxes is dependent upon communication. Service industries could just as well be called communication industries, for they are almost totally dependent on effective communication.

From all these applications of the word *communication*, it might appear that people have many different meanings for it, but actually the word is applied in only three basically different ways. It may be used as a substitute for the word *message* as in "sending a communication" to someone; it may refer to the process of transferring messages from one place to another (in this case the plural form, communications, is generally used); or it may refer to the process of one person stimulating meaning in the mind of another by means of a message. Telephone communication is an example of the transmission of messages from one place to another. The primary characteristic of this type of communication is that it is concerned with messages rather than with meaning. If a message is picked up by an instrument, carried over a wire to another instrument, and made audible and understandable by the second instrument, telephone communication has been successfully established.

The word *communication* as used in this and the following chapters refers to *the process of one person stimulating meaning in the mind of another by means of a message.* This definition covers three types of communication: accidental, expressive, and rhetorical.

1. *Accidental communication.* Accidental communication occurs when one person stimulates meaning in the mind of another without having any intention of doing so and without necessarily knowing that he or she has done so. People communicate their interests, their needs, their backgrounds, and sometimes their weaknesses without having the slightest desire to do so, and often in spite of a definite desire *not* to communicate these things. For example, in his book *The Silent Language*, Hall[1] tells how North Americans unintentionally communicate unfriendliness to Latin Americans by moving away from them in the course of conversation. Because of cultural differences, the physical distance between people engaged in conversation creates different meanings in the minds of North Americans and Latin Americans. Latin Americans tend to stand very close to one another while conversing but North Americans tend to become nervous and apprehensive if people stand too close to them. Thus, North Americans tend to move away from Latin Americans while conversing and in this way accidentally stimulate Latin Americans to think of them as unfriendly.

2. *Expressive communication.* Expressive communication arises from the emotional, or motivational, state of the individual. One individual produces messages that represent her or his feelings with the intention to communicate with another individual. This intention, however, is not an essential characteristic of expressive communication. If you are hammering a nail and hit your thumb when no one is around, you may produce a message such as "ouch" or a more colorful expression. Communication under the definition given above cannot occur, since no one is present other than the person producing the message. If there were another person present, however, there could be communication, because the other person would be stimulated to attribute meaning to the exclamation. You might, because another person was present, change the nature of your exclamation so as still to represent your emotional state, but at the same time to avoid accidental communication.

3. *Rhetorical communication.* Rhetorical communication is the type with which our book is concerned. We may define it as *the process of a source stimulating a source-selected meaning in the mind of a receiver by means of verbal and nonverbal messages.* Several parts of this definition need to be clarified. "Source" refers to the individual or group of individuals from whom a message emanates. "Source-selected meaning" suggests that the source of the communication has previously determined what meaning it wishes to create in the mind of the receiver. If rhetorical communication is successful, something approximating the source-selected meaning will be so created; but if rhetorical communication is unsuccessful, a receiver-selected meaning that differs substantially from what the source intended will be created. "Verbal messages" refers to symbolic language, which may be transmitted to a receiver either by oral or written means. "Nonverbal messages" include all other types of messages, such as the nodding of one's head, the waving of one's hands or arms, facial expressions, or tone of voice.

Rhetorical communication is *goal-directed.* It seeks to produce specific meaning in the mind of another individual. In this type of communication there is specific intent on the part of the source to stimulate a particular meaning in the mind of the receiver. As a mundane example, let us take the case of trying to get someone to pass the pepper at the dinner table. Through previous experience you have probably found that asking, "Would you please pass the pepper?" ordinarily causes another individual to hand you the pepper. You may therefore transmit this message in the expectation that you will receive the pepper. In addition to transmitting this verbal message, you also may look at the person whom you expect to pass the pepper and point or nod toward the pepper. If you do indeed receive the pepper, you may say that you communicated rhetorically. If you do not receive the pepper, you will most likely construct another message, such as "Excuse me, George. Would you please pass me the pepper?" Typically, you will continue transmitting messages until you either receive the pepper or determine that you are not going to receive it, and so give up.

Our understanding of the process of rhetorical communication will be facilitated by examining several communication models. The next section of this chapter is devoted to models of communication that represent various views on what constitutes the process.

MODELS OF THE COMMUNICATION PROCESS

Figure 2.1 presents what is frequently referred to as the Shannon-Weaver telephone model. It represents message-centered communication. Notice that there is no reference to meaning. We merely have a source, such as a person, putting a message into a transmitter, such as a telephone, with the message then being transmitted through a channel to the receiver. An important element in this model is the concept of noise, which we shall consider at greater length later.

Figure 2.2 presents the model to which we shall refer in the remaining chapters of this book. Let us therefore look at its parts in greater detail. Our model of rhetorical communication includes three essential parts: the source, the channel, and the receiver. As Shown in Figure 2.2, it encompasses more than just the rhetorical communication process. It also takes into con-

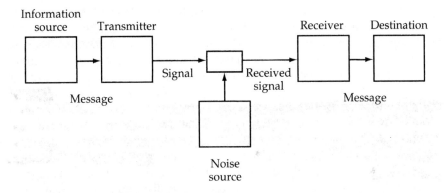

FIGURE 2.1   The Shannon-Weaver model from C. E. Shannon and W. Weaver, *The Mathematical Theory of Communication* **(Urbana: University of Illinois Press, 1949), p. 98. Reprinted by permission of the University of Illinois Press.**

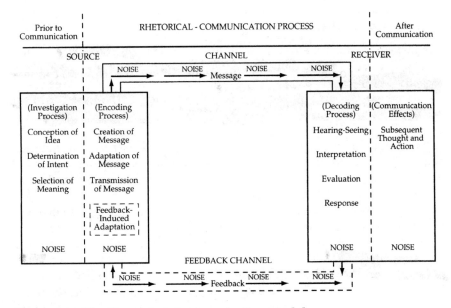

FIGURE 2.2   The Rhetorical Communication Model.

sideration factors that are relevant to the process prior to the inception of rhetorical communication and to projected effects after the completion of rhetorical communication. Thus the first thing you may learn from the model is that rhetorical communication does not occur in a vacuum; it is part of an overall process of daily life.

To understand this process, let us begin with the source of rhetorical communication before the process actually begins. Although we will discuss the source as if it were always a single person, the source of rhetorical communication may be either a single individual or a group of individuals. In some cases, the source may even be some type of organization, such as a government agency. Whatever may be the nature of the source, prior to the inception of rhetorical communication, the source must accomplish three things: (1) conceive the idea to be communicated, (2) determine the intent toward the receiver, and (3) select the meaning he or she hopes to stimulate in the receiver's mind. These three acts must precede verbal communication; unless they are accomplished, rhetorical communication is impossible. In large measure, these three factors distinguish rhetorical communication from the other kinds of meaning-centered communication discussed previously.

Once you have conceived the idea, determined the intent toward the receiver, and selected the meaning wanted in the receiver's mind, you are ready to begin the rhetorical communication process.

The Encoding Process

The first step toward rhetorical communication is the *encoding process*, which may be defined as *the process of translating an already conceived idea into a message appropriate for transmission to a receiver*. This process includes three essential parts: (a) *creation* of the message, (b) *adaptation* of the message to the intended receiver, and (c) *transmission* of the message to the receiver. The encoding process is based on the source's perception of the way the receiver will perceive the messages. This phase of the process is crucial to rhetorical communication. We may create messages without regard for a receiver, but if we do, we are not engaged in rhetorical communication but are instead concerning ourselves with expression.

Classical rhetoric, although it does not refer to the process as encoding, provides considerable guidance for the rhetorical communicator at this point in the process. The classical canons of rhetoric are primarily concerned with the encoding process. Three of these canons are particularly relevant: *invention, disposition,* and *style*. Each of these is audience- or receiver-centered. We invent a message for a given audience. We arrange and apportion the materials of that message with an eye to the effects likely to be produced in the mind of a receiver. We select the words and phrases for our message on the basis of what meaning we believe those words and phrases will create in the mind of a receiver. *Encoding,* then, is a *receiver-centered,* or *audience-centered,* process. Encoding that does not take the receiver into account is not part of a rhetorically communicative act.

Several subsequent chapters will be devoted primarily to the process of encoding messages for rhetorical communication. We shall look not only at the individual parts of the encoding process—invention, disposition, and style—but also at the receiver. We shall consider several factors that influence receivers' perceptions of messages.

Transmission

Once the message is encoded by the source, it must be transmitted through a channel to a receiver. In rhetorical communication, our concern as to what the particular channel may be is somewhat limited. The primary channel may be written or oral. In some cases the channel may be partly visual. The media through which the message is transmitted to the receiver will, in some cases, affect the outcome of the rhetorical communication process. In Chapter 4 we shall consider, for example, aspects of selectivity that determine, among other things, whether or not a receiver may even come into contact with a message that is transmitted.

The Decoding Process

The destination of a message, of course, is always the receiver. The receiver gets the transmitted message through a channel and then engages in the decoding process. This process has four essential parts.

1. *Hearing-seeing.* The first step in the decoding process is always either hearing or seeing the message, or in some cases both. When the message is received through a written channel, the first step is seeing, but when the message is received through an oral channel, the visual channel may also receive a message. For example, when a speaker talks to an audience, the audience not only hears the speaker and the words said, but it also sees the person—the person's facial expressions, gestures, and movements.

2. *Interpretation.* Whether the message is written or oral, the second step in the decoding process is interpretation, the receiver determines what he or she believes the source meant by the message transmitted. This implies that the receiver makes a conscious attempt to interpret the message correctly. It does not mean, of course, that a correct interpretation will always result, but only that normally there is such an attempt on the part of the receiver.

3. *Evaluation.* Once the receiver has interpreted what the source meant by the message, the message is then evaluated in terms of its personal meaning to the receiver. The receiver may, for example, hear a source request money for a cause the source believes to be worthy. The receiver then evaluates that appeal for funds in his or her own terms, deciding whether it comes from a worthy organization and whether he or she has funds that could be allocated to that cause without producing a personal hardship.

4. *Response.* Once the evaluation is completed, the receiver responds to the message as it has been seen or heard, interpreted, and evaluated. This response is in some cases an *overt (observable)* response—an act of behavior—or it may be a *covert* (internal, not observable) response. In many cases, responses are both overt and covert.

Once the receiver has responded, the decoding process is complete, as is the rhetorical communication process as a whole. Subsequent to this time, responses of the receiver, in terms of thought or action, do not belong to the rhetorical communication process. These subsequent thoughts and actions of the receiver, however, are frequently affected by the rhetorical communication process that has occurred. In fact, the intent of the source is precisely this—to affect the subsequent thoughts and actions of the receiver.

We have now looked at the essential parts of the rhetorical communication process: the encoding process, the transmission of a message through a channel, and the decoding process by a receiver.

The model of communication in Figure 2.2 contains other elements too. The primary one is *noise,* which refers to *any element that interferes with the generation of the intended meaning in the mind of the receiver.* We see from the figure that noise may arise in the source, in the channel, or in the receiver. This factor of noise is not an essential part of the rhetorical communication process. In fact, the communication process is always hampered to some degree if noise is present. Unfortunately, noise is almost always present.

Two types of noise occur in the source. The first is "foggy thinking" about the concept to be expressed in the message. This kind of noise affects the rhetorical communication process in a very direct and unfortunate way, in many cases it causing its failure. Examples include cases in which the source is not familiar with important information relevant to the concept that he or she wishes to discuss, has a distorted perception of the information relevant to the concept, or develops an intent toward the receiver that is not in the latter's best interest. The first case involves lack of education, background, or experience on the part of the individual(s) at the source. The second is a problem in the psychology of human beings. The third involves the problem of ethics. The causes of such noise lie outside the province of rhetorical communication; consequently they do not concern us here to any great extent.

The second type of noise in the source is in the encoding process. This is a major concern in rhetorical communication. It can occur when a source does not understand invention, disposition, or style. Subsequent chapters of this book discuss at some length the nature of these elements in the encoding process. In addition, noise in the encoding process can occur when the source has a misconception of the nature of the receivers. The source may encode a message appropriate for audience A, but if that message is transmitted to audience B, the effect produced may not resemble the effect intended. Chapters 4 and 5 in particular are concerned with this type of noise.

Noise in the channel, although it is the essential type of noise to be found in message-centered communication, is not so common or so important in the rhetorical communication process. This type is noise in the more literal sense. If the message is presented orally, for example, loud sounds may so distract the receiver that he or she does not get the message as transmitted. Similar effects can occur when sights or other sensory experiences belonging to the receiver are affected by something in the channel not directly relevant to the source's message.

As a cause of failure in rhetorical communication, noise in the receiver is second only to noise in the source. Receivers of rhetorical communication are people, and no two people are exactly alike. Consequently, it is impossible for the source to determine the exact effect that a message will have upon a given receiver. Within receivers, there are many variables that affect their perception of messages. Chapters 4, 5, and 6 look at these in considerable detail. At this point it is important to remember simply that messages are not like light switches. When light switches are turned on, they invariably produce light (unless the electricity is off). Messages invariably produce responses, but the responses are far from perfectly predictable. The noise within the receiver—the psychology of the receiver—will determine to a great extent what the receiver will perceive.

Another element in our model of the rhetorical communication process is feedback, which is a receiver's overt response(s) to a source's message. In Figure 2.2, in the channel from source to receiver, there are arrows pointing in the direction in which the message is carried. Just below this there is the *feedback channel*, where the arrows are pointing from the receiver to the source. Solid lines represent the main channel (from source to receiver), but broken lines show the feedback channel (from receiver to source), because the channel between source and receiver must always be present in rhetorical communication. Feedback from receiver to source, however, is not an essential part of the rhetorical communication process. In fact, it can occur only when source and receiver are in proximity with one another. When an editorial writer publishes a newspaper commentary, most of the receivers of the editorial have no opportunity to provide feedback to the source. However, in the oral-communication situation, receivers often do make overt responses (that is, feedback) which the source may observe.

When the source observes the feedback, he or she is functioning simultaneously as a source and a receiver. In the function of receiver, the source must decode the feedback message received—the source must hear or see the feedback message, interpret its meaning, evaluate it in terms of its impact upon the original effort to communicate, and respond to it. The response may be negative in the sense that the source does nothing about it. Or the source may respond positively by adapting the message it has been transmitting through the channel to the receiver.

Let us take an example. A saleswoman is trying to persuade a customer to purchase a vacuum cleaner. After presenting some of her message, she notices that the customer appears to be very bored. This may suggest to the saleswoman that her message is not having the desired effect. She must therefore modify her message in such a manner as to raise interest on the part of the customer. This modification of the message from what the saleswoman had originally intended to transmit is what we refer to as feedback-induced adaptation. This is not an essential element in rhetorical communication (hence the broken lines around that term in the model), but it may be the factor that determines the success of a given communicative effort.

As we have noted, feedback ordinarily is not possible in written communication, and hence neither is feedback-induced adaptation. In oral communication, on the contrary, feedback and feedback-induced adaptation usually are possible. This is not true when the medium of transmission of the oral message is radio or television, because the receiver is not in proximity with the source. But in the setting of typical speech making, discussion, or conversation, feedback and feedback-induced adaptation are possible. For this reason, the person-to-person, oral rhetorical communication process is more likely to succeed than any other. Under no other condition can you determine that your message is not producing the desired effect in time to make alterations in that message so that it will be effective. This fact is recognized by most people, particularly those heavily involved in rhetorical communication.

That feedback and feedback-induced adaptation are possible does not mean, however, that they will inevitably emerge. You may perceive that you are receiving feedback but misinterpret that feedback. Thus, any adaptation you make may not be superior to the original message plan. Similarly, some people are incapable of adapting themselves to feedback. This factor will be discussed at greater length in a later chapter on the factor of delivery in rhetorical communication.

INTERPERSONAL COMMUNICATION MODEL

Although our rhetorical communication model (Figure 2.2) can be employed to describe any rhetorical communication transaction between two people, it is most useful for describing a person-to-group type of transaction, such as public speaking, where we can easily identify the source and the receiver. Much more common contexts for rhetorical communication, however, are transactions between two people in relative isolation from other people and

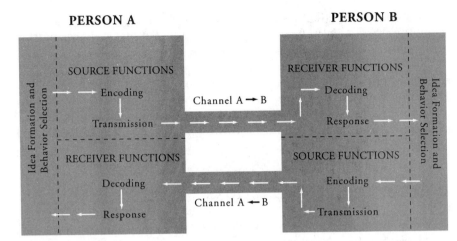

FIGURE 2.3   The Interpersonal Communication Model.

transactions involving a small group of people all interacting with one another. Our rhetorical communication model is much less useful for describing transactions such as these because we cannot easily identify who is source and who is receiver; all parties in the transaction are both sources and receivers.

The two-person rhetorical communication model presented in Figure 2.3 gives a much more accurate picture of communication in this context. As this model indicates, each person serves as both source and receiver. It shows the process of movement from source to receiver and from receiver to source. This is potentially a perpetual cycle, which may be begun at any point. A very important distinction between this and the preceding model is that the concept of feedback is not indicated in the present model. Feedback, of course, consists of receiver-encoded messages that sources may decode. Thus, when we recognize that people in interpersonal communication function as both sources and receivers, we see that the channel from person A to person B is the feedback channel for person B, and the channel from person B to person A is the feedback channel for person A. Similarly, person A's message is person B's feedback, and person B's message is person A's feedback. Feedback consists merely of messages transmitted by a source, whom we formerly called a receiver, to a receiver, whom we formerly called a source.

As the number of people involved in a communication transaction increases, the number of channels among these people also increases. Actually, as the number of people increases arithmetically, the number of channels progresses geometrically. Where we had two channels with two people, we have six channels with three people. If we were to add a fourth person, we would have twelve channels; add a fifth person and we would have twenty channels.

Although the essential rhetorical communication process remains the same, the presence of these additional channels and the messages passing through these channels can have a major impact on any rhetorical communication effort. For example, the effort of person A to influence person B can be either enhanced or impeded by messages emanating from person B. Therefore, whenever there are more than two people present, the rhetorical communicator must take into account messages emanating from other sources when designing the messages he or she hopes will influence the receiver.

SOME IMPORTANT DISTINCTIONS

Now that we have considered the different types of communication and have looked at the rhetorical communication model in some detail, we must stress several important distinctions.

1. *Intentional communication versus accidental communication.* We have noted that rhetorical communication is intentional. That means the source selects the specific meaning he or she desires to stimulate in the mind of the receiver and then goes about the rhetorical communication process in such a manner as to produce that meaning. There are cases in which the source of rhetorical communication makes serious mistakes—what we have referred to as noise in the encoding process—but still is successful in achieving its purpose. We might refer to this process as "serendipitous" communication. *Serendipity* may be considered synonymous with "fortunate accident." Indeed, this type of communication is a fortunate accident. We all know effective communicators who have never studied the process of rhetorical communication and indeed may never have heard of the word *rhetoric*, yet they are highly successful. We also know people who do not do the things that we say should be done in rhetorical communication, and yet they too are successful. It is therefore important to stress the distinction between successful rhetorical communication produced by an intentional, knowledgeable act, and that produced by chance or by a fortunate accident. This book does not intend to suggest at any point that the only way in which to achieve the effects desired from rhetorical communication is to follow the outline of the "proper" procedures, but rather that your chances for success are much greater by following these procedures than by not following them. You may not follow them and still succeed, but your success would then be a truly fortunate accident.

2. *Expressive communication versus rhetorical communication.* The distinction between expressive communication and rhetorical communication has already been noted, but it must be reemphasized. Expressive communication is source-centered, whereas rhetorical communication is receiver-centered. This is in no way intended to derogate expressive communication, but only to stress the difference between these two types of communication. In the public speaking classroom, for instance, both types of communication may be important. Speeches may be given primarily for the purpose of learning how to deliver a message, or they may be delivered primarily for the purpose of learning how to achieve an effect upon the receiver. The distinction between these two must be made so that the potential rhetorical communicator will not attempt to follow procedures acceptable for expressive communication but inappropriate for rhetorical communication. The purpose of expressive communication is merely to represent as clearly as possible the meaning in the mind of the source. The effects of this expression upon the receiver are irrelevant to the source's purpose. In rhetorical communication, on the other hand, it is not uncommon for the communicator to conceal what he or she really thinks. The vital thing in rhetorical communication is the meaning that is to be stimulated in the mind of the receiver.

3. *Investigation versus rhetorical communication.* The model of the rhetorical communication process (Figure 2.2) distinguished between what occurs prior to the process and what is included in the encoding process. Investigation of a concept is not part of the rhetorical communication process. When a communicator goes to a library or to some other source of information to find out about a concept before beginning the encoding process, he or she is not engaged in rhetorical communication. If, however, during the encoding process, particularly during invention, the person decides that a specific piece of information is needed, he or she may have to search for it. The important distinction here is that rigorous logical thought, which precedes encoding, is investigation, not rhetorical communication. As will be discussed in a later chapter, thought processes in rhetorical communication are quite different from those in investigation. The distinction between investigation and rhetorical communication is made at this point to reduce confusion about the explanation of the rhetorical thought process as discussed in later chapters.

MISCONCEPTIONS ABOUT COMMUNICATION

If you are reading this book as a result of enrolling in a basic course in rhetorical communication, your previous formal education in the field of communication is probably somewhat limited. Nevertheless, you may have acquired a number of conceptions about communication that are commonly believed in Western cultures. In many instances, such common conceptions

are at odds with clear thinking about communication. In order to avoid confusion that may be generated by such faulty concepts, it is useful to examine several of the most common ones and try to determine why they should be viewed as misconceptions.[2]

1. *Meanings are in words.* Probably the most common misconception about communication is that meanings are in words. We learn as little children that if we do not understand a word, we should look it up in the dictionary. From this we fail to learn that words are merely codes, symbols for meanings we have in mind. While words (as well as nonverbal symbols) exist in many forms, meanings exist only in people's minds. Thus, *meanings are in people, not in words.*

No word has meaning apart from the person using it. To the extent that two people have different meanings for the same word, communication between those people will be less effective than would be possible if they had the same meaning for that word. To a major degree, successful communication between two people depends on the extent to which they have similar meanings for the words (and for the nonverbal symbols) they use. The meanings we have for words are a product of our culture, our social class, and our experiences. No two people share precisely the same meanings for all words because no two people share the exact same background and experiences. Consequently, the rhetorical communicator who wishes to stimulate some meaning in the mind of a receiver must select words (and nonverbal symbols) to be used on the basis of what he or she expects the receiver's meanings for those words to be.

2. *Communication is a verbal process.* When most people think of *communication,* they think of words, whether written or spoken. This verbal focus is understandable, given that our educational system stresses it from kindergarten through college. However, communication, particularly oral communication, is not just a verbal process, it is also a nonverbal process.

What we say or write, of course, is important. But often how we say it is of equal or even greater importance. Our nonverbal behavior will determine to a major extent whether people even choose to listen to us, but if we overcome that barrier, our nonverbal behavior will have a major influence on what our receivers perceive as the intended meanings of the words we say. Communication is both a verbal and a nonverbal process. The nonverbal elements in communication are so important to the outcome of rhetorical communication that this book devotes an entire chapter to the subject.

3. *Telling is communicating.* This misconception provides the foundation for many interpersonal conflicts as well as other rhetorical communication failures. Many people operate as if saying something is equivalent to communicating it. It is not. As noted previously, encoding (saying and telling) is just the first step in the rhetorical communication process.

This misconception stems from our failure to recognize the active role the receiver plays in the communication process. Receivers are not sponges. They hear or read our messages, interpret them, evaluate them in light of their own experiences, and record in their memories what our messages mean to them. These meanings may be very different from, or even diametrically opposed to, the meanings we intended them to record. Telling is, at best, only half of communicating.

4. *Communication will solve all our problems.* Communication is viewed by many people in contemporary society as the sure cure for whatever ails us. Whether we face a problem with a lover, boss, or parent, or our country faces a problem with another country, the solution that the "experts" are certain to advance is "communication." Unfortunately, communication is no magic cure for all the ills in society.

Communication can sometimes create problems as well as help solve them. People, as well as groups and even countries, sometimes have irreconcilable differences. When such differences are recognized, we realize that communication offers no guarantee of solution. In addition, some less significant differences may be overlooked and thus not present a problem unless they are emphasized by communication. Although effective rhetorical communication may lead to the solution of some problems, it cannot be expected to solve all problems. Furthermore, ineffective rhetorical communication may make many problems worse than if no communication were attempted.

5. *Communication is a good thing.* If people think of communication as a panacea for the world's problems, it is natural that they would view communication as a good thing. But *communication is simply a tool*, and may be used for good or bad purposes. By analogy, communication is like many drugs. Used properly, many drugs can save our lives. Used improperly, those same drugs can kill us. Effective use of the tool of rhetorical communication has led to many benefits in society. But let us not forget that Adolf Hitler was one of the most effective rhetorical communicators of the twentieth century. Few would assign the moral quality of "goodness" to his communication endeavors.

6. *The more communication, the better.* When asked, most people will readily state that when it comes to communication, *quality is more important than quantity.* In reality, however, research studies have consistently demonstrated that people in many cultures, including the United States, hold a stereotype that is the opposite: The more a person talks (within limits), the more positively that person will be viewed by others. People who talk (or write) a lot are perceived to be more competent, more friendly, more attractive, more powerful, and better leaders than people who talk less. Of course, we all know people who talk too much. Actually, it is usually not the *amount* of talk that causes us to perceive them that way, it is that we do not like what they have to say—the *quality* of their communication.

This misconception of "the more, the better" also leads to many problems in organizations. Organizations, particularly bureaucratic ones, often almost bury themselves with paper. The number of messages, particularly from upper levels of the organization, can become excessive and result in little positive impact. Too many messages can lead to what is known as *"communication overload."* When we receive more messages than we can handle, we tend to ignore most of them, and seldom are we able to sort out the important from the unimportant ones. More attempts at communication, therefore, are no guarantee of better communication.

7. *Communication can break down.* When people or even nations attempt to influence one another but are unsuccessful, they often feel a need to place blame for that failure. *"Communication breakdown"* is frequently identified as the culprit. Somehow, it seems, if we can assert that communication broke down, there is no need to assume that anyone is at fault. The concept of communication breakdown should be recognized for just what it is: a cop-out intended to cover someone's failure to communicate effectively.

When people refer to communication breakdowns, they are usually implying that communication was unsuccessful and was terminated. However, in many of these situations, communication was successful in that the parties involved may have developed an excellent understanding of how the other thought and felt. In other situations the breakdown refers to circumstances where rhetorical communication was attempted and was unsuccessful. In either instance the people involved may stop talking to one another. But the absence of talk often communicates more than talking itself. In a very real sense, *one cannot not communicate*. While the grammar of this statement may appear questionable, the content illustrates a very important concept about communication. Simply to stop talking does not terminate communication or indicate that communication has broken down. The absence of verbal communication often communicates more than would its presence. Remember, communication is both a verbal and nonverbal process.

8. *Communication is a natural ability.* The final misconception about communication we will consider is that one is born with the ability to communicate. *Communication* is not an inborn, natural ability; it *is a learned ability*. Only recently has this fact come to be recognized at the top levels of education and government in the United States. Although reading and writing have long been recognized as basic skills that every child needs to learn, not until the 1980s did the federal and most state governments see the need to include speaking and listening among the basic skills to be taught in schools.

Although the normal child is born with the capacity to learn each of these four basic communication skills, without careful instruction the child will develop little ability in any of them. Such instruction is sadly lacking in many elementary and secondary schools. Thus, the fact that you may not yet have a high level of communication ability is probably far more a function of previous lack of opportunity to study communication than of some inborn limitation. One of the major purposes of this book is to help you overcome this deficit and increase your communication ability.[3]

THE GOALS OF RHETORICAL COMMUNICATION

Much has been written concerning the goals of rhetorical communication. Some writers designate the goals as "to inform or to persuade." Others break down the latter category and suggest that the goals of rhetorical communication are "to inform," "to convince," "to stimulate," or "to actuate." Other writers describe goals in terms of message descriptions. Messages are frequently described as expository or persuasive.

None of these category systems is quite adequate for our purposes, nor has any been adequate in the past. They have led, indeed, to considerable disagreement among writers in communication as to the existence of some of these goals. In particular, there has been much controversy concerning whether "to inform" is truly a goal of rhetorical communication. Many writers contend that all rhetorical communication has persuasive intent. Thus there would be no place in their theory for what are frequently called *informative messages*. Other writers prefer to define goals of rhetorical communication in terms of receivers' responses. They suggest that whenever a message is received by an individual, it has persuasive effect. In other words, receivers' attitudes or behavior are always affected by any message received. Another group of writers prefers to define the goals of rhetorical communication in terms of the perceived intent of the source. They suggest that in some cases sources merely wish the receivers to understand something, while in others they wish the receivers to modify an attitude or behavior. They distinguish the goals, on the basis of this type of intent, as informative or persuasive.

   This book tends to avoid the controversy about whether there is such a rhetorical goal as "to inform"; instead it identifies rhetorical communication goals in terms of the desired response of the receiver. In order to determine what those goals may be, it is necessary to examine the possible responses a receiver may make to any communicative message.

Possible Receiver Responses

Chapter 4 will discuss the nature of attitudes. Here it is important to remember only that no attitude exists until the receiver develops an evaluation of the object of the attitude. For example, we do not have an attitude toward some imaginary concept we shall call "exokir" until we evaluate it. Messages about "exokir" may produce four different kinds of responses: understanding, formation of attitude, strengthening of attitude, and/or changing of attitude. These responses—and only these—are possible in a receiver. If the communicator is going to be talking about "exokir," and we have not heard of it before, our first response should be to try to understand what "exokir" is. When this is done, we will probably have formed an attitude. Later on we may receive further messages that will strengthen our evaluative response or cause us to change that response.

   Considering these possible responses to messages, we conclude that there are four possible goals of rhetorical communication. The rest of this book refers to these four goals as *to create an understanding, to form an attitude, to strengthen an attitude,* and *to change an attitude.* Later chapters discuss, at some length, characteristics of messages that may differ when the goal of the communicator varies.

DISCUSSION QUESTIONS

   1. Other than rhetorical communication, what means do we have to control our environment? Are any of these means completely independent of rhetorical communication?

2. Does expressive communication serve any useful purpose in modern society?

3. How can we as receivers determine in any given case whether the meaning we perceive from a communicator's message is source-selected or receiver-selected? Can the meaning ever be both?

4. How are the Shannon-Weaver telephone model (Figure 2.1) and the Rhetorical Communication model (Figure 2.2) similar? How do they differ?

5. What are the eight common communication misconceptions? Can you provide, in a single phrase or sentence, a better refuting concept to replace each of the eight?

6. Is there such a thing as informative intent in rhetorical communication?

NOTES

1. E. T. Hall, *The Silent Language* (New York: Fawcett Books Group-CBS Publications, 1959).

2. The ideas in this section are based on similar ideas in J. C. McCroskey and L. R. Wheeless, *Introduction to Human Communication* (Boston: Allyn and Bacon, 1976), pp. 3–10.

3. This is not to say that there are no inborn characteristics of individuals which impact their communication behavior. In fact, an extensive body of research has accumulated which indicates that a substantial portion of the variability among people in terms of personality and temperament is largely due to genetic factors. For a discussion of this work and its implications for communication see M. J. Beatty, J. C. McCroskey, and A. D. Heisel, "Communication Apprehension as Temperamental Expression: A Communibiological Paradigm," *Communication Monographs* 65, (1998):197–219.

■ ■ ■ ■ ■

CHAPTER 3

STAGE FRIGHT:
A NORMAL PROBLEM

(Before reading this chapter, please read and complete the brief question-naire presented in Figure 3.1)

A nationwide survey revealed that the primary fear of Americans is the fear of giving a public speech.[1] Even the fear of death came in a poor third! In his extensive work at Stanford University, Zimbardo found that three out of every four college students, like other Americans, have a very great fear of public speaking.[2] My own research, involving over fifty thousand college students and other adults in various parts of the United States, strongly supports Zimbardo's findings. Stage fright—the fear of speaking in public—is experienced by an overwhelming majority of people in this society.

The questionnaire in Figure 3.1 is known as the Personal Report of Communication Apprehension (PRCA-24).[3] It is designed to provide an indication of how much apprehension (fear or anxiety) you feel in a variety of communication contexts. Figure 3.2 provides information on how to score the PRCA. Compute your scores.

The higher the score you obtain, the more apprehension you feel in the various communication contexts. Scores on the various contexts can range from a low of 6 to a high of 30. Any score above 18 indicates some degree of apprehension. If you score above 18 for the public speaking con-text, you are like the overwhelming majority of Americans.

A NORMAL PROBLEM

The title of this chapter is intended to suggest that stage fright is a normal problem. Normal people experience stage fright. But what is "normal"? This term presents definitional problems even to psychiatrists and psychol-ogists. What is meant by use of the term *normal* is *that which characterizes most people.* To be afraid of plastic pens or objects falling from outer space is

Directions: This instrument is composed of twenty-four statements concerning your feelings about communication with other people. Please indicate in the space provided the degree to which each statement applies to you by marking whether you (1) Strongly Agree, (2) Agree, (3) Are Undecided, (4) Disagree, or (5) Strongly Disagree with each statement. There are no right or wrong answers. Many of the statements are similar to other statements. Do not be concerned about this. Work quickly; just record your first impressions.

_____ 1. I dislike participating in group discussions.

_____ 2. Generally, I am comfortable while participating in group discussions.

_____ 3. I am tense and nervous while participating in group discussions.

_____ 4. I like to get involved in group discussions.

_____ 5. Engaging in a group discussion with new people makes me tense and nervous.

_____ 6. I am calm and relaxed while participating in group discussions.

_____ 7. Generally, I am nervous when I have to participate in a meeting.

_____ 8. Usually I am calm and relaxed while participating in meetings.

_____ 9. I am very calm and relaxed when I am called upon to express an opinion at a meeting.

_____ 10. I am afraid to express myself at meetings.

_____ 11. Communicating at meetings usually makes me uncomfortable.

_____ 12. I am very relaxed when answering questions at a meeting.

_____ 13. While participating in a conversation with a new acquaintance, I feel very nervous.

_____ 14. I have no fear of speaking up in conversations.

_____ 15. Ordinarily I am very tense and nervous in conversations.

_____ 16. Ordinarily I am very calm and relaxed in conversations.

_____ 17. While conversing with a new acquaintance, I feel very relaxed.

_____ 18. I am afraid to speak up in conversations.

_____ 19. I have no fear of giving a speech.

_____ 20. Certain parts of my body feel very tense and rigid while giving a speech.

_____ 21. I feel relaxed while giving a speech.

_____ 22. My thoughts become confused and jumbled when I am giving a speech.

_____ 23. I face the prospect of giving a speech with confidence.

_____ 24. While giving a speech, I get so nervous I forget facts I really know.

FIGURE 3.1 Personal Report of Communication Apprehension (PRCA-24).

The PRCA-24 permits computation of one total score and four subscores. Subscores relate to communication apprehension in each of four common contexts—group discussions, meetings, interpersonal conversations, and public speaking. To compute your scores, merely add or subtract your scores for each item as indicated below.

Subscore Desired	**Scoring Formula**
Group Discussions	18 + scores for items 2, 4, and 6 − scores for items 1, 3, and 5
Meetings	18 + scores for items 8, 9, and 12 − scores for items 7, 10, and 11
Interpersonal Conversations	18 + scores for items 14, 16, and 17 − scores for items 13, 15, and 18
Public Speaking	18 + scores for items 19, 21, and 23 − scores for items 20, 22, and 24

FIGURE 3.2   How to Score the PRCA-24.

not normal; most people do not have those fears. To be fearful of giving a public speech is normal, since most people experience that fear.

To place the label "normal" on the experience of stage fright is not to suggest that it is not a problem; it is. However, most people who experience stage fright are of the opinion that most other people do not experience it. They think they are among the few who do, and this makes them feel abnormal. This misperception makes an already troublesome problem even worse than it needs to be. The first step in learning to control your stage fright is to recognize it for what it is: a normal reaction to a potentially threatening experience.

Although we have indicated that experiencing stage fright in a public speaking setting is quite normal, we do not wish to imply that all experiences of apprehension in communication are normal. Some are distinctly abnormal. Stage fright is one form of communication apprehension. In order to understand it better and move toward bringing it under control, we need to look at communication apprehension within a broader context.

COMMUNICATION APPREHENSION

Communication apprehension is an individual's level of fear or anxiety associated with either real or anticipated communication with another person or persons.[4] There are four types of communication apprehension: trait-like, context-based, audience-based, and situational.

Traitlike Communication Apprehension

Much of the research on communication apprehension has taken the view that it is a predisposition, based in the individual's personality, that exists across communication contexts.[5] This type of communication apprehension represents a general orientation, or trait, of the individual. The questionnaire in Figure 3.1 (the PRCA) is designed to measure that general orientation. The total PRCA score you computed will give you some idea of the degree to which you experience traitlike communication apprehension. Total scores may range from 24 to 120. Any score above 72 indicates that you are more generally apprehensive about communication than the average person. Scores above 80 indicate a very high level of traitlike communication apprehension. Scores below 59 indicate a very low level. Extreme scores (below 50 or above 80) are abnormal. They suggest that the degree of apprehension you may experience in any given communication situation may not be associated with a realistic response to that situation. That is, very high scores suggest that you will often experience a high degree of fear or anxiety in communication situations in which there is no rational reason for such an experience. Very low scores, on the other hand, suggest that you often will not experience either fear or anxiety even in situations in which you reasonably should be expected to have such an experience. In contrast, the average, or normal, person will experience fear or anxiety in some situations but not in others, depending on the situation itself.

Although stage fright is not the same as general shyness[6] or communication apprehension, they are related. People who are generally shy or have a generally high level of communication apprehension are more likely to experience stage fright, and the experience is more likely to be severe. Changing personality orientations is not easy, and it can seldom be accomplished without professional help. However, such a change may be necessary for shy or highly apprehensive persons to develop fully the ability to control their stage fright.

Context-Based Communication Apprehension

Traitlike communication apprehension is an orientation toward communication across varied contexts and situations. Context-based communication apprehension is restricted to a single generalized context. Thus, you may have high context-based communication apprehension with regard to one or more contexts and moderate or low communication apprehension with regard to other contexts. The questionnaire in Figure 3.1 (the PRCA) is concerned with four of the more common contexts: conversing with one other person, interacting in a small group, talking at a meeting, and public speaking. Compare the scores you computed for these four contexts. If you are like most people, the scores will not all be alike. Typically, the highest scores are reported for public speaking and the lowest for interpersonal conversations. However, for some people the opposite is true. Many professional performers, for example, have very low scores for public speaking but very high scores for some, or all, of the other contexts.

Stage fright, as we view it here, is one form of context-based communication apprehension—specifically, that which relates to public speaking. Having a very high or very low level of context-based communication apprehension causes one to behave and feel just like a person with a very high or very low level of general communication apprehension (or shyness), but only in situations representing that generalized context. Thus, a person with a high level of context-based communication apprehension about public speaking would be expected to experience a high degree of stage fright when confronted with a situation requiring public speaking, but the same person may be completely relaxed in other communication situations. Unless this high level of context-based communication apprehension is joined by a similarly high traitlike level of communication apprehension, however, it is quite possible for most people to learn to control the resulting stage fright through sufficient training and experience.

Audience-Based Communication Apprehension

Context-based communication apprehension represents an orientation of the individual toward a given communication context, or generalized situation, regardless of the other people involved, but audience-based communication apprehension represents an orientation of the individual toward communication with a specific person or group of persons, regardless of the context in which the communication takes place. The high-school principal generates this type of communication apprehension in many students. It does not make any difference whether they are to talk to the principal alone, in a small group, in a meeting, or as a member of an audience for a public speech; the students experience high apprehension.

We all have people in our environment with whom we feel comfortable, and most of us have some that uniformly make us uncomfortable. Our level of audience-based communication apprehension, therefore, varies sharply depending on to whom we have to talk. Some people feel little stage fright if they are asked to give a speech before a class of their friends but succumb to panic if asked to speak to a group of strangers. Many others have exactly the opposite reaction. For some students, giving a speech is not that big a problem, but to have to give it in front of the teacher is terrifying. They are probably experiencing audience-based communication apprehension and would have a similar response to asking a question in that teacher's class, having the teacher join a small discussion group in which they are participating, or having the teacher call them in for a conference. Stage fright, then, can be a function of the people to whom one is speaking and, consequently, can be highly variable in severity from one audience to another.

Typically, people report the most communication apprehension when talking with strangers, quite a bit less when talking with acquaintances, and the least when talking with friends. Having a very high or very low level of audience-based communication apprehension causes one to behave and feel just like a person with a very high or very low level of general communication apprehension, but only in situations involving that particular type of audience. Thus, a person with a very high level of audience-based communication apprehension about talking to strangers would be expected to experience a high degree of stage fright when presenting a speech to a group of strangers, but the person might be completely relaxed when presenting a speech to a group of friends. Unless this high level of audience-based communication apprehension is joined by a similarly high traitlike level of communication apprehension, however, it is quite possible for most people to learn to control the resulting stage fright through sufficient training and experience.

Situational Communication Apprehension

Situational communication apprehension is experienced by virtually everyone at one time or another. This form of communication apprehension represents the orientation of the individual to communicating with a given individual or group, at a given time, in a given context. Although personality orientation, context orientation, and orientation toward an individual or group will have a bearing on the degree of fear or anxiety felt in any communication situation, the unique combination of influences generated by audience, time, and context is what generates situational communication apprehension. Although we may neither have a generally high level of communication apprehension or shyness, nor normally be bothered by this particular group of people or by public speaking in general, the unique combination of these factors may generate a high level of stage fright. Giving another speech to the same group next week may not have a similar effect.

To illustrate this type of communication apprehension, I will describe a true experience of my own. I have a very low level of general communication apprehension. I thoroughly enjoy public speaking and give many speeches every year. While I was a college student, I was an intercollegiate debater and spoke before numerous student body assemblies in the small college I attended. During my last year of college, I was invited to serve as master of ceremonies for an all-college talent show. I immediately accepted the invitation and looked forward to the experience. I never received any more information about the show before the day it was to be presented. There was no dress rehearsal. Until fifteen minutes before the start of the show, I did not even know the number of performers or who

was presenting each act. When I went on stage to start the show, I was as near to panic as one can be and still function. That level of stage fright did not decline until the show was completed. I had extreme situational communication apprehension. Never once in the decades since that time have I experienced stage fright as badly, although I have had similar situational communication apprehension in non-public-speaking contexts.

The key point to be drawn from this illustration is that no matter who you are or what may be your general orientation toward communication, toward a generalized-communication context, or toward an individual or group of people, you can find yourself in a communication situation that will provoke situational communication apprehension. In the public-speaking context this is called stage fright. To conclude the illustration, even though I was near panic, no one noticed my stage fright, and many commented that I did a good job. They could not see that the shirt under my jacket was wringing wet, nor could they hear my rapid heartbeat (which sounded deafening to me). They also did not know I drank over two gallons of water while offstage during the acts in a vain attempt to conquer "dry mouth." The final point, then, is that even though you experience stage fright, even severe stage fright, with sufficient training and experience you can learn to control it so that, despite your misery, your public-speaking attempt can be successful.

CAUSES OF STAGE FRIGHT

We have noted that most stage fright is a normal response to a threatening situation and have suggested that recognition of that fact is the first step toward learning to control your stage fright. Now that we have placed stage fright within the broader context of communication apprehension and shyness, we can turn our attention to what causes stage fright.[7] We can place these causes into three groups: internal, general external, and situational external.

Internal Causes

Stage fright is an internal, very private experience. Although people experiencing stage fright may have higher physiological arousal (for example, more rapid heartbeat and increased sweating) than they would otherwise have, and they may exhibit distracting mannerisms and vocal cues that are observable to listeners, it has long been known that the internal experience of stage fright has little relationship to either the degree of physiological arousal or observable characteristics of speaking.[8] *Stage fright primarily is a mental, not a physical, phenomenon.*

If you have ever experienced stage fright, the assertion that this is a mental problem rather than a physical one may be difficult for you to accept. You know that when you are experiencing stage fright your heart is beating rapidly, you may be sweating, your hands may be shaking and your knees may be knocking. Aren't those things physical? Of course they are. But what the person who reports having stage fright usually does not realize is that people who do not report having stage fright frequently have many of these same symptoms! In fact, the physical reactions of people who report high stage fright and those who report almost none in some circumstances have been found to differ very little.[9]

As we approach an important public-speaking situation, our bodies become keyed up to perform well. This is a natural physiological response, not unlike that experienced by athletes and musicians. Without that heightened physiological activity, our efforts would be less likely to succeed. People who report not experiencing stage fright often report that just before a speech they are excited and look forward to the experience. People who report a high degree of stage fright describe themselves as fearful and anxious in the same situation. What is happening is that the two types of people are giving different verbal reports of essentially the same physiological responses. They are mentally reacting to the same things in different ways.

In order to control these internal causes of stage fright, it is vital that you do not misinterpret the meaning of your heightened physiological arousal. Your body is not telling you the world is about to end; it is telling you it is getting ready to help you do well.[10]

General External Causes

Although stage fright is an internal response of an individual, things in the external environment affect that response. Our environment in large part determines our learning and thus impacts on our concepts about when to be fearful and anxious.

One of the main reasons that stage fright associated with public speaking is more common than apprehension about other communication settings is that it requires knowledge and skills that are not readily obtained in everyday experience by most people. Consequently, most people have underdeveloped skills in this area. If we do not know how to do something but are in a situation where we must do it, it is certainly normal to become apprehensive. Some communication skills are learned by watching other people and attempting to imitate or model their behavior. We have the opportunity, for example, to interact with other people in conversations every day. We can observe what we perceive to be effective skills exhibited by others and try to model them in our conversations with other people. We may never become outstanding conversationalists in this way, but we are very likely to obtain enough skill development to feel that we can get by in most situations.

In order to obtain knowledge and improved skills in public speaking, many people take public-speaking classes. This is a wise step, but one should not expect such classes to perform miracles. Skill development demands practice. In most public-speaking classes, students have fewer than a dozen opportunities to give speeches. Should you expect this amount of experience to fine-tune your skills to the point at which you will not experience stage fright in the future? Well, if you had only participated in a dozen conversations with other people in your life, how confident do you think you would be in your conversational ability? Public-speaking classes can be an excellent first step, but you will probably need much more experience and practice than one class can give before you can develop full confidence in your skills. As you gain more experience and recognize your improved skills, you can anticipate a gradual reduction in the severity of your stage fright.

Although experience is very valuable, it is no guarantee of improvement. In some cases, *prior experience is a major cause of stage fright*. If we have had a series of unsuccessful experiences, we may learn to be helpless in the face of future similar situations.[11] It is regrettable but true that some students come out of a public-speaking class with worse fright than they had when they entered. If the teacher or other students make the experience highly unpleasant, the results of the class can be very negative. Although a sensitive and competent teacher can do much to prevent this from happening, a person with very high general communication apprehension may interpret the entire experience negatively no matter what the teacher and

Directions: Below are twelve situations in which you might need to communicate. People's abilities to communicate effectively vary a lot, and sometimes the same person is more competent to communicate in one situation than in another. Please indicate how competent you believe you are to communicate in each of the situations described below. Indicate in the space provided at the left of each item your estimate of your competence. Presume 0 = completely incompetent and 100 = completely competent. Your score can be anywhere between 0 and 100, or one of those numbers.

_____   1.   Present a talk to a group of strangers.
_____   2.   Talk with an acquaintance.
_____   3.   Talk in a large meeting of friends.
_____   4.   Talk in a small group of strangers.
_____   5.   Talk with a friend.
_____   6.   Talk in a large meeting of acquaintances.
_____   7.   Talk with a stranger.
_____   8.   Present a talk to a group of friends.
_____   9.   Talk in a small group of acquaintances.
_____ 10.   Talk in a large meeting of strangers.
_____ 11.   Talk in a small group of friends.
_____ 12.   Present a talk to a group of acquaintances.

FIGURE 3.3   Self-Perceived Communication Competence Questionnaire.

other students actually say or do. Thus, if you have very high communication apprehension, it may be wise to seek help in reducing your apprehension level prior to entering such a course; otherwise you may turn a potentially valuable experience into one of the worst experiences of your life.[12]

Self-Perceived Communication Competence

Self-perceived communication competence is discussed under its own heading because it is neither completely an internal cause nor an external cause of stage fright. Rather, it represents an internal perception of external reality. Complete the questionnaire in Figure 3.3 and determine your scores by following the instructions in Figures 3.4[13] and 3.5.

As noted previously, if you have little experience in a particular type of communication, you may have underdeveloped skills for such events. You may have good reason to be fearful and apprehensive. Unfortunately, things are not always as simple as this might suggest. Sometimes our true skill level is not a good predictor of how skilled we think we are. You most likely have run into people who really think they are effective communicators, and who are constantly talking, but they are really not effective. This

To compute the subscores for the SPCC, add the percentages for each item as specified and divide the total by the number indicated below:

Public   Add scores for items 1, 8, and 12, then divide by 3.
Meeting   Add scores for items 3, 6, and 10, then divide by 3.
Group   Add scores for items 4, 9, and 11, then divide by 3.
Dyad Conversation   Add scores for items 2, 5, and 7, then divide by 3.
Stranger   Add scores for items 1, 4, 7, and 10, then divide by 4.
Acquaintance   Add scores for items 2, 6, 9, and 12, then divide by 4.
Friend   Add scores for items 3, 5, 8, and 11, then divide by 4.

To compute the total SPCC score, add the subscores for stranger, acquaintance, and friend, then, divide that total by 3.

FIGURE 3.4   Scoring the SPCC.

Higher SPCC scores indicate higher self-perceived communication competence in the four communication contexts (public, meeting, group, dyad) and with the three types of receivers (stranger, acquaintance, friend), as well as overall self-perceived communication competence. Determine whether you have a high or low score in each case as follows:

Score	High SPCC	Low SPCC
Public	Above 86	Below 51
Meeting	Above 85	Below 51
Group	Above 90	Below 61
Dyad	Above 93	Below 68
Stranger	Above 79	Below 31
Acquaintance	Above 92	Below 62
Friend	Above 99	Below 76
Overall SPCC	Above 97	Below 59

FIGURE 3.5   Interpreting SPCC Scores.

illustrates our key point here: *People make decisions about communication based on their self-perceptions of their own communication skills, not on the basis of the actual skills.* These self-perceptions may be very accurate, but often they are not. If you think you are not competent to give a speech, you will react as an incompetent person, and will almost certainly be highly apprehensive if you are forced to speak. Self-perceived incompetence is associated with higher communication apprehension in all general contexts and with all types of receivers.[14] One reason skills courses often have a positive impact on students' levels of communication apprehension, beyond their acquisition of new skills, is that as a function of taking such classes they learn that they are not incompetent! Feelings of incompetence are associated with increased apprehension, and becoming aware that you really can do something that you previously didn't think possible will go a long way toward reducing that apprehension.

Situational External Causes

The causes of stage fright already discussed apply primarily to a general disposition toward stage fright in public-speaking situations. Other causes of stage fright have been suggested by both theorists and public speakers as a function of their own experiences. The causes examined here will focus on elements that may generate stage fright even for people who do not experience it generally and that make it more severe for those who do. Each of these causes relates to the specific situation in which the public speaking will take place. The most commonly described causes include degree of evaluation, degree of conspicuousness, degree of ambiguity, degree of novelty, and degree of prior success. Each will be described from the vantage point of people who believe they have contributed to their own problems.

Degree of Evaluation.   The more we believe our speaking effort will be the subject of evaluation by the audience or others, the more stage fright we are likely to experience. Of course, if we are highly confident that the evaluation will be positive, the severity of the problem will be greatly reduced. Few people have such a high level of self-confidence that they actually enjoy being evaluated. The number of students, for example, who love taking tests is far exceeded by the number who hate to take them. In a very real sense, any public speech is a test. The more evaluative that test is and the more there is at stake, the more likely the speaker is to experience stage fright.

Degree of Conspicuousness.   If you spill a cup of coffee when you are alone, you may be annoyed with yourself. If you do the same thing when you have just been introduced to a new acquaintance, you may be embarrassed. If you are at the head table at a banquet of four hundred people and do the same thing, you may be humiliated. The degree of conspicuousness of your behavior has a major impact on your reactions in these instances. In general, the more conspicuous your communication effort, the more likely you will be to experience stage fright.

The speaker in a public-speaking setting is always conspicuous to some degree. The size of the audience contributes to the degree of conspicuousness, with larger audiences typically generating more stage fright. Similarly, speeches broadcast on radio and television, although the size of the audience may be unknown, tend to raise the degree of conspicuousness and, consequently, the level of stage fright. In addition to size of audience and involvement of the media, being a new speaker (such as the newly elected president of a group), the only speaker, or a representative of an important group may increase conspicuousness even if the audience is small. In any event, the more conspicuous the speaker feels, the more likely stage fright will be experienced.

Degree of Ambiguity.   Fear of the unknown is a common human experience. The more ambiguity there is in a situation, the less certain we can be about how to behave in that situation. Consequently, when the circumstances surrounding a speaking situation are ambiguous, the probability that the speaker will experience stage fright is increased. Some things that can increase ambiguity include uncertainties about how large the audience will be, who will be in the audience, what the audience expects, what previous speakers have said, and what the audience knows about what you are going to say. All of these things make audience analysis and solid preparation more difficult. Such analysis is a crucial part of the rhetorical communication process, as we will explain in more detail in later chapters. When a speaker cannot prepare adequately because of the ambiguity surrounding the situation, stage fright is likely to increase.

Degree of Novelty.   Situations that are novel or unusual, like those that are ambiguous, create uncertainty in the minds of speakers. If we approach a speaking situation unlike any we have confronted before, we may have difficulty determining how we should behave. The more novel or unusual the situation is, therefore, the more likely the speaker will be to experience stage fright.

Degree of Prior Success.   Our experiences in the past build our expectancies for what will happen in the future. If we have failed in our speaking before a group in the past, we probably will expect to fail in the future. If we have succeeded in our speaking before a group in the past, we probably will expect to succeed again. The more we expect to succeed, the less likely we will be to experience stage fright.

A key to appreciating these causes of stage fright is the recognition that each of the causes provides a rational reason for concern. If a number of the aforementioned causes are present, a person *should* be apprehensive about his or her speech. To experience no apprehension would be to be insensitive to a real threat. Such a response would be akin to knowing that a stove is hot but still putting one's hand on it. Most people would see that as quite irrational. We should see stage fright as stemming from these causes in the same way. Although we want to control the stage fright so that a successful speech is possible, the only way to completely eliminate it is to eliminate the cause(s). That may not be possible. In short, we must all learn to live with and handle a certain degree of stage fright.

Research on Situational Causes of Stage Fright

The presumed situational causes of stage fright outlined above are commonly discussed in books and articles concerned with stage fright in public speaking.[15] Most students read these descriptions and see themselves responding with fear or anxiety when such situations are present. In short, these alleged causes of stage fright make sense to most people, both to those who have actually given speeches and to those who are preparing their first one. It comes as a surprise to many, therefore, to learn that research has been reported that calls these presumed causes into serious question. In fact, it appears from this research that these factors may not be causes at all.

The work of Beatty and his colleagues indicates that we need to take another look at the presumed situational causes of stage fright.[16] The results of this research program indicate that, even though speakers' perceptions of situational variables like those discussed previously are substantially correlated with the amount of stage fright those speakers report, this relationship cannot be presumed to be a causal one. That is, just because higher degrees of perceived evaluation or conspicuousness are correlated with higher degrees of stage fright does not mean that either evaluation or conspicuousness caused the stage fright that was experienced.

The research indicates that people have general expectations about each of the supposed situational factors believed to be related to stage fright. As a result, regardless of what the situation *really* is, those people who expect high evaluation (for example) will feel highly evaluated even if no one is evaluating them. Furthermore, these expectations are substantially correlated with general communication apprehension. Thus, people who are generally high in communication apprehension expect high levels of the various situational "causes," perceive those levels to be there (whether they are or not), and experience greater stage fright than those who are generally low in communication apprehension. The latter people expect lower levels of the situational "causes," perceive the actual levels to be lower, and experience less stage fright. Hence, the primary cause of more severe stage fright is a person's high general communication apprehension, not the aspects of the situation that are regularly blamed.

This is not to say, of course, that extreme aspects of a situation can never have an impact on a person's stage fright. My experience as a master of ceremonies for a talent show, discussed previously, clearly illustrates that the situation can have a major impact. Rather, the results of this research suggest that my experience was the rare event, not the norm. Most situations are far less extreme. In these more normal circumstances, our general apprehension level is most likely to determine our expectations of the situation, hence how we see that situation, and the degree of stage fright we experience.

Root Cause of Communication Apprehension

Since people with higher general communication apprehension are likely to suffer more from stage fright, it is important to understand the origin of communication apprehension. For most of the twentieth century scholars believed that communication apprehension was learned as a function of one's upbringing and experiences. This theory was based on the "social learning model." This approach to the study of human behavior generally assumed that children were born with a virtually "blank slate," and learned how to behave from their parents and others within their culture. Thus, if a child grew into an adult that behaved poorly, it was attributed to bad parenting and/or a poor education.

By the end of the twentieth century, it became increasingly clear that this was a very poor explanation of human behavior in many instances. Most importantly the work of neurobiologists and psychobiologists pointed strongly to powerful genetic factors as having a major impact on human behavior. Just as our genes generally determine how tall we will be and the size of our nose and feet, it was determined that our genes also influence our basic temperamental and personality orientations and predispositions. Thus, while experiences in our culture help shape our behavior, our basic orientations and predispositions are impacted very little by our learning experiences.

Work in a new research approach referred to as "communibiology" that has drawn heavily from the work of the neurobiologists and psychobiologists has provided insight into the origins of communication apprehension and other important communication predispositions and orientations.[17] This work indicates that communication apprehension is highly associated with two genetically-based temperament variables— neuroticism and extraversion/introversion. People with high communication apprehension have been found to be high in neuroticism and low in extraversion. More simply, high communication apprehensives are neurotic introverts.

Consequently, it is important to recognize that people are born with neurological structures which influence certain predispositions and orientations toward communication such as communication apprehension (as well as willingness to communicate, assertiveness, responsiveness, verbal aggressiveness, argumentativeness, etc.). These predispositions may be pushed to more extreme or more moderate levels as a function of the person's experiences in their culture from childhood through adulthood. However, the genetic elements work to limit the amount of impact life experiences can have. Thus, it is not unreasonable to expect that some change in a person's communication behavior can be observed over time. However, chances for the environment to produce dramatic changes (going from a high communication apprehensive to a low communication apprehensive, for example) are virtually impossible.

The bottom line is that if you experience stage fright, most of it is probably the result of your genetically-based predisposition toward communication. However, this does not mean you cannot learn to control the severity of your stage fright, or to learn to cope with the stage fright you experience to the extent that you can be an effective communicator. The place to begin this process is to recognize that stage fright comes from within, it is not caused by something "out there."

While most people can learn to cope with stage fright without any medical assistance, some people with the most severe forms of communication apprehension (sometimes referred to as "social anxiety") may not be able to. Recent research has determined that anti-depressant drugs (such as Paxil and Prozac) can have a very positive impact on stage fright as well. If you feel you might be this severely impacted by stage fright, you should consult a physician. He or she may determine that prescribing one of these drugs for you would be appropriate.

EFFECTS OF STAGE FRIGHT

The primary effects of stage fright can be divided into two categories: those experienced internally and those with behavioral impact that is potentially observable by others. We will consider each in turn, but before you read further, please read and complete the questionnaire in Figure 3.6, known as the Willingness to Communicate Scale (WTC).[18]

Internal Effects

Previously we noted that stage fright is primarily a mental response to the communication environment. The most frequent effect of stage fright is the experience of psychological discomfort. When we experience stage fright we feel a lack of control over our environment. Some people become very disoriented and have difficulty remembering the content of their speech. This feeling of being unable to cope, of being inadequate for the task, is the sensation that most people find to be the worst effect of stage fright. It also is the cue that most people use to determine the severity of their stage fright and to recognize when they are able to control that response.

Although a state of high physiological arousal can exist with or without the individual's interpreting such arousal as stage fright, as noted previously,

---

Directions: Below are twenty situations in which a person might choose to communicate or not to communicate. Assume that you have *completely free choice*. Indicate the percentage of time you would choose to communicate in each type of situation. Indicate in the space at the left what percent of the time you would choose to communicate. 0 = never, 100 = always.

_____   1.   Talk with a service station attendant.
_____   2.   Talk with a physician.
_____   3.   Present a talk to a group of strangers.
_____   4.   Talk with an acquaintance while standing in line.
_____   5.   Talk with a salesperson in a store.
_____   6.   Talk in a large meeting of friends.
_____   7.   Talk with a police officer.
_____   8.   Talk in a small group of strangers.
_____   9.   Talk with a friend while standing in line.
_____ 10.   Talk with a waiter or waitress in a restaurant.
_____ 11.   Talk in a large meeting of acquaintances.
_____ 12.   Talk with a stranger while standing in line.
_____ 13.   Talk with a secretary.
_____ 14.   Present a talk to a group of friends.
_____ 15.   Talk in a small group of acquaintances.
_____ 16.   Talk with a garbage collector.
_____ 17.   Talk in a large meeting of strangers.
_____ 18.   Talk with a spouse (or girlfriend or boyfriend).
_____ 19.   Talk in a small group of friends.
_____ 20.   Present a talk to a group of acquaintances.

FIGURE 3.6   Willingness to Communicate Scale (WTC).

when we mentally describe our feelings as stage fright, these high levels of physiological response force themselves into more conscious awareness and can result in additional problems. Common physiological effects associated with stage fright are rapid beating of the heart, increased perspiration, some shakiness, and dry mouth. Sometimes these physiological responses interact with the mental feelings of inadequacy in such a way that both are exaggerated to an extreme level. When this occurs, a person can be subject to nausea or dizziness, which can even be severe enough to cause the person to black out temporarily. While these effects certainly can be serious and distressing to the individual, they are almost always transitory and will diminish once the speech is over. Such severe effects, while not truly rare, occur for only a relatively small portion of the population. Even these individuals, with proper help and experience, can learn to prevent the problem from reaching this level of intensity.

Directions: The WTC permits computation of one total score and seven subscores. The subscores relate to willingness to communicate in each of four common communication contexts and with three types of audiences. To compute your scores, add your scores for each item as specified and divide by the number indicated below.

Group Discussions	Add scores for items 8,15, and 19; then divide by 3.
Meetings	Add scores for items 6, 11, and 17; then divide by 3.
Interpersonal Conversations	Add scores for items 4, 9, and 12; then divide by 3.
Public Speaking	Add scores for items 3, 14, and 20; then divide by 3.
Strangers	Add scores for items 3, 8, 12, and 17; then divide by 4.
Acquaintances	Add scores for items 4, 11,15, and 20; then divide by 4.
Friends	Add scores for items 6, 9, 14, and 19; then divide by 4.

To compute the total WTC scores, add the subscores for strangers, acquaintances, and friends, then divide by 3.

FIGURE 3.7   **How to Score the WTC.**

Behavioral Effects

The most common behavioral effect of stage fright is withdrawal from and avoidance of public-speaking situations. This is a very normal response. If one is fearful of something, whether it be heights, water, insects, or public speaking, the natural human reaction is to try to stay away from it. Thus, many people who have experienced stage fright never, or seldom, experience it again. They just do not give any more public speeches. Although this approach may enable the person to avoid experiencing stage fright, it may also present a severe handicap to the individual in her or his occupation or personal life. There are many advantages to be gained in this society by giving public speeches, and avoidance may cause one to lose opportunities to obtain those advantages. In addition, because stage fright is generally reduced through experience, the avoidance of such experience prevents the individual from overcoming the problem and gaining more self-confidence.

The WTC is designed to indicate how willing you are to communicate in a variety of contexts with different types of receivers. Figure 3.7 provides information on how to score the WTC. Compute your scores.

Total WTC Scale Score	65.1
Subscores:	
Public Speaking	54.2
Meetings	59.7
Group Discussions	70.8
Dyad Conversation	76.2
Strangers	38.5
Acquaintances	72.5
Friends	84.7

FIGURE 3.8 Norms for the Willingness to Communicate Scale.

The higher your total WTC score, the more willing you are to communicate generally. Similarly, the higher your given subscore for a type of context or audience, the more willing you are to communicate in that type of context or with that type of audience. Figure 3.8 presents norms for each type of context and audience based on responses of several hundred college students. Compare your scores with those norms.

Although many other factors may influence a person's general willingness to communicate as well as her or his willingness to communicate in a given situation,[19] in the U.S. culture a person's level of communication apprehension is one of the best predictors of such willingness: the higher the apprehension, the lower the willingness. Thus, it should not be surprising that, because most people experience more apprehension about making speeches to strangers, the normal level of willingness to communicate is lowest for presenting a public speech to a group of strangers. If we fear something and can avoid it, we simply will not do it.

The second type of behavioral effect of stage fright relates to the actual presentation of speeches. The person may, but not necessarily will, have a reduced quality of delivery. While many people are able to control their stage fright so that none of their behavior gives evidence of their internal distress, others will have faltering delivery, poor gestures, distracting mannerisms, inappropriate voice volume, poor eye contact, or loss of organization. When these things happen (and they can and do happen to many speakers who do *not* experience extreme stage fright), the quality of speaking deteriorates, and with this deterioration comes less positive influence over the audience and negative perceptions of the speaker in the minds of the audience members.

Throughout this discussion of stage fright we have discussed only negative effects. Can nothing good be said for it? Unfortunately, no. Although stage fright is normal and is common to most public speakers, it is a negative element that one must learn to control to achieve maximum success in the communication process.

CONTROLLING STAGE FRIGHT

In order to learn to control stage fright we need to direct our attention to the elements that cause it. As we have noted, the stage fright experienced in any particular public-speaking situation is tied to our general level of apprehension about communication and public speaking in particular, and the specific factors of the situation in which we find ourselves, if those factors are particularly unusual. These factors interact to produce the stage fright we feel at any given time. Consequently, we must be concerned with controlling each of these causes.

Controlling General Communication Apprehension

People who suffer from high general communication apprehension or high apprehension about public speaking as a generalized situation often need help beyond what typically is available in a classroom devoted to public-speaking instruction. While such help often is available through the department offering the public-speaking course or through a college's counseling service, relatively few students take advantage of such opportunities. Many never learn that opportunities for help exist. For an estimated 10 to 20 percent of students, such help is central to learning to overcome stage fright.

Programs designed to help people overcome general communication apprehension typically focus on one of several available behavior therapies. Most of these require a relatively brief time commitment, usually less than ten hours spread over two to six weeks. The most commonly employed method is known as systematic desensitization.[20] This method involves two major parts. The first is training in deep muscle relaxation. The person receiving the training learns to relax each of the various muscle groups in the body and to recognize when tension appears in any muscle group. The second part involves learning to respond with relaxation in the face of situations that previously caused the individual to become tense. This method has been found to be extremely effective for between 80 and 90 percent of the people who have received it. If such a program is available, and if you suffer from high communication apprehension or generalized apprehension about public speaking, you are encouraged to take advantage of the opportunity to obtain this help. It can go a long way toward helping you to control your stage fright.

Controlling Public-Speaking Experiences

Unsuccessful public-speaking experiences tend to increase the level of stage fright for later experiences. The main reason people have such unsuccessful experiences is a lack of knowledge about the public-speaking process and a lack of training to use that knowledge. The primary purpose of the remaining chapters in this book is to provide you with the necessary information to build your knowledge of both the public-speaking process and rhetorical communication in other communication contexts. If you acquire this information, you will have the knowledge required to speak in public successfully.

You may be reading this book for a course that will permit you to practice your skills under the guidance of a qualified instructor. If so, you will have the opportunity to apply your knowledge and build your skills. If not, you should seek such an experience. If no qualified instructors are available to critique your speaking, at least seek the comments of friends who will tell you the truth. They may not be experts, but at least they can let you know some of the things you do that they like and some that distract them. In this way you can use the experiences you have to improve your skills for later use.

Controlling Situational Factors

Although it is impossible to control all factors in all situations that may increase stage fright, there is much you can do. The key term is *complete preparation*. The more fully and carefully prepared you are, the less likely any situational factor will be to get to you. The third section of this book is devoted to the steps in preparing your messages. If you follow these carefully, there should be relatively few situations that will raise your stage fright to the level of a severe problem. Inadequate preparation, however, will leave even the most confident speaker open to potentially severe stage fright.

A FINAL WORD

Stage fright is a problem—a normal problem. Almost everyone experiences it at one time or another when confronted with the obligation to speak in public. For some the experience is more common and more severe than for others. It is hoped that after reading this chapter you realize that you are not very different from other people—they also have stage fright. Also, you should now be aware that your stage fright can be controlled so that it does not prevent you from speaking with success. However, you are cautioned not to expect miracles. Stage fright does not disappear overnight. It is a problem you have to learn to live with. But you *can* live with it and become highly successful in public speaking, even when stage fright is present.

DISCUSSION QUESTIONS

1. How is stage fright different from general communication apprehension?

2. Are shyness and stage fright the same thing?

3. What is the relationship between internally experienced stage fright and observable behaviors we often associate with stage fright? Why does this relationship exist?

4. Can a person who has never given a speech experience stage fright? Why or why not?

5. Would you believe a person who said she or he used to have stage fright but does not any more? How about one who said she or he never used to have stage fright but does now?

6. What is your impression of a person who has severe stage fright? Why?

NOTES

1. Bruskin Associates, "What Are Americans Afraid Of?" *Bruskin Report,* no. 53 (1971).

2. P. G. Zimbardo, *Shyness: What It Is and What to Do About It* (Reading, MA: Addison-Wesley, 1977): 37.

3. For earlier versions of the PRCA, see J. C. McCroskey, "Measures of Communication-Bound Anxiety," *Speech Monographs* 37 (1970): 269–77; "Validity of the PRCA as an Index of Oral Communication Apprehension," *Communication Monographs* 45 (1978): 192–203; and the 4th ed. of this book (1982).

4. J.C. McCroskey, "Oral Communication Apprehension: A Summary of Recent Theory and Research," *Human Communication Research* 4 (1977): 79–96.

5. Ibid., for summary of this research.

6. Zimbardo, *Shyness.*

7. Much of the material included in this section is the product of extended interactions with John A. Daly as well as of his writings in this area. The author is indebted to Daly for much of his current thinking, but assumes responsibility for the material presented here; it may or may not represent Daly's current thinking.

8. T. Clevenger, Jr., "A Synthesis of Experimental Research in Stage Fright," *Quarterly Journal of Speech* 45 (1950): 134–45.

9. See, for example, D. T. Porter, "Self-Report Scales of Communication Apprehension and Autonomic Arousal (Heart Rate): A Test of Construct Validity," *Speech Monographs* 41 (1974): 267–76. Some of his later unpublished work is even more supportive of this point. Other research has demonstrated that, under intense public-speaking conditions, the heart rates of apprehensive and nonapprehensive speakers do not differ. See M. J. Beatty and R. R. Behnke, "Effects of Public Speaking Trait Anxiety and Intensity of Speaking Task on Heart Rate During Performance," *Human Communication Research* 18 (1991): 147–76. Under less intense conditions, however, highly apprehensive speakers experience higher heart rates as a result of their expectations of negative situational conditions. See also M. J. Beatty and M. H. Friedland, "Public Speaking State Anxiety as a Function of Selected Situational and Predispositional Variables," *Communication Education* 39 (1990): 142–47.

10. It is, of course, possible to become too aroused. A person can learn to control excessive arousal through relaxation training. This will be discussed later.

11. M.E.P. Seligman, *Helplessness* (New York: W. H. Freeman, 1975).

12. W.D. Brooks and S. M. Platz, "The Effects of Speech Training upon Self-Concept as a Communicator," *Speech Teacher* 17 (1968): 44–49; S. A. Taylor and P. K. Hamilton, "The Effects of the Basic Speech Course on Anxiety, Dogmatism, Cognitive Ability, and Communicative Ability," paper presented at the annual convention of the International Communication Association, New Orleans, 1974.

13. J.C. McCroskey and L. L. McCroskey, "Self-Report as an Approach to Measuring Communication Competence," *Communication Research Reports* 5 (1988): 108–13.

14. V. P. Richmond, J. C. McCroskey, and L. L. McCroskey, "An Investigation of Self-Perceived Communication Competence and Personality Orientations," *Communication Research Reports* 6 (1989): 28–36; A. Sallinen-Kuparinen, J. C. McCroskey, and V. P. Richmond, "Willingness to Communicate, Communication Apprehension, Introversion, and Self-Reported Communication Competence: Finnish and American Comparisons," *Communication Research Reports* 8 (1991): 55–64.

15. A.H. Buss, *Self-Consciousness and Social Anxiety* (San Francisco: W.H. Freeman, 1980); J. A. Daly and A. H. Buss, "The Transient Causes of Audience Anxiety," in J. A. Daly and J. C. McCroskey (Eds.), *Avoiding Communication: Shyness, Reticence, and Communication Apprehension* (Beverly Hills, CA: Sage, 1984); J. C. McCroskey and M. J. Beatty, "Oral Communication Apprehension," in W. H. Jones, J. M. Cheek, and S. R. Briggs (Eds.), *Shyness: Perspectives on Research and Treatment* (New York: Plenum, 1986).

16. M. J. Beatty, "Situational and Predispositional Correlates of Public Speaking Anxiety," *Communication Education* 37 (1988): 27–39; M. J. Beatty, G. L. Balfantz, and A. Y. Kuwabara, "Trait-like Qualities of Selected Variables Assumed to Be Transient Causes of Performance State Anxiety," *Communication Education* 28 (1989): 277–89; Beatty and Friedland, "Public Speaking State Anxiety."

17. See, for example, M. J. Beatty, J. C. McCroskey, and A. D. Heisel, "Communication Apprehension as Temperamental Expression: A Communibiological Paradigm," *Communication Monographs*, 65 (1998): 197–219; M. J. Beatty and J. C. McCroskey, "Interpersonal Communication as Temperamental Expression: A Communibiological Paradigm," (pp. 41–67) and J. C. McCroskey and Michael J. Beatty, "Communication Apprehension," (pp. 215–23) in J. C. McCroskey, J. A. Daly, M. M. Martin, and M. J. Beatty (Eds.), *Communication and Personality: Trait Perspectives* (Cresskill, NJ: Hampton Press, 1998); M. J. Beatty and J. C. McCroskey, "It's In Our Nature: Verbal Aggressiveness as Temperamental Expression," *Communication Quarterly*, 45 (1997): 446–460; and K. M. Valencic, M. J. Beatty, J. E. Rudd, J. A. Dobos, and A. D. Heisel, "An Empirical Test of A Communibiological Model of Trait Verbal Aggressiveness," *Communication Quarterly*, 46 (1998):327–341.

18. J. C. McCroskey and J. E. Baer, "Willingness to Communicate: The Construct and Its Measurement," paper presented at the annual convention of the Speech Communication Association, Denver, 1985; J. C. McCroskey and V. P. Richmond, "Willingness to Communicate," in J. C. McCroskey and J. A. Daly (Eds.), *Personality and Interpersonal Communication* (Newbury Park, CA: Sage, 1987); J. C. McCroskey, "Reliability and Validity of the Willingness to Communicate Scale," *Communication Quarterly* 40 (1992): 16–25.

19. Ibid.

20. J. C. McCroskey, D. C. Ralph, and J. E. Barrick, "The Effects of Systematic Desensitization on Speech Anxiety," *Speech Teacher* 19 (1970): 32–36; J. C. McCroskey, "The Implementation of a Large Scale Program of Systematic Desensitization for Communication Apprehension," *Speech Teacher* 21 (1972): 255–65. For a description of another promising method, cognitive restructuring, see J. Ayres and T. S. Hopf, "Visualization: A Means of Reducing Speech Anxiety," *Communication Education* 34 (1985): 318–23, and "The Long-term Effect of Visualization in the Classroom: A Brief Research Report," *Communication Education* 39 (1990): 75–78.

BASIC THEORY

CHAPTER 4

THE NATURE
OF THE RECEIVER:
ATTITUDE FORMATION
AND CHANGE

The encoding process in rhetorical communication must take into account, as we stated in Chapter 2, the nature of the people for whom the message is being created. People are not all alike; they are individuals. When they gather together into audiences they do not give up their individuality. The differences that most concern communicators are those in people's attitudes and beliefs. It is impossible for you to perceive all of another person's attitudes and beliefs, much less to perceive those of all of the members of a large audience. How, then, are you realistically to adapt a message to your receivers? You should base the message on *audience analysis*. By this we mean that you should estimate the attitudes and beliefs of the audience and base your message on this estimate. Audience analysis will be examined more closely in Chapter 8, in the discussion on the creation of the message. This chapter, however, is more directly concerned with what attitudes are, how they are formed, why they persist, and how you may cause them to change.

THE NATURE OF ATTITUDES

Psychologists use the term *hypothetical construct* to describe realities that we believe exist, but for which we have no sensory measure. We cannot see, hear, smell, taste, or touch them, but we generally agree that they are real. Probably the most familiar hypothetical construct is intelligence. We cannot perceive intelligence through any of our senses, but almost all of us agree that there is such a thing. *Attitudes* also *are hypothetical constructs*. They are not perceivable through our senses, but as with intelligence, we believe that attitudes exist.

An attitude is an individual's predisposition to behave in a particular way in response to something in the external world. We may have attitudes toward anything in the world. If at a given moment we perceive something new, we are likely to form an attitude toward it. This definition may seem to imply that sometimes a person's attitude may be estimated by observing that person's behavior. But appearances may be deceptive; frequently a person may hold a given attitude but behave in a manner that apparently contradicts it. The woman who has a strongly anti-income tax attitude may still pay her taxes. Or the man who is firmly convinced that cigarette smoking is a health hazard may continue smoking two packs a day.

Several interesting studies of such phenomena have been conducted. In 1934, R. T. LaPiere traveled across the United States with a Chinese friend and his wife. In only one of 251 instances in which they sought service at hotels, restaurants, and other public places were they refused service because of the race of LaPiere's friend. But when the same individuals who had provided service to the LaPiere party were surveyed six months later, 92 percent of them replied no to the question of whether they would accept members of the Chinese race in their establishments. Only one person said yes, and the others said that it "depended on the circumstances." Behavior was almost directly the opposite of expressed attitude.[1]

Kutner, Wilkins, and Yarrow report similar results. Their party of three women—two white and one African American—received service in eleven restaurants and taverns. Two weeks later, they sent letters to each establishment requesting information regarding reservations for a racially mixed party. Not a single establishment replied. Seventeen days later, one of the young women phoned each of the restaurants and taverns. The calls received responses ranging all the way from implied acceptance of a racially mixed group to outright refusal. Again, behavior and expressed attitude were not consistent.[2]

In both of these studies, the individuals approached were faced with only two possible choices: they could either serve or refuse to serve the racially mixed party. In a study by DeFleur and Westie, a greater range of behavioral choice was provided. The researchers obtained a measure of 250 white students' prejudice toward African Americans. The 23 students indicating the most prejudice and the 23 students indicating the least prejudice were exposed to a variety of questions, devices, and situations designed to explore their feelings about African Americans. Later, they were presented with an opportunity for overt action. Each student had been exposed to color slides showing a young African American man paired with a young white woman, the two seated in separate chairs in a living room, behaving cordially but not romantically. The researcher told each student that another set of slides was needed for further research and asked if he or she would be willing to be photographed in such a situation. The student was then presented with a mimeographed form and told it was "a standard photograph release agreement." This form contained a graded series of uses for the photograph, from laboratory experiments to publication in the student newspaper and use in a nationwide publicity campaign advocating racial integration. The student was asked to approve the release, item by item, by signing the line below each successive situation. The results of the study indicate a strong tendency for the prejudiced students to avoid being photographed with an African American and for the unprejudiced students to accept being photographed. But there were several exceptions; some of the prejudiced students were willing to be photographed, and some of the unprejudiced students refused to be photographed.[3] It appears from these studies that attitude and behavior are not always consistent.

These studies are now quite old. However, they do appear to represent direct tests of the relationship between attitude and behavior. The results indicate a high degree of inconsistency in that relationship. This inconsistency between attitude and behavior, however, is far more apparent than real, and this is not a function of how long ago these studies were conducted. If similar studies were conducted today, the results would almost certainly be similar.

The primary problem when attempting to infer attitude from behavior is to determine what particular attitude to study. Very few actual behavioral choices are based on a single attitude. We all have literally thousands of attitudes, which tend to become grouped into attitude clusters. These clusters are composed of attitudes that are relevant to one another and that are usually consistent with one another. When they are not all consistent with one another, however, any behavior relevant to the attitude cluster will appear to be inconsistent with one or more attitudes. For example, most of us have a generally favorable attitude toward receiving money without exerting much effort. We also have a generally unfavorable attitude toward stealing. Thus, when we refrain from pocketing a hundred-dollar bill that we observe on a counter in a store, our behavior is consistent with one of our attitudes but inconsistent with another. If, however, someone offers us a hundred-dollar bill to complete a ten-item questionnaire, we are quite likely to accept the invitation. The negative attitude toward stealing is not a dominant part of the attitude cluster relevant to this behavior; thus it does not prevent our acting on our attitude toward obtaining money without exerting much effort.

There is, then, a hierarchy of attitudes that functions in determining which attitudes will lead to behavior and which attitudes will not in given cases. Each attitude cluster forms within such a hierarchy. An observed item of behavior by an individual will usually give us a clue to the structure of the attitude cluster, but it will not provide sufficient information for us to infer the character of all of the attitudes in the cluster. The crucial point to remember is that *behavior is always consistent with one or more attitudes, but what particular attitudes these are is not always immediately apparent.*

Closely related to attitude is opinion, which is the verbal expression of attitude. An opinion is, in a sense, an item of behavior that may be predicted from an attitude. If we hold a particular attitude, it is expected that when an appropriate occasion arises, we shall express an opinion consistent with that attitude. It is dangerous, however, to infer attitude directly from opinion. Many circumstances arise to cause people to express opinions inconsistent with their attitudes. If a boss asks a man what he thinks of the boss's pet project, the man is quite likely to express a favorable opinion, even if he considers the project a complete waste of time. Statements that do not reflect attitude are frequently referred to as "lip service." We pay lip service to many things we do not entirely accept. Generally, however, opinions do reflect attitude. More than that, they tend to reinforce attitude. If we once commit ourselves through our expressed opinion to a certain attitude, it is more likely that we shall retain that attitude.

With this general introduction to the concept of attitude in mind, let us look at the nature of attitudes in more detail. Attitudes have three essential characteristics: direction, intensity, and salience.

1. Direction. The direction of attitude may be favorable, unfavorable, or neutral (no direction). On most questions, we shall find people with attitudes representing each of these directions. For example, on the question of increased trade with China, there are people who favor such a policy, people who oppose it, and people who are neutral. An audience may be composed of all favorables, mostly unfavorables, all neutrals, mostly neutrals, or any imaginable combination of favorables, unfavorables, and neutrals. It is vitally important to the communicator to perceive the prevailing direction of the audience's attitudes. Messages appropriate for an audience with one prevailing attitude are likely to produce opposite effects in other audiences.

2. Intensity. Intensity refers to the strength of the attitude. Any attitude may be held with great intensity or with intensity lessening to almost none. The intensity characteristic should be thought of as a continuum ranging from zero to infinity. Various people holding attitudes in the same direction may differ greatly as to intensity of attitude. In general, the more intensity with which an attitude is held, the more likely it is to produce behavior consistent with itself.

3. Salience. Salience refers to the perceived importance of the attitude for the individual. A young man and a young woman may have similar attitudes, in direction and intensity, toward playing football. But the attitude is probably much more salient for the young man than it is for the young woman, because he is more likely to play football than she is. Or consider two young people, one of whom is a college student while the other does not attend school. Both may have similar attitudes toward grades, but the attitude for the student is probably much more salient than it is for the nonstudent.

Although these three characteristics of attitude may be separated for purposes of description and explanation, they are not completely distinct characteristics. Highly salient attitudes, for example, are usually held with much greater intensity than less salient attitudes.

Neutral attitudes present a special problem. For many years researchers considered neutral attitudes as attitudes with low intensity. However, research has indicated that neutral attitudes may vary in intensity just as attitudes in favorable or unfavorable directions do.[4] Research indicates that there are at least three kinds of neutral attitudes corresponding to three kinds of people: the ignorant neutral, the unconcerned neutral, and the intense neutral. All of us fall into each of these categories for some attitudes. The ignorant neutral is the person who lacks information or experience with the particular topic, so that no real attitude has been formed. Many of us, for example, are ignorant neutrals on the questions of who should be authorized to govern Cyprus. We know little or nothing about the area and even less about the governmental conditions. Many of us who do not live in California are unconcerned neutrals on the question of water distribution in that state. We may have read about the problem, but since it does not directly concern us, we choose not to take sides on the question. Finally, some of us are intense neutrals on the question of who should be chosen in a given election to represent our congressional district. The election of a congressional representative is directly important to us; we may know a good deal about the two candidates for the office but be unable to make up our minds concerning whom to support. We may, indeed, dislike both candidates and so refuse to support either one. The stay-at-home vote in most elections includes many intense neutrals.

ATTITUDES AND BELIEFS

At this point it is important to distinguish between attitudes and beliefs. A distinction frequently made is that attitude relates to the affective component of response, while belief relates to the cognitive component. The terms *affective* and *cognitive* may be loosely interpreted as referring to *feeling* and *thinking*. An attitude is an evaluation of something, such as "I don't like grades." A belief, on the other hand, is the degree of probable truth that we assign to something. For example, the statement "Grades are a detriment to learning" would be assigned different degrees of probability of truth by different people. Some would consider it absolutely true; others would consider it absolutely false. Most of us would have attitudes somewhere in between.

Like attitudes, beliefs have the dimensions of direction, intensity, and salience. A belief's dimension of direction is a continuum ranging between complete belief and complete disbelief. Intensity of belief may better be identified as certainty of belief. Degrees of certainty range from very uncertain to

very certain. Weather forecasters, for example, now predict rain in terms of probability. We hear that rain is forecast for tomorrow with a 40 percent probability. This is a relatively low degree of certainty, suggesting that there is a 40 percent chance that the report will prove to be correct, with an accompanying 60 percent chance that it will not. People hold many beliefs, and the degrees of certainty with which they hold them normally cover a very wide range. We believe, with an almost perfect certainty, that we shall have daylight tomorrow. We also believe that we will do well on most examinations we take in a course; but in many cases, we are not at all certain.

Salience of belief is almost exactly equivalent to salience of attitude. It is the relative importance of a belief to the individual holding it. Religious beliefs provide good examples of the salience dimension. During normal times most of us hold certain religious beliefs that are moderately salient. In times of extreme stress, however, they become highly salient, and in many cases they lead to direct action.

The rest of this chapter will consider the factors that affect the formation and change of attitudes. Although it will not be mentioned at each point in the discussion, what will be said about attitudes also applies to beliefs. *An individual's beliefs and attitudes are generally consistent with one another.* Normally, changing one involves changing the other as well. The main concern of this chapter centers on how to employ some of the receiver's attitudes so as to induce him or her to change other attitudes and beliefs. Chapter 6 concerns how to employ an individual's beliefs so as to induce change in other beliefs or attitudes. Before turning to the process of inducing change of attitude or belief, however, we must consider the process by which attitudes and beliefs are formed.

ATTITUDE FORMATION

All attitudes—favorable, neutral, or unfavorable; of high intensity or low; salient or nonsalient—have one thing in common: They are products of the totality of the individual's experiences. People with essentially similar experiences will tend to have similar attitudes. For example, if two young people are required to take the same course in college and both fail the course, they will both be likely to develop intensely unfavorable attitudes toward the course and the course requirement.

We are not born with attitudes but begin to form them almost immediately after we are born. Our parents feed us and care for us. We find this pleasant. Consequently, we develop favorable attitudes toward them. Psychologists have advanced many theories as explanations of the learning process.[5] There is no universal agreement as to which theory is best; however, "reinforcement" theory has proved useful. The basis of this theory is that we learn to respond to stimuli in our perceptual world. Responses that we find acceptable or rewarding (that are reinforced) tend to become habitual. Those we find unacceptable or unrewarding (that are not reinforced) tend not to be repeated.

Let us take as an example the formation of an attitude that most of us hold: our attitude toward telling the truth. From early childhood we are encouraged to tell the truth. We are told that telling the truth is good and right. We are probably told the legend about George Washington and the cherry tree. All this is designed to persuade us to tell the truth by instilling in our minds a strongly favorable attitude toward truth telling. If we tell the truth and are commended for it, our attitude is reinforced. If we tell a lie and are punished for it, our attitude toward truth telling is likewise reinforced. If, however, we tell a lie and avoid punishment or are rewarded, we are likely to develop a favorable attitude toward telling lies. Our favorable attitude toward telling the truth is weakened. Similarly, if we are punished for telling the truth, we tend to develop a more favorable attitude toward telling lies. If, for example, George Washington had been soundly spanked for cutting down the cherry tree, the next time a tree was cut down he would have been likely to say, "No sir! It wasn't me!" and hide his little axe!

Not all attitudes, of course, are formed by such direct reinforcement. Fortunately, we human beings have a remarkable capacity to generalize in our learning. If we experience several similar stimuli, we generalize to other similar stimuli and respond to all of them in much the same way. For example, if as children we are reprimanded by police officers, we may become nervous and apprehensive in the presence of police officers for the rest of our lives.

Generalization also functions in the formation of attitudes. In the example above, the person reprimanded by an individual police officer will probably develop an unfavorable attitude toward that particular person. In addition, the person will tend to extend the attitude to other police officers with whom he or she comes in contact. By generalizing, the individual may even extend the attitude to any person wearing a uniform. In short, people can shift the focus but maintain the same attitude. In the case of the police officer, the attitude shifted from an individual to a group.

Attitudes, then, are learned responses. They are based on the totality of our experiences. Experiences we have frequently occur with another person or a group of people present. We are all members of society as a whole, but more important, we are members of many smaller groups. These groups range from the very small (bridge club or bowling team) to the very large (political party or religious denomination). Our attitudes are not independent of the attitudes held by the groups of which we are members. Attitudes of others tend to "rub off" on us. In this way we vastly expand our universe of attitudes and at the same time stabilize and strengthen it.

Newcomb reports an extensive study of such "reference groups," which involved the entire student body at Bennington College over a four-year period. Newcomb found that the Bennington students tended to change their attitudes toward public issues rather markedly while they were in college. The general trend of change in attitude for the total group was from freshman conservatism to senior nonconservatism. Some students, however, showed much greater change than the average for the group, while others showed no attitude change at all. Careful examination of the group memberships of the students indicated that this wide variance could be explained partly by the students' group affiliations. Attitudes held by groups with which the student developed strong ties tended to be accepted by the student.[6]

That group membership is a strong factor in molding the attitudes and behavior of people other than college students is attested to by methods currently used by political pollsters. With a sample ranging from a few hundred to a few thousand people, these polling organizations have been able to predict the voting behavior of millions. Although their procedure often involves complicated statistical manipulation and the use of highly sophisticated computer programs, the entire process rests upon the assumption that individual attitudes and behavior can be predicted on the basis of group affiliations. The accuracy with which this procedure makes it possible to predict behavior permits political candidates or business organizations to feed data on their proposed persuasive campaigns into computers to find out how likely the campaigns are to be successful if presented to the public.[7]

Since attitudes are learned responses based on all our experiences, direct or vicarious, we may expect that the amount of information an individual possesses will, to some degree, determine the nature of the individual's attitude. To a limited extent this is true. The amount of information possessed by an individual may affect the intensity of his or her attitude, but it does not affect the direction of the attitude.[8] Well-informed people tend to have more intense attitudes than those less well informed. Researchers have been unable, however, to find a relationship between the amount of information an individual possesses and the direction of that person's attitude. Of course, if most of the information one holds supports a favorable attitude, it is more likely the person will have a favorable attitude.

To summarize, attitudes are learned responses. All of our experiences combine to determine our attitudes. These experiences do not have to be direct. The experiences we have with other people also affect our attitude. The more informed we are, the more intensely we will hold our attitude; but the amount of information we possess will not necessarily determine the direction of our attitude.

THE PERSISTENCE OF ATTITUDES

Obviously, some attitudes persist over long periods of time. Consider, for example, the attitudes of some men in the United States toward women. Although massive persuasion has been exerted on the people of this country to accept men and women as equals, many people continue to hold strongly traditional attitudes. Certainly, some of these attitudes persist because they are reinforced by the familiar environment of the persons holding them. Their friends hold similar attitudes, and showing a change in attitude will often cause an individual to be ostracized. Thus, reinforcement is a factor in producing persistence of attitudes as well as in forming them. Four other factors are at least as important in causing their retention. These factors are selective exposure, selective attention, selective perception, and selective recall.

1. Selective exposure. The most important factor in the persistence of attitudes is believed by some to be selective exposure to communicative stimuli. Selective exposure is the tendency of people to seek out communicative stimuli they think will be consistent with their attitudes and to avoid communicative stimuli they think will be inconsistent with their attitudes. Considerable research demonstrating the existence of this phenomenon has been reported.[9] We may see the process in operation in our own experience. If we are Democrats, what kind of political rallies do we attend? We attend Democratic ones. If we go to a football game, which side of the field do we choose to sit on? The home side, if the game is played on a local field; the visitors' side if the game is played elsewhere. We subscribe to newspapers and magazines that have editorial policies consistent with our attitudes. We form friendships with people who have attitudes similar to ours. We join organizations that represent views with which we agree. All these actions are designed (usually unconsciously) either to place us in situations where communicative stimuli will be consistent with our attitudes or to avoid getting us into situations where communicative stimuli will be in conflict with our attitudes.

   2. Selective attention. People cannot always avoid being exposed to communicative stimuli inconsistent with their attitudes. When they do come into contact with such stimuli, the process of selective attention may be employed. In a sense, all attention is selective. Everything in our perceptual world makes some demand upon our attention, but we cannot attend to everything. When we are exposed to a message, we may attend to some parts of it more intently than to others. Thus we are selecting what we shall attend to most closely. This selection is generally an unconscious process. As a result, we tend to pay closest attention to the parts of the message consistent with our attitudes and to pay less attention to the inconsistent parts.[10] Consequently, we avoid full exposure to stimuli that might otherwise change our attitudes.

   3. Selective perception. Frequently, we cannot completely ignore stimuli that are inconsistent with our attitudes. When this happens, we may unconsciously distort the communicative stimuli, so as to perceive them as being consistent with our attitudes.[11] This is the process of selective perception. We may listen to a man expressing an ambiguous view on abortion, but if we are anti-abortion we may perceive his view as being like our own. If the message is such that this is impossible, we may perceive the source as dishonest, uninformed, or otherwise not credible, and simply disregard his message entirely. We tend, then, to perceive what we want to perceive, and what we want to perceive is something consistent with our attitudes. People on both sides of all issues frequently distort communicative stimuli so as to perceive the stimuli as reinforcing their attitudes, even when the stimuli are not reinforcing. The more intense and salient the attitude, the more likely this will happen.

   4. Selective recall. If people are unable to avoid being exposed to communicative stimuli inconsistent with their attitudes, are unable to avoid paying attention to the communication, or are unable to distort the communication so as to perceive the stimuli as consistent, a fourth psychological response may be observed: selective recall.[12] This is the tendency of people to remember communicative stimuli consistent with their attitudes and to forget inconsistent stimuli. For example, if we are pro-choice and are exposed to a communicative stimulus that includes information on both sides of the abortion issue, we tend to recall the pro-choice information but to forget the anti-abortion information.

With all these factors in operation, it is no wonder that attitudes tend to persist. The wonder is that attitudes do get changed under some circumstances. Therefore, let us turn our attention to the question of how attitudes are changed.

ATTITUDE CONSISTENCY AND ATTITUDE CHANGE

Attitudes are changed consciously or unconsciously. In rhetorical communication, conscious changes are produced primarily by arguments to which the individual attends. Chapter 6 will extensively discuss this method of changing attitudes. Our primary concern here is with unconscious changes in attitude.

Several theories of attitude change have been developed. They are frequently referred to as the *tension-reduction* or *homeostatic* theories. Heider's balance theory,[13] Festinger's dissonance theory,[14] and Osgood's congruity theory[15] have all received wide attention. Actually, hundreds of experimental studies tend to support one or more of these theories; many of the studies were even conducted prior to the systematic formation of the theories.

All these theories have a common basis, which has been called the *principle of consistency.*[16] These theories suggest that the human mind has a powerful need for consistency in attitudes and beliefs. Thus, *if two or more attitudes or beliefs are inconsistent with one another, change in attitude or belief occurs as a result of the mind's efforts to establish homeostasis, or consistency.*

All of the consistency theories predict that no change of attitude or belief will occur when a person's attitudes and beliefs are consistent, such as in the circumstances depicted in Figure 4.1. However, these theories predict that changes in a person's attitudes or beliefs, or both, will occur when either or both are inconsistent, such as in the circumstances depicted in Figure 4.2.

Although the principle of consistency may be applied to any pair or group of attitudes, much of the experimental research has been directed toward one particular pair of attitudes: attitude toward the message source and attitude toward the message topic. This research indicates that, in general, when these two attitudes are inconsistent with each other, they tend to move toward each other. That is, if the attitude toward the source is more positive than the attitude toward the topic, a rhetorical communication attempt by the source will usually increase the favorability of the attitude toward the topic but may also result in a less positive attitude toward the source. If the initial attitudes are reversed, an opposite result is probable: the attitude will tend to become more favorable toward the source and less favorable toward the topic. The validity of basing predictions on the principle of consistency is attested to by numerous studies, most notably studies reported by Berlo and Gulley, and by Tannenbaum.[17] In the Berlo and Gulley study, two predictions were made

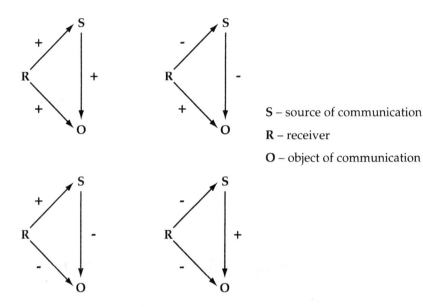

S – source of communication

R – receiver

O – object of communication

FIGURE 4.1 Consistent Relationships. A positive sign indicates a favorable attitude; a negative sign indicates an unfavorable attitude.

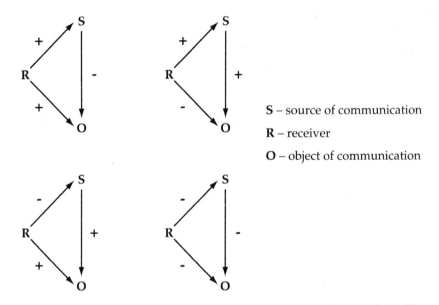

S – source of communication

R – receiver

O – object of communication

FIGURE 4.2 Inconsistent Relationships. A positive sign indicates a favorable attitude; negative sign indicates an unfavorable attitude.

for change of attitude on the part of each of 174 members of an audience. The first prediction was about change of attitude toward the communicator. The second prediction was about change of attitude toward the concept. Of the 174 predictions of direction of attitude change toward the source, 117 were confirmed. One hundred twelve of the predictions of direction of attitude change toward the concept were confirmed. In both cases the number of confirmed predictions far exceeded what would be expected by chance.

It should be noted, however, that many of Berlo and Gulley's predictions were not confirmed. In other studies even more predictions have gone unconfirmed. Therefore, although we can make many accurate predictions based on the homeostatic theories, change of attitude is far from perfectly predictable. Nevertheless, an understanding of the basis of these theories can be very helpful to a source in the construction of a message. Although obviously imperfect, these theories provide some of the best guidelines available at this time for preparation of messages.

This book has suggested that you will profit from understanding the basic concept of the homeostatic, or consistency, theories of attitude change. They provide useful guidelines to follow in constructing messages designed to produce attitude change. It is not essential, however, that you know all the minute workings of these theories. If you remember the principle of consistency, you will be able to secure most of the benefits these theories have to offer. A favorable attitude should be viewed as a bank account. You may draw from that bank account and spend the surplus where there is a deficit. As we shall observe in the following chapter, the attitude the audience has toward you may provide your greatest bank account. But any other favorable attitude may serve also. If your audience has a strongly favorable attitude toward democracy, the establishment of the idea that your program is democratic will increase the support for it. In many cases it is useful to build favorable attitudes other than the one with which the message is primarily concerned so that you may "cash in" on the supplementary attitudes to produce change in the primary attitude.

MESSAGE DISCREPANCY
AND ATTITUDE CHANGE

On the basis of the homeostatic theories of attitude change, we would expect that generally the degree of attitude change will increase as the degree of inconsistency between attitudes is increased. In general this is true. There is a limit, however, to the amount of inconsistency the mind will tolerate. Selective exposure, selective perception, and selective recall are more likely to appear when inconsistency is great. Hence, when a message generates more than a tolerable amount of inconsistency; less attitude change occurs rather than more.

To reexplain this phenomenon, we must introduce several new terms into our discussion. A *discrepant message* is any message that expresses a view different from the one held by the audience. The *latitude of acceptance* is the range of positions that are acceptable to an individual on a given question. The *latitude of rejection* is the range of positions that are objectionable to an individual. The *latitude of noncommitment* is the range of positions toward which an individual feels no commitment.[18]

We have previously discussed attitude in terms of suggesting that it is a single position on a question. In addition to this single most acceptable position, the individual tends to be quite tolerant of other attitudes that are relatively close to that position. This latitude of acceptance is ordinarily quite wide when the attitude is nonsalient. For example, we probably are quite tolerant of most attitudes toward local governmental policies in Peru. They do not affect us, so we are not very much concerned. On the other hand, if the attitude is highly salient to us, we tend to have a much narrower latitude of acceptance. Our attitude toward the college we attend is a good example. If we think it is a very good college, we would probably be quite upset if someone suggests that it is merely adequate. We may become incensed if someone says it is an inferior institution.

Messages expressing views that are within our latitude of acceptance may be referred to as mildly discrepant. These messages cause little inconsistency in attitude. We may *assimilate* the view expressed in the message without feeling that the new view represents a change in attitude. We may not even perceive that the mildly discrepant view is different from our own.

Moderately discrepant messages, however, are perceived as advocating positions quite different from our own. These positions may fall within our latitude of rejection. Considerable inconsistency in attitude will be generated, and quite possibly the inconsistency will exceed tolerable limits.

What are the effects of increasing the discrepancy of a message? Figure 4.3 is a diagrammatic representation of the general trend. It will be noted from this figure that, up to a point, the more discrepant a message is, the more likely is favorable attitude change to occur. After this point, favorable attitude change decreases. Eventually, if the message becomes extremely discrepant, attitude change may actually be in the direction opposite from that intended by the communicator. This unfavorable change is usually referred to as the boomerang effect.

Figure 4.3 is based on the *actual* discrepancy of the message. It must be noted that the effects of perceived discrepancy are quite different. As *perceived* discrepancy increases, change of attitude in the direction advocated by the communicator decreases.[19] When very large discrepancies are perceived, it is not unusual for the individual to shift negatively.

We have previously mentioned assimilation in reference to views expressed in messages falling well within our latitude of acceptance on a given question. At this point we must mention the opposite effect, *contrast*.

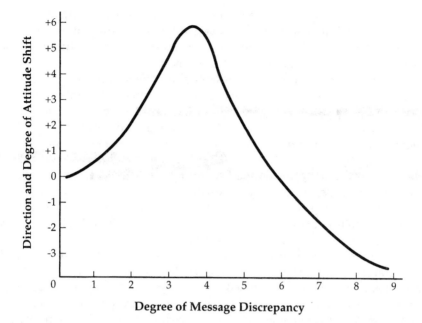

FIGURE 4.3 The effects of message discrepancy on attitude change.
Numbers are arbitrarily selected to illustrate the relationship between attitude
change and message discrepancy and are not meaningful in themselves.

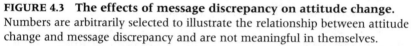

When we are confronted with a view in a message that is well within our
latitude of rejection, we are likely to perceive it as much more extreme than
it really is.[20] In short, overly strong messages usually produce effects counter
to those intended. When we are exposed to them, our attitude toward the
topic is likely to be even more divergent from the speaker's after hearing her
or him than it was before.

All of this has very important implications. To achieve your goal, you
must estimate not only the attitude of the members of your audience on the
point in question, but also their latitudes of acceptance and rejection. The
view you have toward the point may not be the one that should be
expressed in the message. You may need to express a more moderate view
in order to achieve the maximum persuasive impact, or at least to avoid the
boomerang effect. A change in expressed view, of course, raises a rather
substantial ethical question. Such questions will be discussed in Chapter 15.

RETENTION OF ATTITUDE CHANGE

Although attitudes are self-reinforcing and have a strong tendency to persist,
they can be changed. Although it may appear from the foregoing discussion

that changing attitudes is very difficult, this is not necessarily true. Obtaining the maximum change in attitude is a very difficult process and requires considerable skill. Obtaining some change, on the other hand, is usually quite easy. Getting it to stay changed is another matter.

Some persuasive efforts are designed to obtain immediate effect only. Frequently, however, the action we desire an individual to take will occur days or weeks after the communicative event. To produce immediate change of attitude in these cases is not enough; the attitude must stay changed. The question of retention of change, then, is a crucial one. Research indicates that the length of time a change of attitude is retained varies from a few minutes to a number of weeks.[21] Some changes, of course are permanent. Very little is known about the factors affecting retention, indicating that much research is needed in this area. From the limited research already done on retention of change in attitude, however, we are able to extract a few relevant factors.

The main factor seems to be the individual's awareness of the new attitude. That is, if he or she knows the attitude has changed, it is more likely to stay changed. We have discussed how change of attitude can occur on an unconscious level. Such changes appear to be highly susceptible to a gradual decline. The attitude gradually moves back to where it was. This may be explained in terms of selective recall and selective exposure. If we are unaware of changes of attitude that have occurred, we may continue to function with our old attitude. The old attitude has been disturbed, and we may either seek out new communicative stimuli to reinforce it or simply forget the stimuli that induced immediate change. This suggests, of course, that in your persuasive efforts *you should strive for conscious as well as unconscious change of attitude.*

Closely related to the factor of awareness of immediate change of attitude is the vividness of the communicative stimulus that produced the change. If a message is memorable, we tend to reinforce the change by recalling the message as time passes. That is, *a vivid and memorable message will interfere with the natural process of selective recall.* By making important points of the message memorable, *you* can select what your audience will recall.

We indicated before that salient attitudes tend to be held more intensely and are less subject to change. This suggests that if the communicator arranges the message in such a manner as to make the new attitude highly salient for an individual, the change of attitude will be more persistent. Salience is closely related to perceived self-interest. Thus, if the new attitude is perceived to be important to the individual's self-interest, that attitude is more likely to be retained.

In general, the greater the immediate change of attitude, the greater will be the change that is retained over a given period of time. This is not to suggest that major shifts are more persistent than minor shifts. Actually, experimental research tends to show that greater changes decline more rapidly than lesser ones. Nevertheless, at a given time after the communicative event that produced the original change, a person who has made a major initial shift will be more favorable to the communicator's position than a person who has made a minor shift. This is true simply because a ten-point shift, for example, takes longer to decline to zero than a five-point shift. Therefore, the communicator who seeks a long-term change of attitude should strive to achieve as large an immediate attitude change as may be feasible.

In a series of studies designed to test the effects of evidence (facts or opinions attested to by someone other than the communicator) in persuasion, inclusion of evidence in a message was found to enhance retention of attitude change over periods varying from three to seven weeks.[22] The results of a subsequent study suggest that the reason for this impact of evidence is that it serves to inhibit the effects of counterpersuasive sources with whom the receiver comes in contact subsequent to exposure to the original source.[23]

What happens to the individual subsequent to the initial exposure to a communicative stimulus is the final factor directly affecting retention of change of attitude. If the person is subjected to counterpersuasion, the attitude may be expected to change back toward the original position much more rapidly. There is little that a communicator can do to control the persuasion the individual is exposed to after the initial change of attitude. He or she can, however, influence the degree of impact counterpersuasion may have. This is accomplished by "inoculating" the audience against later messages. This inoculation takes the form of exposing the audience to the arguments that may be leveled against the communicator's position and then showing the audience why these arguments are irrelevant or unacceptable. The process of inoculation will be further explored in Chapter 6 in relation to the handling of reservations in persuasive argument.

In summary, although retention of attitude change tends to decline over a period of time, a communicator may cause more change to be retained by making the receiver aware that he or she has a new attitude; by making the message vivid and memorable; by relating the new attitude to the individual's self-interest; by achieving the maximum initial change of attitude; by including evidence in the message; by inoculating the audience against counter persuasion.

RHETORICAL THOUGHT

It may appear from our discussion that people are unthinking dupes who can be manipulated at will by skillful communicators. Or it may at least appear that people are terribly naive. To a limited degree this is true, but people do think. They are usually aware of what is going on around them. They do have some critical capacities. Moreover, the fact that most of the time they are not unreasoning dupes provides the communicator with other means of securing change of attitude. It is important to consider just how people actually think in communicative situations so that we may better understand the communicator's function in guiding their thinking to desired conclusions.

Essential to our understanding of rhetorical thought is an understanding of human nature. Humans are basically self-centered creatures. They normally do things because they think they will benefit from their actions. They normally believe a thing because the belief fits nicely inside their little ego-centered world. Self-interest is the primary motivating factor in human life. But this does not mean that human nature is bad—quite the contrary. Most noble aspirations and acts also are prompted by self-interest.

Altruism is another term for "enlightened self-interest." Most of us repeatedly do good things for other people. When we do, we feel good about it. Others tend to like and respect us more. We are taught from childhood what is right and what is wrong. At an early age we learn that to do what is right is generally in our self-interest, if for no other reason than that if we do not do what is right, we will be punished. Usually the knowledge that we have done right is enough to satisfy us. There are times, however, when we choose to do what we know is wrong. We feel that we receive more benefit from such action than we would obtain from merely knowing we had done right. As a case in point, take the completion of individual income tax returns. If all the people who had cheated "just a little bit" on their tax returns were put in jail, there might not be enough of us left on the outside to guard those who were on the inside.

As we come to understand thought processes in rhetorical communication, we must keep this facet of human nature constantly in mind. As people listen to or read communicative messages, they are constantly dominated by personal concerns: How shall I do this? What does this mean to me? Will I benefit from this? These are the kinds of questions people bring to communicative situations. As you read this book, these questions will constantly be coming to mind. The decoding process in rhetorical communication is primarily a function of integrating message stimuli with perceived self-interest.

All of this suggests that there is little room for logical thought in the communicative process. This certainly is true if "logic" is used to mean strictly formal logic. But there is great need for rational thought. The rational process in rhetorical communication involves giving reasons rather than reasoning. Our problem in constructing messages for rhetorical communication is not that of determining how to get our receivers to think logically; rather it is the problem of getting them to follow our reasons to our conclusions. Many factors that are logically irrelevant enter into the process. Yet these factors make a major impact on the thinking of the receivers.

Rhetorical thought, then, is the process of guiding an audience's thinking in such a manner as to get them to believe that the source's proposed idea or action is consistent with their self-interest. Rhetorical thought, therefore, is neither strictly logical nor illogical; it is psychological.

DISCUSSION QUESTIONS

1. Are there factors other than those discussed in this chapter that could cause attitude and behavior to appear (or to be) inconsistent?

2. Speakers and editorial writers present many opinions. May we infer their attitudes from these opinions? Why or why not?

3. During the frequent wars between Arab countries and Israel, public opinion in the United States has been extremely varied. Some people support the Arabs, some support the Israelis, and some take a neutral stance. Considering the attitude dimensions of intensity and salience, can you explain this wide variation in opinion?

4. Because attitudes are learned, some people argue that persuasion and teaching are the same thing. What do you think?

5. This chapter indicated that selectivity has a major influence on the persistence of attitudes. What relevance does this have to the planning of a political campaign? Would you, if you were the candidate and had the choice, choose to spend your money allotted for television coverage on one-minute spot advertisements or on half-hour to full-hour specials? Why?

6. Assume that Adolf Hitler were to return "from exile" and speak to an audience in your home town. His speech is in favor of capitalism and opposed to socialism. What change of audience attitude, if any, would you predict on the basis of the tension-reduction theories?

7. Many people do not agree with the view of rhetorical thought developed in this chapter. They feel that humans are rational animals and that self-interest is not our primary motivation. What do you think?

NOTES

1. R. L. LaPiere, "Attitudes vs. Actions, *Social Forces* 13 (1934): 230–37.

2. B. Kutner, C. Wilkins, and P. Yarrow, "Verbal Attitudes and Overt Behavior Involving Racial Prejudice," *Journal of Abnormal and Social Psychology* 47 (1952): 649–52.

3. M. L. DeFleur and F. R. Westie, "Verbal Attitudes and Overt Acts: An Experiment on the Salience of Attitudes," *American Sociological Review* 23 (1958): 667–73.

4. See J. C. McCroskey, "Latitude of Acceptance and the Semantic Differential," *Journal of Social Psychology* 74 (1968): 127–32.

5. B. R. Bugelski, *The Psychology of Learning Applied to Teaching* (Indianapolis: Bobbs Merrill, 1971).

6. T. M. Newcomb, "Attitude Development as a Function of Reference Groups: The Bennington Study" in *Readings in Social Psychology*, E. E. Maccoby, T. M. Newcomb, and E. L. Hartley (Eds.) (New York: Holt, Rinehart & Winston, 1959), pp. 265–75.

7. See I. D. Pool, R. P. Abelson, and S. L. Popkin, *Candidates, Issues, and Strategies: A Computer Simulation of the 1960 and 1964 Presidential Elections* (Cambridge, MA: M.I.T. Press, 1964).

8. See G. Nettler, "The Relationship between Attitude and Information Concerning the Japanese in America," *American Sociological Review* 11 (1946): 177–91.

9. E. Katz, "On Reopening the Question of Selectivity in Exposure to Mass Communications," in R. P. Abelson et al., *Theories of Cognitive Consistency: A Sourcebook* (Skokie, IL: Rand McNally, 1968).

10. H. Gilkinson, S. F. Paulson, and D. E. Sikkink, "Conditions Affecting the Communication of Controversial Statements in Connected Discourse: Forms of Presentation and the Political Frame of Reference of the Listener," *Speech Monographs* 20 (1955): 253–60.

11. See E. Cooper and M. Johoda, "The Evasion of Propaganda: How Prejudiced People Respond to Anti-Prejudice Propaganda," *Journal of Psychology* 23 (1947): 15–25.

12. See, for example, J. M. Levine and G. Murphy, "The Learning and Forgetting of Controversial Material," *Journal of Abnormal and Social Psychology* 49 (1954): 23–28.

13. F. Heider, "Attitudes and Cognitive Organization," *Journal of Psychology* 21 (1946): 107–12.

14. L. Festinger, *A Theory of Cognitive Dissonance* (New York: Row, Peterson, 1957).

15. C. E. Osgood and P. H. Tannenbaum, "The Principle of Congruity in the Prediction of Attitude Change," *Psychological Review* 62 (1955): 42–55.

16. For a summary of this body of theory, see R. Brown, *Social Psychology* (New York: Free Press, 1965).

17. D. K. Berlo and H. E. Gulley, "Some Determinants of the Effect of Oral Communication in Producing Attitude Change and Learning," *Speech Monographs* 25 (1957): 10–20; and P. R. Tannenbaum, "Initial Attitude Toward Source and Concept as Factors in Attitude Change Through Communication," *Public Opinion Quarterly* 20 (1956): 413–25. See also, H. T. Hurt and M.D. Scott, "A Re-examination of the Predictive Power of the Congruity Model: A Multiple Regression Approach," a paper presented at the International Communication Association Convention, Chicago, 1975.

18. For an extensive discussion of these concepts, see C. W. Sherif, M. Sherif, and R. E. Nebergall, *Attitude and Attitude Change* (Philadelphia: Saunders, 1965).

19. O. J. Harvey and J. Rutherford, "Gradual and Absolute Approaches to Attitude Change," *Sociometry* 21 (1958): 61–68.

20. C. I. Hovland, O. J. Harvey, and M. Sherif, "Assimilation and Contrast Effects in Reactions to Communication and Attitude Change," *Journal of Abnormal and Social Psychology* 55 (1957): 244–52.

21. H. Cromwell, "The Persistency of the Effect of Argumentative Speeches," *Quarterly Journal of Speech* 41 (1955): 154–58.

22. J. C. McCroskey, "A Summary of Experimental Research on the Effects of Evidence in Persuasive Communication," *Quarterly Journal of Speech* 55 (1969): 169–76.

23. J. C. McCroskey, "The Effects of Evidence as an Inhibitor of Counter-Persuasion," *Speech Monographs* 37 (1970): 188–94.

CHAPTER 5

ETHOS: A DOMINANT FACTOR IN RHETORICAL COMMUNICATION

Since the days of Corax and Tisias, rhetorical theorists have been concerned with the role of *ethos* in communication. During this twenty-four-hundred-year period, Aristotle's view that ethos is the most potent means of persuasion has seldom been challenged. Plato, Isocrates, Cicero, and Quintilian all expressed similar views, even though their conceptions of ethos were somewhat different from Aristotle's.[1]

Of all the aspects of classical rhetorical theory, the one that has the greatest support from modern empirical research is the theoretical importance of ethos in rhetorical communication. Almost without exception, experimental studies have demonstrated the power of ethos. Before looking at a few of these studies, let us clarify what we mean by ethos.

ETHOS DEFINED

Ethos is the attitude toward a source of communication held at a given time by a receiver. Source credibility, prestige, and personal proof are terms that have been used to refer to constructs similar to what we have here defined as ethos. *Initial ethos* is the ethos of a source prior to the beginning of a given communicative act. It is the speaker's ethos just before he or she begins to speak or the writer's ethos just before the reader begins to read. *Derived ethos* is the ethos of a source produced during the act of communicating. It includes the impact of the message, the effect of the circumstances in which the communication takes place, and (if oral) the delivery of the message. *Terminal ethos* is the ethos of a source at the completion of a communicative act. It is the product of the interaction of initial and derived ethos.

Two things need to be made clear at the outset. First, we shall frequently refer to a source's ethos. This may mislead some people into thinking that a *source* has ethos. The source does not. The receiver has the ethos. It is in the

mind of the receiver, just as any other attitude is. Thus, the ethos of a source may vary greatly from receiver to receiver or among receivers in a collective audience. It is not something a source *has,* but it is convenient to talk about ethos as if this were the case. Second, a source's ethos may vary greatly from time to time, even with the same receiver. Like other attitudes, ethos is subject to change as a result of experiences the receiver has with the source. It will often change markedly in the course of a single communicative act.

It is important to reemphasize the meaning of term *source.* As indicated in Chapter 2, a source is not necessarily a single person. However, because most sources are individual people, we will treat the term *source* as grammatically singular throughout this book. A source may also be a group, an organization, a government agency, or even a country. The United States Department of Labor, for example, is the source of many messages. The individual who speaks or writes on behalf of this or any other organization must develop the message in accordance with the desires and policies of the parent group. While her or his individual ethos may in some cases affect the impact of the message, the primary ethos involved is that of the organization.

An individual presenting a speech may also represent an individual source. The press secretary of a president, for example, represents the president. What the secretary says or writes is presumed to be the view of the president and not necessarily her or his own. The person's individual ethos is ordinarily pretty much irrelevant. The pertinent ethos is that of the source for whom he or she speaks.

Ethos, then, is a dynamic construct. It is always subject to change and may even be said to be volatile. As noted later, even apparently small things can drastically alter a source's ethos.

THE DIMENSIONS OF ETHOS

Ethos is an attitude, but it is a somewhat different kind of attitude from the kind discussed in Chapter 4. Psychologists concerned with measuring attitudes generally agree that attitudes are unidimensional. This dimension has been called the *evaluative* dimension, what was referred to in Chapter 4 as the direction of an attitude. Our evaluations of things range between good and bad, harmful and beneficial, wise and foolish, and so forth. If our attitude is favorable, we think the thing is good, beneficial, wise. If our attitude is unfavorable, we think the thing is bad, harmful, foolish. Our attitude, then, is our evaluation of something.

Ethos, being a somewhat different kind of attitude, is multidimensional. Exactly what these dimensions are has been a subject of speculation for many years. Aristotle identified the dimensions as intelligence, character, and good will.[2] Twenty-three hundred years later, three social psychologists, Carl I. Hovland, Irving L. Janus, and Harold H. Kelley, when studying source credibility, identified the dimensions as expertness, trustworthiness, and intention toward the receiver.[3] When we examine these writings, we find remarkable similarity. Aristotle and the three psychologists agree that a source is judged by an audience in terms of her or his knowledge of the subject of discourse, veracity, and attitude toward the well-being of the audience.

With the advent of modern computers and the sophisticated statistical procedure known as factor analysis, empirical researchers directed their attention to the dimensions of the ethos construct. In the first reported factor-analytic study of ethos, Berlo and Lemert obtained three factors, or dimensions, for ethos.[4] They labeled these competence, trustworthiness, and dynamism. The first two correspond exactly with Aristotle's "intelligence" and "character" and Hovland, Janis, and Kelley's "expertness" and "trustworthiness." The third factor, however, was quite different from the theoretical dimension of will or of intention. The factor that Berlo and Lemert labeled dynamism was concerned with the activity or liveliness of the source, not with evaluation of the source.

In an early series of studies designed to develop instruments to measure ethos, I measured the ethos of hypothetical speakers, tape-recorded speakers, televised speakers, and live speakers.[5] Factor analysis of the data consistently produced two factors. These dimensions of ethos were labeled authoritativeness and character. They were equivalent to the first two dimensions presented by each of the three sources just discussed. It is important to note that the few items that appeared to be related to the theoretical good will or intention dimension of ethos were consistently represented on the character dimension. From this I concluded that good will or intention is important but it may not be independent of the other two dimensions of ethos.

After the early studies, many others were conducted and reported.[6] An analysis of the combined results of all of these studies suggested that there were two clear evaluative dimensions of ethos, which may be conveniently labeled *competence* and *character.* This research isolated additional dimensions on which sources are perceived. The three most consistently observed dimensions of perception were labeled *composure, sociability,* and *extroversion.*

The composure perception relates to the degree of emotional control the source is perceived to have. Sociability appears to represent receivers' perceptions of how pleasant and friendly the source is. Extroversion is similar to the dynamism dimension isolated in the earlier research. It focuses on how outgoing, active, and talkative the source is perceived to be.

These new categories, while important, should not be considered as dimensions of ethos. They represent descriptive rather than evaluative perceptions, and thus are not characteristic of an attitude toward a source; rather they are attributes of a source reflected in receiver perceptions. In this respect they do not differ from a vast number of other perceptions that people have of other people.

Recently, the third evaluative dimension of ethos has received new attention. What was called "good will" by Aristole and "intention toward receiver" by Hovland and colleagues has been reconceptualized as "perceived caring" for the receiver. The components of this perception are seen as being *empathy, understanding,* and *responsiveness.*[7] Empathy is seen as being able to take the view of the other person, to see things from the receiver's point of view. Understanding is seen as knowing and caring about the other person's concerns. Responsiveness is seen as the ability to adapt to the needs of the other, to recognize the receiver's problem and work to help overcome it.

Recent work reported by Teven and McCroskey has confirmed the existence of a goodwill or "perceived caring" dimension of ethos.[8] Of course, it was there all this time, but an appropriate approach to measuring it had not been previously established. Consequently, there is a lack of research exploring the impact of goodwill/caring in rhetorical communication. In our work we tested for the impact of goodwill/caring, compared to trustworthiness and competence, on both the believability and the likeableness of a wide variety of sources, including political figures and public (non-political) figures, as well as interpersonal and organizational contacts. Our results indicated that the impact of goodwill/caring was greater than competence but less than trustworthiness on both of these more general attitudes. Our research also indicated that students who perceived their teachers to have higher levels of goodwill/caring had higher cognitive and affective learning and evaluated their teachers more highly than those with lower levels of goodwill/caring.

Ethos, then, is an attitude that differs from other attitudes. It has three dimensions rather than one. It is composed of the perceived competence, character, and caring of a source of communication. The relationships among these dimensions of ethos are not at all clear. Sometimes they function together; at other times, independently. For instance, if we are confronted with two sources whom we initially perceive to be equally competent, we are more likely to accept the views of the one we believe to be most likely to tell the truth. If we are confronted with two sources whose characters we initially perceive to be equal, we are more likely to accept the views of the one we believe to be most competent on the subject. But if we are confronted by two sources (one who is competent but of doubtful character, and one who is of high character but not competent on the question), it is very difficult to predict whose views we will accept. Even when we are confronted by only one source whom we perceive as initially high in one dimension of ethos but low on another dimension, it is difficult to predict the effect of her or his ethos. In these circumstances, it would appear that other variables in the process of communication (particularly the nature of the message) are the factors that determine acceptance or rejection. Initial ethos tends to assume much less importance. Usually, of course, the dimensions of a source's initial ethos are perceived to be qualitatively comparable. Therefore, let us turn to the effects we may ordinarily expect initial ethos to produce.

THE EFFECT OF INITIAL ETHOS

Most of the experimental research on ethos has concerned initial ethos. The design of these studies has usually been to select or create sources with different initial levels of ethos, attribute an identical message to the different sources for comparable audiences, and measure the differences in persuasive effect (usually attitude change) between or among the sources.

The classic study of this type was conducted by Haiman. In his study, three groups listened to the same tape-recorded speech on national compulsory health insurance, which was attributed to different speakers for each group—to Thomas Parran, then Surgeon General of the United States; to Eugene Dennis, Secretary of the Communist Party in America; and to a "Northwestern University sophomore." The "Parran speech" was significantly more effective in changing audience attitudes than was either of the other two speeches. Using essentially the same procedure, Strother obtained similar results.[9]

Hovland and Weiss used the procedure of presenting an identical message to two groups, indicating in one case that it came from a high-ethos source, and in the other that it came from a low-ethos source. They did this with four separate topics and four pairs of audiences. In three of the four cases, the high-ethos source produced significantly greater shifts of opinion than did the low-ethos source.[10]

Kelman and Hovland presented to three audiences an identical tape-recorded message favoring extreme leniency in the treatment of juvenile delinquents. The speech was attributed differently in each group—to a juvenile court judge, a member of a studio audience chosen at random, and a former juvenile delinquent out on bail after arrest on a charge of dope peddling. The initial ethos levels of the three "speakers" were brought out by means of tape-recorded introductory interviews. The results indicated that the juvenile delinquent was significantly less successful in securing shifts of opinion than were the two other sources.[11]

In all these studies, *initial ethos, based on the background and personal characteristics of the bogus sources, was found to have a significant effect upon the degree of attitude change produced by the messages.* In similar studies that I conducted, it was found that a warden was more successful than a convicted murderer in producing attitude change opposing capital punishment; a former director of educational research for the Rockefeller Foundation was more successful than a Communist who was a high-school dropout in producing attitude change favoring federal control of education; and a former Communist was more successful than a present Communist in producing attitude change favoring federal control of education.[12] Numerous other studies have produced similar results.[13] The results of these studies, to most people, seem quite obvious. What else would we expect? It is important in this type of research to begin by testing the obvious, for often what we expect is not the case. Once the obvious has been tested, there is baseline information for testing the less obvious.

In all the studies discussed above, the factors affecting initial ethos were objectively relevant to ethos. We would expect such things as education, experience, and reputation to influence initial ethos. Several other studies have been concerned with the effects of objectively irrelevant factors on initial ethos. Koehler, McCroskey, and Arnold found that the objectively irrelevant factor of Communist affiliation did not affect a person's ethos when the message was concerned with the desirability of capital punishment but that such affiliation did affect the individual's ethos when the message concerned federal control of education.[14] Aronson and Golden found that the objectively irrelevant factor of race did not affect the ethos of a communicator who was an engineer discussing the value of arithmetic but that when the communicator was a dishwasher discussing the same topic, race did have an effect on ethos.[15] Kerrick compared the effects of objectively relevant and objectively irrelevant factors of this on persuasion. The results of the Kerrick study indicate that objectively relevant ethos factors have a more pronounced effect on attitude change than objectively irrelevant factors but that objectively irrelevant factors have an effect under some circumstances.[16]

It appears from these studies that objectively irrelevant ethos factors ordinarily do not have a major effect on attitude change. *In some circumstances, however, factors that appear to be unrelated to a source's ethos may make a meaningful impact.* Therefore, when we consider the ethos of a source, we should be careful not to overlook factors that appear on the surface to be irrelevant. It is important to note that all the studies we have considered thus far have concerned initial ethos as determined by the receiver's perception of the source's background and personal characteristics. Another determinant of initial ethos has received less attention from experimental researchers, but has been observed to have a significant effect. Termed *sponsorship effect*, it concerns the circumstances surrounding the communicative event. Two studies have indicated that individuals who present a speaker, even an unidentified, tape-recorded speaker, can modify the initial ethos of the source without even being aware that they are modifying it. In these studies, a tape-recorded speaker was found to have significantly higher ethos, and to be significantly more successful in modifying attitudes of college students, when the speech was given with the students' course instructor present than when the instructor was not present.[17]

The implications of the sponsorship effect are important for the source. *One may expect to have substantially higher ethos if introduced by a person respected by the audience than one would have without such an introduction.* If the message appears in a national news magazine, the source may expect to have substantially higher ethos, at least for most receivers, than it will if the message appears in a movie magazine. A speaker, then, may enhance initial ethos by carefully selecting the person who introduces her or him to the audience. Experimental researchers have tended to ignore this effect, to the detriment of many studies, but national political leaders have been aware of it for years. We need only to look at any national political convention to observe the sponsorship effect in operation. The nominators, seconders, and presenters are carefully selected on the basis of their appeal to the voting public.

The appearance of the source has also been found to affect initial ethos in oral communication. In a novel experiment, Mills and Aronson found that an attractive woman modified audience attitudes significantly more than did an unattractive woman. Actually, the "two" women were the same one, merely made up differently. Under both conditions, the audiences were composed of male college students. The experimenter suggested that their completion of some measuring instruments would be facilitated if he could have a volunteer read the questions aloud and indicate what they meant. The "volunteer," of course, was the woman who was planted in the audience.[18]

Because Mills and Aronson reported results only on male subjects, it might be argued that the observed effect was really an interaction of sex and attractiveness. A study reported by Widgery and Webster sheds some light on this question.[19] In this study, photographs from a college yearbook were shown to a group of students who were then asked to rate each picture for its attractiveness. After analyzing the ratings, the picture of the "most unattractive" and the "most attractive" males and females were selected for further study. These pictures were presented to a separate group of experimental subjects who were asked to rate the individuals' competence, character, and dynamism. Large and significant differences between attractive and unattractive individuals were observed on the character dimension. No meaningful differences were observed on the other dimensions, and no differences were observed on the basis of the sex of the source. *These results suggest that the physical attractiveness of a source may have a major impact on the source's credibility and subsequently on attitude change, but that the sex of the source may not be a particularly relevant factor.*

To summarize, initial ethos is a very potent factor in persuasive communication. Background, personal characteristics, and appearance all contribute to a source's initial ethos. The initial ethos may also be affected by the surroundings in which the communication takes place and (if oral) by the ethos of the person introducing the source. In general, the higher a source's initial ethos, the more attitude change that source is likely to produce in a receiver. There is also reason to believe, on the basis of a study reported by Arnold, that initial ethos has a similar effect on overt behavior change.[20]

INITIAL ETHOS AND LEARNING

From the preceding discussion it should be clear that initial ethos has a profound influence upon the effects of persuasive communication. It would seem natural to expect that initial ethos would also be an important factor in messages designed to increase audience understanding (informative communication). There have been several research studies concerned with this problem. The most recent ones have found ethos to have a significant effect.[21]

The main effect high ethos has in informative communication is to increase the attention of members of the audience. If an informative message is presented to us by "John Expert," we will probably pay closer attention than if the message is presented to us by "Bill Nobody." We have all noticed differences in teachers we have had; we may highly respect one teacher and feel another is incompetent. We look forward to the class taught by one teacher but prefer to avoid the class taught by another. It is apparent that an ethos factor is in operation. We tend to expose ourselves selectively to sources whom we perceive to have higher ethos; this gives us a greater opportunity to learn from these sources than from those with lower ethos.

High initial ethos, then, can be expected to increase learning for two reasons: We are more likely to expose ourselves to sources we perceive as having high ethos; and we are likely to pay more attention to such high-ethos sources even if we do not have a choice of whether or not to be exposed.

DERIVED ETHOS

Aristotle advised the communicators of his day not to depend upon their initial ethos but to build their ethos with their messages. This is also sound advice for a communicator today. *A source's ethos is highly subject to modification by the content and presentation of the message.* We do not know exactly what elements contribute to derived ethos. Rhetorical theory and the attitude theories discussed in Chapter 4, however, point to some elements as probable contributors to derived ethos. Unfortunately, experimental studies specifically concerned with derived ethos have been few in number and generally not well conceived.[22]

Aristotle emphasized the importance of a source's "rhetorical choices" evidenced by the message. By rhetorical choices Aristotle meant the things the source chooses to discuss, the arguments used, and the support for the arguments. The available research indicates that Aristotle's observation was quite correct. This research suggests that we tend to feel that sources who express views similar to our own are more credible than are those who express contrary views. As stated in Chapter 4, a source may build ethos by supporting things the audience likes and then draw upon the higher ethos to gain approval for other things. The source, then, should select with care the ideas he or she will support. An unwise rhetorical choice may seriously detract from one's ethos.

How a source supports propositions is also a factor in derived ethos. Assuming that the audience members are not already in agreement with a point the source wishes them to accept, whether the source merely asserts the argument or supports it with evidence may make a considerable difference in derived ethos. An asserted point, unless previously accepted by the audience, is always dependent upon a source's ethos for acceptance. If the source continually asserts, he or she is continually drawing upon ethos. As with a bank account, constant withdrawals from a source's "ethos account" may lead to bankruptcy. By including evidence to support assertions, a source can avoid trading so extensively on ethos and, in some instances, may actually increase it. This theory is generally supported by a series of experimental studies I conducted.[23] These studies found that a source with moderate to low ethos could increase ethos by including factual material and opinions attributed to qualified sources. This effect, however, was not found in connection with all topics. The audience's familiarity with the evidence the source uses, or with similar evidence, appears to determine whether the source may build ethos by including evidence in the message. If the evidence is unfamiliar to the audience, it has a favorable impact. Otherwise, it has no effect. Suffice it to say at this point that evidence is a factor that can improve a source's derived ethos. Poor evidence, of course, can have a negative effect.[24]

Another such factor is delivery, which applies most directly to oral communication. In Chapter 14 we shall direct our attention to delivery in some detail. At this point we are concerned only with the effect of delivery on ethos. Its effect is clear. *Good delivery tends to increase a source's derived ethos; bad delivery tends to decrease it.* This effect was first suggested by Aristotle when he theorized that ethos is a cause of persuasion if a speech is so uttered as to make (the source) worthy of belief. Some experimental research has been directed toward the effect of delivery upon ethos. Winthrop found that good delivery significantly increased ethos.[25] Harms found that people can judge the social status of an individual by oral cues alone.[26] Similarly, Allport and Cantrill found that people perceive personality characteristics of an individual from vocal cues alone.[27] In a study I conducted in collaboration with Arnold, which included both oral and visual aspects of delivery, it was found that a live speaker's ethos was significantly lowered by poor delivery. In a subsequent study involving a videotaped speaker and an audiotaped speaker, I found that poor delivery lowered the experimental speaker's ethos. Both the oral and the visual aspects of poor delivery contributed to this reduction of ethos. While the audiotaped speaker's ethos was significantly lowered by poor delivery (only the oral aspects, not the visual, were observed by the experimental subjects), the videotaped speaker's ethos was lowered still more by the visual aspects of poor delivery.[28] In a study I conducted in collaboration with Mehrley, it was found that the fluency of the source had a significant effect on the ethos of both an initially high-ethos source and an initially low-ethos source.[29] A nonfluent presentation tended to lower the ethos of an initially high-ethos source, whereas a fluent presentation tended to increase the ethos of an initially low-ethos source.

Another factor that we intuitively believe is related to derived ethos is the sincerity of the source. A sincere source should be more credible than an insincere one. This is another of those "obvious" results we come to expect. Research reported by Hildreth suggests, however, that sincerity does not make a difference but that *apparent* sincerity does. Hildreth found that the people in his study could not distinguish between sincere and insincere sources, but those the people *perceived* as sincere received significantly higher ratings for effectiveness than those they perceived as insincere.[30] Although the design of Hildreth's study makes it difficult to generalize from his findings to other communication events,[31] his results are quite easily explained. We all know that actors can portray characters quite unlike themselves and yet be very convincing. It should not be surprising to anyone, then, that a skilled source can give the impression of being sincere in the beliefs he or she is expressing, even though the individual is insincere. Of course, it is probably easier to appear sincere if one really is sincere. But even the most sincere source must take care that the message and the presentation of the message also make her or him appear sincere. If one does, one's ethos will probably increase; if not, one's ethos will be likely to decline.

The factor of organization of the source's message has been observed to have a significant impact on the source's ethos.[32] This effect of the structure of the message appears to be more influential on the competence dimension of ethos than on the character dimension.[33] A poorly organized message tends to reduce the source's ethos.

"Fear appeals" are appeals that emphasize possible harmful consequences that may befall the receivers if they do not make attitude or behavioral choices recommended by the source. These may be phrased so as to be vivid (strong fear appeal) or mild (weak fear appeal). *Strong fear appeals have been found to reduce the credibility of an initially low-ethos source*[34] *but to increase the credibility of an initially high-ethos source.*[35] We will further consider the effects of fear appeals in a later chapter.

Two other language usage variables have been observed to have a significant effect on the ethos of the source. Corley found that use of "militant" language (that typical of a black militant speaker in the 1970s) by an initially moderately credible source tended to lower the source's perceived ethos.[36] Similarly, Mehrley and I found that a source employing "opinionated-rejection statements," when the receivers held intense attitudes on the message topic, tended to have ethos lowered.[37] Opinionated-rejection statements are statements that not only indicate the source's attitude toward the topic, but also her or his attitude toward those who disagree. An example of such a statement is, "Only a warmonger would favor sending U.S. troops to the Middle East."

The factors mentioned above are probably the most important for determining a source's derived ethos. Rhetorical theory, however, provides several additional suggestions for the source concerned with increasing ethos. The suggestion that has received the most support from experimental research is that *the source should establish common ground with the audience.*[38] This means that the source should make the audience aware of any similarities between the source's background, experience, and attitudes and the audience's own, assuming, of course, that they are favorably disposed toward the given similarities. If members of the audience have been caught cheating on their income tax returns, it may not increase a source's ethos to indicate that he or she has been caught also.

Such similarities do not even have to be real in order to have a positive effect, although for a source to posit a false similarity raises a rather important ethical question. Ewing found that if sources state in the introduction that their attitude is similar to those of the members of the audience, they will be more successful in modifying their attitudes, even if the source then proceeds to present a message in opposition to this stated attitude.[39] The effect of establishing common ground, therefore, appears to be a strong one indeed.

Closely related to establishing common ground is establishing good will. As already noted, since the days of Aristotle it has generally been accepted that a source's ethos will be higher if the audience believes that he or she has their best interests at heart. Good will may be established by a message that indirectly suggests that the source desires good things for the audience. It may also be established by the source's directly stating such desires. The latter method, however, may raise doubt in the minds of members of the audience who are prone to be skeptical of do-gooders.

The establishment of good will is primarily a process of getting the audience to perceive the source as having the right attitude toward them. Sources may also improve ethos by getting the audience to perceive them as having other right attitudes. Most people consider open-mindedness a desirable quality. Therefore, sources should avoid giving the impression that they are strongly biased on the topic being considered.[40] This is not to suggest that the source should try to appear indecisive—quite the contrary. Sources will probably appear much more sincere if they clearly state and support their positions. In oral communication, direct and forceful delivery is helpful. But to appear objective is to appear open-minded; therefore, considering the other side of the question will tend to improve a source's ethos.

The discussion of initial ethos stated that it is based on the audience's prior knowledge of, and prior experiences with, the source. In many communicative situations, the audience is not fully aware of the source's background. Therefore, tactful references to relevant factors in one's background and in one's experience will tend to improve a source's derived ethos.[41] The key word here is *tactful.* If not carefully handled, such references may appear boastful and have a negative effect.

A source may also profit from references to affiliation with worthy organizations. Such references tend to transfer some of the ethos of the organization to the source. An important consideration here is to determine what a worthy organization is. In such a situation, the merit of an organization is determined by what the audience thinks of that organization. Affiliation with the Federal Bureau of Investigation will probably not increase a source's ethos if the audience is a group of Cosa Nostra members. Nor will being a county chairman of the Democratic Party be helpful when the audience is predominantly Republican. However, being a Rotarian should be helpful when communicating with Rotarians.

The technique of the irrelevant or humorous digression is useful primarily in oral communication. When speakers sense that the audience is becoming hostile, they may protect their ethos by straying from the point for a few moments and talking about something that the hearers will find pleasant. This tends to relax the audience and reduce their hostility. The source may then return to the point and continue the speech as planned.

A study by Carlson indicates that a source may use unfamiliar words and phrases in order to increase derived ethos.[42] The practical utility of this finding, however, is somewhat limited. While employing unfamiliar words may increase a source's ethos, it may also, as indicated in Chapter 2, prevent the audience from understanding what the source is trying to convey. This technique for improving derived ethos seems most appropriate for ethos-centered, rather than concept-centered, communication, a distinction we will consider later.

To summarize, sources are most likely to find their ethos increased if they carefully select propositions to support so as to be certain that they are not highly discrepant with the audience's attitudes; support arguments with evidence from well-qualified sources; present the message in a sincere manner to establish credibility; establish common ground and good will with the audience; appear to be open-minded; and make the audience aware of the favorable aspects of their background, experience, and affiliations. In some cases, sources may also benefit from using unfamiliar words and irrelevant or humorous digressions. The source who makes a serious attempt to employ these methods whenever appropriate is not likely to have ethos reduced as a result of the communication.

TERMINAL ETHOS

As stated earlier, terminal ethos is the product of the interaction between initial ethos and derived ethos. Terminal ethos should always be considered by the source prior to a communicative act. In some cases it will be the source's prime concern; only in a very few cases will it be relatively unimportant.

We may classify rhetorical communication as either *concept-centered* or *ethos-centered*. In concept-centered communication the primary purpose is to modify an audience's attitude toward, or understanding of, some topic. In ethos-centered communication the primary purpose is to enhance the ethos of the source.

The majority of rhetorical communication falls into the first category, but ethos-centered communication is not at all uncommon. Speeches delivered by candidates for public office are typical. The famous Kennedy–Nixon television debates of 1960 offer an excellent example of ethos-centered communication. To view these encounters as debates over substantive issues would be to miss their basic function.[43] They were designed and executed to permit the American public to view these two men defending their views under pressure. Each man took great pains to appear in a good light. There was great concern over such apparently minor things as makeup and lighting. Few question the fact that the Kennedy image was enhanced by the debates. Some even suggest that his showing in the debates won him the election. The presidential candidate debates held since those early Kennedy–Nixon encounters have, for the most part, served similar purposes. However, most have not generated either the interest or the impact of the earlier contests.

Many corporations and unions concerned about their public images prepare speeches for their representatives to give to local groups. The prime function of these speeches is to make the corporation or union look good. Numerous organizations and individuals employ public relations experts to project favorable images for them. All these communicators are involved in ethos-centered communication.

Most of this book is devoted to theory related to concept-centered communication. This body of theory, for the most part, is directly applicable to ethos-centered communication but with one crucial distinction. *In concept-centered communication, the source trades on ethos to increase the favorability of the audience's attitudes. In ethos-centered communication, the source trades on the audience's favorable attitudes to increase ethos.*

Our division of communication into concept-centered and ethos-centered is not intended to suggest that in the former the source is unconcerned with ethos. Usually, the source will want to communicate with the same audience again at a later date. The terminal ethos of today is the initial ethos of tomorrow. Therefore, one must take care to build and preserve ethos each time one communicates with a given audience. Only in the case of one-shot communication may the source be unconcerned with terminal ethos. Failure to be concerned about terminal ethos may place a source in an extremely unfavorable position for later communication. A major political candidate in the United States—Richard Nixon—provides a striking example of an individual who forgot to consider terminal ethos. After being defeated at the polls in California, he held a press conference, carried by nationwide television and radio, at which he presented a stinging denunciation of the American press. He claimed that the newspapers had been unfair to him and had caused his defeat, implying that those involved were the lowest kind of human beings. He presented no substantive support for his assertion, so it was almost impossible for the average citizen to evaluate his claim. Because most people held the press in very high regard, they tended to perceive his outburst as bitterness from a loser. Their estimation of his character was greatly lowered. His initial ethos for subsequent communication, therefore, was significantly lowered also. Although the average citizen probably forgot this outburst in time, it is doubtful that members of the press ever would. The probable effect of this politician's communication, therefore, was to damage temporarily his communicative potential with average citizens but to damage it permanently with the press. The press certainly took delight in later years in publishing Nixon's role in the Watergate affair. We may learn from this unfortunate incident that to ignore our terminal ethos in one communicative situation may seriously reduce our potential for later communicative situations. It is vital to consider our terminal ethos if we wish to communicate with the same audience again at a later date.

LONG-TERM EFFECT OF ETHOS

Thus far the discussion of concept-centered communication has made no distinction between the effects of ethos on immediate change of attitude and on the retention of ethos-induced change. Such a distinction must be made. Experimental research clearly indicates that ethos has a powerful effect in producing immediate change of attitude. Some of the research, however, suggests that ethos has no major long-term effect in this respect.

In the Hovland and Weiss experiment referred to previously, high ethos produced significantly greater immediate change of attitude than did low ethos. When measured again four weeks later, there was no difference in the attitude change produced by the two sources.[44] Similarly, it was found, in the Kelman and Hovland study, that after three weeks there was no difference in attitude change.[45] An unexpected finding in these studies was that while the high-ethos source lost some of its effect over time, the low-ethos source *gained* effectiveness. The researchers labeled what they found the "sleeper effect." The explanation Hovland and Weiss gave for the sleeper effect was that, in the absence of stimuli reinstating the ethos of the source over a period of time, the audience remembers the message but forgets its source. In support of this explanation, data from these experiments show that if the members of the audience are reminded of the source three to four weeks after the communication, and their attitudes are then measured, there are significant differences in effectiveness between the high-ethos and the low-ethos sources. Thus, if the audience is permitted to forget the source, the sustained effect of the communication is dependent, as Hovland, Janis, and Kelley put it, on the "argument and evidence" originally presented by the source.[46]

In a series of studies designed specifically to examine the cause of the sleeper effect, I varied the quality of evidence used from excellent to very poor. It was hypothesized, in accordance with the Hovland-Janis-Kelley explanation, that there would be a markedly greater sleeper effect when a source employed good evidence than when he or she employed poor evidence. The hypothesis was not confirmed. No sleeper effect was observed for either four or seven weeks after exposure to the message, whether the use of evidence was good or poor. This finding was consistent for speeches on two separate topics and was repeated in two experiments. In all cases there was a loss of attitude change for both high- and low-ethos sources over a period of time. In no cases did the low-ethos source gain in effect as time elapsed. In most cases, when there was a significant difference in attitude change produced by variations in the source's ethos measured immediately after the communication, the difference was sustained over time.[47] It will be noted that these results are similar to those found by Hovland, Janis, and Kelley in their reinstatement condition. This suggests, of course, that in these studies reinstatement of the source may have occurred. However, the procedures involved in the Hovland-Janis-Kelley studies and in the McCroskey studies were essentially similar; therefore, this explanation is questionable.

Because of these conflicting results, it is difficult to predict what the effect of ethos will be over a period of time. But one consistent pattern is indicated in these studies: *A high-ethos source always seems eventually to lose some effect.* As the Hovland-Janis-Kelley studies indicate, however, if the audience is reminded of the source at a still later time, most of this loss is regained. Because most communicative events involve sources with ethos ranging from moderate to high, this pattern is particularly important. If such a source can strongly identify itself with the content of the message, recalling the message will tend to reinstate the ethos and cause more attitude change to be retained. The opposite tactic, of course, should be employed by a source with lower ethos. Such a source should strive to reduce identification with the message.

POWER AND ETHOS

Power is the capacity to influence people to do or believe something they would not have done or believed had they not been influenced. When we engage in rhetorical communication with other people, we are attempting to influence them. In other words, we are attempting to exercise our power over them.

French and Raven[48] have provided an excellent framework for understanding how power functions in most human relationships. They suggest that there are five bases or types of power: coercive, legitimate, reward, expert, and referent. Each of these is based on receivers' perceptions with regard to the source of communication and on the motivations of the receivers. Let us consider each type.

A source's coercive power is based on a receiver's perception that he or she can be punished by the source for failing to conform to the source's attempt at influence. The strength of the source's coercive power is based on the receiver's perception of how probable it is that the source will actually punish rejection of influence and on how much the receiver wants to avoid that punishment.

Legitimate power is often referred to as "assigned" power. It stems from the assigned role of the source—such roles as student body president, professor, dean, committee chairperson, fraternity president, and the like. Legitimate power is based on the receiver's perception that a source has the right to make certain demands and requests as a function of his or her assigned position.

Reward power is almost the exact opposite of coercive power. A source's reward power is based on a receiver's perception that he or she can be rewarded by the source for conforming to the source's influence. The strength of the source's reward power is based on the receiver's perception of how probable it is that the source will actually reward acceptance of influence and how much the receiver wants to obtain that reward.

Expert power stems from the receiver's perception of the source as competent and knowledgeable on the topic under discussion. This base of power is virtually identical to the competence dimension of ethos, which was discussed previously in this chapter.

Referent power is based on the receiver's identification with the source. This power stems from a positive relationship between source and receiver such that the receiver sees the source as a person to please and a model to emulate. Both the character and goodwill dimensions of ethos and the receiver's interpersonal attraction for the source impact on the strength of the source's referent power.

How a source chooses to exercise power in rhetorical communication can have a major impact on that source's ethos. Although all five bases of power have the potential to change the behavior of receivers, they may at the same time have very different effects on the source's terminal ethos. Exercise of some bases of power, notably coercive and legitimate, typically results in a major reduction of a source's ethos. In contrast, use of expert and referent power sometimes results in an actual increase in ethos. Use of reward power, on the other hand, usually has little impact on ethos, either positive or negative.[49]

On the basis of the available research related to use of power and ethos, it is clear that a source must be very careful when employing coercive or legitimate power. Receivers tend to resent both and want little to do with sources who employ them. Consequently, sources who employ these types of power tend to lose both expert and referent power, and these are the precise types of power that the source needs over the long term in order to exert continuing influence. The use of coercive power, in particular, tends to create an environment in which only coercive power *can* be used, because over time the other types of power will disappear along with the source's ethos. Coercion will be considered further in Chapter 15 in relation to the matter of ethics and rhetorical communication.

DISCUSSION QUESTIONS

1. What dimension of ethos, other than competence and character, do you think might exist? Why?

2. Is there really such a thing as an "objectively irrelevant" factor that affects ethos?

3. How important is the ethos of a teacher? Does it affect the students' learning?

4. What factors, other than those discussed in this chapter, do you think might have an influence on derived ethos?

5. How common is ethos-centered communication in everyday life?

NOTES

1. W. M. Sattler, "Conceptions of Ethos in Ancient Rhetoric," *Speech Monographs* 14 (1947): 55–65.

2. L. Cooper, *The Rhetoric of Aristotle* (Englewood Cliffs, NJ: Prentice-Hall, 1932), p. 92.

3. C. I. Hovland, I. L. Janis, and H. H. Kelley, *Communication and Persuasion* (New Haven, CT: Yale University Press, 1953), ch. 2.

4. D. K. Berlo and J. B. Lemert, "A Factor Analytic Study of the Dimension of Source Credibility," paper presented at the Speech Association of America Convention, New York, 1961.

5. J. C. McCroskey, "Scales for the Measurement of Ethos," *Speech Monographs* 33 (1966): 65–72.

6. See, for example, J. C. McCroskey and T. Jensen, "Measurement of the Credibility of Mass Media News sources," *Journal of Broadcasting* 19 (1975): 169–80; J. C. McCroskey, W. E. Holdridge, and J. K. Toomb, "An Instrument for Measuring the Source Credibility of Basic Speech Communication Instructors," *Speech Teacher* 23 (1974): 26–33; J. C. McCroskey, T. Jensen, and C. Valencia, "Measurement of the Credibility of Peers and Spouses," paper presented at the International Communication Association Convention, Montreal, Quebec, 1973; J. C. McCroskey, T. Jensen, and C. Todd. "The Generalizability of Source Credibility Scales for Public Figures," paper presented at the Speech Communication Association Convention, Chicago, 1972; J. C. McCroskey, T. Jensen, C. Todd, and J. K. Toomb, "Measurement of the Credibility of Organization Sources," paper presented at the Western Speech Communication Association Convention, Honolulu, 1972; and J. C. McCroskey, M. D. Scott, and T. J. Young, "The Dimensions of Source Credibility for Spouses and Peers," paper presented at the Western Speech Communication Association Convention, Fresno, California, 1971. For the most definitive summary and analysis of this body of research, see J. C. McCroskey and T. J. Young, "Ethos and Credibility: The Construct and Its Measurement after Three Decades," *Central States Speech Journal* 32 (1981): 24–34.

7. J. C. McCroskey, *An Introduction to Communication in the Classroom,* (Edina, MN: Burgess International, 1992), pp. 110–112.

8. J. C. McCroskey and J. J. Teven, "Goodwill: A Reexamination of the Construct and Its Measurement," *Communication Monographs* 66 (1999): 90–103; J. J. Teven and J. C. McCroskey, "The Relationship of Perceived Teacher Caring with Student Learning and Teacher Evaluation," *Communication Education* 46 (1997): 1–9.

9. F. Haiman, "An Experimental Study of the Effects of Ethos in Public Speaking," *Speech Monographs* 16 (1949): 190–202; E. Strother, "An Experimental Study of Ethos Related to the Introduction in the Persuasive Speaking Situation," Ph.D. diss., Northwestern University, 1951.

10. C. I. Hovland and W. Weiss, "The Influence of Source Credibility on Communication Effectiveness," *Public Opinion Quarterly* 15 (1951): 635–50.

11. H. C. Kelman and C. I. Hovland, " 'Reinstatement' of the Communicator in Delayed Measurement of Opinion Change," *Journal of Abnormal and Social Psychology* 48 (1953): 327–35.

12. J. C. McCroskey, "Experimental Studies of the Effects of Ethos and Evidence in Persuasive Communication," Ph.D. diss., Pennsylvania State University, 1966.

13. K. Andersen and T. Clevenger, Jr., "A Summary of Experimental Research in Ethos," *Speech Monographs* 30 (1963): 59–78. See also V. Lashbrook, "Source Credibility: A Summary of Experimental Research," paper presented at the Speech Communication Association Convention, San Francisco, 1971.

14. J. W. Koehler, J. C. McCroskey, and W. E. Arnold. "The Effect of Receivers' Constancy Expectation in Persuasive Communication," Research Monograph, Department of Speech, Pennsylvania State University, 1966.

15. E. Aronson and B. W. Golden, "The Effect of Relevant and Irrelevant Aspects of Communicator Credibility of Opinion Change," *Journal of Personality* 30 (1962): 135–46.

16. J. S. Kerrick, "The Effect of Relevant and Non-relevant Sources on Attitude Change," *Journal of Social Psychology* 47 (1958): 15–20.

17. J. C. McCroskey and R. E. Dunham, "Ethos: A Confounding Element in Communication Research," *Speech Monographs* 30 (1966): 464–66; and P. D. Holzman, Confirmation of Ethos as a Confounding Element in Communication Research," *Speech Monographs* 30 (1966): 464–66.

18. J. Mills and E. Aronson, "Opinion Change as a Function of the Communicator's Attractiveness and Desire to Influence," *Journal of Personality and Social Psychology* 1 (1965): 173–77. See also N. Fensterheim and M. E. Tresselt, "The Influence of Value Systems on the Perception of People," *Journal of Abnormal and Social Psychology* 48 (1953): 48, 93–98.

19. R. N. Widgery and B. Webster, "The Effects of Physical Attractiveness upon Perceived Initial Credibility," *Michigan Speech Association Journal* 4 (1969).

20. W. E. Arnold, "An Experimental Study of the Effects of Communicator Credibility and Attitude Change on Subsequent Overt Behavior," Ph.D. diss., Pennsylvania State University, 1966.

21. P. A. Andersen, "An Experimental Study to Assess the Effects of Source Credibility on Comprehension," paper presented at the Speech Communication Association Convention, New York, 1973; R. E. Dempsey, "Credibility, Attention, and Learning," M.A. thesis, Western Illinois University, 1975; L. R. Wheeless, "The Effects of Comprehension Loss on Persuasion," *Speech Monographs* 38 (1971): 327–30; L. R. Wheeless, "The Effects of Attitude, Credibility, and Homophily on Selective Exposure to Information," *Speech Monographs* 41 (1974): 309–38; L. R. Wheeless, "The Relationship of Attitude and Credibility to Comprehension and Selective Exposure," *Western Speech* 38 (1974): 88–97; and L. R. Wheeless, "The Relationship of Four Elements to Immediate Recall and Student-Instructor Interaction, *Western Speech Communication* 39 (1975): 131–40.

22. For a discussion of this research, see Andersen and Clevenger, "A Summary of Experimental Research in Ethos," and Lashbrook, "Source Credibility."

23. J. C. McCroskey, "Experimental Studies of the Effects of Ethos and Evidence in Persuasive Communication."

24. J. Luchok and J. C. McCroskey, "The Effect of Quality of Evidence on Attitude Change and Source Credibility," *Southern Speech Communication Journal* 43 (1978): 371–83.

25. H. Winthrop, "Effect of Personal Qualities on One-Way Communication," *Psychological Reports* 2 (1956): 323–24.

26. L. S. Harms, "Social Judgements of Status Cues in Language," Ph.D. diss., Ohio State University, 1959.

27. G. W. Allport and H. Cantril, "Judging Personality from Voice," *Journal of Social Psychology* 5 (1934): 37–55.

28. Both these studies are discussed in J. C. McCroskey, "Studies of the Effects of Evidence in Persuasive Communication," *Speech Communication Research Laboratory Report SCRL 4-67*, Department of Speech, Michigan State University, 1967.

29. J. C. McCroskey and R. S. Mehrley, "The Effects of Disorganization and Nonfluency on Attitude Change and Source Credibility," *Speech Monographs* 36 (1969): 13–21.

30. R. A. Hildreth, "An Experimental Study of Audiences' Ability to Distinguish between Sincere and Insincere Speeches," Ph.D. diss., University of Southern California, 1953.

31. For a discussion of this problem, see Andersen and Clevenger, "A Summary of Experimental Research in Ethos," pp. 73–74.

32. H. Sharp, Jr., and T. McClung, "Effects of Organization on the Speaker's Ethos," *Speech Monographs* 33 (1966): 182–83.

33. McCroskey and Mehrley, "The Effects of Disorganization."

34. M. A. Hewgill and G. R. Miller, "Source Credibility and Response to Fear-Arousing Communications," *Speech Monographs* 32 (1965): 95–101.

35. J. C. Gardiner, "An Experimental Study of the Effects of Evidence and Fear Appeals on Attitude Change and Source Credibility," Research Monograph, Department of Communication, Michigan State University, 1969.

36. D. K. Corley, "Effect of Militant Language and Race of Source on Attitude and Credibility," master's thesis, Illinois State University, 1970.

37. R. S. Mehrley and J. C. McCroskey, "Opinionated Statements and Attitude Intensity as Predictors of Attitude Change and Source Credibility," *Speech Monographs* 37 (1970): 47–52.

38. See, for example, F. E. Fiedler and W. G. Warrington, "Unconscious Attitudes as Correlates of Sociometric Choice in a Social Group," *Journal of Abnormal and Social Psychology* 47 (1952): 790–96; D. Byrne, "Interpersonal Attraction and Attitude Similarity," *Journal of Abnormal and Social Psychology* 62 (1961): 713–15; and T. C. Brock, "Communicator-Recipient Similarity and Decision Change," *Journal of Abnormal and Social Psychology* 1 (1965): 650–54.

39. T. N. Ewing, "A Study of Certain Factors Involved in Changes of Opinion," *Journal of Social Psychology* 16 (1942): 63–88.

40. Research findings suggest that bias may not always adversely affect a communicator's ethos. See C. I. Hovland and W. Mandell, "An Experimental Comparison of Conclusion-Drawing by the Communicator and by the Audience," *Journal of Abnormal and Social Psychology* 47 (1952): 581–88.

41. T. H. Ostermeier, "An Experimental Study on the Type and Frequency of Reference as Used by an Unfamiliar Source in a Message and Its Effect upon Perceived Credibility and Attitude Change," Ph.D. diss., Michigan State University, 1966.

42. E. R. Carlson, "Word Familiarity as a Factor in Forming Impressions," *Psychological Reports* 7 (1960): 18.

43. P. I. Rosenthal, "The Concept of Ethos and the Structure of Persuasion," *Speech Monographs* 30 (1966): 114–26.

44. Hovland and Weiss, "The Influence of Source Credibility," pp. 635–50.

45. Kelman and Hovland, " 'Reinstatement,' " pp. 327–35.

46. Hovland, Janis, and Kelley, *Communication and Persuasion*, ch. 2.

47. J. C. McCroskey, "Experimental Studies of the Effects of Ethos and Evidence in Persuasive Communication."

48. J. R. P. French, Jr., and B. H. Raven, "The Bases of Social Power," in D. Cartwright (ed.), *Studies in Social Power* (Ann Arbor: University of Michigan Press, 1959), pp. 150–67.

49. V. P. Richmond, J. P. Wagner, and J. C. McCroskey, "The Impact of Perceptions of Leadership Style, Use of Power, and Conflict Management Style on Organizational Outcomes," *Communication Quarterly* 31 (1983): 27–36; V. P. Richmond and J. C. McCroskey, "Power in the Classroom II: Power and Learning," *Communication Education* 33 (1984): 125–36; K. R. Student, "Supervisory Influence and Work-Group Performance," *Journal of Applied Psychology* 52 (1968): 188–94.

CHAPTER 6

THE NATURE
OF PERSUASIVE ARGUMENT

Oliver has observed that the human mind functions in four distinctly different ways: impressionistically, empirically, logically, and rhetorically.[1] The first three are considered in courses in the arts, science, and philosophy. Most students are well acquainted with these three, although the terms used here may be applied in unfamiliar ways. The fourth function of the mind is the primary concern of communicators. It is also the primary concern of this book.

Although the mind functions rhetorically during a greater proportion of our waking hours than it does in the three other ways combined, only a few students have been exposed to systematic instruction in the rhetorical thought process. As a result, many people approach communication, especially persuasive communication, with inappropriate thought processes. Some present a message to an audience very artfully, almost poetically. They seek to impress the audience with their vocabulary, their stylistic use of words, their resonant voices. Some "let the facts speak for themselves." They overwhelm the audience with all the empirical data relevant to their particular question. Some reason out every point very logically. They assume that the members of their intelligent audience will reach the "right" conclusion if only they see the logic of it.

All these communicators have one thing in common: They base their messages on faulty thought processes. They probably will not succeed in their purpose. If they should succeed, however, it would be by accident rather than by rhetorical design. This chapter concerns the rhetorical thought process, the only thought process appropriate for persuasive communication. Rhetorical thought is neither logical nor illogical: it is psychological. This is not to suggest that rhetorical thought is irrational; quite the contrary. It is rational, but it takes account of the fact that human reasoning does not occur in a vacuum. Research has indicated that reasoning is strongly affected by an individual's attitudes.[2] Consequently, matters of formal logical validity have little relevance for the communicator concerned with influencing an audience.[3] The real test of a communicator's reasoning is acceptance by the audience. The problem of the communicator is to create a message that will guide the audience's reasoning through a maze of attitudes to a particular conclusion. *The function of the rhetorical thought process, then, is guidance, not demonstration.*

In a given rhetorical effort a source will ask the receiver to accept many specific conclusions. Some of them will be main ideas; others will be supporting points. *An argument is a part of a message that is designed to gain acceptance of a particular conclusion.* An understanding of the nature of persuasive argument is crucial to skillful use of the rhetorical thought process.

A PSYCHOLOGICAL MODEL OF ARGUMENT

The first psychological model of argument was set forth by Aristotle. The essence of his model was the *enthymeme*, which he defined as a rhetorical syllogism. Considerable confusion as to Aristotle's meaning of the term *rhetorical syllogism* has existed in this country. Numerous scholarly articles have appeared that purport to explain Aristotle's concept of the enthymeme.[4] There is, however, no general agreement in contemporary rhetorical literature as to his meaning.

A British philosopher, Stephen Toulmin, provided a potentially more useful model of argument. In his book *The Uses of Argument*, Toulmin sets forth a six-part model, which some claim may be used to describe any argument.[5] Unfortunately, this model is based on the logical, rather than on the rhetorical, tradition. Thus, in the form laid out by Toulmin, the model's usefulness for communicators is severely limited.

The model we shall offer was developed within the context of the Toulmin model, but with an Aristotelian view of rhetorical thought. It is, therefore, neither purely Toulminian nor purely Aristotelian, yet it is compatible with the thinking of both of these philosophers. In essence, it is a model of the enthymeme that employs terms set forth by Toulmin as labels for its parts.

There are three essential elements in our model. Toulmin has labeled these elements *claim, warrant,* and *data.* In addition, there is one element that may or may not be present in a given argument, here called "reservations." Let us look more closely at the nature of each of these elements.

The Concept of Claim

A claim is any belief that a source wishes the receiver to accept. It may be the ultimate point of an entire series of arguments, or it may be a point that the source wishes to use as data or warrant for another argument. Whenever a source makes an assertion, he or she is asking the audience to accept a claim. Therefore, theoretically at least, every statement made by a source can be viewed as a claim. This is not to suggest that sources directly express all their claims. Many claims are tacitly implied. If the source indicates that all foreign policies of the United States should work to our benefit and that the policies of the United States toward Latin America are seriously damaging our interests, the source's claim is obvious, whether it is stated or not: The United States should change its policies toward Latin America. Thus, whenever a source asks a receiver to accept a belief not previously accepted, that new idea is a claim.

The Concept of Warrant

A warrant is a belief held by a receiver, which certifies the acceptability of a claim based on relevant data. The warrant is the connecting link, the bridge, between data and claim. No claim will be accepted unless there is a relevant warrant. If a source makes an assertion (claim) that we find unacceptable, we frequently refer to it as an "unwarranted" claim. We mean by this that we cannot connect relevant data to the asserted or implied claim in a psychologically acceptable manner. If a source argues that racial discrimination exists under democracy in this country and that therefore we should adopt a communistic form of government, we are very likely to reject the claim. We say it is unwarranted. We may ask why we should adopt communism just because we have some discrimination within our democracy. Our question is a request for a warrant. The answer is a sign that the source is proposing one.

Our crucial concern with the warrant is that it be believed by the receiver. In the example in the preceding paragraph, the source probably would be faced with an impossible task of trying to find a warrant that would justify the claim in our minds. In short, there may be no way to complete the argument in such a manner as to gain our acceptance of the claim.

The acceptability of a prospective warrant depends upon the nature of the particular audience to which the argument is addressed. For example, the warrant "Wage increases usually produce price increases in the American economy" may be very acceptable to an audience composed of businessmen, but it may be totally unacceptable to a group of union leaders. If a given warrant is not immediately acceptable to the audience to which it is addressed, it must be treated as a claim, and a complete argument must be developed to justify it. The establishment of warrants by this process will be discussed later in the chapter.

The Concept of Data

Data are individual beliefs held by a receiver. Any factual matter or opinion may serve as a datum if it is believed by the receiver. As with the warrant, our crucial concern with data is that they be believed by the receiver. In rhetorical communication, fact and truth are relative matters. Even if a source is firmly convinced that something is true, it cannot be used as a datum unless the receiver also believes that it is true. The presumptive fact that people of all races are are biologically equal may be used as a datum for an audience composed of civil rights advocates, but it will not serve as a datum if the audience is a local chapter of the Aryan Nation. Of course, a source must face ethical factors when selecting data for an argument. But the crucial test as to whether particular facts or opinions can be used as data is their status in the receiver's system of beliefs. Whether the data should be used by the source will be determined by their perceived usefulness for the given argument, and also by ethical considerations. Ethical matters will be considered in a later chapter.

If a source suspects that data he or she wishes to use in an argument have not been accepted by the receiver previously, it may be necessary to treat the data as claims and develop arguments to gain the receiver's acceptance. Other ways data can gain acceptance will be discussed later in this chapter.

Some people find it difficult to distinguish between the data and the warrant in a given argument. This difficulty may be easily understood if we realize that a *a given belief may be used as data in one argument but as the warrant in another.* In a given argument, the distinction between data and warrant turns upon the degree of generality of the belief. The more general belief is the warrant, and the more specific belief is the datum. For example, the belief that "wage increases generally produce price increases" is the warrant when we argue, "Prices of fruit will soon go up because fruit pickers have received a wage increase." It is the datum when we argue, "Whatever causes prices to increase is bad; therefore wage increases are bad." In the former case, the belief that wage increases cause price increases is the more general of the elements of the argument. In the latter case, it is the more specific. Another important distinction between the two is that a warrant, in Toulmin's terms, is an "inference license"; that is, it makes a generalization or states a principle of reasoning for a specific argument, an instance of which is a datum. The numerous examples of warrants given later in this chapter should help in discriminating between data and warrant.

The Concept of Reservations

Reservations are exceptions to an argument; when expressed, they indicate the source's awareness that a claim may not be accurate under certain circumstances. Reservations are not essential parts of an argument. They may or may not be present in a given case. For example, the source may first suggest that a claim about air quality is true unless the government steps in with a new regulation and then indicate that it is most improbable that the government will step in.

Reservations may apply to the data, to the warrant, or to the connection between the two. In a given argument there may be reservations of all three kinds. Figure 6.1 is a diagrammatic representation of an argument with no reservations. Figure 6.2 is a diagrammatic representation of an argument including all three types of reservations. When this argument is

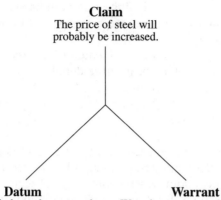

Claim
The price of steel will
probably be increased.

Datum
The steel industry has granted
its employees a wage increase.

Warrant
Wage increases usually produce
price increases in the steel industry.

FIGURE 6.1   Model of Argument with No Reservations.

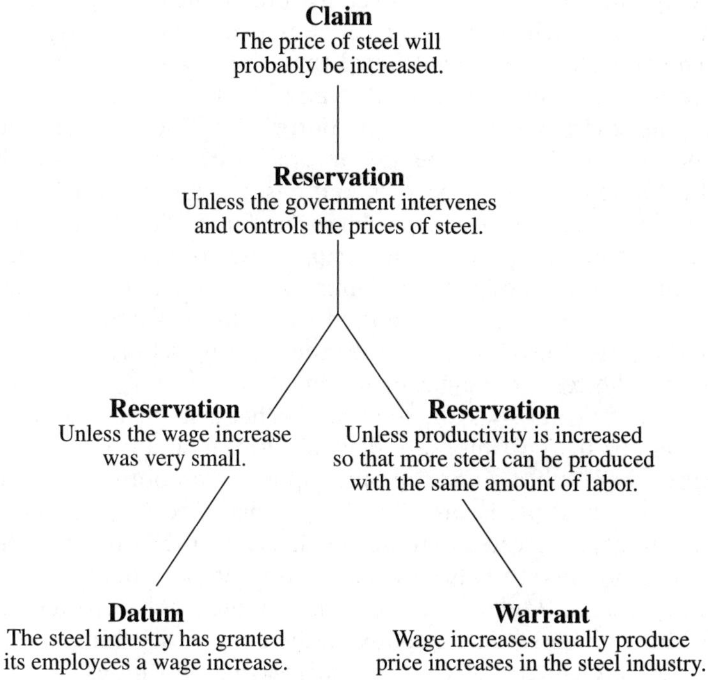

Claim
The price of steel will
probably be increased.

Reservation
Unless the government intervenes
and controls the prices of steel.

Reservation
Unless the wage increase
was very small.

Reservation
Unless productivity is increased
so that more steel can be produced
with the same amount of labor.

Datum
The steel industry has granted
its employees a wage increase.

Warrant
Wage increases usually produce
price increases in the steel industry.

FIGURE 6.2   Model of Argument with Reservations.

presented in a message, any or all of the reservations may be included. Later in the chapter we shall consider the factors relevant to the choice between including and excluding reservations.

With this general view of the elements of persuasive argument in mind, let us look at each element in more detail.

THE TYPES OF CLAIMS

It is vital for the source to perceive what Cicero and Quintilian called the "Stasis," or status, of the argument in the mind of the receiver. There are four different types of issues about which people argue. We may phrase these four types of issues as questions: Is it? What is it? What is its quality? What should be done about it? All arguments are developed as answers to these questions. If the source addresses the wrong issue (in terms of what the receiver perceives to be the right issue), he or she may "win the battle but lose the war." The receiver may accept the individual arguments but not the ultimate claim.

An argument designed to answer any one of the issue questions draws a claim. Thus, for each type of issue there is a corresponding type of claim. Brockriede and Ehninger have labeled these four types of claims as designative, definitive, evaluative, and advocative.[6]

Designative claims answer the question "Is it?" They concern fact: Is or was something so, or will it be so? Several years ago there was fighting along the Chinese-Indian border. In the ensuing international discussion, there was controversy over which soldiers fired first. Did China attack India, or did India attack China? The claims supporting both positions were designative claims. Other designative claims would concern such matters as whether a person exceeded the posted speed limit, whether the price of steel will be raised next year, whether the local bookstore makes a profit, and whether the cost of living is increasing.

Definitive claims answer the question "What is it?" They are concerned with definition. In the Chinese-Indian dispute, it was established after a time that Chinese soldiers had fired first upon Indian outposts. The controversy then raged as to whether this firing constituted "aggression" against India. Indian maps indicated that the area in which the firing took place was inside India's borders, the attack thus meeting norms usually employed in defining aggression. However, Chinese maps indicated that the territory was within China's borders. Consequently, in the eyes of the Chinese, the attack was against "foreign troops" that had encroached on Chinese territory. No matter which view was to be argued, the primary question would be one of definition. Was, or was not, the act aggression? The argument on either side would terminate in a definitive claim. Other definitive claims would be concerned with such questions as how much decline in the value of the dollar is needed in order to constitute "inflation"; whether a six-win and five-loss football season should be called a "winning season"; whether a new federal welfare program is "socialistic"; or whether the alleged taking of life by Smith is "first degree murder."

Evaluative claims answer the question "What is its quality?" They concern values, or the relative merit of an idea, object, or action. Returning to our India-China example, we find that there was considerable international argument over the justifiability of the Chinese attack. The free world generally condemned the attack in terms such as *bad, evil,* and *treacherous.* All these claims were of the evaluative type. Other evaluative claims would concern such matters as the desirability of a tax cut, the evils of cheating on exams in college, the advisability of premarital sexual relations; and the suitability of a political candidate for office.

Advocative claims answer the question "What should be done about it?" They concern policy. In our India-China case, some people in this country argued that the United States should actively intervene in the fighting on behalf of the Indians. Others argued that we should remain neutral. Both sides were drawing advocative claims. Other advocative claims would concern such choices as whether we should vote for a tax cut; whether we should find Smith guilty of murder; whether we should attend the football game; whether we should vote for the incumbent congresswoman; or whether we should enroll for college in the summer.

THE TYPES OF WARRANTS

As we stated previously, warrants are general beliefs held by an audience that certify the acceptability of claims based on relevant data. All warrants have this characteristic of general belief in common. There are, however, major differences between particular warrants. There are three distinguishable types of warrants. Brockriede and Ehninger have called these three types of warrants *motivational, authoritative,* and *substantive.*[7]

Motivational warrants are based upon assumptions concerning the emotions, values, motives, or desires of the receiver. Rhetoricians from Aristotle to those of the present time have recognized the importance of motivational warrants. It would be no exaggeration to suggest that very few advocative claims are established without resorting to motivational warrants. We usually do things because we want to, because they satisfy our desires, or because of some other factor with an emotional basis. Similarly, many evaluative claims are established by means of motivational warrants. Things are usually perceived as good or bad, or beneficial or harmful, because they are perceived as satisfying or not satisfying our needs or desires. The value of a thing, an idea, or an action is relative. The same thing perceived as good by one person may be perceived as bad by another. The determining factor is the motivational warrant accepted by the person. The major problem for the

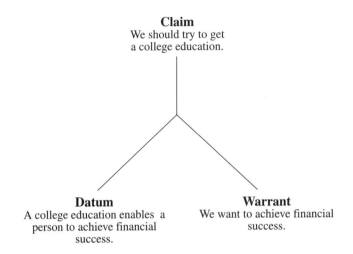

FIGURE 6.3   Argument Using Motivational Warrant.

source is to find the motivational warrant that will enable the particular receiver to accept the source's claim. Figure 6.3 is a diagrammatic representation of an argument with a motivational warrant.

Motivational warrants are frequently implied, rather than expressed in the message. For example, the argument that we should adopt a tax cut because we would have more money to spend if we have to pay less tax proceeds on the motivational warrant that we want more money to spend. Expressing this warrant in the message may add little or nothing to the source's argument. The members of an audience are very likely to fill it in without being specifically reminded that they want more money to spend.

In other cases it is essential that the motivational warrant be expressed. The source can usually determine when the motivational warrant needs expressing. For example, if the warrant "I want better schools" is likely to come up with the tax cut argument above (leading to the claim of "Do not cut taxes"), then the "We want more money to spend" warrant needs to be stated.

Authoritative warrants are based on assumptions concerning the credibility of the source of the data. In arguments utilizing authoritative warrants, the datum and claim appear to be essentially the same thing. An argument may run, for example, like this: Mayor Hoffmann states that our city has adequate parking in the downtown area (datum); Mayor Hoffmann is a credible source (warrant); therefore, our city probably has adequate parking in the downtown area (claim). The assumption is that Mayor Hoffmann is a credible source. Whether this assumption is acceptable depends, of course, upon the receiver. If it is acceptable, the source probably will find the claim accepted also.

Not all authoritative arguments assume the credibility of an outside source; many are based on the credibility of the speaker. Whenever the source asserts a fact or an opinion, an authoritative argument has been introduced. It goes like this: I say X is so (datum): I am a credible source (warrant); therefore, X is probably so (claim). As in the case of a citation from an outside source, the assumption is one of the credibility of the source. If the receiver perceives the source as credible, the claim will probably be accepted. Otherwise, it may be perceived as unwarranted.

As noted in Chapter 5, Aristotle suggested that ethos, the way the receiver perceives the source, is the most potent of the means of persuasion; modern research has tended to confirm this belief. When we realize that it is next to impossible for a source to document every assertion made, we can see why ethos is so potent. *Many of a source's arguments must rest on authoritative warrants that assume the source's credibility for the given audience.* If the assumption is justified, the source is likely to gain acceptance for the claims. However, if the credibility is questionable, it is quite unlikely that claims based on an assertion will be accepted.

As indicated earlier, motivational warrants are useful primarily for establishing evaluative and advocative claims. Authoritative warrants are useful for all types of claims. *Substantive warrants* are based on assumptions concerning relationships among phenomena in the external world. All substantive warrants assume that phenomena in the external world are interdependent and connected. Further, they assume that the connections are sufficiently systematic, regular, and permanent to provide grounds for prediction. In short, substantive warrants involve relationships favorable to prediction.

There are at least six distinct relationships of this sort: causation, sign, literal analogy, figurative analogy, generalization, and classification.

1. Causation. Probably the relationship with which sources concern themselves most frequently is causation. The assumed relationship when a source invokes a causation is that *one thing produces another.* Warrants based on causation include claims such as: A gunshot to the heart produces death; a pay increase produces a higher standard of living; and excessive speed produces auto accidents.

When using the pattern of causation, one may reason from the producer to what is produced (cause to effect), or from what is produced to what has produced it (effect to cause). The assumed relationship is the same in either case. Figures 6.4 and 6.5 illustrate the two types of arguments.

When the substantive warrant is causation, an observed cause may serve as a datum, and the claim of the argument will represent a projected effect of that cause. An observed effect may also serve as a datum, and the claim of the argument will represent the attributed cause of that effect. In either case, when causation is appealed to, a cause and an effect constitute the datum and the claim of the argument. Causal relationships are useful primarily for the establishment of designative claims, that is, for answering "Is it so?" or "Was it so?"

2. Sign. Closely related to causation, yet essentially different, is sign relationship (see Figure 6.6). Sign relationship assumes that *two or more things*

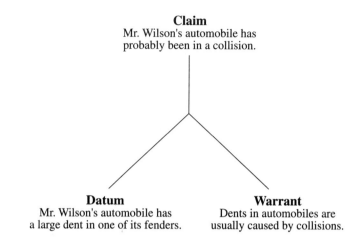

FIGURE 6.4   **Argument Using Causal Relationship: Effect to Cause.**

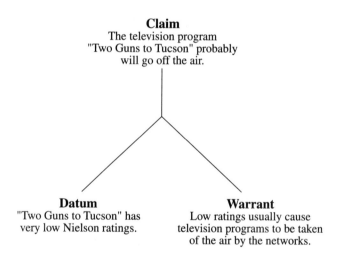

FIGURE 6.5   **Argument Using Causal Relationship: Cause to Effect.**

are coexistent. If the thermometer reads twenty degrees below zero, it is a sign that the local lake is frozen. If we see ashtrays placed in convenient places in our friend's home, it is a sign that our friend will not object to our smoking. If the stock market falls sharply, it is a sign that our economy is undergoing difficulty. If the weather is uncomfortably warm, it is a sign that parks and beaches will be crowded.

As will be perceived from the examples above, sign relationship does not preclude the possibility that a causal relationship is also present. The important distinction is that in sign relationship, the presence, or the assumed presence, of the causal relationship is not vital. We may not know why a car with

Claim
Jimmy probably has the measles.

Datum
Jimmy has a rash all over
his body.

Warrant
A rash all over the body
is a symptom of measles.

FIGURE 6.6   Argument Using Sign Relationship.

its hood raised is parked along a freeway, but we all recognize this as a sign that there is something wrong with the car. We may conclude that we should stop and offer assistance. Later we may find that the car had an overheated radiator, had run out of gas, had a broken fan belt, or had any of a number of other problems. There was a cause of the car trouble, but the specific cause was not directly related to our decision to stop and help the stranded driver.

Sign relationship may best be understood in terms of correlation. Two things may be correlated but not causally related. An enterprising statistician once discovered that the consumption of ice cream in New York City was highly correlated with the death rate in a certain province of India. To assert a causal relationship between these two phenomena would, of course, have been absurd. But if the observed correlation was found to persist over an extended period of time, it would be possible to predict one phenomenon from available figures on the other.

Of course, most argument by sign is not based on such "way-out" relationships as that between ice cream consumption in New York and death rates in India. This example is used here merely to indicate that causation is not a necessary condition of argument by sign. In most cases, argument by sign is a shortcut to reaching a claim when the possible causation is not fully understood, or when an explanation of the causal relationship would be excessively time-consuming. A doctor, for example, may observe a symptom and immediately conclude that the patient has a particular disease. The patient need not be given a complete explanation of the causal relationship between the symptom and the disease. The information that the symptom is a sign of a certain ailment is usually sufficient to convince the patient that he or she indeed has the disease cited by the doctor.

Whenever the assumption of sign relationship is being used as a warrant, the datum for the argument is the observed phenomenon. The claim is that the phenomenon that usually accompanies the observed phenomenon is, was, or will be present also. Sign relationships are useful primarily for the establishment of designative claims—for determining "Is it so?"

The source will do well to approach the use of sign warrants with caution. While it is inevitable that one will find many good arguments with sign warrants, it is also inevitable that many will be fallacious. Most of our superstitions are based on sign warrants. Many of us view walking under a ladder or being confronted by a black cat as a sign of bad luck. These superstitions are based on much the same kind of thought process as that underlying a doctor's decision to administer a given treatment to a patient. The point is that sign relationship is a rather tenuous thought pattern. Some members of an audience, therefore, may balk at accepting claims based upon such assumed relationships. Careful analysis of the audience should precede a decision to base an important argument on a sign warrant.

3. Literal analogy and figurative analogy. Literal analogy and figurative analogy are best understood if examined together. They have one main thing in common: They seek acceptance of conclusions based on comparison. Whenever we think analogically, we reason that if two or more things are alike in one or more respects, they probably are alike in still other respects. In arguments employing analogical relationships in the warrant, the data consist of observed characteristics of one phenomenon, the warrant assumes that this phenomenon and other phenomenon are alike in one or more crucial respects, and the claim asserts that the second phenomenon also has the characteristics attributed to the phenomenon in the data. Figures 6.7 and 6.8 provide examples of the two types of analogies.

The main distinction between the two types of analogy is that, in the literal analogy, the things being compared are essentially similar in their basic nature, whereas in the figurative analogy, the things being compared are essentially dissimilar. If we are comparing two state governments, two baseball teams, two tables, or two sections of the same college course, we are comparing things that are essentially similar. In this we are making use of literal analogy. If we compare driving on a highway to foreign policy (that road will take us nowhere), preventive war to sewing (a stitch in time saves nine), the administration of a government to the operation of a ship (the president is the captain of our ship), or the choice of whom to vote for in an election to riding a horse across a stream (don't change horses in midstream), we are comparing things that are essentially dissimilar. In this we are making use of figurative analogy.

Writers of textbooks frequently deplore the use of the figurative analogy because of the obviously tenuous relationship between the two things being compared. Based on the logical inadequacy of such argument, the criticism is well founded. The logical adequacy of an argument, however, is usually irrelevant to persuasive impact on an audience. For the rhetorical

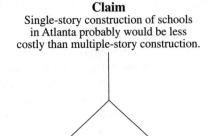

Claim
Single-story construction of schools
in Atlanta probably would be less
costly than multiple-story construction.

Datum
Single-story construction of schools
has been found, in Birmingham, to be
less costly than multiple-story
construction.

Warrant
Atlanta and Birmingham are
essentially similar in all
important respects relevant
to construction.

FIGURE 6.7   Argument Using Analogical Relationship: Literal Analogy.

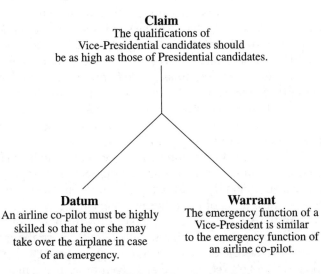

Claim
The qualifications of
Vice-Presidential candidates should
be as high as those of Presidential candidates.

Datum
An airline co-pilot must be highly
skilled so that he or she may
take over the airplane in case
of an emergency.

Warrant
The emergency function of a
Vice-President is similar
to the emergency function of
an airline co-pilot.

FIGURE 6.8   Argument Using Analogical Relationship: Figurative Analogy.

context, therefore, such criticism is misguided. The figurative analogy is a powerful persuasive instrument, and the source should not hesitate to make extensive use of it.

On the other hand, the literal analogy is accorded high status by many writers because the things being compared are essentially similar in nature.

Hence, greater logical validity is present in such an argument. Unfortunately, this does not guarantee either accuracy or acceptance of claims based on the literal analogy warrant. Since World War II, a standard literal analogy has been invoked against foreign governments with whom our government has found itself in disagreement. Comparison is made between the policies of Hitler's Germany and presently distrusted foreign governments. We are asked as members of the audience to accept all sorts of claims based on such a comparison—all the way from preventive war to deliberate appeasement.

What is the point of the preceding discussion? Is it to suggest that figurative analogies are to be preferred to literal analogies? No. Our point is that both types of analogies are valuable means of gaining acceptance of claims, and that neither is a guaranteed path to "logical" truth. We stress once more the difference between logical thought and rhetorical thought. In persuasion, both types of analogies are powerful instruments.[8] Of the six kinds of substantive warrant, only analogies are useful for all types of claims. The crucial concern of the source in determining whether to employ either type of analogy should be whether or not the given warrant is likely to be sufficient to obtain receiver acceptance of the claim.

4. Generalization and classification. Since these two relationships are almost the exact reverse of each other, we shall consider them together. Figures 6.9 and 6.10 provide examples of them. Generalization assumes that what is true of a sample from a class is also true of other members of that class. This is frequently referred to as the *inductive* thought pattern. Classification assumes that what is true of a class is also true of individual members of that class. This thought pattern is frequently referred to as *deduction*. Both generalization and classification are useful primarily for gaining acceptance of designative and evaluative claims.

Generalization is one of the most common warrants employed by sources. It is characterized by the presence of a limited number of examples (data), the usually implied assumption that these examples are typical of a class (warrant), and a claim that most or all of the other members of the class have the same characteristics as those in the examples do. Probably the best known "generalizers" are the political pollsters. With a sample of one or two thousand people in a given state or across the entire country, the pollster predicts how over sixty million people would be likely to vote at a given time. The remarkable accuracy of these predictions testifies to the acceptability of the assumption in the warrant that the observed examples are typical of the population as a whole.

Unfortunately, most people do not have at their disposal the resources of the political pollsters. We cannot present a thousand examples to an audience. Certainly, most of our assumptions as to how typical our limited number of examples may be are much less subject to verification. Our problem is to satisfy our receiver that our examples are reasonably typical. The generalization based on one example or the "way-out" example is less likely

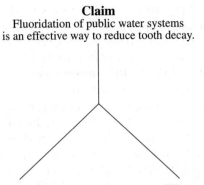

Claim
Fluoridation of public water systems
is an effective way to reduce tooth decay.

Datum
Fluoridation of public water
systems in Springfield, Bay
City, and Lincoln resulted
in decreased tooth decay in
those cities.

Warrant
Springfield, Bay City, and
Lincoln are representative
American cities.

FIGURE 6.9   Argument Using Inductive Relationship: Generalization.

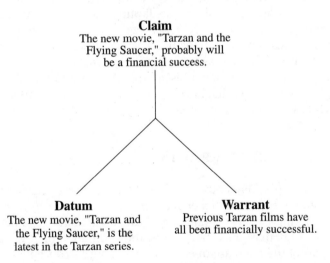

Claim
The new movie, "Tarzan and the
Flying Saucer," probably will
be a financial success.

Datum
The new movie, "Tarzan and
the Flying Saucer," is the
latest in the Tarzan series.

Warrant
Previous Tarzan films have
all been financially successful.

FIGURE 6.10   Argument Using Deductive Relationship: Classification.

to be accepted because the assumption that it is typical is open to question by a receiver with even minimal critical capacity.

Arguments based on the assumption of *classification* involve quite a different problem. The classic example of classification is: Socrates is a man (datum); all men are mortal (warrant); therefore, Socrates is mortal (claim).

It is unfortunate that in rhetorical communication we seldom have "allness" warrants at our disposal. There is usually an exception to the rule in the class to which we wish to refer. Thus, we make more use of the word "most" than of "all." We may argue that because Brown is a Republican and most Republicans support civil rights, Brown is probably a civil rights supporter.

Arguments based on classification include, as data, observations concerning a phenomenon's membership in a class. The warrant assumes a certain characteristic to be typical of the class. The claim then asserts that the member of the class identified in the data probably has the characteristic typical of the class. The primary concern of arguments based on classification is that the receiver believe that the group or class in question is relatively homogeneous and in possession of the given characteristics. Such a belief is usually the product of prior generalization. If we observe all of our teachers through twelve years of schooling, we may classify teachers as a group and perceive that they have certain characteristics in common. Thus, when we meet a new teacher, we assume that he or she will have the characteristics of our classification of teachers. The problem with classification, which may be apparent from our teacher example, is that it makes little allowance for individual differences within a class. Fortunately for persuaders, a flaw in the thought process of most people makes argument based on classification more useful than it probably deserves to be. People tend to overgeneralize, establishing classes where none really exist, or incorrectly assuming that characteristics of a minority of a class are characteristics of the class as a whole. This is sometimes referred to as *stereotyping*. The persuader has at her or his disposal these psychologically based classifications, as well as those that have a more substantive foundation. Of course, use of such false classifications raises a rather large ethical concern.

VERIFICATION OF WARRANTS

Warrants of all types frequently require verifying before a receiver will accept them. In Toulmin's original model of argument, provision was made for what he called "backing," which Ehninger and Brockriede have renamed "support for warrant." In both of these treatments, the verification of a warrant is conceived as part of the main argument. I believe that this conception is misleading. When a warrant is verified for a receiver, the warrant is treated as a claim, and a separate argument is developed to gain acceptance of that claim. The nature of the argument used to establish a warrant varies according to the type of warrant being established. Substantive warrants are usually established by resorting to further substantive warrants in the supporting argument. Authoritative warrants are usually established by sign relationship. Certain characteristics are assumed to be signs of credibility (warrant), and the data consist of characteristics of the source that conform to assumed characteristics of credibility. Motivational warrants are frequently established by analogy with other motivational warrants. Motivational warrants may also be established by generalization or by classification. Occasionally a motivational warrant may be established by an authoritative warrant, but this occurs infrequently.

These suggested methods of establishing warrants should be considered merely as general guidelines. If the source treats as a claim every warrant that needs verification for the given receiver, he or she will have little difficulty in finding methods appropriate for its support. The person needs merely to develop an argument to establish it, just as he or she does to establish any other claim.

THE TYPES OF DATA

There are three distinct types of data: first order, or receiver belief; second order, or source assertion; and third order, or evidence.[9]

1. First-order data: receiver belief. Receiver belief is designated as of the highest order because ultimately it is the only type on the basis of which a meaningful argument may be developed. One example of this type of data is receiver opinion. If the receiver believes that blue-eyed people are inferior to brown-eyed people, this opinion may be used by the source as a datum for an argument. One may not, in this case, use a contrary opinion (that brown-eyed people are inferior or that there is no difference related to eye color) as a datum unless one first instills that opinion into the receiver's mind. Thus, in any given instance of persuasion, the data restrict a source in the choice of arguments that can be found or implanted among the beliefs of the receiver.

A second example of first-order data is receiver knowledge. *Anything that the receiver knows can serve as data for an argument.* If the receiver is aware of wage increases for fruit pickers, this knowledge may be used by the source to obtain acceptance of the claim that increases in fruit prices are likely in the near future. If the receiver is unaware, however, of such wage increases, the source is precluded from using this as a datum until he or she has informed the receiver of the wage increases and has secured in the receiver the belief that such increases have occurred.

There is a narrow line between knowledge data and opinion data. What is knowledge to one person may be opinion to another. This need not concern us, however, because knowledge and opinion operate in almost exactly the same manner. If the receiver believes or knows a given item, it may be used as a datum. If the receiver does not believe or know a given item, it may not be used as a datum.

2. Second-order data: source assertion. Source assertion is of a lower order than receiver belief, although it is essential to a source in nearly every circumstance. This type of data includes asserted opinion and asserted information and depends in every case upon a secondary, usually implied, argument. This secondary argument has as its datum the asserted opinion or information. The warrant is based on the credibility of the source. An example of this would run as follows: I say X's are usually Y (datum); I am a credible source (warrant); therefore X's are usually Y (claim). The datum in this example meets the test of first-order data, for if the receiver hears me say it, the receiver's opinion that I said it is immediately assured.[10] The crucial determinant of whether or not the claim is accepted has to do with whether the source's ethos is high enough for the warrant to be acceptable to the receiver. This is the case whenever a source makes an assertion. As long as source credibility is high enough, there is a warrant that will permit the assertion to become receiver opinion or receiver knowledge. Thus, *assertions by highly credible sources can establish first-order data for further arguments, whereas assertions by sources with lower credibility serve no persuasive purpose.* When a source makes an assertion, the receiver immediately (though usually not consciously) completes the secondary argument. If the source's ethos is high enough, the assertion is accepted by the receiver and becomes either receiver knowledge or receiver opinion. At this point, a first-order datum is present, and the source may continue to develop further argument. (Figure 6.11 illustrates the use of second-order data.)

When appropriate receiver opinion or knowledge is not available and the source's ethos is not sufficient to establish assertions as audience opinion or knowledge, the source must resort to third-order data.

3. Third-order data: evidence. Third-order data consist of opinions of others and facts attested to by others. This type of data will be recognized as what traditionally has been called "evidence." As in the case of the second-order data discussed previously, the introduction of opinions of others, or of facts attested to by others, immediately causes the receiver to complete a secondary argument. This argument has as datum the belief that the outside source made the statement attributed to it, and the warrant is based on the ethos of the outside source.

Actually, a third-order argument is also produced. It goes something like this: The source says that so-and-so said X (datum); the source is credible (warrant); therefore, so-and-so probably did say X (claim). Obviously, the source must have a certain minimal amount of credibility in order for this argument to be accepted. But if it is accepted, the datum for the secondary argument is established. Then the credibility of the outside source (warrant) becomes crucial. If the outside source is credible enough, the secondary argument will be established and new receiver opinion or receiver knowledge will be created. The source may then use this new belief as a first-order datum to develop further argument.

The establishment of first-order data by means of evidence (third-order data), then, depends upon the credibility of the source. Is the source

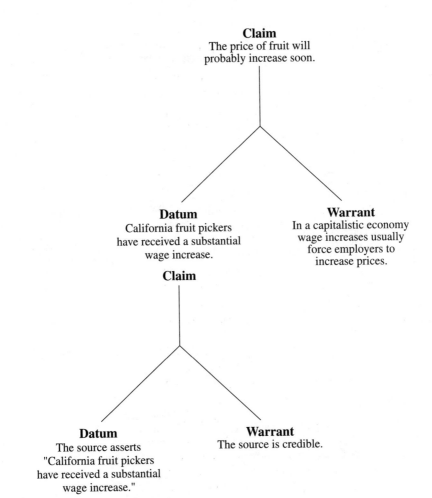

Claim
The price of fruit will
probably increase soon.

Datum
California fruit pickers
have received a substantial
wage increase.

Warrant
In a capitalistic economy
wage increases usually
force employers to
increase prices.

Claim

Datum
The source asserts
"California fruit pickers
have received a substantial
wage increase."

Warrant
The source is credible.

FIGURE 6.11 Argument with Second-Order Data.

at least honest enough to tell the truth about what others say? For the source with very low ethos, evidence would serve no persuasive purpose, since the receiver would reject the evidence because of the person presenting it. But if the source has the minimal ethos necessary to overcome this obstacle, the credibility of the outside source can become crucial. If the receiver is unfamiliar with the outside source, he or she is unlikely to accept the authoritative warrant. Citing and qualifying sources establishes the credibility of the source's third-order data. (Figure 6.12 illustrates the use of third-order data.)

It is important to note here that either second- or third-order data may be rejected by a receiver if the acceptance of them would force acceptance

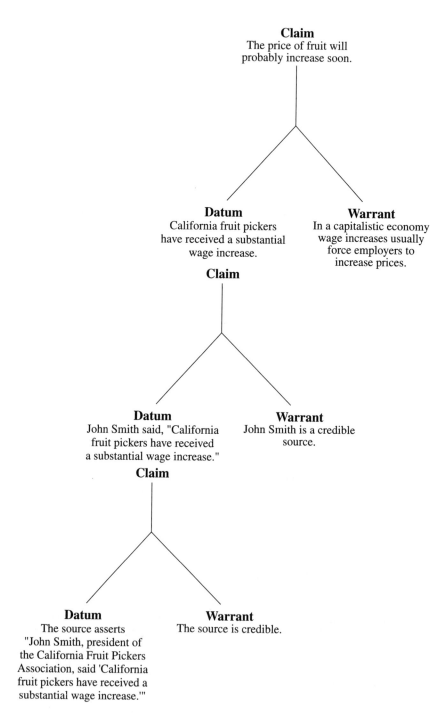

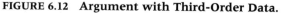

FIGURE 6.12 Argument with Third-Order Data.

of an unacceptable claim. Some of us would refuse, for example, to accept the claim that a dictatorship is a better form of government than democracy, no matter who asserted it and no matter what evidence was brought forth to support the assertion. We find this an unacceptable claim. No first-order data are available that can persuade us of this claim, and no source could establish any such claim by means of second- or third-order data. Some people simply cannot be persuaded to accept some claims.

In summary, there are three orders of data available to a source when persuasion is possible. First-order data include existing receiver opinion and receiver knowledge. If this type of data is available, it is to be preferred on rhetorical grounds to data of a lower order. It is the data most likely to enable the source to achieve the intended goal in persuasion. Second-order data include asserted opinions and information. This type of data is dependent on the credibility of the source. If the source is highly credible, this type of data is rhetorically preferable to data of a lower order. Second-order data are available, however, only to a source with ethos ranging from moderately high to high. Third-order data include opinions of others and facts attested to by others. This type of data is what has traditionally been called "evidence." Its persuasiveness depends on both the credibility of the source and the credibility of the outside informant. Because there are two supplementary arguments introduced each time this type of data is used, there are more chances for this type to be rejected by the receiver than when first- or second-order data are used. Thus, on rhetorical grounds we should consider opinions and facts attested to by others as the least potent of the data options open to the source.

This is not to suggest that third-order data (evidence) should not be used. As we have indicated previously, on some topics the receiver may not have any knowledge or opinion that the source can use as data, and the source's ethos may be too weak to establish assertions as receiver knowledge or receiver opinion. Whenever this is the case, third-order data should be useful, unless the ethos of the source is so low that the receiver will not accept even the evidence presented. Sources with very low ethos may not have any promising options as to data available to them. Therefore, they probably will be unsuccessful as rhetorical communicators, whether they include evidence in their messages or not.

OPTIONS REGARDING RESERVATIONS

It should be apparent from the foregoing discussion of claims, warrants, and data that few claims are developed in rhetorical communication that are completely above reproach. Ordinarily, persuasive argument deals with probability rather than certainty. Whenever our claim is a statement of probability (and it almost always is), there are appropriate reservations. In some cases we shall want, or need, to present these reservations to the receiver; in other cases the reservations may be ignored. A source's handling of reservations is, in large measure, an indicator of probable success. Let us consider several guidelines the source should follow when faced with the question of how to handle reservations.

The first question that comes to mind is whether a particular reservation should be referred to in the message to be presented to the receiver. Whether it should be included or not depends upon three considerations: Is the receiver likely to think of the reservation if it is not included? May the reservation be conceded without losing the receiver's acceptance of the claim? Can the reservation be refuted?

If a reservation is likely to be thought of by the receiver even if it is not referred to in the message, it is usually wise to include it in the message. To avoid reference to the reservation may lead the receiver to think that the source is either ignorant of the limitation of the claim or trying to deceive the receiver. Either interpretation will seriously damage the perceived ethos of the source and reduce her or his potential persuasiveness. This possibility may be avoided by referring to the reservation in the message. On the other hand, if the receiver is unlikely to think of the reservation, the source may choose to omit from the message any reference to it.

The second question is whether the reservation can be conceded without losing the receiver's acceptance of the claim. If a reservation severely limits the source's claim, he or she would be on very dangerous ground to merely mention the reservation and go on to another point. On the other hand, if the reservation would not be likely to cause rejection of the claim, the source might make passing reference to the reservation without losing persuasive impact.

The third question, closely related to the second, is: Can the reservation be refuted? Or, can the receiver discount the reservation and go on to firmly accept the claim? A reservation that can be refuted may provide the source with an advantage in persuasion. A considerable body of research points to the fact that a source may immunize the audience against counterpersuasion by including arguments against the claims (reservations) and then refuting those arguments.[11] This technique makes the receiver aware of, and suspicious of, arguments counter to those presented by the source. Thus, when the receiver is confronted by another source asserting claims that conflict with those originally accepted, the receiver is much less persuasible. Receivers so immunized tend to suspect the motive and the credibility of the new source and to discredit her or his claims. Thus, the source who introduces reservations and then refutes them stands to gain persuasive impact in terms of long-term retention of persuasion.

The question of whether a source should or should not include reservations is related to the purpose of the communication. Research indicates that if the source seeks sustained change of attitude, he or she should include and refute reservations so as to inoculate the receiver against counterpersuasion. If, however, the source is concerned only about the short-range effects of the communication, he or she might be more successful omitting reference to reservations. *Research also indicates that if the receiver is well educated or initially hostile to the source's argument, a message including and refuting reservations is more effective. For receivers who are not well informed or who are initially favorable to the source's argument, a message with no reference to reservations is more effective.* The reason for this seems to be that the well-informed or hostile member of an audience is likely to think of reservations whether the source mentions them or not, but the uninformed or favorable member is unlikely to think of reservations. Support for this explanation is provided by a study conducted by Thistlethwaite and Kamenetsky.[12] They found that including previously known facts in opposition to a source's argument increased effectiveness but that including previously unknown facts in opposition to an argument decreased effectiveness.

Thus, the source has three options in regard to reservations: They may be ignored, conceded, or refuted. The following guidelines are suggested for the source to follow when deciding which option to exercise.

1. If the receiver is likely to perceive the reservation and the reservation cannot be conceded but may be refuted, introduce the reservation and refute it.

2. If the receiver is likely to perceive the reservation and the reservation may be either conceded or refuted, introduce the reservation and refute it if time permits. Otherwise, introduce the reservation and concede it.

3. If the receiver is not likely to perceive the reservation and the reservation may be either conceded or refuted, introduce the reservation and refute it if time permits. Otherwise, ignore the reservation.

4. If the receiver is not likely to perceive the reservation and it can be neither conceded or refuted, avoid any mention of the reservation.

5. If the receiver is likely to perceive the reservation and it can be neither conceded nor refuted, avoid any mention of the reservation.

Whenever one finds guideline 4 or 5 appropriate to the problem, one should proceed very cautiously. *When a reservation may neither be conceded nor refuted, there usually is something seriously wrong with the argument.* The source should question whether he or she is certain of the accuracy of the claim. If so, the source should attempt to develop a different argument that will not present the same kind of problem about the reservation. If no substitute argument is available, the source should reevaluate the entire effort at persuasion. Guidelines 4 and 5 should be recognized as signs of danger. In addition to the obvious ethical consideration, the use of guideline 5 in particular exposes the source to the probability of loss in credibility, possibly so great a loss that the entire effort to persuade will be unsuccessful. In short, guidelines 1, 2, and 3 may be utilized at will, but before employing guideline 4 or 5, one should subject the argument to careful reexamination or seek a substitute for the argument in question.

Finally, research has indicated that the strength of inoculation effects is related not only to whether reservations are refuted but also to the strength of the refutation employed. Messages including strong evidence have been found to increase inoculation significantly in comparison with identical messages without the evidence.[13] Therefore, one should attempt to provide strong evidence against reservations if such evidence is available.

DISCUSSION QUESTIONS

1. What is an argument?

2. Compare Aristotle's enthymeme with Toulmin's model of argument. How are they similar? How do they differ?

3. Select several newspaper, magazine, or television advertisements and diagram the arguments included according to our modified Toulmin model. What consistent pattern or patterns do you observe? Why?

4. Assume that you have six arguments you could include in your message. Each argument has a different type of substantive warrant. Other things being equal, which argument would you choose to include? Why? If you could include five arguments, which one would you omit? Why?

NOTES

1. R. T. Oliver, "Speech as an Academic Discipline," address delivered at the New York State Speech Association Convention, Utica, New York, March 12, 1965.

2. See, for example, D. Thistlethwaite, "Attitude and Structure as Factors in the Distortion of Reasoning," *Journal of Abnormal and Social Psychology* 45 (1950): 442–58.

3. For a summary of research supporting this conclusion, see G. R. Miller, "Some Factors Influencing Judgments of the Logical Validity of Arguments: A Research Review," *Quarterly Journal of Speech* 55 (1969): 276–86.

4. G. L. Cronkhite, "The Enthymeme as Deductive Rhetorical Argument," *Western Speech* 30 (1966): 129–34.

5. S. Toulmin, *The Uses of Argument* (New York: Cambridge University Press, 1958). See also W. Brockriede and D. Ehninger, "Toulmin on Argument: An Interpretation and Application," *Quarterly Journal of Speech* 46 (1960): 44–53.

6. Brockriede and Ehninger, "Toulmin on Argument."

7. Ibid., pp. 125ff.

8. A study that compared the effects of three messages on attitude change found that messages that included either a literal or a figurative analogy produced more attitude change than a message including no analogy, but that the two analogy messages did not differ from

each other in effect. See J. C. McCroskey and W. H. Combs, "The Effects of the Use of Analogy on Attitude Change and Source Credibility," *Journal of Communication* 19 (1969): 333–39.

9. This conception of data was generated as a result of the author's research on the effects of evidence in persuasive communication. See J. C. McCroskey, "A Summary of Experimental Research on the Effects of Evidence in Persuasive Communication," *Quarterly Journal of Speech* 55 (1969): 169–76.

10. This assumes, of course, that perception distortion does not occur. The selective perception phenomenon is discussed in Chapter 3.

11. W. J. McGuire, "The Effectiveness of Supportive and Refutational Defenses in Immunizing and Restoring Beliefs against Persuasion," *Sociometry* 24 (1961): 184–89; D. Papageorgis and W. J. McGuire, "The Generality of Immunity to Persuasion Produced by Pre-exposure to Weakened Counter-Arguments," *Journal of Abnormal and Social Psychology* 62 (1961): 475–81; M. Manis and J. B. Blake, "Interpretation of Persuasive Messages as a Function of Prior Immunization," *Journal of Abnormal and Social Psychology* 46 (1963): 225–30; and E. Crane, "Immunization: With and without the Use of Counter-Arguments," *Journalism Quarterly* 39 (1962): 445–50.

12. D. L. Thistlethwaite and J. Kamenetsky, "Attitude Change through Refutation and Elaboration of Audience Counter-Arguments," *Journal of Abnormal and Social Psychology* 51 (1955): 3–12.

13. J. C. McCroskey, "The Effects of Evidence as an Inhibitor of Counter-Persuasion," *Speech Monographs* 37 (1970): 188–94; J. C. McCroskey, T. J. Young, and M. D. Scott, "The Effects of Message Sidedness and Evidence on Inoculation Against Counter-persuasion in Small Group Communication," *Speech Monographs* 39 (1972): 205–12.

■ ■ ■ ■ ■

CHAPTER 7

NONVERBAL COMMUNICATION

Several years ago, a popular American politician took a trip to Latin America. Upon his arrival at the airport, he emerged from the airplane, stood at the top of the loading ramp, and waved to the people awaiting his arrival. Someone shouted out, asking him how his trip had been. He responded by flashing the common "OK" gesture. Shortly thereafter he left the airport and engaged in a brief visit with a local political leader. Following that visit, he went to the major university in the area and delivered an address on behalf on the American people. During his talk, he emphasized that the United States was most interested in helping this neighboring country through economic aid that would help develop the economy and relieve the difficult economic surroundings of the poor. His speech, in fact his entire visit, was a disaster.

Why? Everything this gentleman did verbally was quite acceptable. But nearly everything he did nonverbally was wrong. To begin with, a photographer took a picture of our visitor just as he flashed the "OK" sign to the person who asked how his trip had gone. That picture appeared on the front page of the local newspaper. You may wonder, What is so bad about that? The gesture that we use in the United States to signal "OK" is a most obscene gesture in this particular Latin American country.

After this faltering start, our representative went to the university to give his speech, apparently unaware of the fact that this university had recently been a scene of violent protest against that government's policies. His choice of that place to speak was interpreted by the government as showing sympathy for the rioting students, but was perceived by the students as an invasion of their territory by a friend of the government. Further, while our representative was presenting an excellent speech in English concerning our interest in helping the poor people of that country, the speech was being translated for the audience by an interpreter in full military uniform. The interpreter was a clear symbol of the military dictatorship that was in control of the country at that time.

It is certainly not surprising that the intended good will visit of our representative had a contrary effect. This is an excellent example of what can happen when people are unaware of, or unconcerned with, their nonverbal behavior.

In other cases, people can be overly concerned with their nonverbal behavior. In 1968 the majority of the American people were very concerned with getting peace talks started in Paris to seek a solution to the Vietnam War, but it seemed that it would take forever before the talks could begin. The problem centered around the seating of the various delegations for the peace conference, and the shape of the table. The United States and South Vietnam each wanted two sides at the table; North Vietnam and the Viet Cong each wanted four sides. Four sides would put the Viet Cong on an equal status with the other three parties in the talks, something that the North Vietnamese and Viet Cong insisted on, but that the United States and the South Vietnamese were unwilling to accept. After eight months and thousands of deaths and injuries on both sides, a compromise was reached whereby the North Vietnamese and the Viet Cong could interpret the table settled upon as four-sided, while the United States and South Vietnam could interpret it as two-sided. Almost anyone not directly involved in those negotiations would agree that the behavior of these parties was absurd. Nevertheless, this extreme sensitivity to the nonverbal communication of the shape of the table resulted in months of delay and thousands of deaths. The importance of nonverbal communication in this setting could hardly be overestimated.

THE IMPORTANCE OF NONVERBAL MESSAGES

Nonverbal messages in communication are always important. Sometimes, as in the two preceding examples, they dominate everything else. In normal human communication, Mehrabian estimates that 55 percent of the social meaning stimulated in the communication process is a direct result of facial and physical nonverbal messages. Further, he estimates that 38 percent of the meaning is stimulated by vocal cues—not the words said, but the way in which they are said.[1] The remaining 7 percent of the meaning is stimulated by the verbal messages. Others have suggested different percentage breakdowns (Birdwhistell, for example, estimates that 65 percent of social meaning is stimulated by the facial and physical nonverbal messages[2]), but most observers agree that nonverbal messages normally account for much more of the meaning stimulated in receivers than do verbal messages under normal circumstances. Clearly there are times when most of the meaning is stimulated by verbal messages, and other times when most is stimulated by nonverbal messages.

This is particularly important when we realize that it is impossible for nonverbal messages to be excluded by either a source or a receiver. Such

messages are omnipresent. They are obviously present whenever two people are in direct proximity with each other during communication. Some nonverbal messages are removed (facial expressions, gestures) in telephone conversations, but the vocal nonverbal messages (tone, pitch, loudness, and so on) still remain. Similarly, the written media eliminate a large number of nonverbal messages, but even then some nonverbal messages remain, such as the type of paper employed, the time chosen to communicate, and the length of the verbal message.

The importance of nonverbal messages is reinforced by the tendency of receivers to place primary emphasis on the nonverbal. *When the nonverbal message and the verbal message conflict, the receiver tends to believe the nonverbal message on the presumption that the nonverbal message is harder to falsify.* Most people can become fairly facile verbal liars, but very few become excellent nonverbal liars. The real skill of the professional actor or actress is in the ability to connect appropriate nonverbal messages with the verbal messages that the playwright has provided. When we describe someone as a "poor actor," we are really saying that the nonverbal messages do not coincide with the verbal messages. Few people are ever aware of all the nonverbal messages they are presenting in a given communication transaction. Even fewer are able to control those messages in order to enhance desired effects in receivers. In order to better understand the range of nonverbal messages available in communication and to attain some measure of control over them, let us consider the major categories of nonverbal messages available.

PROXEMICS

Proxemics refers to the way space is used in communication. Research has indicated that different types of communication transactions require different use of space by the participants.[3] For example, in the North American culture, if individuals are in intimate conversation, they tend to stand between six and eighteen inches apart. In a normal conversation between friends, the interpersonal distance is normally between three feet and four feet six inches. For conversations of a strictly business nature, such as those between employer and employee or between student and teacher, the distance is between five and seven feet. When formal speeches are presented, there is normally at least fifteen feet between the speaker and the nearest audience member.

It must be stressed that these distances are estimates for the general North American culture. The distances for interpersonal communication vary substantially from one culture to another. For example, Greeks and citizens of several Latin American countries try to establish a much closer proximity than North Americans when engaged in a normal, friendly conversation. This difference between North Americans and Latin Americans can produce some very strained exchanges when the two are trying to converse with one another. The North Americans will have a natural tendency to step away from the Latin American, while the Latin American will step closer. Each is striving to establish what he or she considers to be the correct interpersonal distance, but the perception of the other individual in the transaction may be quite different. The North American is likely to perceive the Latin American as pushy and aggressive, while the Latin American is likely to perceive the North American as distant, aloof, and unfriendly. The relationship between the North American and the Latin American is almost the opposite of that between the North American and the person from Somalia. Somalis consider the appropriate distance for friendly interpersonal transactions to be about five to six feet. Hence, the North American appears to be the pushy, aggressive individual, and the Somali the distant, aloof, and unfriendly one.

When people are seated, space again has a major impact on interpersonal communication. For example, when seated at a rectangular table, people tend to talk primarily to the person directly across the table or the person diagonally across the corner of the table. The person an individual is least likely to speak to is the one seated next to her or him.[4] Whoever happens to sit down at the head of the table will almost always be perceived as the leader of the discussion. Much of this changes, however, when people are seated in a living room, in a situation such as a party. The tendency here is for people seated next to one another to engage in conversation. Depending on the individual circumstances, not only does space itself communicate a message, but it also determines whether people will communicate with one another.

People tend to be very space-conscious in their everyday lives, although they are usually unaware of their concern. Each individual tends to carve out an area in whatever circumstances he or she happens to be. For example, in a classroom, it normally takes only one or two class periods for each student to select a specific seat and to consider it her or his own. If someone else comes in and takes that seat, it makes the first person quite uncomfortable and is usually likely to stimulate hostile reactions toward the interloper. Similarly, in their homes, people have certain spaces that are considered theirs. Not only do individuals have their own rooms, but in the larger environment of the household, they are quite likely to have their own chairs. In the family or living room in most homes, the husband and wife have their own chairs. When guests arrive, they may be offered either "her" or "his" chair, but if they actually sit in the offered chairs, the ensuing conversation is likely to be quite strained.

The place selected for communication also communicates something. For example, if an instructor wishes to talk with a student about an academic matter, he or she might ask the student to meet privately in an office. The classroom is somewhat closer to neutral territory and, if the student is asked to remain after class, is not very threatening. But the teacher's office is clearly the teacher's space, and to ask the student to come there clearly indicates that the instructor is going to be the dominant member of the conversation. This is quite likely to increase the student's anxiety about the communication transaction.

CHRONEMICS

Chronemics refers to the use of time in communication. An individual's use of time communicates much about him or her to other people. When talking to another member of their culture, Americans tend to leave very little time between statements. A pause by one of the participants in the conversation generally indicates that it is the other person's turn to speak. In some other cultures, the length of pauses between contributions by the various participants is very much longer. Americans feel strained and uncomfortable if the pause between one person's statement and the next person's statement is more than a few seconds long, and that communication pattern in other cultures will cause the American to interject himself or herself into the conversation more often and more quickly than is customary in the other culture. Consequently, the American is very likely to be perceived as overbearing.

In addition to this direct effect of time on communication, time affects nonverbal communication in many other ways. For example, being kept waiting communicates a message. Americans are not conditioned to accept waiting very gracefully. If kept waiting for more than five minutes, they tend to become uneasy and to perceive the person who is making them wait as unconcerned with their well-being or disdainful of them. Other cultures do not conform to the time habits of Americans. For example, our five-minute waiting period is roughly equivalent to a forty-five minute waiting period in some parts of Latin America. An American kept waiting forty-five minutes is very likely to become incensed, but the intention of the Latin American who would keep someone waiting forty-five minutes would be not unlike that of the American executive who keeps someone waiting for five minutes.

Arrival time for meetings also varies sharply. The variability here is not only that between cultures but that within a given culture, depending on the purpose and place of the gathering. In most parts of the United States, if an individual is invited to a party, he or she is expected to arrive between ten and forty minutes after the appointed hour. But when invited for dinner, one is expected to arrive approximately on time or up to fifteen minutes late. However, for a business appointment, a person is expected to be on time or not more than five minutes late. Of course, not everyone in the United States follows the same time pattern. An example of a substantial deviation is the Mormon time pattern in Utah. Mormons believe rigidly in being on time. Consequently, Mormons tend to arrive either on time or early. Being late is definitely considered an offense. On the other hand, some segments of American society consider being on time an undesirable social attribute. To be on time is to be graciously late.

Although various segments of American society utilize time somewhat differently, they all have a pattern that is understood by most members of the given segment. To violate the time pattern of that segment tends to cause a person to be perceived unfavorably. Some other cultures have no sense of time as the American knows it. Americans can systematically categorize time periods from seconds through weeks, months, and years, but in some Middle Eastern societies, time beyond one week in the future does not exist. That is, the time period a week from now and the one a hundred years from now are perceived in much the same way. Although it is not at all uncommon in the United States to plan a meeting for a month in the future, to do so in some Middle Eastern societies would be perceived as exceedingly strange behavior.

Time serves as a nonverbal communication message in yet another way—the hours in which individuals choose to communicate. A phone call received sometime after midnight will almost always cause immediate concern. This time for calling is reserved by most people for emergencies and for reporting deaths or accidents. Similarly, business calls are normally made between nine and five during the week. A business call received on Sunday is perceived as strange. The time chosen in which to communicate may have a major impact on the effect of the communication. For example, if a person is invited at four in the afternoon to a party to be held that evening, he or she may refuse despite interest in attending. The person has not been given enough "lead time" according to our cultural norms. To accept at that late time would suggest that one is not very popular.

Most individuals begin learning about the importance of choosing appropriate times for conversation as children. Children learn not to ask their father for something when he first wakes up in the morning. They also learn not to ask for extra money for the movie just after they have been punished for misbehavior. Even though people do begin learning about timing for communication at an early age, many occasionally violate the timing expectations of others and, as a result, are less effective in their communication attempts than they could otherwise be.

OCULESICS

Oculesics refers to the use of eye contact in communication. Direct eye contact with another individual normally communicates interest and attention. The absence of direct eye contact, inversely, communicates lack of interest and lack of attention. Most people learn to utilize the nonverbal message of eye contact better than any other nonverbal message. But most of this learning and its use is subconscious. Completely consistent, direct eye contact makes most people uncomfortable, so they unconsciously break contact from time to time when talking with another person. But because individuals are taught from childhood to distrust people who refuse to look them in the eye, they try as much as possible to look at the other person during interpersonal communication.

Eye contact is often used to control a communication transaction. When an individual does not wish to be interrupted while talking, he or she often glances away from the person to whom he or she is speaking and continues talking. The individual will look back at the other person as he or she finishes the current thought, and this communicates to the other person that it is now his or her turn to speak. A pause in a conversation accompanied by direct eye contact almost demands that the other person speak.

Courtship behavior of Americans depends quite heavily on eye contact in the early stages. In particular, the male will tend to establish what is sometimes referred to as the "courtship stare" with the female. This overlong, direct eye contact communicates strong interest on the part of the male. It says to the female, "I am interested in you; are you interested in me?" If the female turns away, the answer is no. If she smiles or in some other way indicates approval of the male, the answer is yes. Meaningful verbal communication may begin at this point.

The use of eye contact is also heavily influenced by culture. Not all cultures treat eye contact in the way that Americans do. A Peace Corps volunteer in Nigeria, for example, had considerable trouble getting any discipline in class. It became evident that the students did not respect him because he was perceived as showing no self-respect. He was unaware that his problem stemmed from the fact that he insisted that his students look him in the eye while he was speaking to them to show attentiveness. In that culture, prolonged eye contact is considered disrespectful. Much can be communicated by the nonverbal messages of direct eye contact, but across cultural barriers, much unintentional communication may occur.

HAPTICS

Haptics refers to the use of touch to communicate feelings and emotions. This use varies sharply from one culture to another. More than any other nonverbal element, the use of touch within American society depends on the somewhat distant cultural heritage of the individual within the society. Italian-Americans tend to touch much more than do Anglo-Americans. This difference represents a direct transfer of an individual's cultural heritage, a heritage that has survived the intermixing of cultures in the United States. Unlike some of the other nonverbal elements, the use of touch does not seem to follow any cultural norm to which nearly all Americans subscribe. There are, however, some general differences between Americans and people from other cultures. For example, males in the United States will almost never be seen holding hands, because in the American culture it is a symbol of homosexuality. However, in many other parts of the world, such as southeast Asia and some Arab states, hand-holding among males is very common and has no sexual overtones. For males to hold hands as they walk down the street or as they sit in a waiting room is a sign of friendship. This difference in touching behavior caused considerable problems in communication between U.S. servicemen and Vietnam servicemen during the Vietnam War. American GIs simply could not develop much confidence in the fighting ability of their allies after seeing the sergeant and the corporal holding hands on the battlefield.

Courtship behavior of males and females within the American culture involves distinct standards for permissible touching behavior. During the early stages of courtship, for example, the male is not expected to touch the female except when they are dancing. However, the female may, under certain circumstances, touch the male without generating any undesirable perceptions. Such touching communicates interest on the part of the female. If she and the male are standing near one another, she may touch him lightly on the forearm or upper arm; if they are seated near one another, she may gently touch his thigh. Either touch says to the man, "I like you. I would like to date you. Ask me."

Considerable difficulty in communication can arise between Americans as a result of differences in touching behavior. For example, the Anglo-American male will tend to perceive the Italian-American female as very warm-blooded, possibly much more warm-blooded than she actually is. This can often encourage him to engage in more amorous advances than the female is willing to tolerate. She then may perceive the male as overly aggressive and reject him. He will go home wondering what on earth he did wrong. On the other hand, the differences between the Italian-American and the Anglo-American may have the opposite effect when we reverse the sexes in our example. The Italian-American male is likely to perceive the Anglo-American female as very cold and distant and thus have nothing to do with her. The Anglo-American female then perceives the Italian-American male as totally uninterested in her and can't understand why she is so unattractive to him.

Even more major differences in touching behavior will be readily apparent as one goes from one culture to another. For example, it is very common to see the political leaders of many European countries hugging and embracing when they meet one another at an airport. Can you imagine what the electorate of the United States would think if they were to turn on their television sets and see the vice-president hugging the president upon his return from a foreign trip? Americans as a whole seldom touch one another, but when they do, it is normally intended and normally perceived as a very intimate gesture indicating warm, friendly relations.

KINESICS

Kinesics refers to body movement in communication—any movement of the head, arms, legs, and so forth. Body movements are the most pervasive form of nonverbal messages in interpersonal communication transactions. At the same time, body movements are the hardest to bring under complete control. Birdwhistell has estimated that there are over 700,000 possible physical signs that can be transmitted through body movement.[5] To indicate how complex the nonverbal communication of body movement can be, Birdwhistell has isolated twenty-three separate and distinct eyebrow positions that communicate different meanings to receivers.

The individual's use of the body in communication is learned from childhood. Although the use of gesture and movement seems completely natural, it is highly culture bound. A few examples will clarify this point.

A Peace Corps staff member received an emergency call to come to a town to deal with reports that one of his volunteers was treating Ethiopians like dogs. When he arrived, he found that the volunteer, working at a health center, would go into the waiting room and call the next patient. She did this as she would in America—by pointing with her finger to the next patient and beckoning her or him to come into the examining room. In Ethiopia her pointing gesture is appropriate only for children and her beckoning signal is appropriate only for dogs. In Ethiopia one points to a person by extending the arm and hand and beckons by holding the hand out, palm down, and closing it repeatedly.

Americans make no distinction between gesturing for silence to an adult or to a child. An American will typically put one finger to her or his lips in both cases; an Ethiopian will use only one finger for a child but four fingers for an adult. To use only one finger for an adult is a sign of disrespect. Similarly, Ethiopians make no distinction along age or status lines in gesturing to indicate emphatic disagreement. They shake their index finger from side to side to an adult as well as to a child. In America this gesture is reserved only for children and is a direct affront when used with an adult.

The gesture of slitting one's throat—drawing the hand or finger across the throat—says, in America, "I have had it," or "Stop." In Swaziland, that same gesture means "I love you."

In the United States, when individuals agree, they often nod their heads; when disagreeing they shake the head from side to side. Certainly, this seems to be a universal gesture, but in parts of Africa and the Middle East these gestures are reversed: Nodding indicates disagreement, and shaking the head from side to side indicates agreement. Another interesting example is the gesture traffic police use to mean "Stop!" In Greece, motorists use this sign when nonverbally "cursing" other motorists.

As a final example, let us not forget that our gesture for "OK" is fine in America but is highly offensive—in fact one of the most obscene gestures possible—in parts of Latin America. It is similar to the wrong half of a peace sign.

Indeed, then, kinesics is based on cultural norms. Although many gestures do remain the same across cultures, many others do not. Within a given culture, however, individuals do generally attribute similar meaning to gestures and bodily movements. An example of the latter case is a group of gestures and bodily movements commonly employed during courtship behavior in the United States. Both males and females, when they are romantically interested in the person they are with, tend to sit unusually straight, tense the stomach muscles, often rearrange their clothing in minor ways, engage in hair stroking and other preening-type behavior, and often sit with their legs crossed in such a manner as to exclude other people from their conversation. This "exclusionary" leg crossing is accomplished by crossing the outside leg over the inside leg. For example, if the man is sitting to the right of the woman and is interested in her, he will likely put his right leg over his left leg, which will turn his body toward the woman and tend to exclude other people to his right. Other common gestures used by males who are interested in the female and with whom they are communicating include tie straightening, sock tugging, and leaning toward the female. If the female is interested in her male companion, she will often jiggle her leg while she is seated and, even more often, will tend to arch her back so that she obtains maximum breast protrusion.

Seldom will either the male or the female engaged in courtship behavior be aware of the nonverbal cues that he or she is sending. Similarly, the receiver also will seldom be aware of what is happening. But the nonverbal cues of body movement do communicate. Both the male and the female are quite likely to understand that their companion is interested in them. For the typical communication transaction between young, unmarried people, this produces no problem. But you can imagine the future of the young business executive who finds the boss's wife quite attractive and unconsciously engages in this type of nonverbal behavior while the boss is watching. Therefore, an understanding of the power of body movement can help people not only communicate their intended message, but also avoid unintentional communication.

OBJECTICS

Objectics refers to both the use and choice of objects in nonverbal communication. People are surrounded by objects and, when they communicate, these objects are often brought into play. By their use or just by their presence, objects in the communication transaction may communicate something of considerable importance to the receiver.

Choice of clothing tends to communicate a great deal about personality. Is it stylish; is it neat; is there one unbuttoned button more than normal in the shirt or blouse? The answer to each of these questions implies something about the person wearing the clothing. Further, if it is a man, does he have a flag in the lapel of his suit coat? If he does, he is trying to communicate something to other people.

The handling of objects often gives cues as to the internal state of the individual. For example, there are definite masculine and feminine ways of handling a cigarette. And if a person is clicking a ball-point pen, it generally indicates nervousness or boredom.

Other choices relating to objects communicate about people. The type of automobile a person chooses may say a lot about the person and his or her attitudes toward other people. The man driving the nine-passenger station wagon will normally be perceived differently from the man driving the bright red convertible. Often those two men have consciously chosen to set forth the image that they project. As with automobiles, living surroundings (including office surroundings) communicate a lot about the inhabitant of the environment. What type of art, if any, is displayed on the walls? Is the furniture traditional or ultramodern? Is the magazine on the table *Atlantic Monthly, Cosmopolitan,* or *Playboy?* Is the desk clean and neat, or does it look as though a month's work is still sitting there?

Most of the examples used above refer to choice in use of objects that unconsciously reflect upon the individual. In some cases there is a conscious use of objects to communicate a certain idea. Many people wear religious medallions in order to communicate their faith. Some place religious statues in their cars. Some are likely to hang crosses or stars on the walls of their homes or offices to communicate their faith to other people. Some of these people engage in this use of objects in a sincere effort to communicate their faith. Others use objects of this sort as a facade to create a false impression. This latter group is similar to the young businessperson who carries a briefcase home every night to make it appear that he or she is working at home, even though there is hardly enough work to keep busy in the office during the day.

In summary, the mere presence of objects communicates nonverbally, as does their use. No one can avoid communicating through choice and use of objects. The individual must be aware of what nonverbal messages he or she is presenting when using objects.

VOCALICS

Vocalics refers to the use and quality of the human voice in communication. In all oral communication the nonverbal elements of the voice have considerable potential for influencing the meaning of the verbal message as interpreted by the receiver.

People use inflection to give their words special meaning. For example, "*That* is good?" and "That *is* good" can have almost exactly opposite meanings. The first suggests that it is not good at all, whereas the second definitely suggests that something is good. The verbal message is the same, but the nonverbal use of the voice is what produces the intended meaning.

Research has indicated that receivers perceive a communicator's personality through the voice.[6] It is important to note that they do not necessarily perceive the personality accurately; rather, they attain personality perception by stereotypes that they have developed. For example, the female with a breathy voice is perceived as more feminine and prettier than the female without a breathy voice, and the male with a high-pitched voice is perceived as effeminate. Both males and females who speak with a rapid rate are perceived as animated and extroverted. Since they are based on stereotypes, these perceptions may or may not be correct in a given case. The breathy-voiced female may be grossly overweight and ugly, and the man with the high-pitched voice may be a heavyweight boxer. Nevertheless, personality is perceived by listening to the voice, albeit often incorrectly.

Some other characteristics of sources can be perceived quite accurately through the voice. For example, research has indicated that the voice can clearly indicate the sex, race, size, and age of the source, as well as his or her level of education, region of origin within the United States,[7] social status,[8] and, to some extent, the source's emotional state while speaking.[9]

The point to remember about the effect of the voice in producing nonverbal messages in communication is that the voice often tells more about oneself than one really wants known and, in addition, it may often tell things that are not true. Similarly, people see others through their voices, and not always accurately.

It is important to remember that many areas of nonverbal communication have not yet been thoroughly researched. In addition, some that have been researched have not been discussed in this chapter. A complete discussion of all nonverbal messages in communication is not possible in the space available here, so we have concentrated on those considered most important.[10]

The source in rhetorical communication must be aware of the nonverbal elements in communication and control them as much as possible in order to have the intended effect. Similarly, the receiver must attend to the available nonverbal cues to try to sort out the meaning and motives of the sources with whom he or she comes in contact. Although the major focus of this book is on the verbal elements in rhetorical communication, the nonverbal elements are often dominant. One who ignores this fact does so at one's own peril. Nonverbal communication will be further considered in Chapter 14 in relation to the role of delivery in rhetorical communication.

DISCUSSION QUESTIONS

1. Several research studies have indicated that receivers tend to believe nonverbal messages when they conflict with verbal ones. Why do you think this is the case?

2. Observe some advertisements on television. What proportion of the total number of messages in the ad is nonverbal? Do you think the typical receiver is aware of most of the nonverbal messages?

3. Try to recall the first day of class. When you first saw your instructor, what was your impression on him or her? What nonverbal messages contributed to that impression?

4. Observe the objects in your classroom. What might these objects communicate to a nonstudent who enters the room for the first time?

5. Marshall McLuhan was famous for his assertion that "the medium is the message." How might this idea be explained with reference to nonverbal communication?

6. Do you believe that deaf people differ from others in their awareness of nonverbal messages? Why, or why not?

7. In the context of public speaking, what are some important nonverbal messages related to:

   a. proxemics?
   b. chronemics?
   c. oculesics?
   d. haptics?
   e. kinesics?
   f. objectics?
   g. vocalics?

NOTES

1. A. Mehrabian and M. Wiener, "Non-Immediacy between Communication and Object of Communication in a Verbal Message," *Journal of Consulting Psychology* 30 (1966).

2. R. L. Birdwhistell, *Introduction to Kinesics* (Louisville, KY: University of Louisville Press, 1952).

3. E. T. Hall, *The Silent Language* (New York: Fawcett Books Group-CBS Publications, 1959)

4. R. Sommer, "Leadership and Group Geography," *Sociometry* 24 (1961): 99–100. See also "Further Studies of Small Group Ecology," *Sociometry* 27 (1965): 337–48.

5. Birdwhistell, *Introduction to Kinesics.*

6. D. W. Addington, "The Relationship of Selected Vocal Characteristics to Personality Perception," *Speech Monographs* 35 (1968): 498.

7. G. P. Nerbonne, "The Identification of Speaker Characteristics in the Basis of Aural Cues," Ph.D. diss., Michigan State University, 1967.

8. L. S. Harms, "Listener Judgments of Status Cues in Speech," *Quarterly Journal of Speech* 47 (1961): 164–68.

9. J. R. Davitz, *The Communication of Emotional Meaning.* (New York: McGraw-Hill, 1964).

10. For a more thorough discussion of nonverbal communication, see V. P. Richmond and J. C. McCroskey, *Nonverbal Behavior in Interpersonal Relations,* 4th ed. (Boston: Allyn & Bacon, 2000).

CHAPTER 8

DIVERSITY AND CULTURE

Throughout the previous chapters of this book we have stressed that in rhetorical communication it is vital that sources adapt to their audiences. This basic concept has permeated classical rhetorical thinking from Aristotle to the present. If the rhetorical communicator expects to be effective with a group of receivers, he or she must adapt her/his messages to the receivers he/she wishes to influence. Contemporary social science research on attitude and attitude change has consistently confirmed this injunction.

Throughout its history, the United States has been populated with highly diverse populations. While the majority of the immigrants until recent years came from Europe, they came from vastly different cultures on that continent, ones that had histories of wars and conflicts spanning many centuries. Thus, although many of these people appeared physically similar, they represented extremely different religious, economic, and cultural orientations—ones which considered each other to be enemies. Some, for example, left Europe in search of freedom to practice their religion and culture, only to attempt to force their religious and cultural views on others in the new country. Strife, hatred, prejudice, and stereotyping among the various European minority groups in society (Irish, Welsh, German, Italian, Slavic, Polish, French, Russian, Norwegian, Swedish, Danish, Scottish, Dutch, Greek, Spanish, Portuguese, English, etc.) has existed since these groups arrived, and continues to this day. Prior to the arrival of Europeans, Asians (now commonly referred to as Native Americans) lived in what is now known as the United States. They were far from a homogeneous group of people. In fact they were distributed through hundreds of groups (or tribes), some of which got along with their neighbors, but most of whom had long histories of wars and conflicts much as did the Europeans who followed them.

Some people were moved to the United States against their will—predominantly African slaves. Some were enticed to come only to find themselves living as quasi-slaves—primarily Chinese but also some other Asians and Pacific Islanders.

Diversity, then, is not something new to the United States. However, throughout most of U.S. history, there has been a conscious attempt to integrate the various ethnic subgroups into a general "American" culture employing the "melting pot" metaphor. For the most part, this effort has been highly successful. The "American" culture is very recognizable to virtually all non-Americans in the world. In fact, it is so pervasive, not only in North America but throughout the world, it is deeply resented in many areas because of its perceived negative impact on local cultures.

The most difficult culture to recognize as "different" from other cultures, is one's own culture. What people learn from their culture (attitudes, beliefs, preferred behaviors, etc.) is simply seen as "normal" for all "normal" human beings. Hence many subgroups within the general American culture see themselves as much more different from other subgroups than they really are. They see the differences but are blind to the similarities. Of course, some subgroups really are less integrated within the general culture than others. Most notably the descendants of African slaves have been less accepted within the general American culture than other groups, in spite of their extemely important contributions to the overall culture.

Today the "melting pot" metaphor is no longer accepted by many. Instead of working to merge all of the cultures of the various subgroups into one general culture, peoples are encouraged to "celebrate" diversity. Unfortunately some of the "celebrations" are seen as rejections of "the American way" by others, and strife, prejudice, and stereotyping have been increased in some areas. Whether this change of world view will be beneficial or harmful to society in the long run remains to be seen.

Dealing with diversity is a major concern for rhetorical communicators today, much more so that it was in the past. It's not that diversity is new. It definitely is not. It is "as American as apple pie." The difference is that more and more people who will be in audiences which rhetorical communicators wish to influence prefer rhubarb pie—and the rhetorical communicator her/himself may actually prefer pear pie. Simply put, the homogeneity one could expect in both U.S. speakers and audiences is a thing of the past, if it ever really existed. What is expected, much more now than in the past, is sensitivity to the diverse nature of U.S. audiences. Is that more of a problem today than it was in the past? Probably not. It just may be that most of us are more aware of the problem than we used to be. We recognize that we need to be more sensitive to other cultures.

CULTURAL SENSITIVITY

If we are all people of the same culture, we all do what is "normal" and "right." Of course, that is because all of us were taught the same version of "normal" and "right." Under these circumstances being sensitive is easy— and also meaningless.

In contrast consider two very real possibilities in today's world:

1. Our family is composed of cat fanciers. We love cats. We have been raised with cats and been around them since we were infants. Our new neighbors just moved in a few weeks ago. They seem like nice people—clean, neat and quiet. We notice a small out-building behind their house, but never think much about it until we see that there are several cats living there. The next time we see our neighbors we comment on their cats because we appear to have something in common. To our horror our neighbors comment on how delicious that breed is and indicate they will have to have us over soon for dinner so we can try some. Now be sensitive—

2. Our family has lived in ranch country for over 100 years. We know nothing is quite as good as brisket smoked for 24 hours with our special barbeque sauce. When we move to a metropolitan area, we are careful to bring our barbeque equipment with us. When we move in, our neighbors welcome us with open arms and are very helpful to us while we are getting settled. Once we are settled, we want to pay them back for their kindness, so we invite them over for barbeque. When they arrive we notice the look of horror on their faces as they see the beef cooking. We can't imagine what is wrong, so we ask them, What is the matter? They tell us that it is very difficult for them to see what they just looked at. In their religion, cows are sacred. Again, be sensitive!

Sensitivity is not always easy. In fact, usually it is not. Sensitivity is being willing to tolerate (not necessarily *accept*) what we "know" is wrong. How do we "know" what is wrong? Our cultural upbringing taught us.

CULTURE

Defining culture is difficult because it is such an encompassing concept. Rogers and Steinfatt define culture "as the total way of life of a people, composed of their learned and shared behavior patterns, values, norms, and material objects."[1] Klopf tells us that a culture can be thought of as "a set of rules for constructing, interpreting, and adapting to the world."[2] Gudykunst and Kim tell us that "culture" is a term which usually is reserved for the ordering of systems at the societal level.[3] These systems, or cultures, often coincide with political or national boundaries between countries and we refer to them in such ways as "U.S. culture," "Mexican culture," and "German culture." However, they may also encompass more than one political entity, such as "Arab culture."

Often cultures exist within larger cultures. As Gudykunst and Kim indicate, the term traditionally used to refer to this cultural ordering is *subculture*.[4] Examples of such subcultures include the academic subculture (people who teach and do research in colleges and universities), the medical sub-culture (people who work in medicine), and the Washington (D.C.) subcul-ture (people who work for the Federal government). This term is also used to describe the cultures of racial or ethnic groups living within a larger cul-tural system (Texas subculture, Hispanic subculture, or African-American subculture). However, the term *co-culture* is now frequently used in this con-text because the suffix "sub" (as in subculture) is taken by some to suggest a lower status, not just lower ordering according to size.

It is useful to think of a culture like a living thing. Cultures (including sub- and co-cultures) are not static. They constantly grow and change, although the changes may not be very noticeable to people living within the given culture because these changes, like changes in human beings, typi-cally occur very gradually. Most cultures have very high "self-esteem" and their devotees are often fiercely loyal—to the point of being willing to die to protect the values and orientations shared by the people in that culture.

A group's culture is cumulative, it grows, expands, and adapts to changes. A group's culture is passed on to its children through a learning process called "enculturation." While schools are the most obvious instru-ments of enculturation for children, religious groups, parents, peers, senior members of communities, writers and artists, the mass media, and even gov-ernment agents function to enculturate the young. When new people move into a culture, the host people attempt to "acculturate" the newcomers by directly and indirectly influencing them to adopt new ways of thinking about and doing things—the ways of the host culture. Acculturation almost always works in this direction—the host culture influences the newcomer. Efforts by newcomers to change the host culture are usually rejected, and often new-comers who persist in making such attempts will be ejected from the host culture or at least made to feel extremely unwelcome. The current effort on the part of leaders of the U. S. culture to get their members to be more "sen-sitive" to newcomers' cultural orientations and behaviors, therefore, is an effort that has no guarantee for success. In fact, historically, there are few examples where such efforts have succeeded anywhere in the world.

ON BECOMING ENCULTURATED

Regardless of what your music teacher may have said, you are cultured! Even if you grew up in one of the many "less sophisticated" parts of the United States (as I did), rest assured. You are cultured. Even if you hate opera, would rather go deaf than hear Shastakovich one more time, find Shakespeare hopelessly boring, and think most of modern art was painted by monkeys, you are cultured. However you were probably not born into the Italian, German, or English cultures.

See if any of the following are so familiar to you that you take them for granted: supermarkets, interstate highways, free public education, barbecue, pickup trucks, cowboy boots, button-down collars, aloha shirts, cin-emaplexes, rodeo, baseball, basketball, football, jeans, deodorants, pizza, Dr. Pepper, Mr. Clean, Kleenex, fast food, talk radio, cable TV, commercial TV, Playboy, public colleges and universities, grits, apple pie, black eyed peas, tacos, TV dinners, American music (like jazz, rock, country, Broadway, rap, gospel, hip hop, easy listening, etc.). These are just a few of the things that are part of the American culture. Can you imagine living where none of these things exist? Strange as it may seem, it is quite possible to do so. Many cultures have none of these things. In Chapter 11 we will direct attention to a large number of American values. There are places where virtually none of those values exist. It isn't the "things" that define our culture, it is the val-ues, beliefs, attitudes, orientations and assumptions we share which result in the things that we find so common. Of course, in different parts of the United States there are slight subcultural differences. If you are not familiar with black eyed peas, you probably didn't grow up in the South. Pizza? I never heard of it until I was out of college. It wasn't around where I grew up. Do you like guns? If you do, you probably live in an area where hunting is com-mon. Enjoy skiing? If so, You probably don't live in Miami. It might get expensive for you. Certainly, as these examples illustrate, there are subcul-tural differences among people who call themselves "American." But gener-ally we all have more in common with each other than we do with people from cultures anywhere else in the world. The differences among the sub-cultures of American culture are vastly smaller than the differences between our general culture and most other cultures in the world.

CULTURE AS COMMUNICATION CONTEXT

All communication, rhetorical or not, exists within a context. The largest part of that context is the culture in which communication occurs. We talked about nonverbal behavior in Chapter 7. The vast majority of our non-verbal behavior comes as a function of our culture. Similarly, we are all born with the capability of learning any or all of the languages of the world. But what one(s) do we learn? With extremely few exceptions, only the lan-guage (or languages) that we hear while we are infants or young children become part of our culture. The tools for our communication, both verbal and nonverbal, are provided to us by our culture. Unfortunately, if we take our tools to another culture, they will have limited effectiveness—or may be completely ineffective. They may even be highly offensive, particularly in the case of our nonverbal behaviors.

Today, we do not need travel around the world to find ourselves in contexts where our culture is not the primary culture defining the context of our communication. Intercultural communication is at our fingertips on the Internet. It is also available in our neighborhood, in our work environ-ment and in our vacation environment.

At this point, it is probably useful to draw some important distinctions. Three are particularly valuable:

1. Intracultural Communication. This is communication between two (or more, in the case of public presentations) people who identify with the same general culture. They are very similar in their use of language and nonverbal behaviors. They adhere generally to the same value system. They usually see the world in the same or highly similar ways. This is the type of communication with the highest likelihood of success.

2. Intercultural Communication. This is communication between a source and receiver(s) who identify with distinctly different cultures. They employ different languages and nonverbal behaviors. Their value systems may have some things in common but are likely to differ greatly, particularly in the ordering of individual values. They may have world views very different from each other. This is the type of communication with the lowest likelihood of success.

3. Interethnic/Interracial Communication. This is communication between a source and receiver(s) who identify with different ethnic and/or racial subgroups within the same overall cultural group, or one who identifies with an ethnic/racial subgroup while the other identifies only with the overall cultural group. Communication is enhanced in this context by some shared orientations as a function of membership the same overall cultural group, but it is impeded by the differences characterized by the ethnic/racial group(s) involved. These may be related to values, language (or dialect/accent of the language), and/or nonverbal behaviors. The chances for this type of communication being effective depend on the degree to which all parties involved try to focus on the elements which they have in common. When the focus is on the differences, the chances for a positive outcome are minimal.

Of course, when engaging in rhetorical communication with a sizeable audience in today's society, all of these types of communication may be present simultaneously. This is the type of situation which places maximum stress on the communication source to be sensitive to the complexity of the process unfolding and the cultural "land mines" which may be in her/his path. We will address some of these "land mines" in the next section. Please complete the scale presented in Figure 8.1 and score your responses according to the instructions in Figure 8.2 before reading the next section.

XENOPHOBIA AND ETHNOCENTRISM

Xenophobia is the fear of strangers. Being somewhat reticent when encountering strangers is very common. It is a trait shared by most people. In fact,

Directions: Below are 22 items that relate to the cultures of different parts of the world. Please indicate the degree to which you agree or disagree with each item, in the space before that item, using the following five-point scale: (5) Strongly agree; (4) Agree; (3) Undecided; (2) Disagree; (1) Strongly disagree. Work quickly and record your first reaction to each item. There are no right or wrong answers.

_____ 1. Most other cultures are backward compared to my culture.
_____ 2. My culture should be the role model for other cultures.
_____ 3. People from other cultures act strange when they come to my culture.
_____ 4. Lifestyles in other cultures are just as valid as those in my culture.
_____ 5. Other cultures should try to be more like my culture.
_____ 6. I am not interested in the values and customs of other cultures.
_____ 7. People in my culture could learn a lot from people in other cultures.
_____ 8. Most people from other cultures just don't know what's good for them.
_____ 9. I respect the values and customs of other cultures.
_____ 10. Other cultures are smart to look up to our culture.
_____ 11. Most people would be happier if they lived like people in my culture.
_____ 12. I have many friends from different cultures.
_____ 13. People in my culture have just about the best lifestyles of anywhere.
_____ 14. Lifestyles in other cultures are not as valid as those in my culture.
_____ 15. I am very interested in the values and customs of other cultures.
_____ 16. I apply my values when judging people who are different.
_____ 17. I see people who are similar to me as virtuous.
_____ 18. I do not cooperate with people who are different.
_____ 19. Most people in my culture just don't know what is good for them.
_____ 20. I do not trust people who are different.
_____ 21. I dislike interacting with people from different cultures.
_____ 22. I have little respect for the values and customs of other cultures.

FIGURE 8.1 Ethnocentrism Scale. A revised version of a scale originally developed and reported by J. W. Neuliep and J. C. McCroskey.[7]

some people believe that this fearfulness is the result of the long process of evolution in humans. In the distant past, it is believed, humans who did not have this response and were friendly and open to strangers were more likely to be captured or killed by those who were foraging in the woods for the necessities of life. As some put it, the warm, friendly humans were "food."

Step 1: Add scores for items 4, 7, and 9.

Step 2: Add scores for items 1, 2, 5, 8, 10, 11, 13, 14, 18, 20, 21, and 22.

Step 3: Subtract the score of step 1 from step 18.

Step 4: Add scores from step 2 and step 3.

The result is your Ethnocentrism score. Higher scores = higher ethnocentrism.

FIGURE 8.2   Scoring the Ethnocentrism Scale

Whether this is the origin of the most common human response to strangers or not is uncertain, but whatever the cause, the response is extremely common. To get an estimate of how xenophobic you are, compared to others, turn back to Chapter 3. Look at your responses to the WTC scale in Figure 3.6 and the scores you computed from the instruction in Figure 3.7. More specifically, look at your score for the "Strangers" subscale. If you scored below 70, you show distinct signs of being xenophobic. The odds are that you did score in that range, since the average person who has completed this scale in the past scored under 40. As you can see, xenophobia is normal in humans, and is not necessarily a problem in and of itself. However, being fearful of something (heights, snakes, spiders, strangers) typically leads to suspicion and dislike of the feared object. Thus many people, if not most, view strangers with suspicion and dislike, and maintain those perceptions until the stranger becomes well-enough known to be reclassified as an acquaintance. Most strangers never achieve such a level with us. People from other cultures, and sometimes even from subcultures or co-cultures within one's own general culture, have a particularly difficult time overcoming this basic xenophobic response.

When you are planning to engage in rhetorical communication, it is critical that you take the xenophobic response into account. If you are speaking to a group of strangers, xenophobia is likely to impact both you and your audience—and the impact is not likely to be positive. Your suspicion of the members of the audience might show through, if you are not careful. Since you are a stranger to them, it is likely that your ethos will be in question in their minds. You may have to go out of your way to build your credibility with such an audience. Identifying similarities with the audience members is critical, and you may want to ensure that this begins with the person who introduces you.

The problem of xenophobia is compounded by another common orientation of humans—*ethnocentrism*. If you correctly followed the instructions in Figure 8.2, you have your ethnocentrism score. Any score above 15 indicates a certain degree of ethnocentrism. If your score is above 45, you have a very high degree of ethnocentrism.

The term "ethnocentrism" is derived from two Greek words: Ethnos which is Greek for "nation" and kentron which is Greek for "center." In combination these words suggest that one sees her or his nation (or culture) as the center of the universe. This is a view held by many people and is as old (at least) as recorded history. For a simple example, look at the map of the world that is available where you live. If it is designed by North Americans, North and South America are in the middle of the map, with Europe off in one direction and Asia in the other. If you are an American, it is likely that this is the only kind of map you have ever seen. However, if you were to look at the French or German map of the world, you would find Europe in the middle with Asia and the Americas off to opposite sides. Similarly, the Chinese map has Asia in the middle and Europe and the Americas off to opposite sides. Just as individual people are self-centered (or ego-centric), and view all others from the perspective of themselves (they are the center of their universe), cultures are ethnocentric and view all others from the perspective of themselves.

It is useful to continue our comparison of self-perceptions with cultural perceptions. We encourage children to develop high self-esteem. However, if they get "too much" self-esteem they may boast about how great they are and how worthless others are by comparison. Similarly, people are taught that their culture is great and they should feel very fortunate to have been born into it. Viewing one's culture in high esteem is a positive thing. However, if we get highly ethnocentric we may begin boasting about how great our culture is and how inferior other cultures are. Whether it is our view of self or our view of our culture, moderate esteem is generally preferable to either one of the extremes.

In any event, to the extent that we are ethnocentric, we all tend to view other cultures (and subcultures) from that vantage point. That is, our culture is the standard by which we evaluate other cultures—and the people from those cultures. Any deviation from that standard is usually (but not always) viewed negatively and will be used as evidence of people from the other culture's inferiority. Of course, that is the basis from which people from other cultures also evaluate us. Their culture is best in their minds, and the extent to which we deviate is usually viewed as an indicant of our inferiority.

Positive Ethnocentrism

Ethnocentrism provides the foundation for the existence of a culture or a subculture. It helps people making up cultures and subcultures develop a sense of collective identity and group pride. It helps maintain the integrity of the culture or subculture in the face of external threats from people from other cultures (who also believe their culture to be the best one). Some people suggest that if there were no ethnocentrism, there would be no culture. Ethnocentrism gives the people of a culture an identity and helps make them more homogeneous and cohesive. It promotes positive and effective communication among people within the culture. It results in people being more willing to follow the formal and informal practices of the culture, since the people of the culture consider these practices to be the correct ones and the best ones for all normal people to follow. When conflict occurs with people from other cultures (or subcultures), blame can be placed on the other group which, in turn, reduces potential conflict within the cultural group. Ethnocentrism provides the foundation for patriotism—a critical factor in building internal support in times of conflict with out-groups. If we see our culture as the best, it obviously is worth defending—even if at the cost of one's life—so that loved ones can continue to enjoy the blessings that culture provides (democracy, freedom, the "American way", etc.). This defensive reaction is not always completely rational. For example, more wars have been fought and more people have been killed to protect or advance a culture's religion than for all other reasons combined throughout human history. Each culture is convinced their religion is the best, and is often seen as "the only true religion." This belief permits the slaughter of people who believe differently even though these people's only "crime" is to follow another religion.

Clearly, ethnocentrism is the first line of defense for a culture. Without it, a culture is open to rapid and extreme changes and is subject to losing its very existence. Over the centuries, many cultures and subcultures have thrived, then perished. For this reason, people who lead subcultural groups within a larger general culture often resort to very militant communication in the ethnocentric defense of their subculture and their attacks on the larger culture. They recognize that in the absence of high ethnocentrism among the members of the subculture, it will lose its distinctiveness and blend into the larger culture (and the leaders will lose their leadership status). If too few people think a subculture is worth preserving, it will not be preserved.[5]

Negative Ethnocentrism

Like many other things, ethnocentrism in moderation can be positive, as indicated in the previous section. However, if taken too far, ethnocentrism can become a very negative orientation. It is particularly dangerous for people to have strongly ethnocentric beliefs and not recognize that they do. It is considered easy to see ethnocentrism in others, but it is usually difficult to recognize it in oneself. After all, our view of the world is the correct one, isn't it? All normal people share it, don't they? Some of the people who complain the most about being mistreated by some other cultural or subcultural group are also among the most ethnocentric people you will find. However, they will deny their ethnocentrism loudly while proclaiming this very evil in others around them.

There are three potentially serious problems for rhetorical communication which emanate from excessive ethnocentrism: culture shock, stereotyping, and prejudice. We will consider each of these in turn.

Culture Shock.   While culture shock has been experienced by people for centuries, it was not fully identified and described until 1960.[6] Culture shock is something almost everyone experiences when they move to a new cultural environment. Whether the move is from one continent to another, one state to another, one town to a neighboring town, or just from home to a nearby college, some degree of trauma is likely to be experienced. That trauma is now commonly referred to as "culture shock." If you have ever experienced it, "shock" will not seem too strong a word to describe it. At the extreme, culture shock has been found to result in complete mental breakdown and even suicide. The greater the actual difference between the old and new culture (or subculture), the greater the shock. Similarly, the higher one's ethnocentrism, the greater the shock.

While there are real differences among cultures and subcultures, people who are highly ethnocentric tend to exaggerate their perceptions of those differences. They tend to feel that literally everything is different, even if only a few things actually are. This often leads to depression and loneliness, accompanied by a powerful desire to be "back home," to have some "normal" food, and to talk to someone "who makes sense." Communicating with people from the new culture becomes extremely difficult, and attempts are likely to lead to very negative perceptions on the part of everyone involved.

It is not necessary for a person to move to a new culture to experience many aspects of culture shock. Even traveling on vacation in a new culture can generate many of these same feelings and negative experiences for the person who is highly ethnocentric. Research indicates that some people who have moderate ethnocentrism actually become more ethnocentric as a function of contact with other cultures.[7] Overcoming culture shock and reducing one's ethnocentrism while in constant contact with another culture or subculture may take many months, or even years. People do not necessarily become more culturally sensitive as a function of contact with people from other cultures. They may become more ethnocentric rather than less, particularly if their ethnocentrism was not very low in the first place.

Clearly, attempting to engage in cross-cultural rhetorical communication while one is experiencing culture shock is unwise (at best). The first thing people need to do if they plan to have more than fleeting contact with people from other cultures or subcultures is get control of their ethnocentrism. Establishing effective rhetorical communication requires accurately analyzing and adapting to one's audience, and high ethnocentrism makes such an effort impossible. Of course, reducing one's own ethnocentrism does not guarantee that one can become an effective intercultural rhetorical communicator. The receivers need to have their ethnocentrism under control as well.

Stereotyping.   When we view a group of people from a culture or subculture as sharing one or several common characteristics, we have formed a generalization commonly known as a "stereotype." Such generalizations serve as a means of organizing our experiences with others. We need these kinds of generalizations so that we may better predict how people will respond to our rhetorical communication efforts. Unfortunately, even when stereotyping people from our own culture, the accuracy of the stereotypes is often low. Not all stereotypes are inaccurate, however; many are accurate.[8] These accurate stereotypes are very valuable to the rhetorical communicator.

We know so little about most people, and even less about people from another culture or subculture, that any attempts we make to individualize our communication are likely to be based on misunderstandings. Hence, stereotyping is not an option; it is a mandate. The issue is not how we can avoid stereotyping, it is how we can generate better stereotypes. High ethnocentrism makes generating better stereotypes much more difficult. The first stereotype category we are likely to create is the dichotomy of "like me" vs. "not like me." If we are highly ethnocentric, few if any people for other cultures or subcultures will qualify for the first category. Thus virtually everyone with whom we come in contact that is from a different culture or subculture will be immediately branded as "different." This usually leads to making any one of three kinds of errors about the other person(s): we can overestimate differences, we can underestimate differences, or we can see what we expect to see.

When we overestimate differences we tend to ignore similarities, hence the others are seen as odd, unfamiliar, and often, dangerous. These stereotypes are likely to lead us to avoid attempts at communication with others. The absence of communication may lead to increased fear or distrust. It is only a short step from fear or distrust to disliking and hating—a step which all too often is taken even by the most well-intentioned person.

When we underestimate differences we fail to recognize that people from other cultures vary a lot among themselves, just as people do in our own culture. Some people in any given culture are really wonderful people, and some in the same culture are rotten eggs. When we stereotype people from another culture we often fail to recognize such variability which we take for granted in our home culture. We encounter one rude person in Japan, and all Japanese people become "rude." We meet one Russian who is an alcoholic, and all Russians become a "bunch of alcoholics."

The final error is seeing what we expect to see even though what we expect is not there. If we have heard that farm women in Iowa are overweight and that is included in our initial stereotype, and we meet a dozen thin Iowa women and three heavy ones, we confirm our "overweight" expectation. Strong stereotypes are often resistant to change, even in the presence of obvious exceptions. We see what we expect to see—even when it isn't there.

Given these common errors to which everyone is prone (although more ethnocentric people are even more prone), it is no wonder that once stereotypes are formed, they are highly resistant to change. In fact, if we encounter people from another culture or subculture with our stereotypes firmly in place, we are likely to reinforce those stereotypes through our selective perceptions (recall Chapter 4) of those around us and our choices of people with whom to communicate in that culture. Oddly as it may seem, it may be easier to function with people from the culture that fit our stereotype but are atypical of the culture itself than it would be with those who are more typical of the culture but don't fit our stereotype. This leads us to the final error.

Prejudice. Prejudice refers to a priori judgements based on inadequate stereotypes. The term "a priori judgements" refers to judgements which are made in advance of the time when they are employed. The expression "based on inadequate stereotypes" suggests that the basis for the judgement is limited and very possibly inaccurate.

While "prejudice" suggests a negative judgement, that is not always the case. There are instances where the pre-judgement is positive. However, this is the exception rather than the rule—and much more likely to occur within one's home culture than in intercultural encounters. Like stereotyping, the root cause of prejudice is ethnocentrism. And since virtually all of us are ethnocentric at least to some degree, it is likely that we have some negative stereotypes of people from other cultures or subcultures, and it is likely that we have some prejudices about some groups of people and their culturally based behaviors—including communication behaviors. And, of course, it is highly likely that people from other cultures and subcultures have negative views of us for the same reasons.

The Ethnocentrism Continuum

According to DeVito[9] ethnocentrism exists on a continuum. He has outlined five steps on that continuum. We shall examine these five steps in ascending order.

Equality. This is lowest level of ethnocentrism. This person communicates with others on the basis of equality. While differences in cultural practices and ways of behaving are acknowledged, they are not considered inferior to one's own, just different. If everyone in a communication encounter enters at this level of ethnocentrism, the probability of successful communication is high. Ethnocentrism will be irrelevant. Unfortunately, this is the least common circumstance under which intercultural communication is likely to occur.

Sensitivity. This is a moderately low level of ethnocentrism. The person at this level is sensitive to the fact that he or she is somewhat ethnocentric and wants to communicate without offending people from another culture. If all people in an intercultural communication encounter are at this level of ethnocentrism or lower, the likelihood of successful communication is good. It closely resembles the "cultural sensitivity" which we referenced early in this chapter. This the type of communication encounter frequently experienced at international conferences where everyone is "on their best behavior" and highly sensitive to problems which may need to be confronted.

Indifference. This is a moderate level of ethnocentrism; the amount a typical person would have in a typical culture. Such people are happy with their own culture, or at least they don't think negatively about it. Such people really don't know or care much about how people from other cultures or subcultures differ from people in their own culture or subculture. They prefer to communicate with people who are very much like themselves, and prefer not to think about people with different attitudes and values at all. If they are forced to interact with people from other cultures or subcultures, they are likely to become much more ethnocentric as a result. The majority of people in most cultures are in this group. Passing contact between people from different cultures with this level or a lower level of ethnocentrism are likely to be civil and can even be pleasant. However, more in-depth contact can be problematic.

Avoidance. This is a moderately high level of ethnocentrism. It is more common in environments where different cultures or subcultures have frequent contact with each other. At this level people know they are ethnocentric (although this term my be foreign to them), and they want little to do with people from other cultures or subcultures. They do their best to avoid communicating with people from other cultures and subcultures and have a difficult time communicating effectively enough with them to have a good working relationship, much less a personal relationship. The probability of their communication leading to conflict is much higher than the probability of a successful, smooth interaction. The more intercultural contact these people have, the more ethnocentric they are likely to become.

Disparagement. This is a very high level of ethnocentrism. A person with this high a level is likely to be seen by people from another culture or subculture as a racist, sexist, or bigot. Communication between this person and a person from another culture or subculture is most likely to involve hostility. This person is likely to belittle the other person and/or their culture—in some cases including the use of very derogatory terms. The possibility of effective communication when even one person is at this level of ethnocentrism is practically nonexistent. The possibility of physical violence occurring when two or more people in an interaction are at this level of ethnocentrism is very high. Such circumstances should be prevented if at all possible.

It would appear that our goal should be to reach at least the sensitivity level if we are to attempt to engage in rhetorical communication with people from other cultures or subcultures. If we can't achieve that goal, it would be best if we have those who can communicate on our behalf to avoid making things worse instead of better. We should also work to learn to recognize what level people from other cultures or subcultures are so that if they are not at least at the sensitivity level we refrain from influence attempts with them. Again, absence of communication is better than making things worse.

IMPROVING RHETORICAL COMMUNICATION ACROSS CULTURES

Rhetorical communication is difficult under the most positive circumstances. Dealing with others who are culturally different from one's self is even more difficult. Given today's realities, however, the probability of one needing to communicate to influence a person or persons from another cultural or subcultural group is extremely high. Below are suggestions which should improve your chances of being an effective rhetorical communicator under such circumstances. It is important to note that even following all of them, does not guarantee success.

1. Recognize your own ethnocentrism. Ethnocentrism is the number one enemy of effective intercultural communication. While you are entitled to believe that your culture is the best culture in the world, it is vital that you also recognize that such judgements are a matter of opinion, not a matter of fact, and that a person from any other culture or subculture is most likely not to agree with you. Think what you like, but keep such thoughts to yourself.

2. Avoid derogating anyone else's culture. Be sensitive to the ethnocentric feelings of people from other cultures. They, like you, are proud of their culture. You can gain nothing by making negative references to another person's cultural views or practices. Such references will only serve to "make an enemy" and ruin your chances for establishing effective intercultural communication with that person. The more a person's culture is attacked, the more ethnocentric that person will become.

3. Demonstrate respect for other people and their cultures. The principle of reciprocity operates in both intracultural and intercultural communication. This principle suggests that if you show respect and sensitivity toward the other person and her or his culture, it is more likely that you will be shown similar respect in return. In intercultural relationships people do not have to like one another's cultural orientations, but they do need to be sensitive to them and show respect for them if there is to be any positive communication in the relationship.

4. Be empathic. Try to see things from the vantage points of other people's culture. You may view things differently, but if you can empathize with other people and understand why they have views different from your own, it is more likely that you can accommodate their views in your communication efforts.

5. Develop a higher tolerance for ambiguity. Intercultural communication encounters regularly involve a high degree of ambiguity. If you can provide a measure of acceptance of things which you do not fully understand, it often will be possible to avoid needless unpleasantness. If the ambiguity is cleared up subsequently, you will be in a better position to deal with matters that you want changed at that time.

6. Reduce the level of evaluation in your messages. People in the general North American culture tend to be highly evaluative in their verbal observations of the world around them. It is critical that when communicating with people from other cultures that one soften such observations. In many cases requesting someone to explain why things are as they are is vastly superior to giving one's evaluations of those things.

7. Do not assume that nonverbal messages are pancultural. We learn our nonverbal behavior from our culture, and we learn it so well we assume it is "natural" for all humans. It isn't. In fact, some of the most innocuous nonverbal behaviors in one culture can be seen as offensive or even obscene in other cultures. If you are going to attempt to communicate with people from a different culture, try to learn as much about that culture's nonverbal behaviors as you can.

8. Be sensitive to both the differences and similarities. As we noted previously, two of the common errors people make is to over- or under-emphasize either differences or similarities. It is very important that before you attempt to communicate with people from a different culture or subculture you have a good command of both the similarities and the differences between your culture and theirs. While it is important that you emphasize the similarities, it is equally important that you are constantly aware of the differences so that you can avoid issues which may involve those differences.

9. Work to build better stereotypes. You are going to find it necessary to build generalizations about how to expect people to behave in different cultures. The more you read about and study those cultures, the better generalizations you will be able to make, and the more you will be able to adapt to those behaviors. To refine those stereotypes, engage in as much communication with people from those cultures as you can.

10. Never forget that meanings are in people, not in cultures. Remember that people in any culture do not all behave, much less think, alike. Therefore, while it is fine to start with cultural stereotypes, try to monitor the behavior of the people with whom you communicate in order to identify the important ways that they differ from the cultural stereotypes and then adapt to those differences.

Just as considerable study and practice are necessary to become an effective rhetorical communicator within one's own culture, it is necessary to learn new behaviors and practice those behaviors to expand one's skill to the intercultural context. Remember, the guidance given in the following chapters is directed toward developing your skills in the context of the General American culture. If you are going to be communicating in a different cultural or subcultural context, some adaptation is almost certain to be necessary. To determine what adaptations are necessary, you must learn about the particular culture or subculture with which you are going to come in contact.

DISCUSSION QUESTIONS

1. Read the speech in Appendix A by Hillary Rodham Clinton. Was that speech directed primarily to people in the general American culture or to another culture? How can you tell?

2. Identify three subgroups that exist within the general American culture. Identify two positive and two negative stereotypes you have for each subgroup. Which task was more difficult? Why?

3. Identify an example where you have had a prejudice concerning people from another culture or subculture which you believed was positive. Do you think a member of that group would see that prejudice as positive or negative?

4. Is it ethical to engage in behaviors which are characteristic of another culture in order to influence members of that culture when those behaviors are not normal in your own culture? Why or why not?

NOTES

1. E. M. Rogers and T. M. Steinfatt, *Intercultural Communication* (Prospect Heights, IL: Waveland, 1999), p. 79.

2. D. W. Klopf, *Intercultural Encounters: Fundamentals of Intercultural Communication* (Englewood, CO: Morton, 1995), p. 26.

3. W. B. Gudykunst and Y. Y. Kim, *Communicating with Strangers: An Approach to Intercultural Communication*, 3rd ed. (New York: McGraw-Hill, 1997), p. 18.

4. Ibid.

5. Many of the views developed in this and the following sections were first advanced in J. C. McCroskey and V. P. Richmond, *Fundamentals of Human Communication: An Interpersonal Perspective* (Prospect Heights, IL: Waveland, 1996).

6. See K. Oberg, "Cultural Shock: Adjustment to New Cultural Environments," *Practical Anthropology* 7 (1960): 176–182.

7. J. W. Neuliep and J. C. McCroskey, "The Development of a U.S. and Generalized Ethnocentrism Scale," *Communication Research Reports* 14 (1997): 385–398.

8. Y. T. Lee, L. J. Jussim, and C. R. McCauley, *Stereotype Accuracy; Toward Appreciating Group Differences* (Washington D.C.: American Psychological Association, 1995).

9. J. A. DeVito, *Human Communication: A Basic Course*, 6th ed. (New York: HarperCollins, 1994).

PART

MESSAGE PREPARATION
AND PRESENTATION

CHAPTER 9

MESSAGE PREPARATION: PRELIMINARY CONSIDERATIONS

The first two sections of this book were devoted to presenting material necessary for an understanding of the rhetorical communication process. We have considered the nature of rhetorical communication and how it is different from other forms of communication. We have looked at the nature of receivers, the importance of ethos and nonverbal messages, and the nature of persuasive argument. Information in Parts One and Two was presented with the firm belief that a thorough understanding of the rhetorical communication process is necessary for the individual who wishes to be an effective rhetorical communicator. The following chapters are devoted to the application of the theories developed in the preceding section to the practical matter of preparing messages and presenting those messages to an audience. This section is concerned with rhetorical communication in a one-to-many context, such as public-speaking and editorial-writing situations.

The model of the rhetorical communication process (Figure 2.3) in Chapter 2 made a distinction between the elements that occur prior to the inception of that process and those that are involved in the encoding process, the first phase of rhetorical communication. The present chapter concerns the things that the source must consider prior to the inception of the encoding process.

SELECTION OF A TOPIC

One problem confronting the student who is first exposed to the study of rhetorical communication is selecting a subject for the communicative act. It is ironic that this causes students of rhetorical communication so much concern, for it is a matter of relatively small importance in rhetorical communication outside the classroom. To understand the process of selecting a subject, let us consider the circumstances under which people normally involve themselves in rhetorical communication.

The first circumstance is spontaneous conversation or discussion. In this, the individual does not have prior warning that he or she will be considering a given subject. A subject for discussion simply occurs. The individual does not necessarily select the subject; it arises from the situation.

In the second circumstance the audience seeks out the source. It is not uncommon for a person to receive a telephone call asking her or him to give a talk to a particular club or organization several days hence. At this time the caller usually suggests a topic, or the individual called asks the caller what the organization would like her or him to talk about. It is obvious that in these two circumstances calling for rhetorical communication, the selection of the subject causes little difficulty. The potential source does not choose the subject.

In the third circumstance, an individual has an idea he or she wishes to communicate and seeks an audience to convey it to. Salespersons, ministers, and politicians are obvious examples of this type of individual. All of us, however, fall into this category at one time or another. We all have axes to grind: ideas that necessitate our securing an audience to influence.

All of this suggests that selecting the subject for rhetorical communication is seldom a major problem. The student who has been assigned a speech or an essay in the classroom and is worried about selecting a subject probably is not really concerned with *rhetorical* communication but with *expressive* communication. The student has been asked to give a speech or to write an essay, which he or she perceives as a performance for the class. If the student's classmates and instructor are perceived as an audience to influence, the choice of subject will be a much smaller problem. The prospective communicator who has not selected a subject could ask the question, "What do I know or believe that I would like others to know or believe?" The person should explore her or his own background, knowledge, and interests. If one sincerely examines one's motivations, one will not be short of subjects about which to communicate but will have such a varied selection that there may be some difficulty deciding which idea is the most important. At any rate, approached in this manner, selecting a subject is only a minor difficulty.

SELECTION OF A PURPOSE

With a subject in mind, the source must determine the intent toward the audience. This intent is what we shall refer to as the source's purpose.

The first decision relating to purpose is the basic intent of the communication. In Chapter 5, we discussed the distinction between concept-centered and ethos-centered communication. Choosing between the two must be the first decision the source makes. Is the goal to change the attitudes or understanding of the audience in terms of a concept, or is the primary concern one of changing the audience's perception of herself or himself as a source? Nearly every decision in preparing a message will hinge upon this choice.

The source's second decision is whether the concern is with a long-term effect or only with the initial response of the audience. As we indicated in Chapter 6, for long-term effect there are certain procedures a source may employ to inoculate the audience against counterpersuasion to which they may be subjected later. A message created with the idea of long-term, as well as short-term, effect in mind may well be quite different from a message created only for short-term effect.

If the source's basic purpose is to persuade the audience, he or she must choose one of three operational aims, each directed toward a different kind of response: (a) to generate an attitude not previously held, (b) to reinforce an attitude already held, or (c) to change an attitude already held.

Generating a new attitude may involve a subject (the governmental situation in Lebanon, for example) about which the audience already knows a little but on which they have not yet adopted a definite position. But if the audience members already hold an attitude on the subject, the source may wish to reinforce that attitude so as to increase its intensity. Or if the audience members hold an attitude on the subject that is contrary to the view the source would like them to hold, then the purpose will be to change the attitude. In this case the source becomes concerned with both the intensity and the direction of the attitude of the audience.

Most rhetorical communication fits within these three categories of persuasive purpose. But there is a fourth: In some cases, sources are concerned with their audience's understanding. They wish to inform the audience but are not concerned with the attitudes stimulated by this information. Finding an example of purely informative communication in the "real world" is not a simple task. Ideally, for example, the report of a congressional investigating committee should have informative intent. The purpose of such investigations is supposedly to find the facts relevant to a given matter and to report them to Congress. But examining such reports will indicate to even the most naive observer that their intent rarely is the mere presentation of the facts. Ordinarily, if the investigating committee did not have a preconceived persuasive purpose, it certainly would develop one during the investigation. The report naturally would reflect this purpose.

Truly informative intent can exist only if the source is comparatively free from bias on the question. Such freedom from bias, however, is rare. Many people contend that there is no such thing as purely informative intent. This view holds that, even though the source may think the intent is informative, closer examination of the motivation would show that the desire is really to cause the audience to form an attitude, to reinforce an attitude, or to change an attitude. In short, the actual motivation is basically persuasive. But at this point, whether informative intent is common or not is irrelevant; it is clearly possible even if it is uncommon. Chapter 10 will consider the distinctive characteristics of a rhetorical communicative act with informative intent.

Some writers say that there is a fifth category of purpose: to provide the audience with enjoyment. The classification "entertainment" is frequently included in communication textbooks. The after-dinner speech is cited frequently to distinguish this type of communicative act from the others we have discussed. But we shall not consider entertainment as a separate type of communicative act. We hold that there is no intention strictly to provide enjoyment. By this we mean that speeches or writings that amuse or entertain an audience either are not rhetorical communication or have informative or persuasive intent. Humor is frequently used to make a point. The humorous point almost invariably is a persuasive one. Similarly, speeches given at banquets also make points. Sometimes the point clearly fits within the pattern of asking the audience to form, reinforce, or change an attitude toward a concept. In other cases the function of such speeches is clearly ethos-centered. The source merely desires the audience to think better of her or him and feels that, by providing them with enjoyment, he or she will be perceived as a more desirable individual.

The selection of the purpose for a given act of rhetorical communication, then, involves three choices. The source must determine whether the purpose is to be ethos-centered or concept-centered; whether to seek both short- and long-range effects or only short-range effects upon the audience; and whether he or she wishes to get the audience to develop a new attitude, reinforce an old attitude, change an old attitude, or merely have the audience understand material relevant to the chosen subject.

Once these decisions are made, they should be reflected in a specific statement of purpose, which should be written down by the source. A typical purpose statement would begin with, "The purpose of this speech (essay) is to get my audience," and be followed by such statements as: "to form a positive attitude toward intercollegiate wrestling"; "to change their attitude and become supportive of a tuition increase at this school"; "to be more favorable toward eliminating final examinations in courses"; or "to understand the new rule changes in intercollegiate basketball." This purpose statement should become the guiding light for the preparation of the message. The function of this specific statement of purpose will be very simple and direct. Anything that aids in the accomplishment of the purpose is potentially appropriate for inclusion in the final message. Anything that fails to contribute to the accomplishment of this purpose is inappropriate for inclusion.

GENERAL AUDIENCE ANALYSIS

At numerous points in the preceding chapters, we have emphasized the point that rhetorical communication is, and must be, audience centered. To

be audience-centered, a message must be specifically adapted to the particular audience for which it is intended. In order to adapt a message, then, the
source must know something about the audience. Every step in the communication process, as well as the parts leading up to it, must take into consideration the specific audience for which the message is intended. The
process of audience analysis is constant throughout rhetorical communication. In a sense, it never begins or ends. The discussion of selection of subject and purpose stated that these things must be done with the audience in
mind. Therefore, it is essential that the source undertake a general analysis
of the audience prior to the inception of the encoding process. During the
encoding process the source will become involved in more specific audience
analysis in relation to the individual ideas, or parts of ideas, that are considered for inclusion in the message. At this point, however, we are concerned
only with the general audience analysis.

The things that all audiences have in common are relatively few. We
have pointed out most of these in Chapter 4 and discussed them at some
length. In our general analysis of our audience, what we are seeking are the
distinctive characteristics of the particular audience for which we are going
to create a message. Some of those characteristics will be readily perceivable;
others will be very difficult, or even impossible, to determine. Let us look
first at some of those that are readily perceivable in most cases.

The first readily observable characteristic of an audience is the gender
of its members. Is the audience composed of all males, all females, or is it a
mixed audience? In many cases, men and women have different interests.
In addition, they may have very different attitudes toward certain concepts;
on other points men and women may think the same way. The question the
source must ask is, "Is the gender of the audience relevant to my specific
topic and to my purpose?" If the answer is yes, then the source will need to
consider gender further in developing the message.

As Aristotle noted in the *Rhetoric,* the ages of members of an audience
are highly relevant to their attitudes and to their political positions. Young
people, for example, tend to be somewhat more liberal than their elders.
That is quite understandable. The environment in which the young must live
is usually not primarily a product of their efforts. As one grows older, however, one becomes more responsible for the circumstances in which one finds
oneself. Consequently, a person tends to perceive past decisions as being
right ones, and anyone who wishes to change the person's beliefs is asking
the individual to admit that he or she was wrong in the past. Because this is
difficult for most people to admit, it is not surprising that older people tend
to be somewhat less susceptible to persuasion in the direction of change than
young people are. Similarly, older people have a greater respect for tradition
than do the young because they took part, in many cases, in establishing that
tradition. Although there are many individual exceptions, as people grow
older there is a tendency for them to become less impetuous, less given to
domination by their emotions, less idealistic, more pragmatic, more cynical,

and more suspicious. Thus, if the source is faced with an audience on primarily one age level, these factors of personality attributable to age must be taken into consideration.

Although age and gender may be readily observed, numerous other characteristics of an audience need to be perceived as well. The politics of an audience is of considerable importance. If it is composed entirely of people of the same political party—or rather, of the same wing of the same political party—their attitudes are likely to be very similar. Also, the religion of an audience may be important. For example, if a speaker is to talk on the subject of birth control, it would be wise to attempt to determine whether or not the audience is predominantly, or even partly, Roman Catholic. Also, what region of the country does the audience come from? People from Honolulu, Hawaii, from Platte, South Dakota, from State College, Pennsylvania, and from Norfolk, Virginia, are quite likely to have different attitudes, but are likely to have attitudes similar to those held by people in their own areas. It is also important, in many cases, to determine the socioeconomic level of the audience. If the audience comes primarily from one socioeconomic group, its attitudes on some topics are somewhat predictable. For example, a source discussing taxation will probably find a lower socioeconomic group more favorable to the income tax than to a flat-rate sales tax. Conversely, if the source is going to speak to an upper socioeconomic group, that group will be more likely to have unfavorable attitudes toward the income tax.

Examining these characteristics of audiences is important not so much for the particular characteristics in themselves but rather because of what we may be able to infer from them. Merely to know the age or the gender or the socioeconomic group the audience comes from really does not tell us anything. The question then becomes, "What is it that we should try to infer?"

Our main concern in the general audience analysis is to answer the following questions: *What are the audience's expectations? What motives are likely to be in operation in the audience? What are their major relevant attitudes? What will this audience probably perceive as the ethos of the given source?* We can seldom determine the answers to these questions with perfect precision. Rather, we are forced to guess what they might be. The more we know about the general characteristics of the audience, the better our guesses become.

Our general audience analysis must also include the circumstances surrounding the communicative event. We need to know where, when, and under what circumstances the communicative event will take place. Will it be in a large hall? Will it occur on a holiday? Will our message be published in a major news magazine? Shall we be speaking at a regular meeting of a club? Shall we be speaking in the morning, in the afternoon, or in the evening? Who will speak before us? Who will introduce us? As has been noted in the preceding chapters, all these factors are relevant both to the nature of the audience that will choose to expose itself to our message and to their perception of us as a source.

In short, in the general audience analysis, the source should attempt to find out everything possible about the audience and about the circumstances under which the communication will take place. In the specific message preparation, it will be necessary to make many decisions. These decisions are more likely to lead to effective rhetorical communication if the source properly perceives the nature of the audience. A source who prepares a message based on what is known about the audience is more likely to accomplish the intended purpose, and the more the source knows about the audience, the better.

CHANNELS AND FORMS FOR PRESENTATION OF MESSAGES

Another major decision the source must make prior to the inception of the encoding process is to select the channel to be used for transmitting the message. The two primary channels, of course, are written and oral-visual. Research reported by Knower indicates that this choice should be in favor of the oral-visual channel whenever possible. Knower observed that the transmission of messages through such channels produced significantly greater effects in the desired directions than messages transmitted through written channels.[1] *Whenever possible, the source should transmit the message through an oral-visual channel.*
        The selection of the oral-visual channel necessitates further choice. The transmission of the message in this way may occur either in a person-to-person situation or in the larger context of a person-to-group situation. Knower's research indicated that in the one-to-one situation, there is greater likelihood of the source's achieving the intended purpose than there is in the person-to-group situation.[2] Sometimes the source may actually choose the channel to use, but much more commonly the source has no choice at all. You may have been invited to speak, so you have the opportunity to employ the oral-visual channel, but you must speak to a group as a whole rather than to each individual member in isolation. Or you may be in a situation where you cannot speak to the audience at all, and the only way you can reach the audience is through the written channel. But if the source does have a choice, he or she should choose the oral-visual channel in the one-to-one situation. This is not to say that success in achieving communicative intent is foreclosed by using either the written channel or the oral-visual channel in the person-to-group situation; it is only to suggest the priority for the source in terms of where the greatest likelihood of success lies.
        The primary rhetorical communication format with which we are concerned in this section is the person-to-group format employing the oral-visual channel. Once this format is selected, the speaker must also choose among the four forms for the presentation of the message. These four forms have been called impromptu, extempore, manuscript, and memorized.

The *impromptu* speech form is employed when the source has had no opportunity for previous specific preparation. This does not mean that the source is ignorant on the subject, but only that he or she has not had an opportunity to follow procedures such as those outlined in the following chapters on message preparation. The source must analyze and adapt to the audience and create on the spot an appropriate message. *Extempore* speaking is a form in which the speaker has previous knowledge that he or she is going to speak and has an opportunity to engage in thorough preparation. The source is able to go through all such phases of preparation discussed in the following chapters and ordinarily presents the message with a limited number of notes. The *manuscript* speech is a step beyond the extempore speech. It is, in effect, an extempore speech that has been written out completely and then read to the audience. The *memorized* speech is simply a manuscript speech that has been memorized and presented to the audience from memory. Each of these forms has certain advantages and disadvantages.

The impromptu speech has the major advantage of being spontaneous. It provides opportunity for the source to react to feedback received from the audience and, thereby, to adapt to the audience on the spot. Its major disadvantage, of course, is that there is no previous preparation and, consequently, the likelihood of success is greatly reduced. The extempore speech, like the impromptu speech, has the advantage of permitting adaptation to feedback from the audience. It is a speech that is thoroughly prepared but is delivered from notes and consequently can vary as a result of perceived audience feedback.

The manuscript speech permits full use of the knowledge of style and language in communication. When the potential extempore speech is written out and becomes a manuscript speech, it may then be polished by the speaker to such a point that every word and phrase is carefully considered.

The main difficulty with the manuscript speech is presentation. Since it must be read to the audience, it is difficult for the speaker to maintain good delivery, particularly good eye contact with the audience. When the eye contact is not good, of course, it is very difficult to perceive audience feedback. However, even if this feedback is perceived, an additional disadvantage of the manuscript speech comes into play: It is difficult to adapt to an audience in a manuscript speech. This is because, once the adaptation is made, it is extremely difficult for the speaker to get back to the point in the manuscript where he or she left off. Even if the source gets back to the exact point, what has been written out may not necessarily follow from what has just been inserted as adaptation to the audience.

The memorized speech has the advantage over the manuscript in that direct eye contact is possible. It also has the advantage over the extempore speech in that full treatment of style is possible, as in the manuscript speech. The main disadvantage of memorized speaking is that it is extremely hard to adapt to the audience feedback that has been perceived. While it is difficult in the manuscript speech to adapt and then get back to the place where the speaker left off, in the memorized speech, it is almost impossible. Also, memorized speaking usually increases the tendency to suffer from stage fright.

Each of the forms for the presentation of a speech to an audience has certain advantages and certain disadvantages. The question is then, which form should the speaker normally select? *Select the extempore form in most circumstances.* The impromptu speech should be avoided when possible. It does not permit adequate preparation and thus severely restricts the opportunity for the speaker to develop the means of persuasion best suited to a given audience. The manuscript form provides stylistic superiority over the extemporaneous speech, but, practically speaking, precludes adaptation to audience feedback. Since such feedback greatly enhances the possibility of the source's being successful in carrying out the purpose, it is generally of greater importance than minute perfections of style. Since the memorized speech provides little advantage over the manuscript speech and also presents increased problems of stage fright or nervousness, it is far inferior to the extemporaneous form.

Because of the paramount importance of thorough, specific preparation and of adaptation to audience feedback, the extempore speech form is normally preferable to the three other forms. The exception to this generalization occurs when adaptation to feedback is precluded by the circumstances in which the communicative event takes place. Radio and television disturb the normal relationship between extempore and manuscript speaking. In these two contexts of person-to-group communication, there is no possibility of immediate feedback from the audience or of subsequent adaptation. Therefore, the stylistic superiority provided by the manuscript form makes it preferable to the extempore form. The manuscript form is also to be preferred in circumstances in which minute choices of wording are of paramount importance. In a presidential address, for example, every word the president speaks will be carefully scrutinized by the world press. Inadvertent word choice, such as may occur in extemporaneous speaking, sometimes can cause severe problems. For this reason, many government speakers, as well as speakers representing business, industry, or labor, will choose the manuscript style of speech to avoid such problems.

In general, then, the extemporaneous form should be used whenever possible except when word choice is of paramount importance. The following chapters presuppose the employment of the oral-visual channel, the person-to-group format, and the extemporaneous form. This is certainly not to suggest that the material included in these chapters has relevance only under these circumstances. In most cases this material is directly relevant to communication in other channels, formats, and forms. It is important, however, that the reader be aware of the context for which the material in these chapters is intended while being exposed to it.

SELECTION OF SOURCE FOR PRESENTATION

So far we have used the term *source* to designate the person who has the idea and who will be responsible for generating the message to be transmitted to an audience. This is not always the same person or group that the audience perceives to be the source. One of the definite choices that must be made in rhetorical communication is who shall be the source to transmit the message. Normally, of course, the person who generates the idea and the message is also the person who transmits the message and who is perceived by the audience to be the source. If the originator of the idea and the message is a group of people or a person with the power to hire or delegate a representative, this selection of source is important. Certain guidelines should be followed. Obviously, the higher the ethos an individual has with a given audience, the better that person will serve as the source to transmit the message. In addition to this factor, three others should be taken into consideration.

On the basis of Knower's research, it appears that a source's gender is important. Knower observed that male sources were more influential with female audience members and females were more influential with male audience members.[3] Consequently, if the audience is all male or all female, or predominantly one or the other, and there is a choice between a male and a female speaker, the choice should take into consideration Knower's findings. Another important factor is how close an identification a prospective source has with a given audience. In most cases we tend to pay more attention to people in our own group and in some cases tend to identify with them more and thus believe them more. Of course, this is not always the case. Sometimes a remote individual will have a greater impact. Finally, the selection of the source should take into consideration the abilities of the prospective speakers in delivery. Certainly the speaker chosen should have adequate delivery and, other things being equal, the speaker with the best delivery should be chosen. Naturally, all of the other factors contributing to source credibility and ethos should be considered in the selection of a source, as discussed in Chapter 5.

PERCEPTION OF THE POSSIBLE

One of the most common weaknesses of people who hope to be effective rhetorical communicators is to attempt to accomplish too much. The power of the spoken and written word is certainly great, but is not as great as we sometimes think. The speaker who hopes to convert an audience composed of members of the Right to Life movement to support federal aid for abortion in one ten-minute speech is hoping for far too much. If the source should succeed in accomplishing this goal with even one member of such an audience, he or she will be remarkably successful.

The source must, therefore, attempt to perceive what is possible with a particular audience. *Attempting to achieve more than is possible often causes the source to achieve far less than is possible.* In many cases, this fact necessitates modifying the most desired purpose of the source. This does not mean that a person must compromise her or his beliefs, but that he or she should attempt only to get an audience to accept that part of the overall structure of belief that is possible within the time and the circumstances surrounding the communicative event.

This chapter has been concerned with the preliminary considerations that you should take into account before beginning the encoding process. Once all of these factors have been considered, you are ready to begin the preparation of the message for the audience. The remaining chapters in this part of the book are concerned with the essentials of message preparation. The essential activities of message preparation may be classified, as rhetoricians for centuries have classified them, according to the classical canons of rhetoric: invention, disposition, style, delivery, and memory (we shall not consider memory separately in this book). Although these classifications are useful for purposes of exposition of theory, it should be kept in mind that these categories are far from discrete. Invention, disposition, and style are heavily dependent upon one another and so interrelated that it is often difficult to determine precisely with which activity a source is involved at a given moment. This interrelationship will be discussed further. In order to find that discussion meaningful, it will be necessary to develop some understanding of invention and disposition, the subjects of Chapters 11 and 12. Before turning to these vital matters, however, we will consider the construction of informative messages. Such messages are not only important in their own right, but they also provide the foundation for other messages.

DISCUSSION QUESTIONS

1. Many people consider audience analysis the first step in the preparation of a message for rhetorical communication. Do you agree? Why, or why not?

2. What demographic data about an audience, in addition to that discussed in this chapter, might be helpful to a source?

3. A preference for extempore speaking over other forms of oral presentation, and over the written channel, was expressed in this chapter. Do you agree with this preference? Why, or why not?

NOTES

1. F. H. Knower, "Experimental Studies of Changes in Attitude; (11) A Study of the Effect of Printed Argument on Changes in Attitude," *Journal of Abnormal and Social Psychology* 30 (1936): 522–32.

2. F. H. Knower, "Experimental Studies of Changes in Attitudes; (1) A Study of the Effect of Oral Argument on Changes of Attitudes," *Journal of Social Psychology* 6 (1935): 315–47.

3. See also G. E. Steffens, "An Experimental Study of the Effects of the Sex of the Communicator on Perceived Ethos and Attitude Change," M.A. thesis, Michigan State University, 1967. Steffens was unable to replicate the Knower findings. The changes in gender roles and stereotypes in contemporary society may make sex differences less important than they were in the past. Nevertheless, the safe choice is the one recommended here.

CHAPTER 10

INFORMATIVE MESSAGES

All messages in rhetorical communication are designed to influence the thoughts or actions of other people. The source's intent is always to influence. Informative messages are designed to influence how other people understand things. They are not designed to influence people's attitudes. They may, however, have such an effect.

PERSUASIVE VERSUS INFORMATIVE INTENT

Chapter 2 approached the question of whether there is such a thing as informative communication. The text at that point indicated an avoidance of controversy over the question. At this point, however, the question must be considered directly. Is there such a thing as informative intent? The fact that the present author chooses to include this chapter indicates his belief that there is. This is not to suggest that everything that goes under the term *informative* conforms to our conception of informative intent.

Most so-called informative speeches and essays are definitely motivated by persuasive, rather than informative, intent. This distinction between persuasive and informative intent is based on projected attitudinal effects. A source with persuasive intent has a conscious desire to influence the attitudes of the audience. A source with informative intent consciously rejects the desire to influence the audience's attitudes. While these two categories are mutually exclusive, there is a type of intent-message combination that does not fall clearly into either of them. In this circumstance, a source often presents a message that appears on the surface to be informative but that in reality is designed to influence audience attitudes. Thus, some messages are directly intended to influence attitude (persuasive messages); some messages are directly intended to influence understanding and are not specifically designed to influence attitudes in a predetermined manner (informative messages); and some messages are specifically designed to influence understanding but are designed unconsciously to influence attitudes (persuasive messages).

The real problem in distinguishing between persuasive and informative intent is the factor described in Chapter 2 as noise in the source. This book has previously suggested at several points that the communicator must clearly perceive his or her intent with regard to the audience. In such a case, the intent to persuade or inform will be apparent. The messages generated as a result of these two distinct types of intent are easily recognizable and significantly different from one another. The problem comes in when the source is fuzzy about his or her own intent and perceives it as informative when, in reality, it is persuasive. The source may perceive that the intent, for example, is to inform the audience on the question of capital punishment. But the message presents only information leading to the conclusion that capital punishment should be abolished. Our fuzzy-thinking source may never admit that the goal was to persuade the audience to adopt the attitude that capital punishment should be abolished. The source may tenaciously cling to the belief that he or she really wanted the audience to understand the facts about capital punishment. The intent, nevertheless, is a persuasive one.

Only when there is no desire to influence the attitudes or actions of other people can a source truly have informative intent. Thus, *whenever a source has either a conscious or unconscious intent to persuade, he or she does not have informative intent.*

Chapter 12 will discuss the difference between one-sided and two-sided messages within the context of persuasive communication. These terms are actually misnomers, since persuasive communication is always one-sided. A so-called two-sided message in persuasive communication is merely a persuasive strategy for gaining the acceptance of the source's position. In informative communication, however, the real two-sided message can and should exist. It would treat both sides equally in presenting reliable information. This, of course, is quite different from the two-sided approach in persuasion. The reason this difference can exist is that when there is persuasive intent, the source has already determined in his or her own mind what the best side is, and the primary purpose in communicating is to gain the audience's acceptance of that side. When there is informative intent, however, the source is not concerned with the effect the message may have upon the attitudes of the audience. Rather, he or she wishes to present the information relevant to the topic so that the members of the audience may understand it and draw their own conclusions. These conclusions, unlike those in the persuasive situations, are of no concern to the source.

PSEUDO-INFORMATIVE MESSAGES

The pseudo-informative message is a persuasive message presented in an apparently informative format. All the trappings of objectivity are present in the message, particularly during the early portions. The message may look or sound like an informative message, but it is a consciously persuasive device employed by many sources. This persuasive device must be carefully distinguished from informative messages. Both the intent and the effect of these two types of messages are different. This is not to suggest that there is anything wrong with the pseudo-informative message. At this point, the reader should simply note the distinction; the persuasive strategy will be considered in a later chapter.

THE GOODWILL INFORMATIVE MESSAGE

Chapter 5 noted a distinction between concept-centered communication and ethos-centered communication, pointing out that many organizations and individuals present speeches and write pamphlets and other materials in order to enhance their images. As we approach an understanding of informative messages, we must clearly distinguish between such messages and those that are ethos-centered persuasion. Typically, ethos-centered persuasive messages inform the audience about something related to an organization or individual. *The purpose in the goodwill informative message is to enhance the image or ethos of the organization or individual, not to provide understanding for the audience, even though factual information may be provided.* Telephone companies have representatives giving speeches about their companies to clubs and school groups all over the United States. These messages definitely do provide the audiences with interesting information that increases their understanding of how the company operates. However, the source of these messages is primarily motivated by a persuasive intent. That intent is to enhance the audiences' favorable image of the company. It just so happens that presenting information is the device chosen for increasing the tendency of the audience to favor the company. Such messages, while producing some informative effects, have persuasive intent and primarily persuasive effect.

THE MOTIVATION TO INFORM

The motivation to persuade may be described as selfish. We go out of our way to persuade people to accept our ideas primarily because we believe their acceptance of those ideas will be either directly beneficial to us or to those who are important to us, or indirectly beneficial to us through the improvement of society. Perceived benefit is the primary motivation of persuasive communicators. It is rare, indeed, for a human being to attempt to persuade someone to accept an idea that is contrary to the persuader's well-being.

The motivation for informing other people, however, includes more aspects of altruism. It is not uncommon for an informative communicator to receive no direct or indirect benefit from her or his effort. This is not to say that the informative communicator will never benefit, but merely that he or she need not perceive any benefit before choosing to address an audience.

Teachers are the people with whom we most directly identify informative communication. Many teachers are motivated to go into their profession by altruistic goals. While they may believe that if everyone in the country or the world had greater understanding, the whole world would be a better place for themselves and their loved ones to live in, they must realistically perceive that their contribution to the overall good will be minimal. Thus, the benefits that the individual teacher receives through improvement of society are actually slight. The teacher, however, does improve the well-being of students by increasing their understanding of the world about them. Of course, even teachers are not purely altruistic. Although the tangible rewards for their efforts, in the United States at least, are somewhat less than overwhelming, the intangible rewards they receive from knowing that they have made a worthwhile contribution to the lives of other people make up, in some measure, for this difference.

Informative intent, therefore, is motivated by both selfish and altruistic purposes, whereas persuasive intent is primarily selfishly motivated. This is not to suggest that one type of intent is morally superior to another but merely that the two types arise from somewhat different motivations.

UNDERSTANDING AND BELIEF

Although I believe that there is such a thing as informative intent accompanying informative messages, I must admit that I hold this belief only on the basis of definition. I have defined informative intent as distinct from persuasive intent. I have said that one seeks understanding but the other seeks attitude or behavior change. Are these two really different?

Chapter 4 noted the similarities between belief and attitude, further indicating that most of the things discussed concerning attitudes also applied to beliefs. The real problem in distinguishing between informative and persuasive intent in messages is distinguishing between understanding and belief. I do not believe such a distinction can be made unambiguously. What understanding really is, is belief. We may have a very simple message describing how to load a Polaroid camera. The goal of that message is for the receiver to "understand" how to load the Polaroid camera. But what the "understanding" really consists of is a group of beliefs. The message is designed to get the receiver to believe that putting the film in a certain way is the best method of loading the camera. It is designed to get the receiver to believe that inserting the flashbulb in a certain way is the best method of inserting the flashbulb. Certainly many persuasive elements come into play here. If the source attempts to demonstrate the insertion of film and flashbulb, and we see that the film will not go in the way described or that the flashbulb does not fire when inserted in a certain way, we believe that this is not the proper way to load the camera. According to the source, we do not "understand" how to load the camera.

We can also see the difficulty of making a belief–understanding distinction by looking at communication in ordinary classrooms. First, consider the social studies teacher who explains to the fifth grade class, "Slavery was the primary cause of the American Civil War." Teachers, for most fifth graders at least, are seen as credible, and if the teacher says it is so, it is so. Thus, the child "understands" the cause of the Civil War and can provide the correct answer on the test that comes later. Second, consider the college teacher who explains to the upper-division Civil War history class full of history majors, "Slavery was the primary cause of the American Civil War." Such students have heard and read a great deal about the Civil War, and they are very likely not to accept the teacher's assertion about slavery as a fact. From their perspective, they do not "believe" what the teacher says. From the teacher's perspective, they do not "understand" the cause of the Civil War.

A necessary condition for achieving informative effect, then, is an adequate level of credibility for the source. If we do not believe that the source is relatively knowledgeable and trustworthy on the subject being discussed, we may perceive the message as persuasive rather than informative. If the Secretary General of the United Nations comes before us and informs us about the workings of that organization, we are likely, upon the completion of the message, to "understand" the workings of the UN. We believe what the Secretary General says. But if a high school boy comes before us with the same message, we may very well ask, "How does this person know what he is talking about?" He may say the same thing, but we may not believe that it is true. Therefore, we will not "understand" how the U.N. works from the source's point of view.

Clearly, then, there is much persuasion within an informative message. The informative communicator must "persuade" the audience to hear or to read the message. He or she must also "persuade" the audience to believe that the information given is accurate. Understanding is based upon belief, and that belief is instilled in informative messages in much the same manner as it is in persuasive messages, by use of prior belief, source credibility, or presentation of evidence.

UNDERSTANDING: DETERMINING THE INFORMATIVE GOAL

The term *understanding* has been used several times in this and preceding chapters. You have probably felt that you "understood" what was meant by the term. You were probably right. But at this point we need to consider the concept of understanding in more depth so that we can begin to select from among the possible informative goals for our messages.

Irving Lee has suggested seven definitions for the term *understanding*.[1] Each of these definitions provides us with a possible informative goal. Let us consider each of the definitions and the accompanying goals.

1. **The following of directions.** Our receiver understands us when he or she does something the way we want it done. Goal: to enable the receiver to accomplish a task in the manner we prescribe.
2. **The making of predictions.** Our receiver understands us when he or she can predict what behavior we will engage in after receiving the message. Goal: to enable the receiver to specify our future behavior.
3. **The giving of verbal equivalents.** Our receiver understands us when he or she can express our idea in terms that are adequate approximations of the way we would express the idea. Goal: to enable the receiver to adequately express an idea we have selected.
4. **The agreeing on of programs.** Our receiver understands us when he or she undertakes an action that both of us have agreed upon. Goal: to enable the receiver to undertake an action that he or she and we have agreed should be undertaken.
5. **The solving of problems.** Our receiver understands us when he or she can recognize the steps that must be taken to solve a problem. Goal: to enable the receiver to recognize the steps that must be taken to solve a specific problem.
6. **The making of appropriate responses.** Our receiver understands us when he or she is able to make responses to stimuli that we consider appropriate. Goal: to enable the receiver to make a given response to a given stimulus.
7. **The making of proper evaluations.** Our receiver understands us when he or she is able to respond to a stimulus of our selection independent from any other stimuli present. Goal: to enable the receiver to isolate and respond to a given stimulus independent from other competing internal and external stimuli.

As you read the seven goals above, you may have noticed that each was expressed in behavioral terms, that is, in terms of behaviors that the receiver might undertake. As noted previously, the goal of persuasive messages is to stimulate receivers to engage in predetermined behaviors. Thus, it is essential that we make a clear distinction between persuasive goals and the informative goals listed here. The key word is *enable*. The goal of informative messages is to *enable* the receiver to engage in certain behaviors, not to get him or her to do so. Our receiver "understands" us when he or she is *able* to engage in certain specified behaviors; our receiver is "persuaded" when he or she actually *engages* in the behaviors.

Because understanding relates to the ability to act rather than to action itself, it is often difficult for us, as sources, to determine whether we have succeeded in our informative goal. The receiver may have developed the ability to engage in a certain behavior as a result of our message but may choose, for any of a number of reasons not obvious to us, not to engage in that behavior.

Your first step in developing an informative message is to select from the available informative goals those that are appropriate for the communication transaction in which you are to engage. You will often discover that what you really seek to accomplish with your receiver is a behavior change, not one of the informative goals listed. There is nothing wrong with that; but when this happens, your goal is a persuasive rather than an informative one, and your message should be developed with that fact in mind.

CHARACTERISTICS OF INFORMATIVE MESSAGES

The two primary characteristics of informative messages are *clarity* and *objectivity.* Clarity is a stylistic virtue in nearly all messages. In some cases of persuasive communication, ambiguity can be superior to clarity as a means of producing the desired effect.[2] In messages for informative communication, however, clarity is always a virtue. We cannot hope to be understood unless our message is clear. Objectivity is not a necessary characteristic of persuasive messages. Persuaders are biased, or they would not attempt to persuade. They draw their conclusions and then design their messages to gain acceptance of the conclusions by other people. There may be *apparent* objectivity in a persuasive message, but in most cases, it is not real. Informative messages, however, must be objective if they are to be informative. An informative message is concerned with what actually *is*, not with what the source wants to establish.

THE MATERIALS FOR INFORMATIVE MESSAGES

The materials appropriate for informative messages are not, for the most part, substantially different from those appropriate for messages designed to influence audience attitude. The most significant difference is related to argument. Argument, as described in Chapter 6, is not present in truly informative messages. However, an examination of such messages would lead us, in many cases, to conclude that arguments are present. We sometimes observe certain materials within the message that may be interpreted as argument when their true function is not clearly understood. As we have noted, the primary characteristics of informative messages are clarity and objectivity. Objectivity precludes the employment of argument as discussed in this book. Clarity, however, requires that we employ in informative messages materials that could also be used to establish argument. The most useful materials are analogies, factual examples, hypothetical examples, and statistics. A reading of the following discussion will indicate that these categories of materials are not unrelated to one another. The use of a category in order to clarify an idea often requires use of material from one or more additional categories.

Analogies

Analogies are the primary means of clarifying ideas in informative messages. In some cases, complex ideas can be understood only by the use of analogy. Communication models, such as those presented in Chapter 2, are merely complex analogies. Understanding the relationships within the model gives a clearer picture of the communication process. It is necessary to be careful in using analogies, however, because they have a natural tendency either to magnify or to minimize an idea's importance. Thus, our analogies may remove many of the characteristics of objectivity that we seek to incorporate in informative messages. Consider the following examples of analogies, employed to clarify the meaning of three billion dollars as an amount of money spent on a certain government program.

> **Analogy 1.** How much is three billion dollars? Well, let us compare it to something we college students can understand—the cost of our education. With three billion dollars, we could pay for the tuition of every student in our nation's twenty-five largest universities and still have enough money left over to pay for the room, board, and incidental expenses of every one of those students.
>
> **Analogy 2.** How much is three billion dollars? Well, let us compare it to something we have all heard a lot about. Three billion dollars represents approximately two percent of the estimated amount of money Americans spend annually on illegal gambling. It also represents less than one percent of our Federal government's annual budget.

Either of these analogies would help to clarify the meaning of three billion dollars. The first analogy, however, would tend to make the audience perceive three billion dollars as being a very, very, large amount of money, whereas the second analogy would tend to make the audience perceive it as a comparatively small amount of money. Analogies are extremely useful for clarifying ideas because they tend to relate the unfamiliar to the familiar. They must be employed with care, however, so that the objectivity of the informative message is not destroyed. One of the best ways in which to determine whether a given message is informative or persuasive in intent is to examine the analogies employed by the source. If they consistently magnify or minify ideas in a given direction, the message probably is intended to be persuasive. If, however, the magnification and minification produced by the analogies tend to balance out, the message probably is informative in intent.

Factual Examples

A factual example describes a real thing or event. If I say water pollution is an important problem in the state of Michigan, most people will have a general idea of what I am referring to, but they will not have a really clear picture, particularly if they are not native Michiganders. However, if I relate the following story, the example makes the meaning much clearer.

> Last winter I moved to a new home approximately two blocks from the Red Cedar River in East Lansing, Michigan. At that time the river was frozen and there was snow covering it; it was a beautiful sight. Each day as I drove across the bridge on my way into town, I admired the beautiful scenery surrounding the river. However, as the winter progressed, I noticed an increasing amount of trash on the ice. As the days went by, a collection of rubbish appeared. There were boards, beer bottles, waste paper, and a dead rabbit—all visible from the bridge. Hundreds of people crossed that bridge every day, but they, as I, did nothing to remove the trash from the ice. When spring came the ice melted and the trash disappeared. For the first few days after the ice had melted, the Red Cedar River was a sparkling blue stream. But the beauty of the river lasted only a few days. Within a week it had turned a rust color, and there were oil slicks floating by. The level of the river dropped a couple of feet and left a black mass visible on the banks. One day I stopped my car and walked down to the edge of the river. Or rather I walked toward the river. I did not go all the way because the stench from the water was almost overpowering. Instead of a sparkling blue river, stinking, greasy slime flowed between the banks. That is the water pollution problem that we face in Michigan.

Hypothetical Example

The hypothetical example is an imaginary instance that is told to the audience. In many cases a hypothetical example will be as effective as a factual example, if not more so. Consider the following hypothetical example.

> Let us imagine that you are the head of an average American family. You are married and have two children. You have a down payment on your house and are paying monthly installments, and you are doing the same with your car. One day, your six-year-old daughter comes in and claims that she has a pain in her chest. You think it probably is not too important but you decide you had better take her to the doctor to see if anything is seriously wrong. When the doctor tells you that she has a serious heart condition that will require open-heart surgery, you are shocked. Like many young American families, you have health insurance, but it has limits on what it will pay for many kinds of problems.

You check your insurance company and they tell you that their policy will cover $50,000 of the cost. However, the doctor tells you that the total cost, including surgery and the necessary hospitalization, will run over $250,000! You are faced with a choice: You can let your daughter die, or you can subject yourself to financial catastrophe. You will not let her die, so you sell your house and borrow every dollar you can get your hands on. And you spend the next five to ten years trying to pay the money back. This type of financial disaster is what I refer to when I say that medical expenses for families not adequately covered by major medical insurance can produce severe financial hardship. We have one of the best medical systems in the world, but it costs a lot of money, and most of us can't afford it.

Statistics

Statistics can stimulate considerable interest in an informative message when used effectively. The mere recitation of figures, however, is likely to bore the audience rather than interest it. Statistics need to be qualified and made interesting when presented in an informative message. When statistics are employed in conjunction with analogies, factual examples, or hypothetical examples, the statistics take on new meaning and add new interest to the message. Statistics may be inherently clear to the statistician, but they are not inherently clear to the average audience member. Consequently, the source must exert extra effort to be certain that the statistics employed are meaningful and clear to the audience.

VISUAL AIDS IN INFORMATIVE COMMUNICATION

Empirical research on informative communication, unlike that relating to persuasive communication, generally has been unenlightening. As Petrie stated after summarizing this body of research, "Reading experimental literature about informative speaking is disappointing and sometimes frustrating. Such studies are so limited in number and the results are so inconclusive and inconsistent that few, if any, conclusions can be drawn."[3] Although Petrie's conclusion is over three decades old and still remains generally correct, one area of research relating to informative communication has provided relatively unequivocal results: the use of visual aids in conjunction with verbal messages significantly increases the amount of learning by the audience. Estimates of the amount of improvement produced by visual aids run as high as 55 percent.[4] Clearly then, the rhetorical communicator who hopes to increase the audience's understanding should consider the use of visual aids. Photos, drawings, charts, graphs, and maps may be employed by sources using either the oral or the written channel. Oral communicators

have additional visual aids they may also employ, including blackboards, easels, objects, Power Point, and handouts. Sources who wish to enhance audience understanding should always consider using visual aids.

Suggestions for Using Visual Aids

Properly employed, visual aids can be a tremendous asset in clarifying ideas. Improperly employed, they can better be described as visual hindrances. If the suggestions below are followed, the likelihood of these materials being visual hindrances will be greatly reduced.

1. Be certain that the entire audience can see the visual aid. This suggestion is really two suggestions. First, when you are preparing a visual aid, make it large enough so that it can be seen. If you are not making the visual aid but have it available, be sure that it is large enough to be seen before deciding to include it. It cannot be a visual *aid* if people cannot see it. The author recalls a speaker discussing valuable coins before an audience of three hundred people. At one point, he held up a dime that was over a hundred years old. Even the front row could barely see the dime. It was obviously not a visual aid. Second, be certain to display the visual aid in such a manner that it may be seen by all members of the audience. A visual aid held straight forward may be visible to most people in the middle of the audience, but may be totally obscured from the vision of the people to the speaker's left and right. You should turn the picture, or any other visual aid, so that it can be seen in turn by the various sections of the audience.

2. Avoid talking to the visual aid instead of to the audience. One of the most irritating characteristics shown by speakers using visual aids is that, as soon as one is displayed, they begin talking to the aid rather than to the audience. The visual aid seems to become more important in the speaker's mind than the audience is. Certainly if you need to point out things on the visual aid you must look at it, but you can look at it, point to the element of interest, and then turn your attention back to the audience.

3. Remove the visual aid from sight when through with it. Even the most useful visual aid can outlive its usefulness. If it is left in view of the audience after you have finished with it, it is most likely that the audience will continue to look at it. This is particularly true when the speaker is not dynamic. Thus, even a good visual aid may become a distracting element.

4. Ordinarily, keep the visual aid in your possession. Visual aids should seldom be handed to the audience. Only when each person in the audience can have a copy should a visual aid be passed out at all during a speech. Passing things around removes the attention of segments of the audience from the parts of your message that follow. If the visual aid must be closely inspected by each member of the audience before its usefulness can be achieved, you may consider passing it out before the speech begins. Or, if this is not feasible, you may pass it around and simply stop speaking while that is being done. Another alternative is to wait until the completion of the speech to pass the visual aid to the audience. Rarely should a visual aid be handed from person to person in the audience while the speaker continues speaking.

5. Use visual aids that are clear and that need little or no explanation. A very complex visual aid can be more of a hindrance than a help. The visual aid should be used to help clarify what is meant in the verbal message, not the other way around. Of course, there are exceptions to this. In some cases a source might be attempting to explain the function of the complex object. Then the object itself, although very complex, will help to clarify meaning. In most cases, however, the more simple and clear the visual aid is, the greater will be its benefit.

6. Use visual aids that catch attention. Visual aids should be inherently interesting for the audience. In many cases, a little extra effort can make a dull visual aid interesting. Charts can be black and white, but adding colors will increase their attention-getting quality. A caption over a picture will, in some cases, capture attention when the picture itself is not particularly interesting. You should always ask yourself whether anything can be done to increase the interest in the visual aids you plan to use. If there is, generally it should be done.

7. Use visual aids only when they serve a definite purpose. Visual aids should not accompany verbal messages just so as to have a visual aid. All of us at one time or another have heard speeches in which the speaker employed needless and meaningless visual aids. A common practice of some speakers is to write numbers or letters on a blackboard or easel to represent each point in the speech. For the most part this is useless, and in some cases it is distracting. The test of any visual aid is whether it will make a meaningful contribution to the clarity or interest of the verbal message.

8. Beware of electronic devices. The use of aids such as motion pictures, television, overhead projectors, opaque projectors, Power Point, computer imagery, and slides can be of enormous help to a speaker trying to inform an audience. Hence, many beginning speakers turn first to such electronic devices and assume they *must* have these devices to be successful. This is seldom the case; in fact, such devices may have caused the failure of more informative presentations than any other single factor. One of "Murphy's Laws" applies all too frequently: If an electrical device can fail, it will do so just when it is most needed for a presentation. Flashy aids are fine, but simple aids are more likely to work when you need them. When considering use of electronic devices, always be prepared for disaster by having a complete answer to this question: What will I do when this equipment is not available or will not work? If your only answer is "Panic!" scratch the gadget.

DISCUSSION QUESTIONS

1. Some people believe that a communicator always has either a conscious or an unconscious desire to persuade an audience. Do you agree? Why, or why not?

2. An author of a book on rhetorical communication is engaging in an act of rhetorical communication. Do you believe the present author's primary interest is to inform or persuade? Why?

3. Do visual aids serve a different function in messages with informative intent than they serve in those with persuasive intent? Why?

4. Read the student speech "The Proposed Basketball Rule Changes," which appears in Appendix A. Is this an informative message? Why or why not?

NOTES

1. I. J. Lee, "Why Discussions Go Astray," in *Language, Meaning and Maturity*, ed. S. I. Hayakawa (New York: Harper and Rowe, Pub., 1954), pp. 42–43.

2. B. C. Limb, "Speech: The Life of the Diplomat," *Quarterly Journal of Speech* 53 (1957): 55–61.

3. C. R. Petrie, Jr., "Informative Speaking: A Summary and Bibliography of Related Research," *Speech Monographs* 30 (1963): 79–97.

4. H. E. Nelson and A. W. VanderMeer, "Varied Sound Tracks on Animated Film," *Speech Monographs* 20 (1953): 261–67.

■ ■ ■ ■ ■

CHAPTER 11

MESSAGE PREPARATION: INVENTION

The quality of invention is the key to effective rhetorical communication. The purpose of this chapter is to detail procedures for the invention of material appropriate for the desired messages.

INVENTION DEFINED

Baird tells us that invention "refers to the investigation, analysis, and grasp of subject matter."[1] This view of the nature of invention is representative of the views of the majority of the writers on rhetorical communication in the past. Nevertheless, it is misleading. Investigation, analysis, and grasp of subject matter are not part of invention; rather, they must precede invention.

The model of the rhetorical communication process in Chapter 2 (Figure 2.2) distinguished what occurred prior to rhetorical communication from what was part of the first phase of the process, namely, encoding. The text stated that encoding is the process of translating a preconceived idea into a message for transmission to a receiver. The term *translating* is important here. It rightly implies the occurrence of a change. Obviously, something must exist before it can be changed. Therefore, a source must investigate the subject thoroughly, analyze it completely, and secure a very good grasp of it in order to be ready to translate this knowledge into a message appropriate for presentation to a receiver.

Investigation and analysis of materials are processes by which people attempt to identify fact or truth. *Invention is the process by which communicators adapt to an audience what they have determined to be fact or truth, in order to accomplish a predetermined purpose.* The distinction between investigation and invention is a crucial one. Failure to observe it has caused many textbook writers to present platitudes about investigation rather than procedures for invention. In this context, the words of Wilson and Arnold are pertinent.

The authors of this book believe it is not very profitable to enjoin speakers to Think, Read, Digest, and then to leave them with these noble injunctions. Neither do we think speakers are helped much by textbooks and writers who exhaust vocabulary in deploring the undeniable superficiality of much student and other contemporary speaking. Something more practical is wanted. *Method* in inventing what is to be said is more important than hours spent in intellectual and emotional agitation.[2]

Aristotle defined rhetoric as "the faculty of discovering in a particular case what are the available means of persuasion." While this definition probably is not fully adequate for rhetoric, it does seem to be an adequate definition of invention. Invention is the discovery aspect of rhetoric. It is not the discovery of ideas as such; it is rather the discovery of what particular ideas are most likely to be helpful to the source in achieving the intended purpose with the audience. Assuming that thorough investigation has uncovered what is knowable about the subject, invention is the process of discovering what, among the knowables, is sayable by the particular source to the particular audience on the particular occasion to accomplish a particular purpose.

THE BASIC PLAN

The first step in invention is to develop a basic (preliminary) plan for the message. The final plan will be developed later when the source directs attention to disposition. We shall consider that part of message preparation in detail in the next chapter. In this first step in invention, it is necessary only to develop a basic plan that the source can keep in mind during the inventional process. This plan may be, and frequently is, substantially changed during the dispositional phase of message preparation. We may liken the source's problem at this point to that of a woman living in Pennsylvania who decides to take a trip to California. Her first job is to look at road maps to get a general idea of where she must go. After she has examined the states and cities she could possibly pass through, she establishes a complete route for her trip. But before such a detailed route can be developed, it is essential for the traveler to know where she is going and, in general, what path she is going to follow in order to get there.

The first factor the source should consider in developing a basic plan is the problem of selective exposure. Will the people you want to influence be present to hear your speech? You may wish to change people's attitudes on some topic, but those people may choose not to attend your talk because they oppose your views. Messages designed to strengthen the attitudes of people who agree with you may be very different from messages designed to change opponents' views. If you want to generate more supporters for your position, you may need to take special care that selective exposure does not prevent you from speaking to potential converts to your position.

The second factor the source should consider in developing a basic plan for a message is the concept of balance. Since the balance or tension-reduction theories were discussed at length in Chapter 4, they will not be explored in depth here. It is very important, however, to employ these theories at this step in invention. The primary function of rhetorical communication is to move an audience from where it is at the outset of the message to where the source wants it to be at the close of the message. Thus, the source must take the audience as it is and mold that audience into what he or she wants it to be. By employing the concept of balance, we can theorize in advance about what kinds of changes are going to occur in the minds of the audience as the message proceeds. Such an approach has been found very effective in designing messages that will both change attitudes and protect the ethos of the source.[3]

The third factor to consider in developing the basic plan is the audience's experiences subsequent to hearing the message. Is it necessary for the source to include in the message elements that will inoculate the audience against counterpersuasion they will receive later? If the audience is going to be exposed to persuasion contrary to the view of the source, it is vitally important to take this into account, even in the earliest stages of message preparation. A basic plan, then, should always include awareness of points that will require inoculation.

THE GENERATION OF ARGUMENT

Argument constitutes the bulk of the message when the source seeks to form an attitude, to strengthen an attitude, or to change an attitude—three of the four possible goals in rhetorical communication (see Chapter 2). It becomes necessary, therefore, for the source to generate the required arguments. Generating arguments for a message includes determining what arguments are needed and the actual creation of those arguments.

DETERMINATION OF NEEDED ARGUMENTS

To determine the arguments needed, the source should follow a systematic plan. Such a plan begins with determining the ultimate claim for the series of arguments to be developed. Consider a hypothetical situation: Assume that our communicator, a man who is president of a supermarket chain, wishes to convince the board of directors that they should immediately approve a plan for plant expansion rather than waiting until next year. He knows his ultimate claim at the onset: We should expand our plant imme-

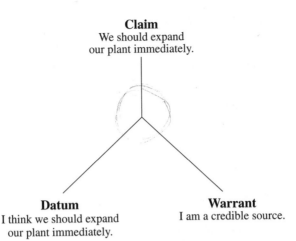

FIGURE 11.1   Argument Based on Source's Own Ethos.

diately. The source's invention must be based on this ultimate claim. He should ask himself, "What data and warrant can I use to lead my audience to accept this claim?"

His first choice might be to base the argument on his own authority. Such an argument could be the one diagrammed in Figure 11.1. Such an argument is very simple and direct. The total message to be presented, if the source decides that this is an adequate argument, will be very brief and to the point. He will simply get the attention of his audience, assert that the concern should expand the plant, and ask the audience's approval. The source will be depending entirely upon his own ethos as his means of persuasion. In audience analysis, he will need to answer the simple question "Will the audience accept my argument on the basis of my personal prestige?" If he can answer yes to this question, he has found his means of persuasion. If he must answer no, he will need to continue this phase of the inventional process.

Let us assume that the source believes his ethos is not high enough to gain acceptance of the claim if it is based strictly upon his assertion. He may then consider appealing directly to the audience's self-interest. He may generate an argument such as the one in Figure 11.2. If this is an argument the source thinks may be employed, he will need to analyze his audience to determine two questions: (1) Does the audience believe that the company will save money by expanding now rather than later? (2) Is the audience motivated by the desire to save money? If both answers are in the affirmative, the source may have found the basic argument for his message. However, if either one of the answers is no, invention must continue. If the audience does not believe that money will be saved by immediate expansion,

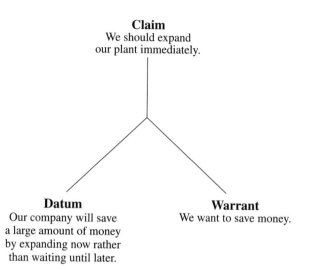

Claim
We should expand
our plant immediately.

Datum
Our company will save
a large amount of money
by expanding now rather
than waiting until later.

Warrant
We want to save money.

FIGURE 11.2   Argument Based on Audience's Self-Interest.

the communicator must treat this proposed datum as a claim and proceed to generate an argument to support it. If the motive of saving money is not important to the audience, the source may seek to establish that motive, or, more likely, to find a motive to replace the one in question.

Assuming for the moment that the audience is motivated by the desire to save money, let us consider how the source may develop an argument to support the data for his basic argument. He may generate an argument like the one diagrammed in Figure 11.3. If we assume the acceptance of this argument, we then have a two-argument message, one argument leading to the acceptance of the other. Assume that the audience does not immediately accept the data of the second argument; they are not aware that construction costs are due to go up after July 1. In this case, the communicator must convince them that it is going to happen. To do this he may generate an argument like the one represented in Figure 11.4. At this point we have three newly generated arguments for inclusion in the message, plus the argument originally excluded, which was based solely on the source's credibility. At this point the source may very well determine that he has adequate argument to gain acceptance of his claim. If so, he is ready to move on to the dispositional phase of message preparation.

In most cases the source will need to develop more arguments than our hypothetical supermarket president did. If the board of directors failed to accept any point the president was going to present to them, his whole message would fail—certainly not a desirable outcome. Therefore, he should create "backup" arguments. They are arguments that may be used if, during the presentation of the message, the communicator perceives that

Claim
Our company will save a large amount
of money by expanding now
rather than waiting until later.

Datum
Construction costs will go up
at least ten percent after July 1.

Warrant
A ten percent increase in
construction costs would
represent a large amount of
money.

FIGURE 11.3   Two-Argument Message.

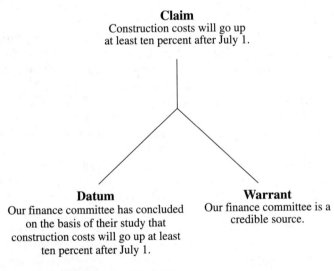

Claim
Construction costs will go up
at least ten percent after July 1.

Datum
Our finance committee has concluded
on the basis of their study that
construction costs will go up at least
ten percent after July 1.

Warrant
Our finance committee is a
credible source.

FIGURE 11.4   Three-Argument Message.

his audience has not accepted a point he believed they would accept. The
backup arguments are what makes adaptation to perceived audience feedback possible.

If the supermarket official stopped after generating just these four arguments and went right on to disposition, eventually producing a message based
upon them, he would be taking an unnecessary chance. The arguments that

first come to mind are not necessarily the best arguments to use. Although the arguments in the supermarket situation seem to be good ones, there may very well be better arguments for the immediate expansion of this supermarket chain. If invention is concluded too quickly, there is always the possibility of overlooking the most potent arguments that may be available. The source, therefore, should always invent many more arguments than can possibly be presented to the audience in the time or space available. The invention of these arguments should be based on knowledge of the source's ultimate claim and upon audience analysis, as in the development of arguments used by the supermarket president.

AUDIENCE ANALYSIS

Exactly what is meant by audience analysis during the generation of arguments? At this point in the preparation of a message, it refers to the predicted reaction of an audience to a specific element considered for inclusion in the message. In general audience analysis, we attempt to clarify this by looking for demographic data and general attitudes of the audience. In audience analysis during the generation of an argument, we look for specific attitudes, motives, and beliefs. General audience analysis will aid us, of course, in this specific audience analysis. But we cannot afford to lose sight of the fact that an audience is not static but is ever changing. The audience that comes to listen to our messages changes as a result of hearing them. Thus, although members of the audience may not believe certain data at the onset of the message, as a result of hearing or reading elements of the message, they may come to believe the data, and consequently the data may be used to further a new argument. This is precisely what we assumed would happen in the case of the supermarket president talking to the board of directors. The directors did not believe, when they came in, that they would save money by immediate plant expansion, but the president hoped that he could get them to believe it by showing them particular data that were pertinent.

Specific audience analysis and argument generation are inseparable. The source cannot depend entirely upon the results of audience analysis conducted during message preparation. Rather, the source looks at the audience as it is and determines what can be done to change it as the message proceeds. Then, with these changes in mind, the source can present a different message from the one conceived as if the audience were unchanging. As Williams has noted, adaptation to audience members necessitates estimating where they *are* and where they *will be* as a result of a certain part of our message, and then adapting to them where they *will be* rather than where they *were*.[4]

Unfortunately, the source will not always be able to analyze the audience well enough to predict confidently its reaction to all data and claims. The source may find that he or she needs to know something about the

audience, but that there is no means of obtaining the information. Whenever this happens, the source should recognize the need for developing additional arguments to supplement or replace the ones in question. The source may, and very probably will, develop dozens of arguments that could be used in the message, all of which may be based upon specific problems uncovered in attempts at audience analysis. If the message is presented extemporaneously, the final decision on some arguments can be made on the basis of observable audience response. This may cause the source to exclude some unneeded arguments and to bring in some that had been held in reserve. Thus, by rigorously applying this method, the source should be able to discover the available means of persuasion with the particular audience and, at the same time, identify most of what does not fit into the category of "available means."

INOCULATION AND RESERVATIONS

As pointed out in Chapter 6, just about every argument has reservations. While generating an argument, you should examine it to determine what are the possible reservations to it. You should remember that there may be reservations to the data, to the warrant, and to the link between the data and the warrant. These reservations should be noted and the probability of the receiver's perceiving them should be estimated. You should consider, at this point, the guidelines for inclusion or exclusion of reservations, as discussed in Chapter 6. In our discussion of inoculation, we suggested that whenever a reservation is noted in a message and refuted, you are likely to increase the inoculation of the audience against counterpersuasion. Obviously, not all reservations can be refuted in the amount of time that is available. Therefore, you must determine which arguments have reservations that require refuting in order to establish inoculation. The time to do this is during the generation of the argument. If an argument has numerous reservations all requiring refutation, the argument is probably not one you should include in the message. Awareness of numerous reservations will suggest to you the need to generate a new argument to replace the doubtful one. At any rate, the problem of reservations and inoculation is not to be put off until later in the process of preparation. Rather, it must be faced immediately at the outset of invention so that the generation of argument is not hampered by shortsightedness.

TOPOI AND THE GENERATION OF ARGUMENT

Thus far we have shown that arguments must be generated and have outlined a procedure to follow during that process. Unfortunately, this does not guarantee that you will be able to generate all the arguments needed, much less the best possible arguments. Sometimes one spontaneously thinks of good arguments, and sometimes one does not. The only way to be certain that you have the best arguments is to make sure that you have *all* the arguments available. You will probably never generate all the available arguments, but some system is needed that will enable you to approach that desirable goal. Aristotle advanced such a system.[5]

The Aristotelian system assumes that there is a limited number of lines of argument that may be employed by any source, on any topic, with any audience. Aristotle referred to these lines of argument as *topoi* (singular, *topos*). All the lines of argument, or topoi, may be divided into two categories: the general topoi and the topoi of specific fields. The general topoi are within the province of our discussion in this book. The topoi of special fields are those that are uniquely used within a given line of endeavor, such as physics, ethics, or politics. The discussion in the following pages will establish several categories of topoi. Neither these categories nor the topoi included under them should be considered as offering a complete presentation of the possible lines of argument. Rather, they are meant to be suggestive of some of the lines of argument with which this author is familiar. Unfortunately, there is an unfulfilled need for research into the lines of argument available to contemporary communicators. Until that research is completed, we must depend upon our own incomplete categorization of them.

THE ARISTOTELIAN TOPOI
OF GOOD AND EVIL

As stated in Chapter 4, attitudes are evaluative in nature. We classify things as good or bad, and this represents our attitude toward these things. Consequently, in almost all discourse designed to influence the attitude of another individual, a source refers to the specific things or behaviors as good or bad. To argue that something is good necessitates a knowledge of what people believe to be good. In the *Rhetoric,* Aristotle provides us with a fairly complete list of topoi of good and evil. As he rightly observed, the opposite of good is evil. Here a list of the goods:

Happiness	Wealth
Justice	Friends and friendship
Courage	Honor
Temperature	Reputation
Magnanimity	Power
Magnificence	Wisdom
Health	Life
Beauty	

where are the evils? (handwritten annotation)

In employing these topoi of good and evil, you should look at each one, raising the question "What can I say about this that will lead to acceptance of my claim?" Obviously you will not be able to employ all fifteen topoi in most messages, but you will almost always be able to employ some of them.

TOPOI OF POLICY ARGUMENT: STOCK ISSUES

Although not all rhetorical communication deals with policy, a very large proportion of it is concerned with the acceptance or rejection of particular policies. Contemporary theory on argumentation suggests another topoi system that may be employed when you are concerned about acceptance or rejection of a given policy. This system includes six topoi, commonly referred to as the stock issues of policy argument.

1. Need. The first stock issue in policy argument concerns the existence of a current problem or need. Before we accept a new policy, we generally insist that there is something wrong with the present system. In other words, there must be a need to change from the present system in order to obtain some benefit.

2. Inherency. Most people, before being willing to reject a present policy in favor of a new policy, must be convinced that the present one has some intrinsic weakness. In other words, there must be something inherently wrong with the present system that cannot be overcome through making minor changes. To illustrate the topoi of need and inherency, take the argument over discontinuance of foreign economic aid. For several years people argued that we needed to abolish foreign economic aid because the money we sent abroad was being used by recipient countries to purchase gold from our own gold reserves, thus placing the American dollar in danger. This was seriously questioned as an inherent weakness of our foreign aid program. Many people held that we could continue to give foreign aid to needy countries without sending them dollars. They suggested that we could send products and services rather than money. In this way foreign aid could continue and the need to change that policy could be overcome. Consequently, there was no inherent weakness in foreign aid, as such, that would produce the gold drain.

3. Policy. A policy is a specific plan the source proposes in order to overcome an inherent need. The first issue concerning this plan, or policy, is whether it will meet the need that has been established in the audience's mind.

4. Practicality. Practicality refers to the reasonableness of believing that the proposed plan can be put into operation; that is, will this plan work? The issue of practicality is a major one. For instance, in discussions concerning the advisability of the federal government's providing funds to help unemployed people move from areas of chronic unemployment to other areas of the country, many people argue, with some substance, that such a program simply is not practical because the people who are unemployed do not wish to move from their homes to other parts of the country. Thus, these people argue, theoretically the plan would work, but practically it would not.

5. Advantages. The topos of advantages concerns whether a proposed plan provides more advantages than disadvantages. Take, for example, the argument over whether the United States should have invaded Cuba during the early 1960s. There was little question but that Cuba posed something of a threat at that time and that the United States had the military power to invade and occupy Cuba. The real question was whether there would accrue to the United States, as the result of an actual invasion, disadvantages outweighing the advantage of ousting Castro. The disadvantages, of course, were the possibility of nuclear war or at least a serious confrontation with the Soviet Union.

6. Counterplan. The topos of counterplan concerns the possibility of there being another policy that can be employed to meet an admitted need, a policy that can provide more advantages and fewer disadvantages than the proposed new policy. An argument employing this topos was widely used by opponents of Medicare under Social Security. These people suggested other programs that would care for the health needs of elderly citizens through general welfare funds administered by the states rather than through a program under federal Social Security.

Argumentation theory suggests that the advocate of a change in policy must take into account all six of these stock issues. However, the person who wishes to oppose a change in policy, and thus support the present system, will need to be concerned with only one out of the six stock issues. In either case, the topoi of policy argument are highly suggestive of possible arguments you may include in the message.

THE TOWNE PUBLIC POLICY TOPOI

Many subjects for rhetorical communication concern public policy. In an attempt to develop means by which his students could better analyze questions of public policy for academic debate, Towne generated nine topoi that apply to questions of public policy.[6] These topoi are worthy of consideration by all sources concerned with public policy questions.

1. **Justice.** Does the present policy, or the proposed policy, provide a just program for the majority of Americans? For the minority?
2. **Waste.** Is the present policy, or the proposed policy, a wasteful program? Are funds or resources expended needlessly?
3. **Confusion.** Is the present policy, or the proposed policy, clear or confused? Do we know what it is doing? Can we understand it?
4. **Security.** Does the present policy, or the proposed policy, provide for increased or decreased security on the part of our nation or on the part of individuals?
5. **Morality.** Is the present policy, or the proposed policy, a moral or an immoral program?
6. **Efficiency.** Is the present policy, or the proposed policy, an efficient one? Does it get the job done with the least amount of effort and expenditure?
7. **Strength.** Does the present policy, or the proposed policy, provide for greater strength for our country, our state, or our locality?
8. **Prestige.** Does the present policy, or the proposed policy, enhance the prestige of ourselves, of our neighbors, or of our friends?
9. **Destruction.** Does the present policy, or the proposed policy, increase or decrease the possibility of destruction of our way of life?

THE TOPOI OF FEAR AND PLEASURE

Chapter 4 stressed that attitudes and behavior patterns are learned through a process of rewards and punishments that the individual receives during the course of life. When we wish to get someone to change an attitude or behavior, we often talk to the person about potential rewards or punishment that may come as a result of attitude or behavior Some people describe the persuasive process as one of guiding a person to see that he or she will achieve more rewards and fewer punishments by adopting a new attitude or new behavior in place of the one held prior to persuasion.

There is little doubt that human beings make every effort to avoid punishments and to secure rewards. We fear punishment, but we find pleasure in reward. Blackburn conducted an exploratory study in which she attempted to identify the categories of things people fear.[7] She asked a random sample of the adult population of Lansing, Michigan, to respond, from the point of view of their own concern, to eighty statements expressing a wide variety of fear situations. From analysis of the resulting data, it is possible to set forth tentatively the following general categories of fears. When considering these categories as topoi, you should remember that arguments may be generated to indicate that punishment will be forthcoming (fear arousing) or that reward will be forthcoming (pleasure arousing) or both. From what research is available, it appears that the way the argument is developed has little bearing on its impact. Both fear-arousing and pleasure-arousing appeals appear to increase attitude change in some circumstances.[8] In each of the cases below, the topos is intentionally stated as fear arousing.

> Loss of national security, nuclear war, loss of democracy
> The power of a Supreme Being, fate after death
> Loss of, or harm to, loved ones
> Inadequacy for success in job or profession
> Loss of life or health
> Social disapproval
> Poor or incomplete family life
> Loss of mind or emotional control
> Lack of money, or financial hardship
> Loss of status in the community
> Being caught doing wrong
> Losing, or being unable to make, friends
> Failure
> Inability to raise children properly
> Inability to establish meaningful love relationships
> Being unknowingly influenced by others
> Harming others

THE TOPOI OF AMERICAN VALUES

One of the biggest problems in generating argument for a message is to determine warrants, particularly motivational warrants, that the audience will accept. Although every audience has unique characteristics, American audiences generally hold certain warrants in common. Although any warrant generally held by the American people must be examined in the light of the particular audience being addressed, knowledge of the general American motivational warrants or values is very valuable when generating argument. Minnick has provided us, under six categories, an excellent summary of these general American values.[9] Over the past thirty years some modification of these values has occurred, particularly with regard to social values for men and women. What used to apply only to men now usually applies to both sexes.

I. Theoretic values of contemporary Americans
1. Americans respect the scientific method and things labeled scientific.
2. They express a desire to be reasonable, to get the facts and make rational choices.
3. They prefer, in meeting problems, to use traditional approaches to problems, or means that have been tried previously. Americans don't like innovations, but, perversely, they think change generally means progress.
4. They prefer quantitative rather than qualitative means of evaluation. Size (bigness) and numbers are the most frequent measuring sticks.
5. They respect common sense.
6. They think learning should be "practical" and that higher education tends to make a man visionary.
7. They think everyone should have a college education.

II. Economic values of contemporary Americans
1. Americans measure success chiefly by economic means. Wealth is prized and Americans think everyone should aspire and have the opportunity to get rich.
2. They think success is the product of hard work and perseverance.
3. They respect efficiency.
4. They think one should be thrifty and save money in order to get ahead.
5. Competition is to them the most important aspect of American economic life.
6. Business can run its own affairs best, they believe, but some government regulation is required.
7. They distrust economic royalists and big business in general.

III. Aesthetic values of contemporary Americans
1. Americans prefer the useful arts—such as landscaping, auto designing, interior decorating, and dress designing.
2. They feel that pure aesthetics (theater, concerts, painting, sculpture) are more feminine than masculine and tend to relegate the encouragement of them to women.
3. They prefer physical activities—sports, hunting, fishing, and the like—to art, music, or literature.
4. They respect neatness and cleanliness.
5. They admire grace and coordination, especially in sports and physical contests.

6. They admire beauty in women, good grooming and neat appearance in both sexes.
7. They think many artists and writers are peculiar or immoral.
8. They tend to emphasize the material rather than the aesthetic value of art objects.

IV. Social values of contemporary Americans
   1. Americans think that people should be honest, sincere, kind, generous, friendly, and straightforward.
   2. They think a man should be a good mixer, able to get along well with other people.
   3. They respect a good sport; they think a man should know how to play the game, to meet success or failure.
   4. They admire fairness and justice.
   5. They believe a man should be aggressive and ambitious, should want to get ahead and be willing to work hard at it.
   6. They admire "a regular guy" (that is, one who does not try to stand off from his group because of intellectual, financial, or other superiority).
   7. They like people who are dependable and steady, not mercurial.
   8. They like a good family man. They think a man should marry, love his wife, have children, love them, educate them, and sacrifice for his family. He should not spoil his children, but he should be indulgent with his wife. He should love his parents. He should own his own home if possible.
   9. They think people should conform to the social expectations for the roles they occupy.

V. Political values of contemporary Americans
   1. Americans prize loyalty to community, state, and nation. They think the American way of doing things is far better than foreign ways.
   2. They think American democracy is the best of all possible governments.
   3. They prize the individual above the state. They think government exists for the benefit of the individual.
   4. The Constitution to the American is a sacred document, the guardian of their liberties.
   5. Communism is believed to be the greatest existing menace to America. [Subsequent to the fall of the Soviet Union, this belief is not a strong as it was.]
   6. Americans believe the two-party system is best and should be preserved.
   7. They think government ownership in general is undesirable.
   8. They believe government is naturally inefficient.
   9. They think a certain amount of corruption is inevitable in government.
   10. They think equality of opportunity should be extended to minority groups (with notable minority dissent).

VI. Religious values of contemporary Americans
  1. Americans believe Christianity is the best of all possible religions, but that one should be tolerant of other religions.
  2. They think good works are more important than one's religious beliefs.
  3. They believe one should belong to and support a church.
  4. God, to most Americans, is real and is acknowledged to be the creator of the universe.
  5. They think religion and politics should not be mixed; ministers should stay out of politics, politicians out of religious matters.
  6. Americans are charitable. They feel sympathy for the poor and the unfortunate and are ready to offer material help.
  7. They tend to judge people and events moralistically.

USING TOPOI IN INVENTION

We have suggested that you will find it necessary to generate arguments for inclusion in your messages for rhetorical communication and that by skillful use of topoi you will be likely to think of potentially good arguments. Research reported by Nelson indicates that the use of topoi is indeed helpful.[10] Several lists of topoi have been included in the preceding pages with some general comments about their use. Unfortunately, merely knowing that topoi can be useful and reading the lists of topoi will not insure effective invention. You must systematically employ these topoi in the generation of argument. The question is, How?

Each topos should be considered separately. With the claim in mind for which you need to generate argument, ask yourself, "What can I say about 'national security' [or any other topos] that might lead *this* audience to accept this claim?" Think of everything you can that anyone else has ever said about national security (or any other topos). Most important, don't give up too soon! Often the original or unique idea doesn't come right away. You may have to stretch a bit. And don't be disappointed if you are forced to answer your question with "Nothing." Every topos does not apply to every claim. On the other hand, some topoi will lead to several arguments. Just because consideration of a topos has already produced an argument, don't immediately move on to another topos. Give the first topos an opportunity to stimulate more and possibly better arguments in your mind.

The employment of topoi in the generation of argument is a valuable aid but not without hard work. The generation of argument is a creative process and for most people creativity is 10 percent "I.Q." and 90 percent "I will."

SECURING DATA FOR ARGUMENT

The beginning of this chapter stressed the idea that it is essential for you to use a systematic method in generating argument for a message. A procedure, based upon a modified Toulmin approach to the analysis of argument, was outlined for your use. Several topoi systems for generating argument and for determining potential warrants for the arguments have been considered. Thus far, therefore, the text has shown procedures by which you may determine the claims you need to develop in the message and how you may determine warrants appropriate for the arguments leading to the claims. There remains a very important consideration: the problem of securing data for the arguments to be included in the message.

In Chapter 6 we discussed three types of data at some length. As noted there, first-order data are the data most desired. This type of data, of course, is that which the audience already knows or believes. If you follow the procedures already outlined in the preceding pages of this chapter, you will discover most of the first-order data available with the audience. In some cases—albeit a very small minority—you will not need to seek further data, for you will have determined that there is sufficient first-order data available for all the arguments to be included in the message. More commonly, however, you will not have first-order data readily available for all of the arguments and will thus need to consider second- and third-order data. Experimental research findings suggest that when first-order data are available, including second- or third-order data often will make no significant contribution to the modification of audience attitudes. If you are concerned, however, with building ethos, or if your purpose is ethos-centered rather than concept-centered, you will wish to include third-order data. The research findings suggest that third-order data will enhance a source's credibility, even though it may not make a significant contribution to attitude change.[11]

As stated in Chapter 6, second-order data are dependent upon the ethos of the source. Chapter 5 indicated that a source may draw upon ethos to gain acceptance of ideas. When one does this, one is employing, in most cases, second-order data. As noted, however, the more you draw upon your ethos, the less powerful it is as a persuasive instrument and the lower your ethos tends to become. Therefore, the source who draws heavily upon her or his ethos as second-order data in argument faces the very real possibility of significantly lowering ethos by the time the message is completed. Even though you may be a relatively high ethos source with a particular audience, and the purpose is concept-centered rather than ethos-centered, you will generally find it desirable to include third-order data to protect credibility from serious loss. In ethos-centered communication, no matter how high the initial credibility, you will usually find the employment of third-order data a major asset.

The concern here, therefore, is primarily third-order data. Before we consider how to obtain third-order data or evidence, we need to determine the criteria for its inclusion. As mentioned previously, it should always be included in ethos-centered communication, because research indicates that it tends to enhance the credibility of the source. When the rhetorical communicator is a moderate- to-low-ethos source, he or she needs to include evidence to increase the amount of attitude change to be secured from the audience. Additional criteria for third-order data are primarily concerned with the source of the data.

Sources of evidence may be roughly classified into three categories: unbiased, reluctant, and biased. Unbiased evidence comes from a source that has no particular personal involvement in the question. For example, a professor of economics at Kansas State University would normally be considered an unbiased source on the question of whether labor unions produce inflation through their wage demands. Reluctant sources of evidence are people or groups who have a stake in the question at issue but who provide evidence supporting the position contrary to their own best interest. For example, if a labor leader should state that there is little question that labor's wage demands are a primary cause of inflation in the United States, this would be reluctant testimony. Biased evidence emanates from a source who has a stake in the question at issue and provides evidence that supports the source's own best interests. For example, if an executive of United States Steel should make the same statement attributed to the labor leader, it would be considered biased testimony. The appropriate way of determining whether testimony is unbiased, reluctant, or biased is to ask, "What would the receiver expect this source to say?" If we expect it to say the opposite of what it does say, the evidence is reluctant. If it says precisely what we would expect it to say, the evidence is biased. If we cannot determine what we would expect it to say, the evidence is unbiased.

Considering these three categories of sources of evidence, we would probably conclude that the biased source is the least desirable in terms of its effect upon the audience. Research evidence clearly suggests that this is true. A study by Seward and Silvers found that reluctant testimony was believed much more readily than biased testimony.[12] Another study also found this difference in favor of reluctant testimony but further found that unbiased testimony was slightly superior to reluctant testimony.[13] Anderson also found that reluctant testimony was perceived as more credible than biased testimony.[14] We may conclude from these studies that the source should seek evidence that emanates from unbiased or reluctant sources. On many questions, however, there is little or no reluctant or unbiased testimony, and you will need to resort to biased evidence. When this happens, you will need to go to extra lengths to show that the evidence, although emanating from a biased source, is apparently accurate.

TESTS OF EVIDENCE

Although the primary test of evidence, as we have seen, is to determine the motivation of the source for providing that evidence, you should make several additional tests of the evidence before determining that it is satisfactory for inclusion in your message.

1. Is the source of the evidence competent? It is not enough that a source be reluctant or unbiased. It must also be competent on the subject matter with which the evidence is concerned. A submarine commander is probably an unbiased source concerning the educational system in the United States; such a person is not competent, however, to make authoritative pronouncements on the system. A competent source is something of an expert on the subject matter. When evaluating evidence, you should ask, "How is this person uniquely qualified to provide evidence on this subject?" Not only should this question be answered to your satisfaction, but you should also include this highly relevant information in the message so as to induce the audience to perceive the quoted source as competent.

The competence of a source, although theoretically vital, sometimes may not be as important in actual practice as we might like. Research reported by Dresser, for instance, indicated that even relatively intelligent and critical college students were as much influenced by incompetent sources as they were by competent sources.[15] But we should not conclude from the results of the Dresser study that competence is universally an irrelevant criterion for the selection of a source of evidence. In the Dresser study the experimental source was probably perceived by the experimental subjects as a relatively high-ethos source. In such circumstances, it is not unreasonable to believe that the evidence presented was not a significant factor in the message, but rather that second-order data, being so readily available, provided the impetus of the persuasive thrust. In a more recent study it was found that evidence from an unqualified source and evidence not directly related to the point for which it was cited, when presented by a speaker who was not initially highly credible, not only reduced the amount of attitude change produced but also severely damaged the speaker's credibility.[16] A primary criterion in your selection of evidence, therefore, should be the competence of the source of evidence.

As we have suggested, the expertness of the source of evidence is an important consideration in its selection. In some cases, however, nonexperts provide evidence of considerable value. This is particularly true when there is a group of nonexperts. For example, in the discussion of whether the United States should adopt a form of socialized medicine, the nonexpert testimony of average British citizens would be of considerable value. Although these people are not experts in medicine, they have lived under a system of socialized medicine for a considerable length of time. Thus, if it could be shown from a survey of British citizens that the overwhelming majority of these nonexperts believe that socialized medicine is a good thing, we would have a very strong datum suggesting that socialized medicine is beneficial to average citizens.

2. Is the evidence relevant to the point at issue? For evidence to be valuable in a message, it should be directly relevant to the argument in which it is included. If the source is trying, for example, to get the audience to accept the claim that rear seat air bags should be required in all automobiles sold in America and presents the evidence that more people are killed in auto accidents on the way to the airport than are killed in airplane accidents, we may expect the audience to ask, "So what?" Evidence must be relevant to the point at issue, and you should make that relevance very clear in the message.

3. Is there enough evidence? In the models of argument introduced in Chapter 6, we used the term *datum* (singular) rather than *data* (plural). In practice, however, it is more common for the word *data* to be applicable in the generation of argument, for in many cases one piece of evidence (a datum) is insufficient to establish the argument. If we wish, for example, to get our audience to accept the claim that the foreign aid program of the United States is very wasteful, providing only one example of waste will most likely be insufficient. Building a highway into the middle of a jungle that ends up nowhere is probably wasteful. But if the expenditure for this project is only .001 percent of the total foreign aid budget, most reasonable people will not conclude from this single example that our foreign aid program as a whole is wasteful.

4. Is the evidence consistent with other known evidence? During the 1966 elections, a candidate for political office claimed that the Kennedy and Johnson administrations were systematically antiblack. He cited in his message several cases in which agencies of the federal government under Kennedy and Johnson had practiced discriminatory policies. The audience, however, was very much aware of the strong positions taken by both Kennedy and Johnson in support of civil rights and of the implementing bills passed under their administrations. Although the candidate's evidence probably was correct, it was not consistent with other evidence with which the audience was familiar, and it did not cause them to accept his claim. Whenever you plan to include in the message evidence that is not consistent with evidence already familiar to the audience, it is essential to explain the inconsistency. If you cannot do so, the new evidence may not produce the desired effect.

5. Is the evidence recent? Other things being equal, the most recent evidence is the best evidence. When you are trying to decide whether to include a specific piece of evidence, you should always be concerned with the possibility that there is more recent evidence that may show things to be different. For example, average income levels of people residing in the United States in 1960 may be secured from the *Statistical Abstracts of the United States.* They are accurate and they emanate from an unbiased source. But if you are hoping to gain acceptance of a new policy by basing it on this evidence, you may find yourself in considerable difficulty. The 1960 figures are far out of date, and most critical audiences will consider such evidence virtually useless.

In discussing the tests of evidence, frequent reference has been made to "critical" listeners. The astute reader has probably already wondered, "How many people in the audience will really be critical listeners?" To be perfectly realistic, the answer to that question must be, "Not very many in most cases." To develop a message assuming the audience to be noncritical, however, puts you in a precarious position. If it does happen to be critical and you have included unsatisfactory evidence, the audience will notice this and reject your claims. On the other hand, if you assume that the audience is critical and develop the message appropriately for a supposedly critical audience that turns out to be noncritical, nothing will have been lost. Clearly, the best practice to follow is to think of the audience as being highly critical and then to be sure to include in the message only evidence of high quality.

HOW TO OBTAIN EVIDENCE

As stated early in this chapter, you should have completed a thorough investigation prior to beginning invention. If you do so, you will probably have a considerable amount of evidence available and will need only to apply the criteria suggested, selecting the evidence appropriate for inclusion in the message. In many cases, however, the investigative phase will be less than perfect. In such circumstances it will be necessary for you, during or subsequent to invention, to secure needed evidence. This kind of research is quite different from that which occurs in the investigation itself. When seeking evidence during or after invention, you know what you are looking for and search specifically for that material only. Although the procedures employed to obtain needed evidence may be different from those used in investigation, the sources of evidence are not different. This chapter has assumed that you are already familiar with proper procedures for investigation, but it is appropriate at this point to suggest some of the sources that you may employ in your search for additional evidence.

Interviews

A frequent source is other people. If you are discussing the local school system and need information on costs, one of the best ways of obtaining it is to go to the superintendent of schools and ask for it. A similar procedure may be used to secure evidence on many other topics. If there is a person in the vicinity who has the information, probably the best way of obtaining it is to interview that person.

An extension of the interview technique is the use of correspondence. Providing there is sufficient time, you may seek much information by writing to organizations or persons having special knowledge. Such correspondence, if tactfully written, normally produces a favorable result. Most important people will reply, or have a member of the staff reply, to specific requests for information. The important thing here is to make the request specific. If you write to the head of a labor union and ask him for whatever information he has available on labor unions, the response will be less than satisfactory. However, if the request is for the specific criterion of membership in the United Auto Workers Union, you will very likely receive the information requested.

Reading

In many cases, unfortunately, there is no one available to interview, and there is not sufficient time to correspond with a source familiar with the information needed. You will normally need to resort to reading in order to find evidence for the message. We shall not attempt here to develop a short course in library use. We suggest, however, several types of sources, and specific references within these types, with which you should be familiar.

1. Encyclopedias. Encyclopedias provide ready reference for background material. They treat few subjects definitely, but in many subjects they are useful at least in a general way. Specific historical information, for instance, may be obtained in any of the popular encyclopedias. You should consider *World Book Encyclopedia, Collier's Encyclopedia, Encyclopedia Americana, Encyclopaedia Britannica,* and *The New International Encyclopedia.* Also check the yearbooks each of these sources provides for more up-to-date data.

2. Statistical sources. Sources often need specific statistical material. They may need to know, for instance, the percentage of women drivers involved in fatal automobile accidents in the past year. Or they may want to know how many people were executed in the United States in 1942 or exact figures on the federal budget. Several sources are specifically devoted to such information. Some of those with which you should be familiar are *Statistical Abstracts of the United States, Statesman's Yearbook, World Almanac, Information Please,* and *New International Yearbook.*

3. Biographical sources. We have stated that whenever one presents evidence from a literary or personal source, one should indicate who or what that source is and why the source is competent. In some cases you may have evidence available but not know much about its source; thus you are unable either to determine on your own whether the evidence is satisfactory or to present to the audience such supporting information so that it will consider the evidence satisfactory. It is important, then, to determine what the qualifications of the source are. Some biographical sources are *Who's Who, Who's Who in America, Dictionary of American Biography, Who's Who in Education, Dictionary of National Biography, National Cyclopedia of American Biography* and *Dictionary of American Scholars.*

4. Periodicals. People depend upon periodicals for their evidence more than upon any other category of evidence sources. There are literally thousands of periodicals on all kinds of subjects. To obtain specific information you should not merely pick periodicals off library shelves at random; rather, you should be familiar with the numerous periodical indexes, which classify articles in the many periodicals according to subject matter. You may look up your subject in the index and find specifically in what periodicals, in what volumes, and on what pages you will find articles pertaining to the subject. Some of the periodical indexes with which you should be familiar are *Reader's Guide to Periodical Literature, Public Affairs Information Service, International Index, Education Index, New York Times Index, Annual Magazine Subject Index, Essay Index, United States Catalogue, Vertical File Service Catalogue,* and *Federal Register.*

5. Government documents. People frequently overlook a wealth of available information in the vast store of government publications. The United States government publishes information on everything from abalone to zebras. If you live in the vicinity of a library that has a Government Depository, all these publications are available. Check with the librarian in order to obtain this material. If you live in an area where there is no Government Depository, this material is available by writing to the Superintendent of Documents, Washington, D.C. Such a letter should request a list of materials relevant to the subject. Upon receiving the list, you may order specific materials directly from the Superintendent of Documents at a nominal cost. In some cases these may also be secured by writing to the congressional representative from your district. Most members of Congress employ staff members to secure such information and forward it to their constituents.

6. The Internet. Probably the largest and most accessible storehouse of information on just about anything today is available through the Internet and the World Wide Web. This electronic medium serves everything from the latest news to the most arcane interests. If you have not yet learned to "surf the net," you are not in touch with the twenty-first century. Take the time to learn to use this tremendous facility. It will be time very well spent.

Caution in the use of the World Wide Web (WWW) is essential. While many of the excellent sources noted above are also available through the Internet, far more sources are available through the WWW. Unfortunately, most of these sites are not devoted to providing accurate, unbiased information. The vast majority of these sites are commercially based or politically motivated. Others are operated by "inexperienced and unreliable individuals" with personal agendas. While such material is also available through other media, the newness of the WWW encourages many people (not just young people) to give information available through this medium far more credibility than it deserves. All of the criteria for testing evidence noted above should be applied to information on the WWW with even more care than might be used with more established media. As one writer with extensive experience reviewing web sites put it, "There is a lot of junk out there." Information present on the WWW which cannot be confirmed through other sources outside the WWW should be treated with considerable suspicion until such confirmation can be obtained.

RECORDING EVIDENCE

All potential evidence discovered must be recorded. Any systematic procedure for recording is acceptable. Figure 11.5 offers one form you may wish to follow. This figure illustrates a note card (usually four inches by six inches) that includes all the necessary information to be recorded. The card includes the name of the source of the evidence, his or her qualifications, where the evidence was published (if it was published), the specific statement of evidence, and a code number. This code number may refer to the point in the outline of the message where the evidence applies (the code is added to the card, of course, after the message itself has been organized).

Recording evidence on cards such as the one in Figure 11.5 permits you to have the material at your fingertips both during the preparation of the message and during its subsequent presentation if it is presented in the extemporaneous oral form. When the message is given extemporaneously, you will normally read the evidence directly from the card. This procedure increases the probability that the evidence will be presented accurately.

DISCUSSION QUESTIONS

1. What is the distinction between invention and investigation? What is the importance, if any, of this distinction?

IIA13

Smith, John W. (F.B.I. Agent)
"The Cost of Crime," Time, July 14, 1999

Official F.B.I. estimates place the annual cost of crime in the U.S. at approximately $275 billion per year.

FIGURE 11.5   Note Card for Recording Evidence.

2. Reread Minnick's summary of general American values, which was published in 1957. Has the general acceptance of any of these American values changed in recent years?

3. Invention can be an indefinitely prolonged process. How may a source know when to stop it?

NOTES

1. A. C. Baird, *Rhetoric: A Philosophical Inquiry* (New York: Ronald Press, 1965), p. 15.

2. J. F. Wilson and C. C. Arnold, *Public Speaking as a Liberal Art* (Boston: Allyn and Bacon, 1964), p. 95. Reprinted by permission of Allyn and Bacon, Inc.

3. J. C. McCroskey and S. V. O. Prichard, "Selective-Exposure and Lyndon B. Johnson's January 1966 'State of the Union Address,'" *Journal of Broadcasting* 11 (1967): 331–37.

4. K. R. Williams, "Audience Analysis and Adaptation: A Conceptual Clarification," Ph.D. diss., Pennsylvania State University, 1964.

5. For an excellent examination of the Aristotelian system and somewhat similar systems advanced by other classical writers, see R. J. Brake, "Classical Conceptions of 'Places': A Study of Invention," Ph.D. diss., Michigan State University, 1965.

6. R. L. Towne, Jr., " 'Topoi' in Analysis," *Pennsylvania Speech Annual* 22 (1965): 89–91.

7. B. G. Blackburn, "The Typologies of Anxiety-Arousing Cues," M.A. thesis, Michigan State University, 1967.

8. J. C. McCroskey and D. W. Wright, "A Comparison of the Effects of Punishment-Oriented and Reward-Oriented Messages in Persuasive Communication," *Journal of Communication* 21 (1971): 83–93.

9. W. C. Minnick, *The Art of Persuasion*, 2nd ed., pp. 218–20. Copyright 1968 by Houghton Mifflin Company. Used by permission.

10. W. F. Nelson, "Topoi: Functional in Human Recall," *Speech Monographs* 37 (1970): 121–26.

11. J. C. McCroskey, "Experimental Studies of the Effects of Ethos and Evidence in Persuasive Communication," Ed.D. diss., Pennsylvania State University, 1966. See also *Studies of the Effects of Evidence in Persuasive Communication*, Speech Communication Research Laboratory Report SCRL 4-67, Department of Speech, Michigan State University, 1967.

12. J. P. Seward and E. E. Silvers, "A Study of Belief in the Accuracy of Newspaper Reports," *Journal of Psychology* 16 (1943): 209–18.

13. W. E. Arnold and J. C. McCroskey, "The Credibility of Reluctant Testimony," *Central States Speech Journal* 18 (1967): 97–103.

14. L. Anderson, "An Experimental Study of Reluctant and Biased Authority-Based Assertions," *Journal of the American Forensic Association* 7 (1970): 79–84.

15. W. R. Dresser, "Studies of the Effects of Satisfactory and Unsatisfactory Evidence in a Speech of Advocacy," Ph.D. diss., Northwestern University, 1962.

16. J. Luchok and J. C. McCroskey, "The Effect of Quality of Evidence on Attitude Change and Source Credibility," *Southern Speech Communication Journal* 43 (1978): 371–83.

■ ■ ■ ■ ■

CHAPTER 12

MESSAGE PREPARATION: DISPOSITION

When you complete the process of invention as described in the preceding chapter, there should be considerably more arguments and supporting material available than can possibly be included in the eventual message. You face the problem of putting all of this material into some sensible form so that it may be presented to an audience with some hope of its achieving the desired effect. This process of formulating the essence of the message is commonly referred to as disposition.

Hermagoras held that disposition includes three mental operations: selecting, apportioning, and arranging. *Selecting* is the process of choosing the arguments and supporting materials for the message. *Apportioning* is the process of determining the amount of emphasis individual arguments and supporting materials should receive in the message. *Arranging* is the process of organizing the arguments and supporting materials in such a manner as to produce the desired effect.

SELECTING

The process of selecting materials to be included in the message is one of the most difficult, and yet one of the most important, of all the steps in the preparation of a message. This process must be based upon audience analysis. During invention you normally find that there is more than one argument available to support each of the claims. You will therefore be faced with a choice as to which argument or arguments to include from among the many that are available. In addition, there will be supporting materials of varying types and quality. You must choose from all of this material also. The process of selecting involves carefully scrutinizing each argument and each portion of an argument in order to estimate its quality. This process involves hypothesizing the character of the expected audience reaction. You must take into account everything known about the audience's reactions, then you can rank order all of the arguments and supporting materials. Ultimate selection is made on the basis of this subjective rank ordering.

APPORTIONING

The processes of selecting and apportioning are not entirely separate. Part of the process of selection is based on a determination of how much argument or supporting material is needed to establish a certain claim. During the apportioning phase of disposition, you again determine how much argument or supporting material is needed. To do this you must hypothesize the probable nature of audience response to a series of arguments or supporting materials. You are deciding whether, with a particular audience, you will need one, two, or seven arguments in order to gain acceptance of the idea and whether one, two, or twenty pieces of supporting material in a given argument will be needed. In general, apportioning should be guided by one basic principle: In most cases, the stronger an argument is, the more emphasis it should receive in the eventual message. This principle, of course, may be violated. In some cases, weaker arguments need to be emphasized by providing much more supporting material in order to gain acceptance at all. But, in general, the stronger arguments should receive the bulk of the total time available for the message.

During the apportioning process the source must consider whether to include reservations, and if so, how many. Chapter 6 presented the guidelines for handling reservations and stated that, in most cases in which a reservation is likely to be thought of by an audience, it should be mentioned in the message and specifically refuted. Decisions about the number of reservations to be mentioned and about the thoroughness of the refutations required are apportioning decisions. With a limited amount of time for the presentation of a message, it is obvious that not all reservations can be mentioned, much less refuted. You must determine, during the apportioning process, which arguments need to have reservations stated and refuted and which arguments are less in need of this special consideration. Again, it should be emphasized that selecting and apportioning are not entirely separate processes. The refutation of a reservation is in itself an argument. Consequently, when determining the apportionment of time for the arguments in the message, you are also determining which arguments will need supplementary arguments to refute reservations. The processes of selecting and apportioning, therefore, must go hand in hand.

ARRANGING

The process of arranging, or organizing, a message consists of two parts: The message as a whole must be placed in some pattern, and the various parts of the message must be structured.

Pattern of the Whole

Contemporary theory of the organization of messages suggests that they have three essential parts: the introduction, the body, and the conclusion. The suggestion that messages should have at least three parts dates back as far as Plato:

> Every speech ought to be put together like a living creature, with a body of its own, so as to be neither without head, nor without feet, but to have both a middle and extremities, described proportionately to each other and to the whole.

Not all writers on disposition, however, have recommended three parts of the message. Aristotle, for one, wrote that the only indispensable parts of the message are the statement of the case and the proof. He acknowledged, however, that in most cases an introduction and a conclusion would be appropriate.

One of the most influential treatments of disposition appeared in the *Rhetorica ad Herennium.* Its unknown author suggested six parts for the message: *exordium, narratio, divisio, confirmatio, confutatio,* and *conclusio.* The *exordium* was designed to attract the audience's attention and gain their good will; the *narratio* presented factual information; the *divisio* presented a summary of the main points to be developed in the remainder of the message; the *confirmatio* presented constructive arguments; the *confutatio* consisted of rebuttal; and the *conclusio* was the conclusion. Other rhetoricians have proposed from four to nine parts that are necessary in a message. The generally accepted contemporary theory, however, is that there are normally three parts. While the other systems of from four to nine parts are appropriate in some circumstances, most of them are so limited in application that we shall consider only one of them here, Monroe's Motivated Sequence.

The late Alan Monroe developed an overall pattern for a message that is based on "the normal process of human thinking" and includes five parts: *attention, need, satisfaction, visualization,* and *action.* Although Monroe stated that this pattern is useful for both informative and persuasive messages of all types, it is particularly useful for persuasive messages that advocate changes in policy.[1]

The step Monroe calls "attention" is similar to what we usually refer to as the introduction. Its function is to arouse the attention of the audience and obtain its good will. The steps Monroe calls "need," "satisfaction," and "visualization" are included in what is usually referred to as the body. "Need" examines the present situation, identifies what is wrong and why it is wrong, and frequently indicates why the problem has not already been overcome. "Satisfaction" presents a policy, suggests how the policy will work to overcome the problem, and indicates why this policy is better than other policies that possibly could be employed. "Visualization" may be developed positively, negatively, or by the method of contrast. Positive visualization looks to the future, with the new policy having been accepted, and points out the desirability of that policy in light of its overcoming problems. Negative visualization also looks to the future, but assumes that the new policy has not been adopted and considers the harm the problem will continue to produce. Visualization by contrast is basically a combination of positive and negative visualization. It considers the future both in light of the policy's being adopted and in light of its not being adopted and then contrasts the two circumstances. The phase of "action" in Monroe's Motivated Sequence is similar to what we ordinarily call the conclusion. In some cases, there will be a summary of the arguments presented in the message, and there will usually be a direct appeal for acceptance of the proposed policy and, in some cases, a request for specific action to be taken.

Monroe's Motivated Sequence is well adapted to the way in which people ordinarily think. It is a very simple and yet thorough structure for a message advocating a change in policy. The source who hopes to achieve acceptance of a new policy should always consider employing Monroe's Motivated Sequence as the overall pattern for the message.

Organization is one of the major problems for the most inexperienced communicators, and for many experienced ones. But properly understood, organization is one of the easiest functions of the rhetorical communicator. It is the process of arranging material in a pattern that is easy to follow and that enables the receiver of a message to understand what is being communicated. Basically, there are only two patterns of organization: *chain organization* and *parallel organization.*

The distinction between chain and parallel organization is a matter of dependence or independence. When chain organization is appropriate, a series of arguments or supporting materials are inherently linked with one another. For example, if we have two arguments, one that is the central argument and another that is used to establish the datum for the central argument, we have a circumstance calling for chain organization. One of these arguments must lead into the other. Consequently, when the message is developed, these two arguments must be placed in proximity to each other so that the thinking of the audience is led from one point to the next. Normally, this will mean that the supplementary argument is developed first so that its claim may become established and then be used as datum for the next argument.

Parallel structure is quite different. In this case the arguments or the supporting materials are not dependent upon one another. For example, if we have three arguments leading to the same claim that we plan to include in our message, it is not important which of these arguments is presented first. Each argument is independent of the two others. For example, if we are trying to convince a board of education that it should purchase television sets for the classrooms, and we have two arguments, one claiming that we should purchase television sets because they will improve education and

the other claiming that we should purchase television sets because they will save money, we have two separate arguments. It is not essential that the audience accept one in order to be able to accept the other.

When arranging arguments and supporting materials into a message, you must examine the materials to determine when chain structure is necessary and when it is not. Whenever a number of arguments are interdependent, chain structure of some type must be used. The Monroe Motivated Sequence is one of the overall patterns employing chain structure. In this, we first have arguments that establish a problem, and then we employ the awareness of this problem in order to achieve the acceptance of a new policy. As Monroe has rightly observed, the problem must come before the solution in most cases. After examining the materials, the source normally will find some need for chain organization and some need for parallel organization. In persuasive communication, the overall pattern of the body of the message is generally a chain structure, but within this chain there are numerous parallel and chain substructures.

Specific Patterns of Organization

The best organization is the one that arises from the materials. Organization is seldom good when it is selected and imposed upon the materials. Unfortunately, organization does not spontaneously jump from the materials; it must be sought within them. In order to discover the proper organizational patterns to be employed in a particular message, you must be aware of the possible patterns. This is similar to the situation you face in invention when looking for arguments. The arguments are there within the vast supply of materials available, but you must somehow discover them. The preceding chapter suggested that topoi systems are useful, and the same applies here. The following list of twelve organizational patterns should be considered the topoi of organization. You should be familiar with each of them and examine the materials to see which of them most closely approximates the natural organization of your material.

1.   **Problem solution or need-plan-advantages.** This pattern of organization is best illustrated by our earlier discussion of Monroe's Motivated Sequence. The body of the message presents a problem, suggests a solution to it, and indicates the advantages that are likely to accrue if the solution is put into effect. This is probably the most frequently used organizational pattern in persuasive communication.

2.   **Reflective thought pattern.** This pattern is similar to the problem-solution sequence. It is particularly useful when you wish to use the pseudo-informative approach. There is some evidence from research indicating that when people know the source is trying to persuade them, they are much less susceptible than when they are unaware of it.[2] The pseudo-informative approach suggests to the audience that it is being informed by the source rather than being persuaded. The method of inquiry suggested by the philosopher John Dewey is a five-step pattern, commonly referred to as the Pattern of Reflective Thinking. The five steps are locating and defining the problem, describing and limiting the problem, suggesting possible solutions, evaluating the solutions, and adopting the preferred solution. When they are applied to the pseudo-informative message, the source gives the audience the impression that he or she is leading it through the reflective thinking process. Of course, the source already knows the conclusion to be reached, but does not tell the audience ahead of time what it is. Instead, the source locates and defines the problem, describes and limits the problem, suggests possible solutions, and evaluates and tests the solutions in an apparently objective and open-minded manner. During this supposedly objective process, of course, the source leads the audience to believe that there is a problem and that, of the possible solutions, one is clearly superior to the others. Thus, by the time the source actually comes to advocate it, the audience has been prepared to accept the desired solution. This is an excellent organizational pattern to employ when you perceive that the audience is not initially in favor of the proposal. It should also be useful even when the audience is initially favorable.

3. Causal patterns. Chapter 6 discussed the different types of substantive warrants, among which was causal relationship. We observed that sometimes we reason from a known cause to an effect, and at other times we reason from a known effect to a cause. When the message is presented, arguments based on this type of warrant have a natural organizational pattern. The cause-to-effect pattern operates something like this: Here are the things we see in existence today; now let us see what they produce. The effect-to-cause pattern operates something like this: Here are the things we see in existence today; now let us consider what has produced them. Clear organization in either case requires consistency in the pattern. The causal pattern is one of the most common patterns of organization employed in rhetorical communication. During invention, when you analyze arguments, you frequently will find that they are based upon causal warrants. Whenever this is so, it is a cue that a causal pattern of organization will probably be appropriate in disposition.

4. Chronological order. In messages arranged in chronological order, arrangement may move from past to present, from present to future, or the reverse of these. Chronological order is particularly useful when it is important for the audience to perceive time relationships between materials in the message. This pattern contributes significantly to the clarity of a message with respect to such time relationships. For example, if you wish to discuss the merits of the American position in the Arab world during the 1990s, the background materials may be arranged in the order of the factors that occurred prior to the establishment of Israel, the wars between 1947 and 1970, the period of the Arab oil boycott, the postboycott period, the invasion of Kuwait and the subsequent Gulf War, and the strife following that war. You may even subdivide these major points chronologically by considering the events of each year within the period, or even of each month within one of those years.

5. Spatial order. The spatial pattern is a structure based on the relationships of objects, areas, or people as they exist in relation to one another in space. New reports on election evenings make use of spatial order. They divide the election returns according to the sections of the country and subdivide these according to the states within those sections. Spatial order is seldom useful for the overall structure of a persuasive message, but it frequently is useful in the development of individual points within the persuasive message.

6. Degree of familiarity. A source often desires to present a series of informational points or arguments that are comparatively equal to each other in importance (parallel). In some cases a few of these points will be very well known by the audience, others will be partially known, and others will be completely new to the audience. Thus a useful method of organization is to move from the familiar points, through those that are somewhat familiar, to the new points. This pattern is particularly valuable when you are making considerable use of analogy. It is also valuable when the purpose of the message is to increase the favorableness of an already favorable audience. The message begins with arguments the audience has strongly accepted, moves through those with which they may be somewhat familiar, and brings in new highly favorable arguments. This pattern is also useful in developing the need step in a persuasive message being directed to an unfavorable audience. The message then begins with points with which the audience is familiar and gradually leads into new points with which the audience has not previously been familiar but which support your contention that there is a problem in the present system. The pattern or degree of familiarity may be used in conjunction with other patterns and should not be considered the only pattern in the development of either a group of arguments or a total message.

7. Structure-function. When employing the structure-function pattern, a source first describes the structure of an entity and then considers the function of each of the elements within that structure. For example, a discussion of the United States government might first describe its tripartite structure and then look in turn at the functions of Congress, of the presidency, and of the judiciary. This pattern of organization is infrequently appropriate, but in the small number of cases in which it is appropriate, it does provide a system by which clarity may be enhanced.

8. Process. The process pattern of arrangement is similar to chronological order. The steps in an operation are described in their natural order. For example, if you wish to explain the operation of a camera, the process plan may be employed. You will go through the step-by-step processes involved in taking photographs with the camera. This pattern of organization is particularly useful in explaining a new policy. Quite frequently, policies include a series of steps leading to completion. Then the natural organization is to discuss the steps in the order in which they would be implemented.

9. Elimination or residues. As we have stated in preceding chapters, it is frequently desirable for the source to present some of the arguments against his or her own position that the audience may encounter later. In presenting these contrary arguments, of course, the source usually either minimizes them or directly refutes them. The pattern of elimination or residues is often employed when presenting this supposedly two-sided position. In this pattern, several possible interpretations of the cause of a problem or of the solution to a problem are considered and all but the one the source wishes to have accepted are shown to be undesirable, impractical, or incorrect. This is a particularly useful and effective method of arranging arguments when a two-sided message is desired. Whenever you are concerned with inoculating the audience against later counterpersuasion this pattern of organization should be considered.

10. Comparison-contrast. Arrangement by comparison-contrast has two applications. The first is within the elimination or residues pattern discussed above. Various alternatives are compared and contrasted in order to determine which is the best. The other application of the comparison-contrast arrangement is an argument by analogy. The presentation of an analogy itself necessitates the use of comparison or contrast. Of course, if you wish to gain the acceptance of the analogy, the arrangement is primarily comparison. But if you wish to have the analogy rejected, contrast is employed.

11. Climactic, anticlimactic, and pyramidal structure. In any argument or series of arguments, there is a point of maximum interest and strength. Where this point occurs in the overall argument or series of arguments determines whether the structure is climactic, anticlimactic, or pyramidal. In climactic structure, the strongest, most interesting point comes at the end of the series. In anticlimactic structure, it comes at the beginning of the series. In pyramidal structure, the point appears in the middle. Climactic structure probably is best employed when the audience is not initially favorable to your position. You work to gain acceptance of minor points and gradually build to a climax where you put in the "clincher." Anticlimactic structure is most appropriate in the reverse condition. It is also appropriate when there is a question of whether the audience will pay attention to the message. By the use of the strongest, most interesting argument at the onset, attention is often captured when it would otherwise be lost. Pyramidal structure is seldom appropriate. Probably the only circumstance that calls for it is being faced with an audience that is both hostile and inattentive. You should try to allay some of the hostility with minor points, then capture the attention with the strongest, most interesting point, and finally follow this up with other, weaker points. These three approaches are patterns for the overall structure of a message. Unless there is good reason to do otherwise, you should always plan to employ either the climactic or the anticlimactic structure.[3]

12. Topical, or classification, patterns. Most textbooks on rhetorical communication include this pattern in their list of organizational structures for the same reason it is included here—to serve as a catchall. The organizational patterns discussed above will normally provide sufficient options for structuring the message. In some circumstances, however, none of these patterns will seem appropriate. There will seem to be in the materials some logical pattern that simply does not fit into any of the preceding classifications. We refer to this type as the topical, or classification, pattern. In addition, you will often find that the materials seem to have absolutely no pattern. You must then create some kind of pattern. This too will be a topical, or classification, pattern. The only essential in creating such a pattern is that the audience see it as sensible and understandable. If it does, the structure is successful.

Organization of Single Arguments

An argument is designed either to gain acceptance of a new idea (constructive) or to cause rejection of a claim the audience has been believing (refutatory). To determine the organization of each single argument, you must at first determine whether it is a constructive or a refutatory argument. Once this is done, choices in organization are greatly reduced in number and are relatively simple.

1. Constructive organization. The development of a constructive argument may follow either of two patterns. The first and more common pattern covers (a) statement of the conclusion of the argument, (b) support of the argument, (c) restatement or summary of the argument, and (d) transition to the next point in the message. In some cases the source does not wish the audience to know the conclusion before support has been provided, so the original statement will be omitted. The structure of this second pattern is to present material leading to a particular conclusion, to draw the conclusion, and then to make a transition to the next point in the message. How the supporting material is developed and given structure will depend upon the selection of one of the patterns of organization we have discussed. But the overall pattern for the individual point in a message is necessarily restricted to these two.

2. Refutatory organization. For refutatory argument, as for constructive argument, there are two organizational patterns available. The normal pattern is (a) to state the point to be refuted, (b) to state the alternate position, (c) to attack the point to be refuted and defend the alternate position, (d) to summarize the argument, and (e) to make a transition to the next point. In some cases the source does not wish to have his or her position clearly known at the outset; therefore, he or she merely states the point to be refuted and then, in an apparently open-minded manner, suggests that this point needs to be investigated. The source provides material that refutes the point at hand and that tends to support a contrary point. Then he or she draws the conclusion that the contrary point is correct, summarizes the argument, and makes a transition to the next point. As was the case with constructive argument, the organizational pattern for the supporting materials themselves will be selected from the list of twelve patterns in the preceding section. But the overall patterns for refutatory arguments are restricted to the two mentioned here.

INVENTION AND DISPOSITION: THE SIAMESE TWINS

Once in every several hundred thousand births twins are born connected to each other. These "Siamese twins" often share a circulatory system or some vital organ. If they are separated by surgery, they ordinarily die. Consequently, most Siamese twins are forced to live out their usually short lives joined together. Invention and disposition are like the Siamese twins. They have many "vital organs" in common. To separate invention and disposition is satisfactory for purposes of description, but it is next to impossible to separate these two mental operations in practice. Although we have allocated the operations of invention and disposition to two different chapters in this book, it is essential to emphasize the point that these two mental operations must be carried on together. Let us examine the specific operations of disposition to see how they are inextricably interwoven with invention.

1. **Selecting.** We can readily see that this dispositional process is also a vital part of invention. In fact, much of invention is simply a matter of selection based on audience analysis. Each datum and each warrant is selected on the basis of a hypothetical audience reaction to it, and further data and warrants are selected as validation or support for those previously selected. When invention is complete, few problems of selection remain to be considered. Only if we treat invention as divorced from considerations of the audience can it be otherwise. Of course, we refuse to do this. If invention is the creating of arguments in a vacuum, then selection can follow it. But if invention is based on the audience, selection is an integral part of the process.

2. **Arranging.** The dispositional process of arranging is also partially completed during invention. The main factor determining the strategic importance of an argument is what it leads to. If an argument is invented to validate data, then it must be presented in a speech in such a manner as to lead to that end. The dispositional process is similar to building a bridge over a river. The engineer must know the nature of both banks and then plan a bridge that will lead from one to the other. Similarly, the source must know what the audience's present position is on the issue and what he or she wants it to be. Then the source may build a message that will lead to the desired end. The wisdom of an engineer who would build six spans and ninety-six supports for a bridge and then try to figure out how to arrange them for functional use would be doubtful indeed. Each span of a bridge is planned and built to fit into a certain position to connect properly with the spans on either end of it; it is the same with the supports for the structure. The arguments and materials of a message need to be planned and built in the same way.

3. Apportioning. To understand how this dispositional process interrelates with invention, we must remember that invention is predicated upon the need for argument in order to gain acceptance of claims. The source must hypothesize audience responses to an idea to determine how far to go in the invention of argument leading to that idea. This is actually an apportioning decision. If you wish to leave all apportioning until the completion of invention, you may never determine when it is time to conclude invention. At best, you will have no accurate guide by which to decide to terminate at a given point. You probably will invent far too many or too few arguments.

"Preview" and "Review" Disposition

The lines between invention and disposition are far from sharply drawn. Rather than being two separate processes, invention and disposition are complementary phases of the same process: analyzing the audience and developing a message to evoke a predetermined reaction from that audience. As noted, we cannot completely separate invention and disposition, but we can make some distinctions. During the nineteenth century, writers on English composition made a distinction between "preview" and "review" dispositional thought processes, a distinction that has become lost in contemporary writings. Thus far we have been discussing primarily the preview operations—those inextricably bound to invention.

Once you are satisfied that it is appropriate to terminate invention, many of the dispositional choices have already been made. These have been preview dispositional choices. At this point you will go back over all of the material and determine whether these preview dispositional choices were correct and useful for the actual message to be developed. Although you are still concerned with selecting, arranging, and apportioning as you review the products of inventional thoughts, remember that your mind is now functioning with these processes at a different level. The reviewing process provides a more definitive focus for dispositional thought. There are obvious differences in what one has to select, apportion, and arrange. For instance, a question of arrangement might be, "Should the claim be stated before or after the data?" A question of selection might be, "Since this message is too long for the time allowed, what evidence can I omit?" The mind is now manipulating information already derived from similar processes at an inventional level.

It is important to remember that dispositional thought occurs at two points in the development of audience-centered messages. It takes place during invention as a preview process and again as a distinguishably separate process in the review stage. A source who thinks that all disposition occurs after invention is completed may be a captive of inadvertent dispositional choices. It is impossible to complete invention without making many dispositional choices. If you are unaware that you have made them, you may be unaware that they were wrong.

RESEARCH ON ARRANGEMENT

Because appropriate arrangement of materials is so highly dependent upon the nature of the audience to which the message is to be directed and upon the materials themselves, research on arrangement is very difficult to design and execute. It is not surprising that comparatively little good-quality research on arrangement has been reported in the literature of rhetorical communication. A discussion of the limited research findings practically applicable to the communicator follows.

1. The general importance of organization. A study reported by Smith indicates that general organization of a message is extremely important.[4] In his study, Smith developed a speech on socialized medicine that was divided into six main parts: attention, need, satisfaction, visualization, refutation, and action. Several variations of this basic speech were created by moving one or more parts out of the normal sequence. Smith found that moving a single part of the speech out of the normal sequence did not affect the amount of attitude change achieved by the message. However, when two or more parts were transposed, there was a significant decrease in attitude change. In fact, with the parts rearranged completely at random, the audience's attitude change was significant, but in the negative direction. Smith also found, as have several other researchers, that people can distinguish between organized and disorganized messages and show a clear preference for an organized message.[5]

The results of the Smith study and of other, similar studies suggest that minor disorganization probably will not have much effect. Major disorganization, however, will be a serious handicap to effective rhetorical communication. While this emphasizes the importance of the dispositional choices discussed earlier in the chapter, it offers some reassurance to the source faced with a specific decision in disposition that seems difficult. As long as the source does not make too many bad decisions, minor disorganization will probably not negatively affect the eventual success of the message.

2. Organization and comprehension. Several studies have attempted to determine the effect of disorganization upon the comprehension of members of an audience. Studies reported by Thompson,[6] Darnell,[7] Thistlethwaite, deHaan, and Kamenetsky,[8] and Weaver[9] suggest that general structure and the employment of transitions within a message have major effects upon comprehension. As disorganization increases, audience comprehension tends to decrease. Good organization, therefore, is important to the success of communicators, whether they have persuasive intent or informative intent.

3. Organization and ethos. Since organization has been observed to have an effect on comprehension and upon attitude change, we may expect it also to affect the source's ethos. In one study, Thompson took a measure of the terminal ethos of the source of communication. He observed that while disorganization had a major effect upon comprehension and upon the audience's perception of the quality of the message, it had no such effect upon ethos. The meaning of this finding is unclear. Thompson merely asked the members of the audience to answer the question "Do you consider the speaker to be (a) very well informed, (b) well informed, (c) poorly informed, or (d) very poorly informed?" The answers of the audiences hearing organized and disorganized messages, respectively, were not significantly different.[10]

Sharp and McClung, however, in a further study of the effect of disorganization on ethos, employed messages developed by Thompson. Using a more sophisticated method of measuring perceived ethos, they observed a large and significant decrease produced by disorganization.[11] McCroskey and Mehrley found similar effects for both initially high-credibility and initially low-credibility sources.[12]

Though more research concerning the effects of organization on ethos is needed before we can draw definitive conclusions, it appears that poor organization may have a seriously harmful effect on a source's ethos.

4. Support for Monroe's Motivated Sequence. Earlier this chapter described Monroe's Motivated Sequence, stating that it operated as people normally think and recommending it as the best organizational structure for a source to employ when desiring to gain acceptance of a new policy. An experiment by Cohen provides support for this recommendation. Cohen presented two different messages to comparable audiences. In the first message, he presented a threatening argument concerning problems of grading and necessary reforms and followed it with a proposal for grading on the curve, suggesting that this would solve the problems. In the other message, he presented his grading-on-the-curve solution first and then developed the problem. The motivated-sequence pattern, problem-solution, was significantly more successful in achieving attitude change. Cohen explained these results in terms of clarity in understanding the message. He suggested that when the need was developed first and then followed by the solution, interest was heightened; and the solution was understood because the audience members were able to place it in their own contexts. On the other hand, in the treatment in which the solution was presented first, Cohen speculated that the audience could not see its relevance until after the need had been developed. By that time they had probably already forgotten much of the solution because they had failed to pay close attention when it was originally developed.[13]

5. Most desirable point first. When you are going to discuss some ideas with which you and your audience are in agreement and some with which you are in disagreement, it is generally better to discuss areas of agreement first. McGuire theorized that if a source presented ideas the audience liked at the beginning and then followed them with less desirable ideas, the source would be more successful than by following the reverse procedure.[14] He explained this in terms of attention. Theoretically, if we hear something we like, we will pay attention to it, and our attention is likely to carry over to the next idea even though we are not particularly in favor of it. This permits greater opportunity for the undesirable idea to penetrate the selectivity of the listener and succeed in persuasion. Results of McGuire's research support this theory.[15]

6. **"Pro-con" in two-sided messages.** At several points in this and preceding chapters, we have suggested the desirability of presenting the apparently two-sided message. In this type, the source includes both the normal arguments supporting his or her position and arguments that tend to oppose the position. Along with these con arguments, the source normally includes refutation. The question arises as to which should be presented first. Should the source present his or her side (the pro arguments) and then the other side (con arguments)? Or should the structure be con-pro? Studies by Janis and Feierabend,[16] Miller and Campbell,[17] and Anderson and Barrios[18] all point to the pro-con order as being better. In these studies the con arguments were not even refuted, but the pro arguments still gained greater acceptance. No research has been reported that specifically investigated the pro-con with refutation of con, but these other studies strongly suggest that the pro-con would prove to be superior. The basic theory here is that if the audience receives the pro arguments first, they are already convinced to some extent, and thus are on your side when you attack the opposition. If, however, you attack the opposition first, before presenting the preferred side, you may very well be attacking the audience. This will, of course, be particularly true when you are facing an initially hostile audience.

OUTLINING THE MESSAGE

One of the greatest aids to disposition both in the process of preparation and in the eventual presentation of the message is an outline. Only in impromptu speaking is the rhetorical communicator precluded from the opportunity to benefit from outlining the message.

References are often made to the speaker's or writer's outline. This is a misnomer. Actually the speaker will normally have at least three outlines, and the writer at least two. Outlining should begin as soon as you know that you are going to attempt to communicate with another person in any formal manner. The first outline, which may be called the preliminary outline, is sketchy and incomplete but represents your first thoughts about what the nature of the message will be. In most cases, it will undergo considerable revision during invention.

The second outline, developed during the review phase of disposition, may be called the preparation outline. The second outline—produced by extensively revising the preliminary outline—should include references to all major ideas, all subordinate ideas, and all supporting materials.

In extemporaneous speaking, you will normally develop a third outline, called the speech notes. This will be the outline you will employ during the presentation of the message.

Outlines of messages may take either topical, key-word, or complete-sentence form, but there is considerable disagreement among writers on rhetorical communication about which of these forms should be used. There is no clear-cut answer to this question. Complete sentence outlines cause a problem for many sources who plan to present their messages in the extemporaneous speaking format. When they stand before the audience, if they have a complete-sentence outline as their speech notes, there is a strong tendency for them to read far too much and to lose contact with the audience. Consequently, they do not really give an extemporaneous speech; rather they are giving a manuscript speech, but their manuscript happens to have some letters and Roman numerals on it. Even when the speech notes are in topical or key-word form, if the preparation outline is in full-sentence form, there is a tendency on the part of many speakers to try to recall the wording used on the preparation outline. This promotes an almost memorized type of preparation, with all the accompanying detriments. As an extemporaneous speaker, therefore, you must determine for yourself whether the topical, key-word, or the complete-sentence outline better fits your needs. The only way you will be able to determine this is through experience.

Although the topical or key-word outline is better for some extemporaneous speakers, and the complete-sentence outline is better for other extemporaneous speakers, there is little question that the complete-sentence outline is the best for manuscript and memorized speeches and for writers. All the drawbacks that may occur with the complete-sentence outline are irrelevant to these other formats. There is one major advantage for the complete-sentence outline. It permits thorough examination of every major point, every subpoint, and every item of supporting material. With the complete-sentence outline in hand you may thoroughly examine the proposed message to see if all the elements are in their proper places.

The Rules of Outlining

Since most Americans study the principles of outlining in elementary school and in the first years of high school, it is not necessary here to go into the rules of outlining at any great length. Following are a few of the rules that are particularly important for outlining messages for rhetorical communication.

1. Organize the outline into three parts: the introduction, the body, and the conclusion. The body of a message should always be completely developed before the introduction and conclusion are even seriously considered. Many people find it useful to use separate sheets of paper for these three parts.

2. Use a consistent set of symbols to indicate main ideas, subordinate ideas, and supporting materials. It is unimportant what the symbols are, but it is important that the symbols be used consistently to avoid confusion. Generally, but not universally, the order of division is indicated by symbols in the following order: Roman numerals, capital letters, Arabic numbers, lowercase letters, Arabic numbers in parentheses, and lowercase letters in parentheses.

3. The symbol system within each part of the outline (introduction, body, and conclusion) should function as a separate unit. While it is not absolutely essential that this rule be followed in all cases, it will enhance clarity if it is followed. By just a glance at the outline it will be possible to tell when a new point is part of the body rather than the introduction or of the conclusion rather than the body.

4. Employ indentation along with subordination of symbols. Indentation also serves to enhance the clarity of the outline. If two points do not have the same symbol and are not indented equally, it is a clue that they are not considered coordinate.

5. Single subpoints are sometimes appropriate, but not often. You should always examine the outline to find any single subpoints. If the subpoint is merely a clarifying statement, a definition, or a single piece of evidence, it probably is all right. But you should be careful that the subpoint is not intended as a division of the point immediately superior to it. By definition, nothing can be "divided" into one part.

DISCUSSION QUESTIONS

1. What effect is likely to occur when a source employs the pseudo-informative approach with a hostile audience that knows in advance the source's real purpose? Why?

2. Is there an ethical question involved in the use of the pseudo-informative approach?

3. What effect(s) on the ultimate message may be produced by a source's treating invention and disposition as separate, distinct steps in message preparation?

4. Research findings suggest that poor organization interferes with communication. Why may this be true?

5. Research findings indicate that a moderately high-ethos source loses ethos if the message is disorganized. Do you think a moderately low-ethos source gains ethos if the message is well organized? Why, or why not?

6. Would a communicator ever profit by intentionally presenting a disorganized message?

7. Read the speech by George Bush in Appendix A. Do you consider it well organized? Why or why not?

NOTES

1. A. H. Monroe, *Principles and Types of Speech,* 5th ed. (Glenview, IL: Scott, Foresman, 1962).

2. C. A. Kiesler and S. B. Kiesler, "Role of Forewarning in Persuasive Communications," *Journal of Abnormal and Social Psychology* 68 (1964):547–49.

3. Numerous experimental studies have investigated the relative effectiveness of these three patterns. The results have indicated that climax was more effective in some cases and anticlimax in other cases. Pyramidal structure was seldom found to be superior to either of the other patterns.

4. R. G. Smith, "Effects of Speech Organization upon Attitudes of College Students," *Speech Monographs* 18 (1951):292–301.

5. Ibid.

6. E. Thompson, "An Experimental Investigation of the Relative Effectiveness of Organizational Structure in Oral Communication," *Southern Speech Journal* 26 (1960):59–69.

7. D. K. Darnell, "The Relation between Sentence-Order and Comprehension," *Speech Monographs* 30 (1963):97–100.

8. D. L. Thistlethwaite, H. deHaan, and J. Kamenetsky, "The Effect of 'Directive' and 'Non-Directive' Communication Procedures on Attitudes," *Journal of Abnormal and Social Psychology* 51 (1955): 107–18.

9. J. F. Weaver, "The Effects of Verbal Cueing and Initial Ethos upon Perceived Organization Retention, Attitude Change, and Terminal Ethos," Ph.D. diss., Michigan State University, 1969.

10. E. Thompson, "Some Effects of Message Structure on Listeners' Comprehension," *Speech Monographs* 34 (1967):51–57.

11. H. Sharp, Jr., and T. McClung, "Effects of Organizations on the Speaker's Ethos," *Speech Monographs* 33 (1966):182ff.

12. J. C. McCroskey and R. S. Mehrley, "The Effects of Disorganization and Nonfluency on Attitude Change and Source Credibility," *Speech Monographs* 36 (1969):13–21.

13. A. R. Cohen, *Attitude Change and Social Influence* (New York: Basic Books, 1964), pp. 11ff.

14. Ibid., p. 12.

15. Ibid.

16. Ibid., pp. 12 ff.

17. N. Miller and D. T. Campbell, "Recency and Primacy in Persuasion as a Function of the Timing of Speeches and Measurements," *Journal of Abnormal and Social Psychology* 59 (1959): 250–53.

18. N. H. Anderson and A. A. Barrios, "Primacy-Effects in Personality-Impression Formation," *Journal of Abnormal and Social Psychology* 58 (1961): 346–50.

CHAPTER 13

MESSAGE PREPARATION: STYLE

As discussed in Chapter 2, meanings are in people, not in words. But the meaning in the minds of people can be stimulated to awareness by words. During invention, we generate the ideas for our message. During disposition we select, apportion, and arrange these ideas to make the skeleton of a message. In each of these phases of message preparation, we make choices based upon our analysis of the audience and the hypothesized reactions of that audience. When our attention is directed to style, we are concerned with the completion of the message, that is, giving the skeleton its "flesh." Stylistic choices concern the ways in which ideas are expressed. The stylistic phase of message preparation, therefore, is the phase in which you direct full attention to choosing language to express the ideas.

THE FUNCTION OF STYLE

Referring to the function of style as giving the skeleton its flesh may suggest that style serves a purely decorative function, merely covering the skeleton. This is an erroneous impression. Style, like flesh, has a much more useful function than merely covering the skeleton. Style is what makes ideas effective. An important and potentially persuasive idea that is improperly worded loses most, if not all, of its persuasive power with the audience.

It is important to refrain from thinking of style as something we put into our ideas or something we do to our ideas. Every idea, no matter how it is expressed, has some stylistic form. The real question is not whether ideas will be expressed "stylistically," but rather, in what style the ideas will be expressed. *Style determines, to a major extent, the meaning that is stimulated in the mind of the receiver by a message.* It determines whether the message has probative power and whether it is even understood in the context you desire. Good style may therefore be defined as style that stimulates the desired meaning in the mind of the receiver. Poor style, of course, is style that distorts the intended meaning. With this general concept of good style in mind, we turn to the specific characteristics of good style in rhetorical communication.

CHARACTERISTICS OF GOOD STYLE   APEV

1. Accuracy and clarity. The primary requisite of good style is that it accurately and clearly express the meaning intended by the source. The criterion for determining whether style is accurate and clear, of course, is the meaning stimulated in the mind of the receiver. If the receiver understands the meaning intended by the source, the style is most likely accurate and clear. Accuracy refers specifically to the choice of words that express the idea. Style is accurate if the wording represents the meaning intended by the source. Clarity refers to understanding on the part of the audience. Language may accurately represent the meaning intended by the source but be unclear to the audience. The phrase "recalcitrant procrastinator" may accurately describe a person being referred to in the discourse. This phrase, however, may not be understandable to the audience. Thus, though it is accurate, the style is unclear and the message does not stimulate in the receiver the desired meaning.

It is also important for the message to be grammatically correct. Although errors in grammar do not always cause misunderstanding, they frequently do, and even more frequently, they cause an audience to perceive the source to be of somewhat lower ethos than it otherwise would. As audience members, we are somewhat tolerant of grammatical errors when listening to an extemporaneous speech, but we tend to lose our tolerance when the message is a manuscript speech or in written form. Grammatical errors in these two latter cases are avoidable; and if they are present, they indicate either ignorance or carelessness.

2. Propriety. Language should be appropriate to the source, the subject, and the audience. A college student who, while talking to other college students about a football game, employed the ministerial style of Billy Graham would appear ludicrous. But so would Billy Graham if he spoke to a rally of 20,000 supporters with the style of a college student talking to other college students about football. Language appropriate for discussing supermarket shopping is not appropriate for discussing the gallantry of American soldiers on Iwo Jima. And language appropriate for a college professor discussing nuclear fission is not appropriate for a high-school student discussing the same subject.

Although language should be appropriate to the audience, we must be careful not to adapt too much. We must never forget that language must also be appropriate for the source and for the subject matter. If a man who is a professor of agriculture visits a farm in an outlying and impoverished

area, he should not adapt his language fully to the language of that area. He would most likely be perceived as phony if he adapted too much, and his motives would come into serious question.

3. Economy. Verbosity, a common fault of many sources, is the use of more words that necessary to communicate an idea, and frequently is caused by lack of accuracy and clarity. The source presents the idea, but perceives that the idea is not understood and so presents the idea repeatedly. Initial choice of good language will provide accuracy and clarity without needless repetition. Thus, accuracy, clarity, and economy are not completely separable.

One study of the effects of economy in style in persuasive communication has been reported. Ragsdale found that brief messages produced significantly more attitude change than wordier versions of the same message that were indirect, repetitive, or included numerous compound sentences.[1] Apparently, then, economy in style enhances the effectiveness of a persuasive message.

4. Vivacity. Vivacity is the quality of interest or impressiveness in the language employed in the message. A message that is striking when heard or read is more memorable. Most famous quotations are remembered because of their vivacity. In most cases these quotations do not voice ideas no one else had thought of, but they express the ideas in unique ways. When John F. Kennedy said, "Ask not what your country can do for you; ask what you can do for your country," he was not expressing an idea completely new to his listeners. He expressed it, however, in such a way that it immediately caught on and finally became such a common saying that it now seems almost trite. Another example of vivacity in President Kennedy's Inaugural Address was his expression of the idea that we should always be willing to negotiate with other countries, but that we should never do so because of a threat from those countries. He expressed it this way: "Let us never negotiate out of fear. But let us never fear to negotiate."

Chapter 4 discussed the problem of selective attention, indicating that people tend to let their attention wander and that they listen to what seems to conform to ideas they already hold. This problem of the selectiveness of attention can be overcome to a major extent by a message that has vivacity. When an idea is expressed in a unique and striking way, we not only direct our attention to it, but frequently continue to think about it even after the completion of the message. Thus, vivacity not only has an important immediate effect during communication but also tends to have a sustained effect over time.

DIFFERENCES IN ORAL AND WRITTEN STYLE

Since Aristotle, most writers on rhetorical communication have observed that there are important differences in usage between oral and written language. That such differences exist is obvious to any of us who study specimens of oral and written language. But the precise nature of the differences between oral and written style is not as yet completely clear. Considerable empirical research has been directed toward this question, but the problems in obtaining representative samples of oral and written style have made it difficult to generalize from the findings of most of them.[2] On the basis of these studies, the following appear to be major differences between oral and written style:

Oral language includes fewer different words.

Oral language includes words with fewer syllables.

Oral language includes shorter sentences.

Oral language includes more self-reference words (I, me, mine).

Oral language includes fewer quantifying terms or precise numerical words.

Oral language includes more pseudoquantifying terms (many, few, some).

Oral language includes more extreme and superlative words, such as none, all, every, always, never.

Oral language includes more qualifying statements (clauses beginning with unless, except).

Oral language includes more repetition of words and syllables.

Oral language uses more contractions.

Oral language includes more interjections (Wow!, Really?!, No!).

Oral language includes more colloquial and nonstandard words.

These differences between oral and written style are derived primarily from specimens of the two types of discourse obtained without the source of a given message being aware that it was going to be used for empirical purposes. It is reasonable to infer, therefore, that these observed differences are natural differences rather than having been specifically imposed upon style by the respective sources. It is natural to ask why such differences exist. Examination of the list reveals that most of the differences lead to greater clarity in the oral form. There is a definite need for increased clarity in this form because of the manner of presentation. When a receiver reads a message at leisure and then rereads it as many times as desired, there is an opportunity for relative obscurity in the message to be understood. A receiver of oral communication, on the other hand, usually does not have an opportunity to go back over what he or she has heard. Consequently, an oral message must be instantly intelligible if it is going to be understood by receivers.

The need for clarity in all communication emphasizes the fact that, when trying to present a message in the oral form, the source needs to take care that the style is also oral rather than written. In the preceding chapter we approached the question of what type of outline one should use in preparing a message. We noted that some people prefer to use full-sentence outlines and others prefer to use topical or key word outlines. The main defect of style with many speakers is that it approximates the written much more than the oral form. The approximation of written style in the oral form leads to a lack of clarity and to obscurity. One way of avoiding this problem in extemporaneous speaking is to take care not to write out the speech before it is delivered. For some extemporaneous speakers, even full-sentence outlines will produce written style of delivery.

The problem of ensuring an oral style of manuscript speech is somewhat more difficult to overcome. Most people do not naturally write in the oral style. Consequently, when preparing a manuscript speech, they need to devote specific attention to increasing their approximation of the oral mode. The source may profit by using the list of the twelve distinctions between written and oral styles as a checklist in examining a manuscript message. If it is found, for example, that there is a rather large number of long sentences, pains should be taken to break some of them down into shorter sentences. The use of a tape recorder would be helpful. Failure to achieve oral style in extemporaneous or manuscript speaking tends to reduce the source's chances of being effective. Consequently, the oral characteristic of effective style is a value the source should never ignore.

CCHPVE

FACTORS OF ATTENTION AND INTEREST

Nearly every writer on rhetorical communication, from Aristotle's time to the present, has recognized the importance of gaining and maintaining attention if a source is to influence an audience. None, however, has stated the point more cogently than Winans. "*Persuasion*," he wrote, "*is the process of inducing others to give fair, favorable, or undivided attention to propositions."*[3] As Winans implies, attention is crucial to rhetorical communication. Whether you wish audience members to understand, to believe, or to act, you must secure their attention to the message. You cannot hope to influence a person who is unaware of the stimuli being presented.

As noted in Chapter 4 one of the severe problems facing a rhetorical communicator is that of selective attention. At that point we observed that it is impossible for any person to pay attention to everything going on in the environment. Consequently, a person must select the things to which he or she will attend. The effective source serves as a guide to the audience's selection.

Attention and interest in the listener are phenomena that must be consider together. As Oliver has stated, "Attention and interest are twin words that, although not synonymous, are always in company. Whatever we attend to is interesting, and to whatever is interesting we freely give our attention."[4] Thus, the more interesting the message is, the more likely the audience will be to pay attention to it and be influenced by it.

In some cases, what the communicator has to say is inherently interesting to the audience members, and consequently they pay close attention. For example, on December 8, 1941, Franklin Delano Roosevelt stood before Congress to ask for a declaration of war against Japan. Because of the events of the preceding twenty-four hours, every member of Congress was vitally interested in what Roosevelt was going to say, and attention was as nearly undivided as possible.

In some cases sources of communication are interesting in themselves. When a radical and outspoken figure visits a college campus to speak, there will usually be a large and attentive audience, not because the students necessarily agree with the person but because the speaker represents something unusual or novel. For example, when the late George Lincoln Rockwell (until 1967 the head of the American Nazi Party) visited a university campus, students would turn out by the hundreds, and in some cases by the thousands, to hear him. Probably not even one percent of them agreed with what he had to say, but he was interesting, and the students therefore attended and, in most cases, listened.

Unfortunately, most people are not such captivating sources, and most of the propositions they include in their messages are not so compelling. As a rule, sources select propositions that they want to have accepted. In some cases though, particularly in ethos-centered communication, sources do select propositions primarily because of their interest value to the audience, but this is the exception rather than the rule. However, there is no reason why initially low-interest propositions should be uninteresting. This is where good style can help. Interest and attention can be generated by the manner in which something is said, regardless of its substance. Let us take a few examples.

Proposition: America has the necessary resources to increase the amount of money currently being spent on education.

Proposition restated: Any country that can afford to spend $40 billion to put a man on the moon can afford to educate its youth properly.

Proposition: People in this country tend to be too selfish. They are more concerned with what they can get from the government than with what they can do for their fellow human beings.

Proposition restated: Ask not what your country can do for you; ask what you can do for your country.

Proposition: People living east of the city must travel over a dangerous stretch of road in order to get into the city.

Proposition restated: Commuters from the east must negotiate the "mangled mile" in order to reach our city.

Proposition: Last year the United States spent almost $2.5 billion on foreign aid.

Proposition restated: Last year the United States spent 85,000 elementary and secondary school classrooms on foreign aid.

Proposition: The defeat of antipoverty legislation would cause serious hardship and disruption within our country.

Proposition restated: A vote against antipoverty programs is a vote for starvation, ignorance, crime, and race riots.

All of these restated propositions should be somewhat more interesting and attention-getting than the propositions as originally stated. But merely knowing that it is possible to state a point in an interesting manner does not ensure that it actually can be so easily. Therefore, it is important to consider some of the elements of attention and interest so that they may be used as guides for restatement in interesting and attention-getting styles.

1. Concreteness. Abstract ideas often are interesting, but they can ordinarily be made much more interesting by being made more concrete. We are all interested in freedom and democracy. But when the freedom and democracy being discussed is directly related to our present circumstances, our interest becomes much greater. During the middle 1960s the concepts of democracy and freedom were of interest to most students on college campuses, but particularly so to students on certain campuses—the University of California at Berkeley, for instance. There students had real, concrete examples of what they considered to be lack of freedom, such as not being permitted to use certain language in signs during demonstrations. While such censorship was uncommon at that time, the political correctness movement today makes it much more common.

The source should always seek to make ideas as concrete as possible. An abstract description of the good the Peace Corps has done around the world will be not nearly as effective as would a specific example of a specific Peace Corps volunteer irrigating a wasteland and providing food for a village of a thousand people. People like to grapple with ideas, but if they cannot "sink their teeth" into an idea, it soon escapes their minds.

2. Conflict. Most people love a good fight. In Western societies, competitiveness is almost universally admired. The disproportionate amount of attention the American people give to athletic events is indicative of this element of attention. President Harry S. Truman was noted for his skillful use of conflict as an attention-getter in his speaking, earning the nickname "Give 'em Hell Harry." Truman's aggressive and often abrasive style stirred the adrenalin in most of his listeners and caused them to pay attention to what he had to say. This characteristic of his speaking has been credited by some with his winning the election of 1948. Whether this stylistic factor in Truman's speaking was as important as that is not clear, but there is no doubt that it was one of the factors leading to his success as a communicator.

Often, a source may employ conflict by requesting the audience to join in a battle. Stokely Carmichael's almost overnight rise from obscurity to fame in the 1960s is a good example. The militant young African-American's effective use of his famous "black power" slogan was based upon competition and conflict. His reputation as a fighter and the extensive amount of conflict in his oral style stimulated many of the African-American members of his audiences to support him fervently.

3. Humor. People like to laugh and smile, and a source who makes it possible for them to do so will be attended to more closely. Humor does not mean just telling stories. It includes wit, which is probably more compelling. To phrase an idea in a humorous way will tend to call attention to it.

4. Personal touch. Communication of ideas is not possible until the ideas are personalized by an audience. During the late 1950s there was an extensive push in the United States to build fallout shelters as protection against nuclear attack. Just about everyone in the country realized that millions of people would die in the event of nuclear attack unless they had adequate protection from fallout. Some sources sought to impress upon their audiences nationally projected figures for the estimated number of Americans who would die in an attack. Other sources, with a better conception of attention and interest, talked to their audiences about their own children rather than about so many millions of Americans. Sometimes these sources succeeded in having community fallout shelters constructed, and in a few cases, they even succeeded in having elementary schools built underground. These successful rhetorical communicators realized that we attend to things that personally involve us or our loved ones, and that we act when we see that it is personally advantageous to do so.

5. Variety. Probably the most important characteristic of style relevant to attention and interest is variety. A skillful source will not develop all ideas in the same way but, to avoid monotony, will shift from hard-supported argument to humor or satire. Although every point may have specific, documented evidence that could be included to establish the given point effectively, the continuous use of evidence may cause the audience to lose interest. The source may find it helpful to employ a hypothetical instance, rather than a factual one, in order to maintain attention and interest. Other considerations being equal, the source should consider this factor in style when selecting specific supporting materials to be employed in the message.

6. Emphasis. We tend to pay more attention to things that are emphasized than to things that are not. This raises the question of what are the best ways to emphasize an idea. Studies by Jersild[5] and Ehrensberger[6] suggest that repetition is an effective means of emphasis. Specifically, an idea stated three times in the course of a message, or twice at the outset or the conclusion of a message, seems to be better remembered. Other effective methods of emphasis include making a verbal comment that directs attention to an item (for example, "Now get this"), using a short pause before or after the important idea, raising the voice, or making a forceful gesture. You should always consider the factor of emphasis and, whenever possible, specifically select the most effective means of emphasis for the given idea.

SUGGESTION

Suggestion is the process by which meanings are generated in the minds of members of the audience without the presence of specific referents for those meanings in the communicator's message. Suggestion is a pervasive force in rhetorical communication, always present and unavoidable. The effective source will control and use suggestion rather than being controlled by it.

As noted in Chapter 5, the power of ethos in rhetorical communication is great. That persuasive power normally operates through suggestion. In fact, many writers refer to ethos as "prestige suggestion." Meanings affected by ethos suggestion, while probably the most important, certainly are not the only meanings affected by the process of suggestion. All words are suggestive. Words stimulate both connotative and denotative meanings. The denotative, or definitional, meaning is usually the first to be thought of when a word is being selected for a message. But it is necessary to be aware of the connotative meaning also, because this is the meaning through which the process of suggestion operates. The word *farmer* is a good example. This word will stimulate quite a different meaning in the mind of a receiver who was born and raised in Wyoming from that in the mind of a receiver who was born and raised in Manhattan.

As employed by sources, suggestion often evokes uncritical idea acceptance by receivers. This characteristic of suggestion indicates the potential strength of this process as a rhetorical device, and at the same time brings to mind a major ethical question. Is it ethical for a source to employ devices that will gain uncritical acceptance of ideas? Chapter 16 will address questions of this type in the discussion of ethics. At this point we will concentrate on when and how suggestion may be successfully employed to achieve your desired end.

In developing a message, you face the choice of whether to include a direct statement of a point or to develop the point through suggestion. Although suggestion is effective, the first question to be answered is whether suggestion is even more effective than direct statement. Clinical observations by psychotherapists indicate that the answer is yes. Rogers, an exponent of the nondirective school of psychotherapy, claims that decisions made by clients are more lasting when they are reached independently by the client than when they are recommended by the therapist.[7] A relatively small group of experimental studies that bear upon this question have been reported. The results of the studies indicate the following conclusion.[8]

1. When the audience is not well educated and well informed on the topic or when the subject matter is relatively complex, suggestion is less effective than drawing explicit conclusions.
2. When the audience is well educated and the subject matter is not complex, suggestion and drawing explicit conclusions are approximately equal in effect.

On the basis of these conclusions from experimental research, it seems that the source, whenever in doubt, should use direct statement rather than suggestion. When a significant difference was found in these studies, it always favored the message in which the conclusion was explicitly drawn, rather than the message in which the conclusion was suggested. We should be cautious, however, about generalizing from this. Much more research is needed before we can be certain of the effects of suggestion as opposed to explicitly drawn conclusions.

There are at least two circumstances under which we may theorize that suggestion would be more effective than drawn conclusions. The first is when the conclusion has a highly personalized relationship to the individual drawing it. This is the case, of course, in psychotherapy, in which Rogers has observed that suggestion is the more effective practice. No experimental studies directly bearing on this point have been reported. All the studies have dealt with comparatively remote subjects. The second circumstance under which it would seem theoretically preferable to employ suggestion rather than direct statement is when the source of communication is perceived by the audience to be of moderate to low ethos. As we noted in

Chapter 4 in our discussion of the balance of homeostatic theories of attitude change, when a low-ethos source stands in favor of a conclusion, the
audience generally shifts its attitude away from acceptance of that conclusion. Consequently, it would seem reasonable to suppose that a low-ethos
source would be more effective by employing suggestion to avoid being
specifically identified with the conclusion he or she wishes the audience to
draw. If the audience can draw the conclusion without specifically identifying it with the low-credibility source, there is no imbalance to cause it to
reject the conclusion. We may tentatively conclude, therefore, that suggestion is superior to drawing explicit conclusions either when the conclusion
is personally highly relevant to the audience or when the message emanates
from a low-ethos source.

SATIRE AND HUMOR

It is appropriate to consider the effects of satire and humor in conjunction
with our discussion of suggestion. In most cases, satire and humor employ
suggestion rather than drawing explicit conclusions. They are ways of getting around the defenses of the audience and making the desired point in a
supposedly pleasant way so as to make it more palatable.

Relatively little research has been reported on the effect of satire and
humor in rhetorical communication. The conclusions of the studies that
have been reported, however, tend to discourage one from employing satire
and humor. Berlo and Kumata report a study of a satirical dramatic program, "The Investigator," broadcast by the Canadian Broadcasting Corporation. It satirized Senator Joseph M. McCarthy, the well-known former
chairman of the Senate Permanent Investigations Subcommittee. The program was an allegorical satire, in which no specific identification was made
of either McCarthy or of congressional investigations. The conclusions,
then, were suggested rather than explicitly stated. Berlo and Kumata
observed that their college students became more favorable, rather than
more opposed, to McCarthy after listening to the program. The satire, therefore, boomeranged.[9]

Gruner has reported two important experimental investigations of the
use of satire in persuasion. In both these studies, a satirical speech on censorship was employed. In neither study did Gruner observe a significant
overall attitude change on the part of his subjects. In one study, however,
he found that people originally favorable to censorship (the position taken
in the experimental messages) did shift significantly.[10] Although this latter
finding suggests that satire may be somewhat effective with hostile members of the audience, the fact that there was no significant shift overall on
the part of the audience does not permit much confidence in satire as a stylistic device in persuasion. In most experimental studies, almost any kind of
message will achieve a significant attitude change. Not all such changes are

very great, but at least they usually are statistically significant. Thus, if we may compare Gruner's findings with those of the vast body of other studies using the direct-conclusion procedure (which, of course, is a tenuous comparison), we are most likely to conclude that direct statement is far superior to the stylistic device of satire.

A study reported by Kennedy made a direct comparison between two humorous messages and a "straight" serious message.[11] The results indicated no significant differences in the amount of attitude change produced by the three messages. Both Gruner and Kennedy found some tendency for their humorous messages to enhance the perceived character of the message source. Although there is a need for much more research on the effects of humor in communication, the results of the studies reported to date suggest that use of humor may not be a particularly good way to enhance communication effects.

CONTROLLING MESSAGE DISCREPANCY THROUGH STYLE

In Chapter 4 we discussed the effects of perceived message discrepancy on the change in audience attitudes. We noted that, as a message is perceived by the audience as differing greatly from its current attitudes, less attitude change occurs, and in some cases attitude change in the direction opposite to that desired by the source will occur. Perceived message discrepancy may be somewhat controlled by selecting points on the basis of audience analysis and telling the audience what they already believe. This is a dubious procedure. If we merely tell the audience what they want to hear, we may increase our own ethos, but we have little effect upon the audience's attitudes. Thus, in most communicative situations, it is necessary for the source to express positions contrary to those of the audience. The extent of perceived message discrepancy can be controlled in large measure through style. The language we choose to employ in stating a position not originally held by the audience determines, for the most part, how discrepant that position is perceived to be.

Research on the effects of fear-arousing appeals in messages provides insight into the function of style in controlling perceived message discrepancy. A study reported by Miller and Hewgill indicates that a message with a strong appeal to fear obtained significantly more attitude change than one with a mild appeal to fear when the source was of high ethos.[12] (As noted in Chapter 4, a high-ethos source can achieve greater attitude change with a strongly discrepant message than with a mildly discrepant message.) There is no real difference between the mild and strong appeal, but rather in the way the appeal is worded. Strong appeals to fear are so worded as to elicit intense emotional reactions, whereas mild appeals to fear are phrased so as to elicit moderate emotional reactions or, in some cases, only so-called rational reactions. Consider the following example of the same idea worded first as a strong-fear appeal and then as a mild-fear appeal. These appeals were originally used by advocates of increased safety regulation for autos in the 1970s. The success of this campaign resulted in the much safer cars we drive today.

> *Strong-fear appeal.* You may think that the need for safety standards is not very important. You would quickly change your mind if your family had an accident. Seeing your wife impaled on your noncollapsible steering column or seeing your daughter's face after it had collided with your beautiful protruding radio knobs would make you change your mind. This needless death and disfigurement can be prevented by adequate safety standards.

> *Mild-fear appeal.* You may think that the need for safety standards is not very important. You would quickly change your mind if your wife had an accident. Death and disfigurement are produced by unsafe interior construction of automobiles. This needless death and disfigurement can be prevented by adequate safety standards.

The results of the Miller-Hewgill study suggest that the source who believes the audience will perceive her or him as a high-ethos source should employ strong fear appeals that elicit considerable emotional reaction from the audience. The source can accomplish this stylistically by building the emotional reactions from the audience. On the other hand, that same study indicates that there was no significant difference in attitude change between the strong-fear and mild-fear conditions when the source was perceived as a low-ethos source. Thus, the low-ethos source interested in gaining attitude change may not benefit by employing the strong-fear over the mild-fear message. As indicated in the Miller-Hewgill study, however, if the source employs a strong-fear message, he or she will lose more credibility. Gardiner found that a strong-fear appeal by a high-credibility source produced both more attitude change and higher credibility ratings than a mild-fear appeal but that the effects for a low-credibility source were the opposite.[13] Thus, it would appear that a highly discrepant message presented by a high-ethos source produces both greater attitude change and higher perceived credibility, but that the same message presented by a low-ethos source results in both less attitude change and reduced credibility.

From this discussion of the Miller-Hewgill and Gardiner reports, we may conclude that style exercises a very important function in controlling perceived message discrepancy. It seems clear that very intense language magnifies the perceived discrepancy of a message. Whether this magnification is good or bad depends on the initial credibility of the message source. Increasing perceived discrepancy tends to enhance the effectiveness of an initially high-credibility source but tends to reduce even further the effectiveness of an initially low-credibility source.

As yet, insufficient research has been reported to enable specification of all the variables that contribute to language intensity and hence to increased perceived message discrepancy. However, Corley found that messages including language typical of a black militant speaker in the 1960s were perceived as more intense than messages not including such language and that this difference resulted in reduced credibility ratings from her white listeners for her initially moderately credible source.[14] Similarly, Mehrley and McCroskey found that messages including opinionated rejection statements (not only on the source's attitude toward the topic but also on his or her attitude toward those who disagree) increased attitude change among receivers who initially held low-intensity attitudes on the message topic; however, the same statements resulted in source derogation by receivers who initially held intense attitudes on the topic.[15] This result is to be expected when perceived message discrepancy is increased, and it suggests that militant language and opinionated rejection statements may be variables highly related to perception of message discrepancy. Research reported by McEwen and Greenberg indicates that messages including more intense verbs and modifiers result in perceptions of greater intensity for the message as a whole.[16] Employing a moderately credible source, they found that the more intense message resulted in higher perceived credibility than the less intense version.

DISTORTION AND PRIOR KNOWLEDGE OF SOURCE'S ATTITUDE

We noted in Chapter 4 that people tend to perceive what they want or expect to perceive. Through stylistic choices, a source can often control what the audience perceives. Similarly, a source who is not aware of the stylistic choices that have been made can lead the audience to misperceive the message.

The role of expectation in perception must be stressed. We approach most communication situations with pretty clear ideas of what we are going to encounter. In most cases it turns out to be very nearly what we expected. We would not expect to hear a Palestinian leader advocating giving money to Israel. If we did hear him speak, and he was not advocating giving money to Israel, our expectation was confirmed. While this example may be a little extreme, it does indicate a type of situation we get into under normal circumstances. That is, we know what is going to happen, we expect it to happen, and it does happen. Continually experiencing fulfilled expectations reinforces the strength of our expectations.

Such expectations will normally be present in an audience, whether the message is presented orally or in written format. In fact, what the audience members expect the source to say determines, in many cases, whether they choose to expose themselves to the message at all. This is the selective exposure phenomenon discussed in Chapter 4. Consequently, it is vital for you, as the source, to find out what the audience expects you to say. If you already plan to say what is expected, there is little or no problem. However, it would not be uncommon to wish to communicate to an audience an unexpected idea. When this is the case, you must take extra care that the audience correctly perceives your idea.

Several empirical studies have investigated the effects of various violations of audience expectancy and the absence of such violations. In one such study, Koehler, McCroskey, and Arnold created three messages concerning transporting students by bus in order to maintain racial balance in public schools. One message strongly favored it, one strongly opposed it, and one included statements on both sides of the issue, so as to be ambivalent. These messages were variously attributed to Dr. Martin Luther King, Jr., and to Governor George Wallace of Alabama. Six audiences read these messages (prior to Dr. King's death) as being quoted from a recent issue of the *New York Times* reporting an interview with the quoted source. Under the conditions consistent with the prior known attitude of the quoted source (King pro-busing, Wallace anti-busing), the experimental subjects perceived the message as intended. The ambivalent message was perceived as distorted significantly in the direction of the source to whom it was attributed. When it was attributed to King, it was perceived as strongly favorable to busing; when it was attributed to Wallace, it was perceived as strongly opposed to busing. Even when the message was strongly in opposition to the position the audience expected the communicator to take, there was an indication of distorted perception. The Wallace pro-busing message, though perceived as somewhat pro-busing, was perceived as significantly less favorable to busing than the King pro-busing message. A similar effect was found in the King anti-busing message in comparison with the Wallace anti-busing message.[17]

The results of this and similar studies suggest that clarity of style is not enough when audience expectations are contrary to message intent. If you are stating a position substantially different from what the audience expects, you need to inform the audience explicitly that the position is different from what was expected. Otherwise, perception by many members of the audience will not be in line with what you desire.

STYLE, POWER, AND BEHAVIORAL ALTERATION MESSAGES

In Chapter 5 we noted that sources often attempt to exert power to change people's attitudes and behaviors. We also noted that the use of some forms of power tends to lead to a negative impact on the source's ethos. This impact can frequently be increased or reduced as a function of the words that are chosen to make the influence attempt.

Recent research suggests that people use twenty-two different techniques to exert power in their communication with others.[18] Table 13.1

TABLE 13.1 Behavior Alteration Techniques and Sample Messages

TECHNIQUES	SAMPLE MESSAGES
1. Immediate reward from behavior	You will enjoy it. It will make you happy. Because it's fun. You'll find it rewarding/interesting. It's a good experience.
2. Deferred reward behavior	It will help you later on in life. It will prepare you for other jobs. It will help you with upcoming assignments.
3. Reward from source	I will give you a reward if you do. I will make it beneficial to you. I will give you a raise, time off, etc.
4. Reward from others	Others will respect you if you do. Others will be proud of you. Your friends will like you if you do. People around you will be pleased.
5. Self-esteem	You will feel good about yourself if you do. You are the best person to do it. You are good at it. You always do such a good job. Because you're capable of doing it.
6. Punishment from behaivor	You will lose if you don't. You will be unhappy if you don't. It's your loss. You'll feel bad if you don't.
7. Punishment from source	I will punish you if you don't. I will make it miserable for you. I'll give you a reprimand if you don't. If you don't do it now, you will have to do it later.
8. Punishment from others	No one will like you. Your friends will make fun of you. People around you will dislike you. Your peers will reject you.
9. Guilt	If you don't, others will be hurt. You'll make others feel unhappy if you don't. People around you will feel bad if you don't. Your friends will be punished if you don't.
10. Source-power relationship: power	I will like you better if you do. I will think more highly of you. I will appreciate you more if you do. I will be proud of you.
11. Source-receiver relationship: negative	I will dislike you if you don't. I will lose respect for you. I will think less of you if you don't. I won't be proud of you. I'll be disappointed in you.
12. Legitimate: higher authority	Do it, I'm just telling you what I was told. It is a rule. I have to do it and so do you. It's the law. It's the policy.
13. Legitimate: source authority	Because I told you to. You don't have a choice. Don't ask, just do it. I'm in charge, not you.
14. Personal responsibility	It is your obligation. It is your turn. Everyone has to do his or her share. It's your job. Everyone has to pull his or her own weight.
15. Duty	Your group needs it done. Your peers are depending on you. All your friends are counting on you. Don't let your group down. You'll ruin it for the rest of the group.

(continued)

TABLE 13.1 Continued

TECHNIQUES	SAMPLE MESSAGES
16. Normative rules	We voted, and the majority rules. All your friends are doing it. Everyone else has to do it. The rest of the group is doing it.
17. Debt	You owe me one. Pay your debt. You promised to do it. I did it the last time. You said you'd do it this time.
18. Altruism	If you do this, it will help others. Others will benefit if you do. It will make others happy if you do. I'm not asking you to do it for yourself; do it for the good of others.
19. Peer modeling	Your friends do it. People whom you respect do it. The friends you admire do it. All your friends are doing it.
20. Referent (source) modeling	This is the way I always do it. When I was your age, I did it. People who are like me do it. I had to do this when I was starting out.
21. Expert	From my experience, it is a good idea. From what I have learned, it is what you should do. This has always worked for me. Trust me—I know what I'm doing.
22. Source feedback	Because I need to know how well you understand this. To see how well you can do it. It will help me know your problem areas. So I can be of more help to you.

presents a list of these techniques with brief sample messages that people report using in their communication with others. Each of the techniques centers on a warrant the source may use to appeal to an audience for acceptance of his or her claim concerning the behavior in which the audience members should engage.

Examine the messages for each of the techniques listed in the table. Try to design messages for each technique that take into account the characteristics of good style discussed above and that avoid the potential problems noted.

This chapter has discussed some of the important considerations relating to style that you should take into account in the development of a message. Style, like invention and disposition, serves a utilitarian purpose in achieving the effects intended. To the degree that your style does not meet the needs of the communicative situation or is inappropriate to either the message content or the audience, you will lose desired communicative effects. However, if you are skillful in the use of style you will enhance your overall effectiveness.

DISCUSSION QUESTIONS

1. Many people claim that "style is the person." What does this imply? Do you agree?

2. If "meaning is in people, not in words," as is asserted in this chapter, what function does a dictionary serve, if any?

3. If good oral style is clearer and more intelligible than written style, should we attempt to employ good oral style in our writing? Why or why not?

4. This chapter asserts that a vivid and memorable style is desirable. Chapter 4 noted that if perceived message discrepancy is too great, attitude change may "boomerang." Do these statements conflict? If not, why not? If so, how can the conflict be resolved?

5. Which is to be preferred if a choice has to be made: good style or audience adaptation? Why? What implication does this have for the choice of the means of presenting a message to an audience?

6. Read the student speech "The Proposed Basketball Rule Changes," and the address by George Bush, both of which appear in Appendix A. Evaluate the style of each. Why does the style of these speeches differ so much? Do the same with the speech by Heston.

NOTES

1. J. D. Ragsdale, Jr., "Effects of Selected Aspects of Brevity on Comprehensibility and Persuasiveness," Ph.D. diss., University of Illinois, 1964.

2. G.L. Borchers, "An Approach to the Problem of Oral Style," *Quarterly Journal of Speech* 22 (1936): 114–17; G. L. Thomas, "Effect of Oral Style on Intelligibility of Speech," *Speech Monographs* 22 (1956): 46–54; J. A. DeVito, "Psychogrammatical Factor in Oral and Written Discourse by Skilled Communicators," *Speech Monographs* 33 (1966): 73–76; and J. W. Gibson, C. R. Gruner, R. J. Kibler, and F. J. Kelly, "A Quantitative Examination of Differences and Similarities in Written and Spoken Messages," *Speech Monographs* 33 (1966): 444–51.

3. J. A. Winans, *Public Speaking* (New York: Century Co., 1917), p. 194.

4. R. T. Oliver, *The Psychology of Persuasive Speech* (New York: Longmans, Green and Co., 1957), p. 119.

5. A. T. Jersild, "Modes of Emphasis in Public Speaking," *Journal of Applied Psychology* 12 (1928): 611–12.

6. R. Ehrensberger, "An Experimental Study of the Relative Effectiveness of Certain Forms of Emphasis in Public Speaking," *Speech Monographs* 12 (1945): 94–111.

7. C. R. Rogers, "Some Observations on the Organization of Personality," *American Psychologist* 2 (1947): 358–68.

8. C. I. Hovland and W. Mandell, "An Experimental Comparison of Conclusion Drawing by the Communicator and by the Audience," *Journal of Abnormal and Social Psychology* 47 (1952): 581–88; D. L. Thistlethwaite, H. deHaan, and J. Kamenetsky, "The Effects of 'Directive' and 'Non-directive' Communication Procedures on Attitudes," *Journal of Abnormal and Social Psychology* 51 (1955): 107–13; H. Leventhal, R. Singer, S. Jones, "Effects of Fear and Specificity of Recommendation upon Attitudes and Behavior," *Journal of Personality and Social Psychology* 2 (1965): 20–30.

9. D. K. Berlo and H. Kumata, "The Investigator: The Impact of a Satirical Radio Drama," *Journalism Quarterly* 33 (1956): 287–98.

10. C. R. Gruner, "An Experimental Study of Satire as Persuasion," *Speech Monographs* 32 (1965): 149–53; and "A Further Experimental Study of Satire as Persuasion," *Speech Monographs* 32 (1966): 184ff. See also C. R. Gruner, "The Effect of Humor in Dull and Interesting Informative Speeches," *Central States Speech Journal* 21 (1970): 160–66.

11. A. J. Kennedy, "An Experimental Study of the Effect of Humorous Message Content upon Ethos and Persuasiveness," paper presented at the convention of the Speech Communication Association, New Orleans, 1970.

12. G. R. Miller and M. A. Hewgill, "Some Recent Research on Fear-Arousing Message Appeals," *Speech Monographs* 33 (1966): 377–91.

13. J. C. Gardiner, "An Experimental Study of the Effects of Evidence and Fear Appeals on Attitude Change and Source Credibility," Research Monograph, Department of Communication, Michigan State University, 1969.

14. D. K. Corley, "Effect of Militant Language and Race of Source on Attitude and Credibility," M.A. thesis, Illinois State University, 1970.

15. R. S. Mehrley and J. C. McCroskey, "Opinionated Statements and Attitude Intensity as Predictors of Attitude Change and Source Credibility," *Speech Monographs* 37 (1970): 47–52.

16. W. J. McEwen and B. S. Greenberg, "The Effects of Message Intensity on Receiver Evaluations of Source, Message, and Topic," *Journal of Communication* 20 (1970): 340–50.

17. J. W. Koehler, J. C. McCroskey, and W. E. Arnold, "The Effects of Receiver's Constancy-Expectation in Communication," Research Monograph, Department of Speech, Pennsylvania State University, 1966.

18. P. Kearney, T. G. Plax, V. P. Richmond, and J. C. McCroskey, "Power in the Classroom IV: Alternatives to Discipline," in R. N. Bostrom (Ed.) *Communication Yearbook 8* (Beverly Hills, CA: Sage, 1984), pp. 724–46.

CHAPTER 14

INTRODUCING AND CONCLUDING MESSAGES IN RHETORICAL COMMUNICATION

Several of the preceding chapters have been devoted to the procedures by which the bulk of a message for rhetorical communication may be developed. For the most part, these chapters have been concerned with the development of the body of the message. After the body of a message has been developed, you must consider how to introduce that body to the audience and how to conclude the message. In this chapter we shall discuss the functions of introductions and conclusions and suggest some specific ways that messages may be introduced and concluded. As you proceed through this chapter, you should keep clearly in mind that introductions and conclusions are functional units within messages. They are not merely means of beginning and ending messages. Rather, if skillfully employed, they are means of enhancing the effectiveness of the rest of the message.

INTRODUCTIONS

Primary Functions of Introductions

There are three main functions an introduction may serve: to arouse audience attention, to enhance the ethos of the source, and to preview the body of the message.

The preceding chapters have stressed that a receiver must pay attention to a message before the message can exert an influence. In some cases, although very few, an audience knows a subject beforehand and is very much interested in it. In these circumstances the audience's attention level is probably already satisfactory. In most cases, however, the level of interest and attention must be increased. Since the introduction is the first part of the message that the audience either hears or sees, it must stimulate attention

and interest. If the audience's attention is not drawn by the introduction, usually all is lost. In written communication, the reader may not even read the rest of the message if the introduction is not interesting. In oral communication, the situation is quite similar. If the speaker does not arouse the attention of the audience members at the outset, they will probably be lethargic in their response to the rest of the message. If the circumstances surrounding the communicative event permit it, receivers may even leave and not listen to the rest of the message at all. Thus, *the first and foremost function of an introduction is to arouse attention and interest on the part of the audience.*

The second function of a good introduction is to enhance the ethos of the source. As noted in Chapter 5, the three dimensions of ethos are competence, trustworthiness, and goodwill. Goodwill may be enhanced by establishing common ground with the audience. If you indicate that you have interests in common with the audience and are concerned with their well-being, the audience members are more likely to perceive you as a person with goodwill towards them, and maybe as more trustworthy and competent as well. In most cases, you will not specifically include materials designed to enhance your perceived competence. At this point in the message, such references may be perceived as boasting and cause a reduction in the character dimension of ethos. If your competence needs a boost, try to have someone introduce you who can include such material in their introduction. At this point, however, you must take care that the introduction to your speech does not lower perceived competence. In oral communication, there is a tendency on the part of many speakers to apologize to an audience during their introduction. If a speaker arrives forty-five minutes late for a scheduled address, an apology is not only appropriate but almost mandatory. However, in the normal scheme of things, apologies are out of line. Remember, you may be ignorant, incompetent, and a miserable speaker, but let the audience figure that out for themselves. Who knows? Some people in the audience may not perceive your shortcomings.

In many cases, the introduction serves a third function: it previews the material to be discussed in the body of the message. This is not, however, a necessary function of an introduction. Indeed, in many cases, such a preview would hamper the effectiveness of the message that follows. To understand better when to preview the body and when not to, we must consider the problem of forewarning and its effects on rhetorical communication.

THE PROBLEM OF FOREWARNING

When the members of an audience know that a source is going to attempt to persuade them, the likelihood of that communicator's success is greatly reduced. A study by Kiesler and Kiesler indicates that forewarning not only reduces the persuasive effect of a message but in some cases completely precludes persuasion. The results of the Kieslers' study also suggest that forewarning may produce boomerang effects; the receivers may shift their attitude in the direction opposite to the one the source desires.[1]

This finding from the empirical research of the Kieslers seems to suggest, then, that you should never preview the body of the message in the introduction. This conclusion, however, must be tempered. In many cases receivers know, before the source ever begins the message, that the source is going to attempt to persuade them. In this circumstance, a preview of the body does not provide a forewarning that should reduce the persuasive effect. The receiver already has been forewarned, so such a preview has no additional effect. The preview of the body may, however, considerably enhance the clarity of the message and thus increase the probability of achieving the desired effect. The problem of forewarning is also not important when the purpose is to strengthen an attitude the receiver already holds. Forewarning can then be perceived by the receiver as the establishment of common ground. Further, when you have informative intent, the problem of forewarning is not relevant, for the loss of persuasive effect is of no concern in messages with informative intent.

We may conclude from all of this that you probably should not preview the body of the message in the introduction if the audience is not yet aware of the persuasive intent. However, when the audience is already aware of this, when it is in agreement with your position, or when your intent is to enhance understanding, the introduction may include a preview of the body of the message.

Identification of Audience with Message

Related to the question of forewarning is the question of whether you should attempt to identify the audience with the subject of the message. There is a considerable body of theory that suggests that this should be done.[2] As observed in preceding chapters, the source tends to be most effective if he or she identifies the subject with the receiver's self-interest. This suggests the necessity of relating the subject directly to the audience. It also suggests that such identification should probably be begun in the introduction.

However, some research intimates that specifically relating the subject to the receiver may be an ineffective means of communication. A study by Walster and Festinger found that messages perceived by the receivers to be directed to other persons were significantly more effective than were messages the receivers perceived to be directly intended for them.[3] This finding, again, indicates that a receiver will be more likely to be persuaded if he or she does not perceive that the source is trying to be persuasive. It suggests that indirect rather than direct means of identifying the subject with the receiver are more effective. Yet if receivers are already aware that the message is directed to them, if they are already in agreement with the point of the message, or if the message is designed to enhance understanding rather than to persuade, the more direct means of identification are appropriate.

Ways of Beginning Messages

An effective introduction arouses attention and interest, enhances the ethos of the communicator, and in many cases previews the body of the message that follows. It is now time to consider specific ways in which these objectives can be achieved. Following are sixteen ways of beginning a message. Some of them are appropriate for one kind of message but not for another. The different methods are by no means mutually exclusive. You may employ two or more of them in one introduction. These suggestions are provided as a checklist that you may consult if you are having difficulty determining how to develop your introduction.

1. **Startling statement.** Things that startle or surprise us capture our attention. The unexpected is much more attention-getting than the expected. Consider the following example from a speech delivered in Honolulu.

> Paradise Island. The Pearl of the Pacific. The melting pot of the races. Yes, beautiful Hawaii. America's model for racial harmony. Poppy-cock! We have more racial disharmony here in Hawaii than anywhere else in the United States. There are more racial bigots per square mile in Honolulu than in any other city in the world. The only reason that we don't note this fact, call it to

everyone's attention, and root this festering blight from our midst is because most of these bigots, unlike their brothers on the mainland, are nonwhite.

2. Striking question. A striking question in many cases can achieve much the same effect as a startling statement. It piques attention and gets people's minds working. Of course, an ordinary question, like an ordinary statement, captures little attention. The effective use of a striking question is demonstrated in the following example taken from an antiwar speech delivered by a recently returned Korean War veteran shortly after the close of the Korean conflict.

> How many prostitutes have you bought lately? Most of you moral, upright citizens may think you haven't bought any. But I suggest you're wrong. You have bought prostitutes and provided them to men like me through your government. War does things like that to people and to governments. Here at home our government frowns on prostitution. But the moment a war breaks out, all of a sudden prostitution becomes a highly desired profession. Oh, of course, not here. Only where our American boys are outside of the country is prostitution so desired. Now, in most of the countries where we visit on our way to war, or on our way back, prostitutes are readily available. But whenever they aren't, our government, with your tax money, makes sure that they are provided.

3. Suspense. The use of suspense is one of the most effective methods of arousing attention and interest. Curiosity is a very strong motivating factor in most people, and the use of suspense appeals to this motive. The basic idea in the use of suspense is to arouse interest before the audience knows what it is that you are going to talk about. An essay on automobile safety began with the following introduction.

> There is an epidemic raging in this country. It is getting out of hand. Last year, it orphaned over 35,000 children. It caused the deaths of 47 high school homecoming queens. Between 1974 and 1995 it accounted for the deaths of more American servicemen than all the deaths attributable to hostile enemy action. It cut short the promising careers of seven Merit Scholars last year. Even doctors have developed no immunity to this epidemic. Over 500 doctors have succumbed in the last year. What is this epidemic? Is it plague? Cancer? Heart disease? Influenza? No. It is an epidemic of careless and irresponsible use of automobiles.

4. Quotation. What a famous or respected person says is normally of interest to people. The quotation employed may either be well known or obscure; the important thing is that the quotation be interesting and relevant to the point to be developed in the message. Particularly famous quotations usually are not as desirable as less famous or obscure ones because they may have become trite through overexposure. The following paragraph could be used to introduce a talk designed to stress the importance of curricular, as opposed to extracurricular, activities in school.

> The famous actor and comedian Bill Cosby was recently asked the question "What has been the biggest disappointment of your life?" His answer was published in Family Weekly. "The fact that I didn't take advantage of my education. I was bright enough, but spent all my time on sports. Even when I went to college, I had an athletic scholarship. To this day, I regret not learning more. It's a sin to have an opportunity to be educated and ignore it. Some day I hope to return to school." Bill Cosby is an unqualified success in his chosen profession. He is admired and respected by millions of Americans. Yet Bill Cosby recognized that had he devoted more of his energy while in school to his curricular work, he could now live a fuller life. It's probably too late for Bill Cosby to go back to school to learn. But it is not too late for you.[4]

5. Illustration. An illustration may be either a factual or a hypothetical example. An important characteristic of a good illustration is that it permits the receiver to visualize the circumstance being described. The following example of an introduction employing an illustration is taken from a speech delivered by a supporter of the American position in South Vietnam. The speaker had recently returned from a tour of Vietnam in 1966.

> While I was in Vietnam I saw many sights that shocked and startled me. I remember one incident in particular. I came upon a village which had survived a severe bombing from American planes. It was one of the many villages that were accidentally attacked. I visited the field hospital that had been set up in the middle of the village. One of the first sights that I saw as I entered the hospital was a section where injured children were placed. One child in particular caught my eye. I learned that this child was just seven years old. The child was burned over 90 percent of her body. She had lost both legs and one hand. The doctor told me that she would survive and was receiving the best treatment possible under the prevailing conditions. As I looked at this pitiful little girl, I wondered just how we as Americans could justify what we are doing in Vietnam. How are we any better than the Viet Cong? As I was standing by this little girl's bedside and talking with the doctor, I realized the answer to that question. The doctor told me that this little girl was an orphan but that her parents were not killed by American bombing. It seems her parents had been loyal to the South Vietnamese regime, and the Viet Cong had kidnaped them from the village several weeks prior to the accidental American bombing. The day after the kidnaping, an ARVN patrol had found the little girl's parents' decapitated bodies only a mile from the village. It was then that I realized the difference between us and the Cong. It is true that we do it; it is by accident. The Cong systematically torture and murder thousands of Vietnamese. And they do not do it by accident.

6. Humor. Humor can be an excellent method of securing audience attention, but it is frequently misused. Humor, to be well used in the introduction, will be appropriate to the audience, relevant to the subject matter to be discussed, and usually brief. The following example is taken from the speech presented by a person known to the audience as a supporter of the lottery system for drafting men into the Armed Services. It was delivered at a meeting of a local medical society.

> When people know that I am a supporter of the lottery system for drafting men into the Armed Services, they almost invariably ask the same question, "Well, how do you plan to get the doctors the Army needs if you're going to select the men to be drafted purely by chance?" I have a very simple suggestion for solving that particular problem. I think that the Selective Service should merely go to the Yellow Pages, look under physicians, and start making telephone calls. All the doctors who agree to come for a house call receive a deferment. All the others get drafted.

7. Reference to occasion or place. In some cases, the occasion or the place in which a speech is being presented is of particular relevance to the audience, the speaker, or both. In such cases it is highly desirable to open with a reference to this significant circumstance. In fact, in some cases the audience will be offended if the message does not make reference to this occasion or place. The following excerpt is taken from an introduction to a speech delivered at the dedication ceremony for a new bridge.

> Our program here today says that we have gathered to dedicate a bridge, a bridge that spans a mighty river that divides our state. But this occasion is more than just a bridge dedication. It marks the commencement of a new life for thousands of people living on both sides of the river. Most of our lives will never again be quite the same once this bridge is opened. Let us lean back and contemplate for a few minutes the magnitude of the changes that are going to occur in our lives.

8. Appeal to self-interest of receiver. As stated at several points, receivers are highly motivated by self-interest. If the receiver perceives what is being said as something that will aid him or her in achieving a happier or fuller life, that piques interest and attention. This type of introduction is often used to establish a main motivational warrant that will be employed later in arguments in the body of the message. It is also frequently employed in messages designed to increase understanding. The following example was once heard by the author as a student in a classroom. The instructor opened the class session in this way:

> I am quite certain that everyone in this room is interested in getting as good a mark as possible on the final exam, since it counts 60 percent of your final

mark. Questions based on the material that I will include in today's lecture will constitute 25 percent of the final examination.

9. Challenge to the audience. If a man walks up to us and stamps on our toes, we notice him. We may also hit him in the mouth. Issuing a challenge to an audience is similar to stamping on their toes. It must be done carefully, or they will, figuratively speaking, hit us in the mouth. To issue a challenge to an audience means to go directly and bluntly against their beliefs. Although this is an excellent method of capturing attention, it is ordinarily accompanied by a loss of ethos. Thus, the source who wishes to employ such a method must take care, later in the message, to rebuild his or her ethos. The following introduction was employed in 1963 by a guest speaker addressing a Unitarian congregation in a Southern community that was avowedly liberal in both religion and politics.

> It is customary for a speaker addressing a group at their invitation to indicate that he is pleased to stand before them. I find it quite difficult to say that today, because I am a political and religious liberal. Nothing irritates a liberal more than to be confronted by a phony liberal. As I stand before you this morning, I look out upon a sea of white phony liberal faces. The fact that there is not one negro in this audience says more to me than all of your noble pronouncements of your liberalism. So does the fact that in yesterday's march not one of you was present. Birchers and Klansmen can impede the progress of liberal programs in our state and country, but phony liberals like you can kill these programs right on the spot. And you're doing it.

10. Personal reference. In many a case, a person has a unique experience or background that makes him or her a particularly interesting source on the topic to be discussed. In such circumstances, the source may capture attention and enhance ethos at the same time by making a personal reference relevant to this unique background. The following example is an introduction employed by the author in a speech he presented to a group of students who were planning to take a trip to Hawaii.

> As some of you know, I had the unique opportunity to teach for one year on the beautiful University of Hawaii campus on Honolulu. That was clearly the most enjoyable and beneficial year I have ever spent in my life. Hawaii has been appropriately labeled the Paradise of the Pacific. It lives up to that description in nearly every detail. Unfortunately, most people who visit Hawaii see only the glitter and the surface beauty of the islands. Tonight, I want to talk to you about a few things you can see in Hawaii if you know where to go and where to look.

11. Statement of purpose. In some situations you may begin the message by a direct statement of purpose. This may be done when the audience is already familiar with the purpose, or when the purpose is particularly interesting to the audience. This method, however, is generally not desirable. The following is an example of an introduction appropriately stating the source's purpose. The source was speaking at a hearing before the city council in a small community, which was considering an open housing ordinance.

> My purpose in coming before you this evening is to ask you to vote in favor of the pending open housing ordinance. As the Chairman of the Open Housing Committee, I speak for all of our 500 members when I say that this ordinance is the only way we will prevent racial strife in our community.

12. Use of a visual aid. A visual aid that helps to clarify an idea you are going to attempt to get across is often a useful introductory device. In a written message, a story with a picture above it is much more likely to be read than the same story without the picture. A speaker who comes before an audience and exhibits an item that is interesting is more likely to capture attention than a speaker who comes before the group without such an exhibit. The visual aid should be relevant, of course, to the topic of the message. Advertisers, however, learned long ago that a beautiful woman can sell a lawn mower even though she is not really relevant to it. The following example is taken from a talk entitled "The Pill or Poverty." The speaker, an advocate of having birth control devices provided to the public through welfare programs, stood before the audience and held in one hand a large picture of an obviously starving child and in the other hand a small pill. He said:

> Here in America and around the world, mankind is faced with a choice. I refer to this choice as the pill or poverty. Today in this country we are choosing poverty over the pill. This is a picture [holds up the picture] that I took on a recent visit to Mississippi. There are hundreds more children just like this one. In some cases, these children have as many as 10 to 15 brothers and sisters, all of whom are badly undernourished. The parents of these children simply cannot provide for them. As a society, we are confronted with three choices. We may turn our back and let children such as this one die, we can provide welfare assistance to keep them alive, or we can provide welfare assistance to prevent them from being conceived. We will not let people starve in this country so long as we know they are starving, so we are confronted with only two choices: the pill [holds up small pill] or poverty [holds up picture].

13. Reference to recent incident. Often a message is concerned with a topic to which recent incidents familiar to the audience are relevant. These incidents may be employed to capture attention. An editorial concerned with the incarceration and treatment of mentally ill people began with the following introduction.

Less than a month ago, two little girls were molested and murdered in our suburbs by a convicted sexual psychopath who had escaped from our state prison for the criminally insane. Yesterday, two small boys in Detroit met a similar fate at the hands of a known sexual psychopath who had been released as cured. Did these four small children have to die this way? Is there nothing that we as a society can do to prevent attacks on our children by maniacs?

14. Complimenting the audience. One of the most effective methods of enhancing ethos in an introduction is to compliment the audience. Just about everyone likes to compliment the audience. Just about everyone likes to be complimented. We reason that if the other person is wise enough to see our virtues, he or she must have some too. Thus, this method, properly employed in an introduction, tends to increase a source's ethos. A receiver, however, will tend to sense when a compliment is insincere. Thus, the use of a compliment in an introduction should be considered only when there is a sincere basis for it. A college president employed the introduction below when speaking to an audience composed of academic debaters who were visiting on his campus for a debate tournament.

It is indeed a pleasure to have this distinguished group upon our campus. Your schools have reason to be indeed proud of their representatives. Over the past two and one-half days I have had the opportunity to listen to several of you debate this year's topic. The speaking that I heard was intelligent and forceful. Many of our political leaders would do well to come listen to you people. This is the first time that we have been privileged to hold a debate tournament on our campus, and I trust that it will be the first in a long series of rewarding experiences for us. I have no question in my mind but that the group of people seated before me are collectively the brightest and most eloquent group ever to come together on this campus. If there is one thing that we know about debaters, it is that they are the academic and vocal leaders on their campuses. To have so many of you with us at one time is indeed an honor to our college and to me as the president of this institution.

15. Reference to preceding speaker. In oral communication, it is not uncommon for the source to be preceded by another speaker. When this occurs, the audience may still be thinking about what that former speaker has said. An effective means of transferring the attention that remains from the preceding speaker is to relate what that person said to what we are going to say. The employment of this method often is an on-the-spot adaptation rather than a preplanned introduction. We may not know what the preceding speaker is going to say, so we cannot plan in advance to make effective use of what was said. The reference-to-the-preceding-speaker approach is often used in rhetorical communication within a debate format. The second speaker may begin with such a statement as:

Mr. X has given us three reasons that he claims are a justification for our country's adopting a socialized medicine program. I am going to examine those three reasons with you, and I think we're going to see that none of them stands up.

16. Beginning directly with the body. In some cases, the subject matter being discussed is of such major importance to the receiver that no introduction is needed. This is an uncommon circumstance, but not an impossible one. The source should never feel an absolute necessity to include a special introduction. As noted above, an introduction exists primarily to serve three functions: to arouse interest and attention, to enhance the source's ethos, and to give a preview of the body of the message. If all these functions can be fulfilled without a specific introduction, there is no need for one. You are cautioned, however, that if you have any doubt about whether or not an introduction should be included, you should include one.

Integration of Introduction and Body

As noted in this and preceding chapters, the introduction and the body are separate parts of the message. But they should not necessarily be perceived by receivers as distinctly separate parts. The introduction should be integrated into the beginning of the body of the message in such a way that they flow together smoothly. Often this can be accomplished by combining several of the introductory methods just described into one introduction. Several of the preceding introduction examples, although illustrating particular methods, have combined more than one method in the total introduction. Thus, one introductory method may be employed to capture attention and others employed to focus that attention on the body of the message. Whatever introductory technique(s) you employ, you must remember that the attention that it captured in the introduction must be transformed into attention to the body of the message before it can serve a useful function.

Length of Introduction

A question that troubles many beginning students of rhetorical communication is, "How long should my introduction be?" That is a difficult question to answer. The answer "Long enough" is obviously not very helpful, but it is about the only answer possible. The length of the introduction necessarily depends upon the particular communicative circumstances. A study by Miller indicated a range from 1 to 38 percent of the total length of the speech for an introduction. For the fifty speeches studied, the average length of the introduction was 10 percent of the total.[5] Thus, we would normally expect about a one minute introduction for a ten-minute talk. To set that as a guideline, however, could be very misleading. Some introductions last for over half the total message. As an example, consider a speech delivered by Dr. Linus Pauling, the noted atomic scientist, who was invited to speak on the campus of the University of Hawaii. For several days prior to the date of this address, a right-wing political organization inserted advertisements in the local newspapers and made announcements on television and radio to the effect that Dr. Pauling had a background of Communist affiliation. The fact that Pauling had been called to testify before the House Un-American Activities Committee was heavily stressed. Most of the people who were potential audience members for Dr. Pauling were not well informed about his background, but did come in contact with the information brought out by this organization. Consequently, when Pauling faced his audience, these people did not hold him in particularly high esteem. For the first thirty-five minutes of his fifty-five minute talk, Dr. Pauling said nothing about his subject, the elimination of nuclear testing. Rather, he talked about smoking and lung cancer, highway safety, and all sorts of other things. The discussion was light, humorous, and laced with an extensive amount of factual material on the unrelated topics. This thirty-five minute introduction was none too long. Pauling recognized that he needed to enhance his credibility before he could receive a favorable hearing on his main topic and proceeded to accomplish just that. By the time he got to his main point, the audience was friendly, relaxed, and responsive. Although most sources probably will never face as difficult an audience situation as Pauling did, his example should be kept in mind. The introduction should be long enough to accomplish the particular functions required of it—no shorter and no longer.

CONCLUSIONS

Primary Function of Conclusions

Because the conclusion is the last part of the message the audience hears or reads, it *is the part most likely to be remembered if it is well done*. Conclusions for different types of messages may serve a variety of functions.

One function that all conclusions must serve is to end the message gracefully. In this regard, we might consider the so-called *three S's of public speaking: stand up, speak up, shut up*. The last S is the most difficult for many people. A graceful conclusion is the one that focuses attention on what is being said in the body rather than upon itself. We can probably best understand what a graceful conclusion is by looking at what it is not. It is not excessively long. We have all heard speakers who said, "In conclusion," and were still talking ten minutes later. Long-winded, rambling conclusions do not provide a graceful end to a message. On the other hand, a graceful conclusion does not stop abruptly. An abrupt conclusion leaves the audience feeling that there is something missing from the message. A graceful conclusion, then, falls somewhere between the long-winded and the abrupt. It rounds off the message and leaves the audience with a feeling of completeness.

A second function of conclusions is to make the idea or ideas of the message memorable. In a long message, the audience often loses sight of the forest for the trees. The conclusion provides the source with an excellent opportunity to bring the forest back into focus. If the main idea or ideas become memorable through the conclusion, the message has a greater likelihood of maintaining influence.

Conclusions to persuasive messages may serve the additional function of enhancing the ethos of the source. If the message has been well designed up to this point, the audience and the source should have reached communality in interest and belief. Direct reference to this communality will tend to enhance the source's terminal ethos and lay the groundwork for higher initial ethos for later contacts with the audience.

Ways of Ending Messages

These three main functions of conclusions—*to end gracefully, to drive home the main point, and to enhance the source's ethos*—may be achieved through a variety of methods.

1. Make a general summary. A conclusion employing a general summary touches upon the main idea discussed in the body and highlights the main point of the message. It is one of the most commonly used concluding methods. Consider the following example taken from a speech advocating the elimination of capital punishment.

> Well, I don't believe I need to belabor the issue any further. We've examined the facts and seen that capital punishment does not deter crime; we have seen that society can be protected from criminals without killing them; we have seen that the alleged moral basis for capital punishment has been renounced by every major religion in the world; we have seen that discrimination based on race and sex flourishes in the administration of the death penalty; and finally, we have noted that innocent men have been executed, and the only way to prevent that from happening again is to eliminate the death penalty altogether. I have decided what I think should be done about the laws that permit capital punishment. I would guess that you have also.

2. Summarize individual points. This method of concluding messages is similar to the one above, but this one refers to the main support for each point. The following example comes from another message advocating the abolition of capital punishment. It may be compared to the previous example to illustrate the difference between the two approaches.

What can we conclude about capital punishment in the United States? First, it is clear that the threat of the death penalty is not a deterrent to crime. Where it has been abolished the homicide rates are lower than in comparable states where people continue to be executed. Second, capital punishment cannot be justified for economic reasons. As we have noted, executing criminals is far more expensive than maintaining them in prison. Third, capital punishment is discriminatory on the basis of race and sex. Blacks are killed, whites are imprisoned. Men die, but women live. Finally and, in my opinion, most important, capital punishment results in putting innocent men to death. This has not occurred in just a couple of isolated instances, but in virtually every state in the nation in which capital punishment is used.

The big question—the one neither I nor anyone else can answer with certainty—is, "Why?" Why has society allowed this barbaric remnant from the Middle Ages to continue? Why do we continue to direct our law enforcement agents to execute men in hidden rooms of our prisons like the Nazis directed their agents to exterminate Jews in hidden camps like Auschwitz? The only answer I can suggest is that this is just another instance in the long history of man's inhumanity to man. But, whatever the reason, this legalized murder must be abolished!

3. Appeal to the emotions. Frequently, in the conclusion of a message, a source will employ a strong emotional appeal. Such an appeal may be remembered long after the specific factual material in the message has been forgotten. When an emotional appeal is included as part of the conclusion, it seldom is the only method employed. As an example, look at the second paragraph in the preceding conclusion. Even though the conclusion opens with a summary of individual points, it closes with a strong emotional appeal. However, if you are considering the use of emotional appeal, keep in mind that this approach tends to increase perceived message discrepancy unless the groundwork has been laid for it. Therefore, unless you are reasonably certain that the audience is already in fairly strong agreement, you should be very cautious about employing a strong emotional appeal in the conclusion. Rather than highlighting and driving home the main point, such an appeal may cause the receiver's attitudes to boomerang.

4. Point to the future. The visualization step in Monroe's Motivated Sequence (discussed in Chapter 12) may often be employed as a conclusion. As indicated previously, in such visualization you may point either to something desirable or to the undesirable in the future, or you may contrast the desirable and the undesirable. Consider this example of a source who pointed to the future in the conclusion of his talk about air pollution.

The future for the people of our country may be either bright or bleak. It depends entirely upon what we do within the next few years. If we continue to pollute our air as we have been polluting for the past decade, we shall have more disasters such as have occurred in New York and London. People will be forced to wear surgical masks when they leave their homes, merely to stay alive. And even this precaution will not save thousands. However, if the program for the control of air pollution, which our committee has recommended for passage, is adopted, we shall guarantee our children clean air to breathe. The decision is ours. If we decide correctly, future generations will look back at us and admire our foresight. If we decide wrongly, if we do not pass this proposal, future generations, if there are any, will look back and condemn us for our irresponsibility. I leave the decision to you.

5. Indicate personal intentions. A source who indicates a personal intention to follow the recommendations brought forth in the message tends to increase terminal ethos and, at the same time, to induce receivers to follow his or her example. The conclusion to Patrick Henry's famous "liberty or death" speech is generally considered one of the best in the entire history of American public address. This conclusion employs the method of personal intention.

It is in vain, sir, to extenuate the matter. Gentlemen may cry Peace, Peace, but there is no peace. The war is actually begun! The next gale that sweeps from the North will bring to our ears the clash of resounding arms. Our brethren are already in the field! Why stand we here idle! What is it that the gentlemen wish? What would they have? Is life so dear or peace so sweet as to be purchased at the price of chains and slavery? Forbid it, Almighty God! I know not what course others may take; but as for me, give me liberty or give me death!

6. Request specific action. In messages designed to induce the audience to take specific action, the most appropriate method of concluding the message is to request that action. The effective door-to-door salesperson will conclude a pitch by handing the customer a contract and a pen and suggesting, "Please put your name right here." Other rhetorical communicators can learn from the salesperson. If you want people to do something, you must either ask them or tell them to do it. Otherwise, the likelihood of their doing so is greatly reduced. The following example of such a conclusion is taken from a speech advocating the circulation of petitions to put Michigan on Daylight Saving Time.

The special interests are against us, the people are for us. But the people will never have a chance to overcome the special interests unless we put petitions in their hands and get them to sign them. What I want you to do is exactly what I am going to do myself. I am going to pick up one of the petitions that the men standing at the doors are passing out. I am going to take it to twenty-five of my friends and get them to sign it. You do the same. On your way out I want you to do two things. One, sign the petition at the exit door. And two, take one of the blank petitions home with you. If you think cows are more important than people, of course, you won't sign the petition, nor will you circulate a petition to your friends. But if you believe that people are more important than cows, you will do as I ask. All right, let's get at it.

7. Refer to a quotation. Often someone has already made the point the source is trying to make and, in some cases, has made it in an eloquent or memorable way. It is often appropriate, therefore, to quote the other person in the conclusion. Such quotations, particularly if they are familiar to the receiver, tend to make the point stick in the memory and, at the same time, reinforce it through the ethos of the other person. Consider the following example from a talk advocating that the United States be less belligerent in world affairs.

> There are those among us who believe that bombing and bullying are the best ways to get other countries to do what we want them to. They are not, and they never have been. Friendship and cooperation are, and have always been, better means of getting along with other countries than belligerency. But friendship and cooperation do not mean appeasement. We should never be willing to sacrifice the vital interest of our country. We should always be prepared to defend ourselves to the limit if we are attacked. Teddy Roosevelt made the point over a half-century ago, and his words are worth remembering: "Speak softly, but carry a big stick."

8. Appeal to the audience's self-interest. As previously noted at several points in this book, people are motivated primarily by their own self-interests. If you wish to achieve a persuasive goal, you will do well to tie this goal to the self-interest of the audience. You definitely should not wait until the conclusion to accomplish this, but you can reinforce this appeal in the conclusion. The following example comes from a conclusion to a speech calling for opposition to a state law that would permit a city to impose an income tax on nonresidents working within the city.

> Supporters of this law tell us that it will permit property taxes to be lowered. It certainly will. But not *our* property taxes. Only the property taxes of those people living within the city. And how will they be lowered? They will be lowered by letting us pay the difference. We will be paying other people's taxes and getting nothing in return. What will happen to our taxes? They will stay exactly the same. The same that is, except that one percent of our income with no deductions will be removed by the city. That's taxation without representation. That's why our forefathers rebelled against England. And yet our state wants to permit such unfair taxation to be imposed upon us. Now I don't think we should have a tea party, nor do I think we need to have a rebellion. But I do think that we must protect our interests. We must contact our representative in the State Legislature and *demand* that this law not be passed.

9. Refer to the following speaker. In oral communication, it is not uncommon for a speaker to be followed by another speaker who is discussing the same subject. Often, the presentations fall into the debate format. Sometimes you can employ references to the following speaker advantageously. You can focus the audience's attention on potential weaknesses of the following speaker. Of course, if the following speaker is going to be upholding the same position that you are upholding, you may enhance the credibility of the following speaker by complimentary references. The following example is taken from a debate on whether the federal government should exercise more control over elementary and secondary education. The speaker was in favor of more control, and he was scheduled to be followed by a speaker opposing such an increase.

> I see my time is about up. I want to thank you for your courteous attention. I hope that you will be just as attentive to Mr. Williams's talk. I am looking forward to what he will say with great interest. I am quite certain that he will say that my proposal is a socialistic one. But, of course, we've already admitted that and noted that all public education is socialistic. I am going to be most interested, as I am sure you will be, in hearing what Mr. Williams has to say about several important points. I will be interested in hearing what Mr. Williams has to say about how we can eliminate the bigoted control that some Southern governors exercise over education without exercising more federal control over education. I will be interested in what Mr. Williams has to say about how we are going to get more equality in finance for education in the several states without increased federal control of education. And finally, I am going to be most interested in hearing what Mr. Williams has to say about the comparative quality of control of education emanating from the U.S. Office of Education as opposed to local school boards composed of high school dropouts. Listen carefully to Mr. Williams's address. If he has the answers to these problems, he will be the first person in this country who has come up with the answers. But if he doesn't have those answers, I am sure you are going to agree with me that the federal government must exercise substantially more control over public elementary and secondary education than it is currently exercising.

10. Return to the method employed in the introduction. This is one of the most obvious and yet least used methods of concluding speeches. If you have employed an effective device to open the message, the same device very often can also be employed to conclude the message. This method of concluding a message is particularly appropriate when the introduction has included a quotation, an interesting illustration, an anecdote, a reference to an occasion or a place, an appeal to the self-interest of the audience, or a reference to a recent incident. Although we have placed this method of concluding a message last on our list, it is actually the method you should consider first.

Integration of Body and Conclusion

Just as the introduction and the body should flow together so that it is not readily apparent where one leaves off and the other one begins, so should the body and the conclusion. The receiver should sense that the message is being drawn to a conclusion, but it is not essential for you to have a complete break between the body and the conclusion. There should be a psychological movement from body to conclusion that is uninterrupted. Often, when the source is using the climax structure, the conclusion is the high point of the message. The body leads up to it, and the conclusion is the capstone of the message.

Length of the Conclusion

As stated at the outset of the discussion of conclusions, a conclusion should be neither abrupt nor long-winded. But how long should the conclusion be? Generally, the conclusion is shorter than the introduction, but it does not have to be so. The study by Miller indicated that of the fifty speeches he examined, the conclusions varied from 1 to 15 percent of the total content of the speech. The average length was about 5 percent.[6] We cannot say, however, that approximately 5 percent is what you should strive for. The length of the conclusion will depend upon the length of the message, the type of material included in the conclusion, and the needs of the audience.

This concludes the series of chapters on the preparation of messages for rhetorical communication. After messages are prepared, they must be presented. This may take the form of written communication or oral communication. As this section is primarily concerned with the extemporaneous oral form, the following chapter is devoted to the oral presentation of messages.

DISCUSSION QUESTIONS

1. Some people contend that the introduction of a message should always include a "thesis statement," or statement of purpose. Do you agree? Why, or why not?

2. If, in the midst of your conclusion to a speech, you remember an important idea you forgot to mention earlier in your talk, should you include it at this point? Why, or why not?

NOTES

1. C. A. Kiesler and S. B. Kiesler, "Role of Forewarning in Persuasive Communications," *Journal of Abnormal and Social Psychology* 68 (1964): 547–49.
2. R. T. Oliver, *The Psychology of Persuasive Speech* (New York: Longmans, Green and Co., 1957), chap. 8.
3. E. Walster and L. Festinger, "The Effectiveness of Overheard Persuasive Communications," *Journal of Abnormal and Social Psychology* 65 (1962): 395–402.
4. It is interesting to note that after I wrote this example, back in 1967, Bill Cosby *did* go back to school. He is now Dr. Cosby!
5. E. Miller, "Speech Introductions and Conclusion," *Quarterly Journal of Speech* 32 (1964): 181–83.
6. See Miller, "Speech Introduction and Conclusions."

CHAPTER 15

MESSAGE PRESENTATION: ORAL DELIVERY

The importance of delivery in oral communication has been stressed since the days of Aristotle. In the *Rhetoric,* Aristotle said that "success in delivery is of the utmost importance to the effect of speech."[1] But Aristotle also said that "in a fine perspective, delivery is regarded as something vulgar . . . the case should, in justice, be fought on the strength of the facts alone so that all else besides demonstration of fact is superfluous. Nevertheless, as we have said, external matters do count for much because of the sorry nature of an audience."[2]

The Aristotelian view of the role of delivery in oral communication meets with our sympathy. Delivery *should not* make a difference. But it *does* make a difference, and therefore we must study it.

As emphasized throughout this book, rhetorical communication must be adapted to the audience to which it is directed. Audiences are affected by many things other than the specific verbal message prepared for them. Harrison has estimated that "in face-to-face communication no more than 35 percent of the social meaning is carried in the verbal messages."[3] A large portion of the remaining 65 percent of meaning is stimulated by the nonverbal aspects of the delivery of the verbal message. Delivery, therefore, provides ample opportunity for accidental communication to occur. In oral communication, the verbal message is only one of many messages being transmitted to members of the audience. There are also messages in tone of voice, eye behavior, facial expression, and bodily action. Each of these nonverbal messages tends to stimulate meaning. If all of them are coordinated with the verbal messages, rhetorical communication should be enhanced and accidental communication should be reduced. If they are not coordinated, accidental communication is very likely to occur. This chapter will consider several nonverbal elements directly related to the formal presentation of speeches.

THE EFFECT OF DELIVERY
ON ATTITUDE CHANGE

If delivery is as important in rhetorical communication as this book has declared it to be, we should expect delivery to have an effect upon attitude change. Several experimental studies have investigated this possible effect. Studies by Miller and Hewgill[4] and by Sereno and Hawkins[5] investigated the effect of nonfluencies of a tape-recorded speaker on change in audience attitude. In both of these studies, the number of nonfluencies (such word repetitions as "ugh," "er," and the like) varied from none to a very large number. In neither study were the nonfluencies observed to have any significant effect upon attitude change.[6] A similar study reported by Greenberg and Razinsky, which was concerned with written communication, produced similar findings.[7]

The results of these studies suggest that delivery may not have an effect upon attitude change. However, the Sereno-Hawkins and Miller-Hewgill studies both employed a tape-recorded speaker and varied only nonfluencies. A study I conducted with Arnold employed a live speaker and varied delivery in a more extreme manner. In this study, poor delivery included poor use of voice, poor eye contact, poor use of gesture, sloppy posture, excessively rapid rate, and numerous nonfluencies. The good delivery was as nearly opposite the poor delivery as possible. We conducted another version of this test by manipulating the quality of the content of the verbal message. In the strong message, all major ideas were supported by documented evidence, while in the weak message, all such supporting material was removed. The results of the McCroskey-Arnold study support the importance of delivery. With the strong message, good delivery produced significantly more attitude change in the desired direction than did poor delivery. With the weak message, however, there was no significant difference in the amount of attitude change produced by the two variations in delivery.[8] Good delivery is no substitute for good content, but without it good content is less effective.

A subsequent study, which employed a videotaped speaker and an audiotaped speaker, produced results consistent with those of the McCroskey-Arnold study of the live speaker. In each case there was a significant difference in the amount of desired attitude change produced by good delivery as opposed to bad delivery in the strong message condition, but there was no significant effect attributable to delivery in the weak message condition. In addition, poor delivery in the videotaped part of the study produced significantly less attitude change in the desired direction than did the poor delivery in the audiotaped part.[9] This was expected because much of the poor delivery, especially the use of bad physical mannerisms, was obvious in the videotaped condition but was unobservable in the audiotaped condition. A more recent study also found that more attitude change was produced by an otherwise rhetorically strong message when well presented than when presented with numerous nonfluencies.[10]

The results of these studies suggest that delivery is a "nonadditive" factor in rhetorical communication. It is clear that if we add so many units of good delivery we do not get so many more units of attitude change. Good delivery, therefore, is no substitute for a rhetorically strong verbal message. Rather, it appears that good delivery is a *permissive* factor: Good delivery allows a rhetorically strong message to have its normal effect; poor delivery tends to inhibit the effect of a verbal message. Good delivery does not produce attitude change, but it does permit a rhetorically strong message to produce that attitude change.

THE EFFECT OF DELIVERY ON COMPREHENSION OF CONTENT

Although delivery appears to be a nonadditive factor in communication designed to achieve attitude change, it does appear to be an additive factor in communication designed to achieve audience understanding. In two studies by Beighley[11] and one by Leitner,[12] quality of delivery was observed to have a significant effect on the amount of information obtained from the verbal message. In each of these studies, the quality of delivery was manipulated, and the experimental subjects completed a multiple-choice examination on the content of the verbal message after exposure. In each case the subjects exposed to the good delivery achieved significantly higher scores than the subjects exposed to the poor delivery. The results of these studies were what we should expect. Clarity is a very important factor in rhetorical communication designed to increase understanding. Good delivery tends to enhance the clarity of verbal messages, and poor delivery tends to make them less clear. We may conclude, therefore, that good delivery will tend to enhance communication designed to influence audience understanding.

THE EFFECT OF DELIVERY ON ETHOS

The terminal ethos of the experimental speakers in all of the studies of delivery conducted by Miller and Hewgill, by Sereno and Hawkins, by McCroskey and Arnold, by McCroskey and Mehrley, and by McCroskey was measured. In each case, delivery was found to have an effect on terminal ethos. *Sources with good delivery were consistently observed to have higher terminal ethos than those with poor delivery.*

This consistent finding raises a question: Since ethos and attitude change are so closely related, how can delivery affect ethos without also having a significant effect upon attitude change? This question may be answered with reference to the attitude-inconsistency theory discussed in Chapter 4. As stated there, when attitude inconsistency occurs as a result of a source's presenting a message to an audience, those audience members have at least three alternatives for resolving this inconsistency They may disregard the message entirely, they may change their attitude, or they may derogate the source. Assuming that the audience is not going to disregard the message entirely, the audience member is left with two primary alternatives: to change attitude or to derogate the source. These two alternatives, of course, are not mutually exclusive. In many cases, attitude inconsistency is resolved by combining attitude change and source derogation. When a source has poor delivery, it is probably easier for an audience member to derogate the speaker. Similarly, a source with poor delivery must be derogated more in relation to the amount of attitude change in order to resolve the inconsistency. Consequently, we may expect that sources with poor delivery will nearly always be derogated more than those with good delivery, even though the amount of attitude change produced by both would be equivalent.

This explanation is sufficient to account for the results observed by Miller and Hewgill and by Sereno and Hawkins. The results observed in the McCroskey studies, however, need a little more explanation. In those studies there was greater attitude change produced in the good-delivery/strong-message situation than in the others. Terminal ethos in this situation, however, was no higher than the terminal ethos in the good-delivery/weak-message situation. The apparent explanation for this result is the strong message itself. This message presumably produced greater inconsistency in the audience and, consequently, greater attitude change. Derogation of the source in this situation was made more difficult by the factor of good delivery. In the good-delivery/weak-message situation, there was less inconsistency produced by the message and, thus, less need for attitude change or source derogation. Since source derogation was made difficult by good delivery, the terminal ethos of the source tended to remain high and little attitude change was produced.

In the other two situations in these studies—poor delivery and strong message, and poor delivery and weak message—the poor delivery presumably caused the audience to perceive both messages as weak. Consequently, the attitude inconsistency that was generated was not great. Since the delivery was poor, derogation of the source was easier in both cases, and the resulting terminal ethos of the source was lower.

The above explanation, of course, is speculative, as any explanation based upon hypothesized inconsistency within the mind of an audience member must be. We can never be certain of precisely what does go on in a human being's mind. But whether this explanation is correct or not, the results of these studies clearly indicate that delivery does have a direct effect upon the terminal ethos of a source. This fact, important in concept-centered communication, is crucial in ethos-centered communication. We may conclude that the success of ethos-centered communication will be directly related to the quality of the source's delivery. This will be particularly true when the ethos-centered communicator is concerned with enhancing the ethos of a group he or she represents. It may be possible for the audience to dissociate the delivery of the speaker from the ethos of the group the speaker represents. We do not have available, however, any research bearing directly on this question. Until we do, it would be wise for a group seeking to enhance its ethos to look to the indirect evidence of the preceding studies and be particularly careful in selecting its spokesperson. The spokesperson in ethos-centered communication apparently should have considerable skill in delivery.

THE NATURE OF GOOD DELIVERY

We may agree with Aristotle that delivery is a vulgar element in rhetorical communication and may not consider it an elevated subject for study. However, as shown, it is an important factor in oral communication. Therefore, if we are to be effective oral communicators, we must develop good delivery. Before we can begin to develop it, we must understand what good delivery is. The best place to begin is with the words of James Winans.

> Let us imagine all speeches and all memory of speech-making to be blotted out, so that there is no person in the world who remembers that he has ever made a speech, or heard one, or read one; and there is left no clue to this art. "Is this the end of speech-making?" Here comes a man who has seen a great race, or has been in a battle, or perhaps is excited about his new invention, or on fire with enthusiasm for a cause. He begins to talk with a friend on the street. Others join them, five, ten, twenty, a hundred. Interest grows. He lifts his voice that all may hear; but the crowd wishes to hear and see the speaker better. "Get up on this truck!" they cry; and he mounts the truck and goes on with his story or plea.
>
> A private conversation has become a public speech; but under the circumstances imagined it is only thought of as a conversation, enlarged conversation. It does not seem abnormal, but quite the natural thing.
>
> When does the converser become a speech-maker? When ten persons gather? Fifty? Or is it when he gets upon the truck? There is, of course, no point at which we can say the change has taken place. There is no change in the nature of the spirit of the act; it is essentially the same throughout, a conversation adapted as the speaker proceeds, to the growing number of his hearers. There may be a change, to be sure, if he becomes self-conscious; but assuming that interest in story or argument remains the dominant emotion, there is no essential change in his speaking. It is probable that with the increasing importance of his position and the increasing tension, the feeling that comes with numbers, he gradually modifies his tone and diction and permits himself to

launch into a bolder strain and a wider range of ideas and feelings than in an ordinary conversation; but the change is in degree and not in kind. He is conversing with an audience.

. . . I wish you to see that speech-making, even in the most public place, is a normal act which calls for no strange, artificial methods, but only for an extension and development of that most familiar act, conversation. Should you grasp this idea you will be saved much wasted effort and unnecessary worry and embarrassment.[13]

In Winans's excellent hypothetical example he indicates the two primary requisites of good delivery—naturalness and conversational quality.

Naturalness

Good delivery should be natural rather than artificial or mechanical. This view, commonly accepted and taught today, is quite the opposite of the views held by the followers of the elocutionists who taught speech in the eighteenth and nineteenth centuries. This group of pseudoscientists developed highly complex, mechanical, and artificial systems for the use of voice and body in delivering speeches. They taught techniques of delivery that were supposed to provoke specific meanings in the mind of the audience. An extended arm had one meaning, a clenched fist another, and a quavering voice still another. The elocutionists also considered their system to be "natural." Through systematic observation of delivery in communication, the elocutionists attempted to identify delivery characteristics that accompanied the stimulation of certain meanings. When they observed a fairly consistent pattern, they felt they had identified a method by which we "naturally" stimulate a given meaning through delivery. Unfortunately, their good idea went bad. They did not recognize that what is a natural behavior for one speaker often is unnatural for another. Instead of training speakers to have effective natural delivery, the elocutionists wound up training highly artificial and mechanical speakers.

Another group of theorists also sought to find a way to achieve naturalness in delivery. Their overreaction to the evils of the elocutionary movement caused them to develop what has been referred to as an *impulsive* theory of delivery. Their view was that delivery should be left alone and that, on the basis of impulses as one speaks, the speaker will deliver the message naturally. In short, their system was an absence of a system.

The goal of all the systems has been natural delivery. To achieve the truly natural quality we desire, we must first answer the question "What is 'naturalness' in delivery?" That which is natural in delivery is that which does not call attention to itself. Any characteristic of voice or of bodily action that is specifically noticed by the members of the audience and attracts their attention is not natural. Thus, what may be natural for one source with one audience or one subject may not be natural for another source with another audience or another subject. Conversely, a bad characteristic in delivery may be defined as any characteristic that calls attention to itself. A speaker should never be pleased if a member of the audience comes up after the address and compliments her or him on an excellent delivery. If that person paid attention to the characteristics of the delivery, they were bad characteristics rather than good ones. Good delivery, therefore, is so natural that it is not even consciously noticed by the audience.

Conversational Quality

The second requisite of good delivery, according to Winans, is conversational quality. Conversational quality is not the same thing as conversational style. In conversational style, the manner and the choice of words are as similar to actual conversation as is possible in speechmaking. This style is often to be desired and frequently is very appropriate with a particular audience. However, it still is not conversational quality. To understand what conversational quality is in speechmaking, we need to consider what the qualities of conversation are. The two primary characteristics are a conscious awareness of the content of words as they are uttered and, as Winans put it, "a lively sense of communication."

The first characteristic should be present when a speaker is thinking of the entire thought while presenting the message. The speaker is presenting thoughts rather than words. One of the values of the extemporaneous approach to speechmaking is that it forces the source to create wording at the moment of utterance. These words, therefore, must stem from the thought rather than from the printed page.

The second characteristic of conversational quality, "a lively sense of communication," is not so much a characteristic of delivery as it is a characteristic of a rhetorical communicator that manifests itself in delivery. This book was actually referring to this "lively sense of communication" when discussing the need for the source to be aware of the thoughts and feelings of the audience and to adapt to the audience. What is true in invention, disposition, and style is also true in delivery: It must be audience-centered. A speech should not be delivered *to* an audience. If it is, it is a performance rather than a rhetorically communicative act. A source should have an attitude of talking *with* the audience. In conversation, of course, the audience talks back. As a result the speaker will adapt. In speechmaking, the audience provides feedback, but usually not orally. The speaker must adapt to the feedback, and, in doing so, exhibit "a lively sense of communication."

From this discussion we may extract two primary characteristics of good delivery. *First, it does not call attention to itself; it does not distract; it is inconspicuous. Second, good delivery is adaptive delivery.* Like good conversation, good delivery of a public speech involves interaction between source and audience. A pattern of circular response develops. The source begins delivering the message and observes the reaction of the audience. On the basis of that reaction, the speaker adapts to the audience. The audience, in turn, responds to this adaptation. Again the source adapts. This cycle continues throughout the presentation of the message.

The nature of good delivery is so simple that one may wonder why anybody would fail to exhibit it. Two reasons frequently are given for bad delivery. First, some people simply are not audience centered. They do not have "a lively sense of communication." They may know they should have it, but they lack it. Second, some people explain their bad delivery as a manifestation of their nervousness or stage fright. They claim that if only their knees would stop knocking and their hands would stop sweating, they would be able to deliver properly. I believe that these two explanations are really not distinct; they are only two ways of saying the same thing. Let us examine the relationship between nervousness and good delivery a little more closely.

NERVOUSNESS AND DELIVERY

As noted in Chapter 3, nearly all speakers, as they stand before an audience, experience some stage fright. Its severity depends primarily upon the attitude the speaker has toward her or his role in the communicative event. Is the person self-centered or audience centered? The source who is self-centered will be concerned about how he or she sounds and looks to the audience and, as a result, stage fright will tend to become severe. If the source is audience-centered, the concern is not with how he or she sounds or looks. The only concern is whether the audience is getting the idea the source wants them to get. For this source, stage fright will tend to be very minor. The audience-centered speaker will tend to have good delivery unless he or she has developed certain mannerisms or habits that detract from the general quality of the delivery. The self-centered speaker, however, does not have a lively sense of communication. Such speakers are concerned with self, tending to forget the audience except as a possible threat. Nervousness increases and the delivery degenerates. As delivery gets worse, the source becomes increasingly aware of not doing a good job and that he or she probably is being perceived in a lesser light by the audience. This tends to further increase nervousness and decrease the quality of the delivery. In some cases, this cycle of reduced quality in delivery and increased nervousness continues to the point where the speaker can no longer continue.

I know a woman who began a speech before a speech class and proceeded for about a minute and a half, gradually getting worse. Her delivery was very bad, and her nervousness became extreme. Then she stopped abruptly and left the room. A short time later, this same woman, after having attended a convention, stood before a much larger audience and spoke very well. In the first circumstance she viewed her speech as the performance upon which she was going to be graded. She was highly self-centered. She was not concerned with communicating her idea to her audience, but only with sounding good so that the instructor would give her a high mark. In the second circumstance there was no instructor giving her a mark, and her only motivation for standing before the audience was to communicate an idea to them. This same individual, therefore, experienced severe stage fright in one circumstance but almost none in the other. Her delivery was terrible in one circumstance but quite acceptable in the other.

Although the concern of this book is not how to give speeches in the classroom, many of you are in classes where you are expected to give speeches or other presentations. It is appropriate, therefore, to consider for a moment this unique type of communication experience. If you are asked to stand before your class and deliver a public speech upon which you are going to be graded, you are facing probably the most difficult communicative experience in your life! Your primary motivation is most likely that your instructor has required you to stand up to speak. It is very difficult for you to be audience-centered rather than self-centered because the real audience is actually your instructor. You probably will be rated on performance rather than on communication. If you are not bothered by stage fright in this circumstance, you are definitely extraordinary. But to point out these facts relating to the contrived nature of many classroom presentational settings is not to suggest that giving speeches under these circumstances is not beneficial to you. Quite to the contrary, it is probably the best experience you can have. If you can exhibit a lively sense of communication and deliver your speech naturally under these adverse circumstances, it is not unreasonable to assume that you probably can do so anywhere else where you are motivated to speak.

The problems you face in the classroom are not unlike those you face outside. In any situation calling for a speech, you must choose a subject about which you wish to communicate. Outside the classroom the motivation normally precedes the appointment to speak; in the classroom, this procedure is generally reversed. Still, the motivation must be there in either case, so the real problem is not so very different. When you give speeches outside the classroom, your ethos will be affected by the audience's evaluation of your speech. In the classroom this is also true, except that there the evaluation frequently takes the form of a mark; outside the classroom this so-called threat takes a more tangible form.

The degree of a speaker's nervousness and the quality of delivery are directly related, both in the classroom and outside. The primary factor in reducing nervousness and improving delivery is the attitude of the source. The more you develop a lively sense of communication and become audience-centered, the better will be your delivery and the less severe will be the problem of stage fright. Our primary advice, therefore, is to develop the proper attitude. Most people can do this, if not the first time they stand before an audience, at least after some experience. If you are extremely high in communication apprehension, of course, that is a very different matter. It is unlikely you will overcome that problem without outside help.

ELEMENTS OF GOOD DELIVERY

Now that we have an understanding of the general nature of good delivery, we need to look at its specific elements. This section is not intended as a checklist of things for you to memorize and do. You probably already do most of these things properly. If you do not, it is not likely that reading this section is going to make much of a difference anyhow. The point of this section is to help you develop an understanding of the specific elements of good delivery. It is assumed that if you have such an understanding and are made aware of certain deficiencies in your delivery, you will be better able to make the necessary corrections.

The five primary elements in good delivery are direct eye contact, effective use of voice, effective bodily action, variety, and immediacy. We shall consider each of these in turn.

Direct Eye Contact

Direct eye contact contributes more to the establishment of a circular response between speaker and audience than does any other element in delivery. Direct eye contact means just that—the speaker looks the audience members squarely in the eyes, not slightly over their heads, out the window, at their feet, or at the aisles. Direct eye contact suggests audience-centeredness and exhibits "a lively sense of communication." It makes the audience feel they are a part of the communicative event. A source who does not look the audience in the eyes produces accidental communication, tending to be perceived as unconcerned either with the ideas being addressed or with the audience. Without direct eye contact, you cannot adapt to the audience's responses. Unlike the other elements of good delivery, there is no such thing as too much direct eye contact.

Perfectly consistent direct eye contact, of course, is not possible when a speaker has either notes or a manuscript. Thus, the quality of delivery is always reduced somewhat by the use of notes; using them properly, however, can minimize this reduction. (This aspect will be considered a little later.) Speaking from manuscripts, however, usually reduces the quality of

delivery rather substantially as it eliminates adaptive delivery. But again, if the manuscript is well read, this loss is not so severe.

Effective Use of Voice

In oral communication, the voice is the instrument that transmits the verbal message from source to receiver. Several things need to be considered in determining whether the voice is used effectively.

1. Volume. It is obvious that a speech must be uttered loudly enough to be heard by the audience. If the speech is uttered in a voice so soft that it cannot be heard, the message simply cannot have the intended effect. By observing the responses of the people near the back of the room, you can usually tell whether you are speaking loudly enough. If they seem to be straining to hear, you must speak louder. While the problem of speaking in too soft a voice is obvious to most of us, the problem of speaking too loudly is almost as severe and not so frequently acknowledged. Some speakers seem to think that if a little is good, a lot more will be even better, so they almost literally shout their speeches to their audiences. Particularly in a small room or in a room with bad acoustics, the excessively loud voice can be more detrimental to communication than the abnormally soft voice. If the voice is too loud, it can make the audience physically uncomfortable.

But before reaching this severe state, the excessively loud voice can become difficult to understand because of the reverberations of the voice around the room. Therefore, you should speak loudly enough to be heard but not so loudly as too overpower your audiences.

2. Rate. If someone were to stand before us with six oranges and throw them all toward us at once, we probably would be lucky to catch even one. On the other hand, if the person threw one orange to us every hour and fifteen minutes, we might catch the first one, but we probably would not even be around by the time the second one was thrown. Both of our orange problems involve rate. If one orange is thrown to us and we catch it and set it down and the process continues, we could probably catch all six. The same is true with ideas. If the speaker throws out ideas at an excessively rapid rate, the audience does not have the time to digest one idea before it is struck by another and some ideas are lost. On the other hand, the person who speaks extremely slowly tends to lose the audience's attention. The effective rate of speech falls somewhere in between these extremes. Fortunately for the speaker, there is generally a wide range of rates acceptable to the audience. Nevertheless, rate is an important consideration, because many speakers do not speak at their normal rate when they stand before an audience. Many speak much more rapidly; a few speak significantly more slowly.

3. Pitch. An effective speaker uses pitch to clarify and emphasize the ideas in the verbal message. Consider the short sentence "He went to town." If you wish, you may stimulate several different meanings by use of pitch, thus emphasizing different words in the sentence. Assuming that the italicized word is emphasized by variation in pitch, the same sentence will have different meanings, as follows: *He* went to town; He *went* to town; He went to *town.*

Variations in pitch, then, are a major aid to the speaker in stimulating the desired meaning in the mind of the audience. If the pitch always remains the same, it contributes nothing to stimulating meaning. On the contrary, it tends to detract from the overall effect of the message, because it becomes monotonous and difficult to listen to. Similarly, some people have, or develop, an abnormal voice pitch. Women, in particular, in their first experiences as public speakers, often develop abnormally high pitch. Women's voices in general are naturally higher than men's, but the tension of the moment causes their vocal chords to tighten even more and can make their voices quite squeaky. If your voice has abnormal pitch or very narrow range in pitch, you should consider seeing a speech-improvement specialist. Often these problems of pitch can be overcome quite easily through therapy, but in some cases they are physical problems that are more difficult to overcome.

4. Articulation. Words must be spoken clearly or they cannot be understood. In addition, in our culture poor articulation indicates some other undesirable trait, most commonly lack of intelligence or education. Thus it not only causes the verbal message to be less clear and understandable, but it also tends to lower the ethos of the source in the eyes of many audience members. On the other hand, overly precise articulation can be almost as distracting. I recall, in this regard, a professor with whom I studied. This instructor had a favorite word that he constantly overarticulated: "par-tic-u-lar-ly." Every syllable was equally stressed. At the end of class his students compared notes on how many "particularly's" they had counted. Good articulation merely includes all the sounds that normally should be in a word without stressing any of them too much.

5. Fluency. A fluent speech is one that flows smoothly. Repetition of sounds or words, and also vocalized pauses, such as "you know," "uh," or "er," tend to interrupt the flow of the message. As noted earlier, several studies have indicated that nonfluencies tend to reduce the terminal ethos of the source.

6. Pause. Effective use of pause is one of the most important characteristics of effective use of the voice. Pauses may be used to emphasize ideas. Ordinarily, a pause just before or just after an important idea will tend to stress that idea. Pauses also may be employed to give the audience an opportunity to catch up mentally with the speaker. It is important for you to remember that a pause is a *momentary* cessation of sound. Speakers often seem to hate silence, even though it lasts only a fraction of a second. They feel as though they must fill in the void. When they do, we have what we refer to as a "vocalized" pause. Vocalized pauses serve no useful purpose in a speech but tend to distract from its fluency. Therefore, they should be avoided.

Effective Bodily Action

Audience interpretation of verbal messages is influenced by the context in which those messages are transmitted to the audience. One of the major influencing factors in oral communication is the bodily activity of the speaker. Effective bodily action is dependent upon several things.

1. Posture. Good posture is one of the primary means by which a speaker may communicate poise and confidence or the lack of these characteristics. A phrase commonly used to describe good posture is "comfortably erect," meaning that good posture is normally somewhere between the stiff military stance and the slovenly, leaning-on-the-podium or standing-on-one-leg posture. You should appear relaxed but not too relaxed. There are circumstances, however, in which the comfortably erect posture is not necessarily the best. For example, when speaking to a small group of fifteen or twenty people, you may desire to establish an air of informality with the audience. One effective way of doing this is to sit on the edge of a table. If this is done gracefully, poise and confidence are still communicated, but so are feelings of informality and of closeness with the audience. Obviously, such a posture would not be appropriate when speaking to five thousand people in a large hall.

The important thing to remember is that your posture does communicate. If you forget this principle, accidental communication will result. Thus the person who is aware of posture is more likely to communicate effectively through it. The best time to think about posture is just before you begin to present the verbal message. After that, your thoughts need to be on other things. Ordinarily, just a small degree of attention is adequate to keep the accidental communication through posture under control.

2. Movement. Movement—the taking of a step or steps—is not absolutely essential in all speechmaking. When one is speaking into a fixed microphone, in fact, movement is almost impossible. But movement can be employed to emphasize ideas, to add variety to the presentation, and to aid in making transitions from one idea to another. Attention tends to be captured by a moving object. You can, therefore, increase the attentiveness of an audience by skillful use of movement. As with most characteristics of delivery, there are extremes at both ends of the movement continuum. You want to avoid both of these extremes; you should be neither a "post" nor a "pacer."

3. Gesture. Gesture refers to the movement of individual parts of the body, such as the hands, arms, head, or shoulders. Gesture is distinguished from movement in that gesture involves the motion of individual parts of the body, whereas movement entails motion of the entire body. All speakers gesture constantly. Not all speakers wave their hands and arms around constantly, but the body of a speaker during the presentation of a verbal message is constantly active. Nodding or shaking the head, shrugging the shoulders, and leaning the torso forward or backward or to the side are all forms of gesture. The speaker cannot be constantly aware of gestures, since a person cannot concentrate on gestures and ideas at the same time. Gestures, then, are never completely under the conscious control of the speaker.

Gesture is one of the primary means by which a speaker communicates enthusiasm for a subject. A speaker who is comparatively inactive (one can never be completely inactive) accidentally communicates a lack of enthusiasm. Since gestures arise from the feeling state of the speaker, it is next to impossible to improve a speaker's gestures without first changing his or her feeling state. If you are truly enthusiastic, have a lively sense of communication, and are audience centered, you will normally gesture well. However, if any of these elements is lacking, you will probably gesture ineffectively.

4. Facial expression. Facial expression is a form of gesture, but it is so important in oral communication that it needs to be considered as a separate area of bodily activity. An old cliché suggests that the face is the mirror of the soul; like most clichés, this one has an element of truth in it. Of course, skilled actors and actresses can convey in their facial expressions thought and feeling that they do not really feel, but most of us are not so skilled. Our facial expressions arise spontaneously from our state of feeling. Insincerity and lack of enthusiasm are communicated more often by a speaker's facial expression that by any other means. Like other forms of gesture, facial expression cannot be under the complete control of the speaker at all times. But you can exercise control over some facial expression, at least at the outset of the speech. Many people recommend what has been called the "pause-smile" technique. This is simply a matter of pausing for a moment just before beginning the speech and smiling at the audience. This is such a simple and easy technique that one may wonder why any speaker fails to employ it. The answer to that question is the same as the answer to most other questions about why poor delivery occurs: It is a matter of attitude. If you are concerned, at the outset of the speech, with establishing a friendly relationship with the audience, you will smile naturally.

Variety

Many people believe that variety is the single most important characteristic of effective delivery. Because of its extreme importance, this discussion has set variety apart from eye contact, use of voice, and bodily action. Variety is the opposite of monotony. Monotony bores people; variety increases their interest. There is no substitute for variety in voice and action. The earlier statement that the volume of sound in a speech should be loud enough to be heard and yet not so loud as to overpower the audience does not mean that there is one optimum volume level. Rather, variety in volume can be employed to emphasize integral parts of the message. Most people speak at a rate between 120 and 180 words per minute. But that rate should vary in the course of a speech. Whether the rate is at 120 or 180, if it is a constant rate the speaker will sound like a very fluent machine and will become monotonous. Similarly, the pitch of the voice should vary. Emphasis on ideas can be achieved by varying pitch level. Certainly there should be variation in the use of pause. Regular use of pause probably is worse than no pause at all. Gestures should stimulate meaning without calling attention to themselves. Any good gesture will become a bad gesture if it is overused. Variation in gesture, therefore, is just as important as variation in voice.

Immediacy

Immediacy refers to the degree of perceived physical or psychological distance between people in a relationship. An immediate relationship is one in which the people in the relationship see themselves as close to one another.

In general, the more immediate a relationship, the more the people in the relationship like one another and the more willing they are to be influenced by one another.[14]

Formal public speaking, by its very nature, tends to generate a low level of immediacy. The scene of one person talking (often from behind a podium) and a lot of people quietly listening (many at a considerable distance from the speaker) certainly does not naturally lead to feelings of physical or psychological closeness. As a result, a speaker must take special care to try to increase the immediacy in his or her relationship with the audience. The primary means by which this can be accomplished is effective delivery.

Although verbal messages can have some impact on immediacy (using "we" and "us" rather than "you" for example) nonverbal messages are the primary determinant of immediacy. Chapter 7 discussed a variety of nonverbal message systems that function in human communication. A number of these can be manipulated by the effective speaker to enhance immediacy.

The nonverbal variable that is obviously most associated with perceived distance is the actual space between speaker and audience. It is remarkable how few speakers consciously manipulate that space while delivering a talk. If there is a podium or table at the front of the room, you can bet that most people who speak in that room will stand behind that podium or table. But by simply moving in front of the table or podium, the speaker can substantially increase immediacy with the audience.

At the university where I teach, there is a lecture hall that seats about 350 students. It has a very large stage at the front and an open space between the stage and the student seats. Observation of lecturers who taught in that classroom over one week indicated that all but three lectured from the stage. In those classes where the lecturer spoke from the stage, there was no student participation at all. In contrast, one professor began her lecture from a point in the open space between the stage and the first row of student seats. From that point she moved the full width of the room in front of the students and actually moved part way up the aisles between the seats. In that class, students asked questions and provided comments relevant to the content of the lecture. There was an interactive relationship between teacher and students, even though almost every one of the 350 seats was occupied. This lecturer is considered one of the best on campus. She is very highly evaluated by her students, and the attendance in her class is always near perfect. She establishes an immediate relationship with her student audiences.

Physical distance is not the only factor that can be manipulated to increase immediacy. We have noted the importance of eye contact with the audience. Part of the reason why eye contact is so important is that it bridges physical distance and tends to increase immediacy by reducing psychological distance. Similarly, facial expressions can increase immediacy. We feel closer to people who smile at us than to those who frown at us. Even the way we dress can influence immediacy. In general, the more formal our dress, the less immediate we will be. Of course, extremely casual dress for a formal speaking situation will be perceived as inappropriate.

The importance of immediacy cannot be overstated. Immediacy increases the audience's attentiveness; it reduces tension and anxiety for both speaker and audience; it creates greater liking between speaker and audience; and it increases the probability that the speaker's purpose will be accomplished. *Effective delivery is immediate delivery.*

USING NOTES

This discussion of the elements of good delivery has emphasized that you cannot be consciously aware of all these elements, nor should you studiously attend to them to try to make them come out properly. Rather, good delivery must be developed as a habit. We assume that an understanding of what good delivery is will aid you in improving delivery once someone has informed you of certain poor delivery characteristics you have. This section will concentrate on a particular problem in delivery: the use of notes. Good use of notes is not exclusively dependent upon semiconscious habit. As you employ notes, there are several things you can keep consciously in mind that will improve delivery.

As indicated previously, the primary concern of this chapter is with delivery in extemporaneous speaking. Some people suggest that extemporaneous delivery is inherently harmed by the use of notes. I do not support this view. *Properly employed, notes do not necessarily detract from the effectiveness of a speaker's delivery.* They are a definite asset to an extemporaneous speaker in that they tend to ensure against forgetting an important idea or a piece of supporting material. If the suggestions enumerated are followed, the extemporaneous speaker should obtain the benefits of notes without having them hamper delivery to any serious extent.

1. Notes should include only key words. A momentary glance at notes does not seriously impair a speaker's contact with the audience. But if one must take ten or fifteen seconds out of every minute to look at notes, eye contact is going to be seriously interrupted. One way of ensuring that you will not have to look at notes for extended periods is to employ key words on notes rather than full sentences. A brief glance will thus enable you to see these key words and have the idea stimulated back into mind. This momentary glance does not severely impair delivery.

2. Notes should be kept to a minimum. You should have all of the notes that are needed, but no more. There is a tendency on the part of many beginning speakers to include on the speech notes every idea that they plan to mention. As a result, the notes contain more than is required, and, even though they are made up of key words and phrases, the speaker will have to search through these key words and phrases to find the idea with which he or she is concerned.

3. Notes should be on small note cards. You will normally find it beneficial to keep your notes on three-by-five-inch or four-by-six-inch cards. Each main idea should appear on one card. Thus, as an idea is completed, you may remove this card from a small stack of cards, and as soon as you look back at the note cards, you are looking at the card for the next main idea. You will not have to search through a whole sheet of paper to find the next main idea. This procedure also enables you to have quoted material on separate cards and to have it in the appropriate order for inclusion in the speech. One of the biggest drawbacks in using notes in extemporaneous speaking is the speaker shuffling pages of paper while trying to find an idea or piece of supporting material. The use of small note cards, properly ordered, will overcome this problem.

4. Notes should not be used in gesturing. Notes, whether on cards or on sheets of paper, should be laid on the podium or on a table, if one is available, and not waved at the audience while gesturing. If there is no table or podium, you should keep the note cards in one hand while gesturing with the other. As stated earlier, good gestures do not call attention to themselves. But a hand gesture with a handful of note cards is bound to call attention to itself.

5. Do not attempt to conceal notes from the audience. Some speakers seem to be ashamed of the fact that they use notes. They try to hide them from their audience and take furtive glances at them. It is impossible to hide notes completely from an audience, and the more you try, the more attention you draw to the notes. Notes should be laid on the podium or the table, as already suggested, and you should be completely open about looking at them. Most audiences could not care less whether a speaker uses notes or not. But if members of the audience notice you sneaking looks at notes, it detracts from their attention to the speech.

HOW TO ACHIEVE GOOD DELIVERY

This chapter has discussed throughout the importance of good delivery, the nature of good delivery, the relationship between nervousness and good delivery, and the elements of good delivery. At this point you may reasonably be asking, "Well, I understand all of this, but how do I develop good delivery?" You deserve an answer to this question. The primary thing that you must do is to develop a proper attitude toward communication with an audience. You must see your function as a speaker as merely an instrument being employed to stimulate an idea in the audience's mind. Think "audience."

Once this attitude has been developed, you also need to speak where a skilled observer can evaluate your delivery and discuss it with you. These two steps should be taken in this order. Even a trained observer of your delivery cannot know the exact cause of any poor delivery characteristics he or she observes. Only you can know for sure. You are therefore wasting the observer's time unless you have already developed a proper attitude toward communication. Once this attitude is developed, your delivery will be at least moderately good. In most cases, only distracting habits and mannerisms will need to be corrected. This is where the trained observer can be of maximum value to you.

A word about practice. *Practice makes permanent—not perfect.* Some speakers practice their speeches before mirrors or aloud in their rooms. Some books even recommend this procedure. Such practice is often worse than useless. A speech before a mirror or in an empty room is not the same thing as a speech before an audience. People who practice before mirrors and alone in their rooms, and people who recommend that they do so, are concerned with performance, not communication. Such practice will make it even more difficult for you to have the proper attitude as you approach your real audience. You will tend to remember how you looked or sounded in your practice session and will be thinking about yourself rather than about your audience. This is not to suggest that you shouldn't go over your speech several times before you speak to your audience. You definitely should, but not in order to perfect your delivery. Such rehearsal of your speech should be directed to forming and reinforcing the ideas in your mind. It can also be usefully employed to try different ways of expressing an idea. This practice is intended to make permanent the ideas, and is therefore quite useful.

Good delivery is a habit. So is bad delivery. Which habit you will have throughout your speaking career will depend upon the attitudes you develop toward your audience and the willingness with which you approach improvement of the elements of delivery that you become aware of doing wrong. The development of good delivery is your personal concern.

DISCUSSION QUESTIONS

1. How may we distinguish conversation and discussion from public speaking?

2. If good delivery can enhance a source's ethos, why is it that at the same time it may have no effect on attitude change? Is this fact inconsistent with the relationship between ethos and attitude change posited in Chapter 5?

3. What is "natural" delivery?

4. This chapter asserts that nervousness or stage fright is produced primarily by self-centeredness on the part of the communicator. Do you agree? Why, or why not?

5. What is the most important element of good delivery? Why?

6. Do you believe an extempore speaker should use notes? Why, or why not?

NOTES

1. L. Cooper, *The Rhetoric of Aristotle* (Englewood Cliffs, NJ: Prentice-Hall, 1932), pp. 182ff.

2. Ibid., pp. 183ff.

3. R. Harrison, "Nonverbal Communication: Explorations into Time, Space, Action, and Object," in J. H. Campbell and H. W. Hepler (eds.), *Dimensions in Communication* (New York: Wadsworth, 1965), p. 161.

4. G. R. Miller and M. A. Hewgill, "The Effect of Variations in Nonfluency on Audience Ratings of Source Credibility," *Quarterly Journal of Speech* 50 (1964): 36–44.

5. K. K. Sereno and G. J. Hawkins, "The Effects of Variations in Speaker's Nonfluency upon Audience Ratings of Attitude toward the Speech Topic and Speaker's Credibility," *Speech Monographs* 34 (1967): 58–64.

6. Miller and Hewgill did not include their findings concerning attitude change in the report cited above. However, their findings were similar to those of Sereno and Hawkins.

7. B. S. Greenberg and E. L. Razinsky, "Some Effects of Variations in Message Quality," *Journalism Quarterly* 43(1966): 486–92.

8. This study is discussed in J. C. McCroskey, "Studies of the Effects of Evidence in Persuasive Communication," *Speech Communication Research Laboratory Report SCRL 4–67*, Department of Speech, Michigan State University, 1967.

9. Ibid.

10. J. C. McCroskey and R. S. Mehrley, "The Effects of Disorganization and Nonfluency on Attitude Change and Source Credibility," *Speech Monographs* 36 (1969):13–21.

11. K. C. Beighley, "An Experimental Study of the Effect of our Speech Variables on Listener Comprehension," *Speech Monographs* 19(1952): 249–58; and "An Experimental Study of Three Speech Variables on Listener Comprehension," *Speech Monographs* 21(1954): 248–53.

12. M. A. Leitner, "A Study of the Effects of Intraphrase Rate and Pause Time on Information Gain and Speaker Image," Ph.D. diss., University of Wisconsin, 1962.

13. J. A. Winans, *Speech-Making* (New York: D. Appleton-Century Crofts, 1938), pp. 11ff. Reprinted by permission of Appleton-Century-Crofts.

14. V. P. Richmond and J. C. McCroskey, *Nonverbal Behavior in Interpersonal Relations*, 4th ed. (Boston: Allyn & Bacon, 2000).

PART **IV**

RHETORICAL
COMMUNICATION
AND SOCIETY

CHAPTER 16

■ ■ ■ ■ ■

ETHICS AND RHETORICAL COMMUNICATION

The previous chapters of this book have been devoted to basic theories underlying the rhetorical communication process and to techniques that may be employed in the preparation and presentation of messages to audiences. My communicative goal has been to help you enhance your understanding of these theories and techniques.

This chapter sets the treatment of ethical considerations apart from the rest of the book. It is important that you understand the reason for this separation. It is definitely not because I believe that ethics are unrelated to the theory of rhetorical communication or to the techniques employed in preparing or presenting messages to audiences. Rather, it is because of the inherently subjective nature of such a discussion. It has been said that any person who writes about ethics reveals to the reader more about herself or himself than about ethics. Be that as it may, this chapter is a highly subjective discussion of ethics. It represents my personal opinions. It should be read and studied just as the preceding chapters, but this material should be neither accepted nor rejected; it should be considered. Use these ideas as a starting point to develop your own conception of ethics in rhetorical communication. A preceding discussion pointed out that forewarning of persuasive intent on the part of a source tends to produce more critical listening and reading on the part of the audience. Consider yourself forewarned. The persuasive message follows.

THE ETHICS OF MEANS OR OF ENDS

The most pervasive problem approached in most discussions of ethics is whether we should judge things on the basis of the *ends achieved* or upon the basis of the *means used to achieve those ends*. Obviously, a person who uses "good" means to achieve a "good" end is operating ethically. Just as obviously, a person who uses "bad" means to achieve a "bad" end is operating unethically. The difficulty arises when a person either uses good means to achieve a bad end or uses a bad means to achieve a good end.

One of the things many people consider a bad technique in persuasion is the use of strong emotional appeals. Adolf Hitler successfully employed strong emotional appeals to achieve his ends. His use of the emotion of hatred for Jews was highly successful in getting the German people to support his policies. On the other hand, Franklin D. Roosevelt also used strong emotional appeals to achieve his ends. He used Americans' hatred of the Japanese after the bombing of Pearl Harbor, as well as our love of country and patriotism, to get our people behind his policies in World War II. Methods other than persuasion were also used by Germany and America to achieve their ends. Hitler employed mass murder. America employed the atomic bomb. Who acted morally, and who acted immorally? The answer to that question may come easy for most Americans, but the answer does not come so easily for many people in other parts of the world.

Neither Hitler nor Roosevelt used *only* questionable means to achieve his ends. One means of persuasion generally considered ethical is to state the purpose of a message and to make a straight presentation of fact. Both Hitler and Roosevelt employed this technique from time to time. Who was acting morally, and who was acting immorally?

Almost all of us consciously reject the Machiavellian ethic of "the end justifies the means." We say that no matter how desirable an end may be, there are some means to achieve that end that are just not acceptable. The extermination of six million Jews, for example, is not an acceptable means of "protecting the German people from the threat of communism." Because of this anti-Machiavellian attitude, we tend to develop a means-centered ethic for rhetorical communication. We say that propaganda is evil. We read the list of propaganda devices published by the Institute of Propaganda Analysis and condemn such means as the "testimonial" device, the "plainfolks" device, and the "card-stacking" device. Of course, we employ the same devices relabeled positively as "evidence from expert and lay person," "establishing common ground," and using the "two-sided" as opposed to the "one-sided" message.

The big fault in our means-centered ethics is that we seem to apply it only to the other person. When someone else does it, it is unethical. When we do it, we redefine what we do. We are opposed to propaganda, so we establish the United States Information Agency; we tell the "truth" to the other people of the world. But for some strange reason, they perceive us as giving them propaganda. Propaganda can be defined as "what the other guy does to get people to accept ideas I don't agree with." Although there are many more formal definitions of propaganda, this is probably the most accurate one.

Our so-called means-centered ethic, then, is really an ends-centered ethic. If someone else does it, it is wrong; if we do it, it is right. But is there no technique of persuasion that all decent people would oppose? The answer is no.

Let us take an extreme case: lying. Certainly we cannot condone lying in order to persuade people. Or can we? Well, we do. During the Bay of Pigs invasion of Cuba in the 1960s, the United States Ambassador to the United Nations, Adlai E. Stevenson, said that our government knew nothing of the invasion and had no part in it. As we all know, that simply was not true. In only a matter of hours the people of the United States were aware of the fact that we were involved in this invasion. But surprisingly, for all of us who detest lying, there was no significant outcry against the technique our government had used to convince members of the United Nations that we were pure and innocent. Nor is this an isolated instance of people's condoning the use of lying as a persuasive device. For security reasons the State Department and the Pentagon regularly give out false and misleading information. During the Vietnam War these sources released figures on Viet Cong casualties that cumulatively exceeded the total number of Viet Cong and North Vietnamese soldiers! Yet the war continued. At the same time, North Vietnamese sources released figures on the number of American planes shot down, which cumulatively accounted for more planes than the United States had in its entire arsenal. Yet they kept flying. Not too long after the Bay of Pigs invasion, this country faced what has come to be known as the Cuban missile crisis. The American people listened to a speech by President John F. Kennedy, in which he castigated the Russian Ambassador for lying in telling him that Russia was putting no missiles into Cuba. We were shown photographic evidence to the contrary. A great cry went up across the country about the dishonesty of the Russians. Again we see the double standard. When we feel it necessary to lie to achieve a desired end, it seems to be a moral thing to do, but the other person who does it is considered dishonest and unethical.

Nor is it merely governments that use lies as persuasive techniques. Most of us do not like to think of ourselves as liars. We even have a very convenient system of categorizing lies in order to avoid the stigma. We tell "white lies."

It would be nice at this point to be able to say that lies are not an effective technique of persuasion. Unfortunately, common sense tells us otherwise. So does research by Nunnally and Bobrien.[1] Lies, unfortunately, are often just as effective as the truth, sometimes even more so. The person who persists in lying, if he or she is found out, usually loses effectiveness over a period of time, but that is not ordinarily the short-range result, as the Watergate scandal that led to the resignation of President Nixon in 1974 should clearly indicate.

How, then, are we to establish an ethic for rhetorical communication? We must extricate ourselves from the endless controversy over means and ends. Neither a means-centered nor an ends-centered ethic, nor a combined means-centered and ends-centered ethic, will suffice. A viable system for evaluating the ethics of rhetorical communication must be based upon the intent of the communicator.

AN ETHIC BASED ON INTENT
TOWARD THE AUDIENCE

Ethical systems are constructed by human beings. They are not hereditary. Consequently, they must be learned by each succeeding generation. A person who has learned society's ethical system must then choose to accept it or to reject it. If one chooses to accept it, one is called ethical. If one chooses to reject it, one is called unethical. The important consideration here is that a person must have learned the system before being said to act either ethically or unethically. A person who has not learned the ethical system of the society in which he or she lives is neither ethical nor unethical. A person should not be considered unethical for committing what we consider to be a moral wrong if the person is not consciously aware that it is wrong. This principle is recognized by our legal system. If a man is insane and kills a neighbor, he is hospitalized. But if he is sane and commits that act, he is either imprisoned or executed. *Ethics, therefore, is a matter of the conscious choices a person makes.* A person must consciously choose to do wrong before we can condemn him or her on ethical and moral grounds.

We must be extremely careful not to brand a person as unethical or immoral simply because the person commits an act that we consider unethical or immoral. A person who is not aware that behavior is considered to be an immoral act cannot have chosen to do wrong. Similarly, we should not call a person ethical or moral simply because the person does what we consider to be an ethical or moral act. If he or she does not know it is a moral act, he or she cannot have chosen to do right. If we violate this principle, the real usefulness of an ethical system is lost. A person may commit an act on the basis of stupidity, accident, or conscious moral choice. If we evaluate all acts as if they were determined on the basis of conscious moral choice, our evaluation becomes meaningless. Let us apply this concept to some specific examples.

One good end that is almost universally accepted in Western society is saving another person's life. Thus, when a man throws himself on a hand grenade to save his buddies, we say he has committed one of the highest moral acts. But what if this person is trying to climb out of a foxhole and slips and lands on the hand grenade? He still has saved his buddies. Has he committed a highly moral act?

We deplore lying as a means of persuasion. We consider it an immoral act. We noted that Adlai Stevenson made an untrue statement to the United Nations about the Bay of Pigs incident. But a short time after this incident, it was learned that Stevenson had not been told that the United States was involved in the invasion. Stevenson told the United Nations what was not true, but did he commit an immoral act?

The only meaningful way in which we can evaluate the ethics of a source is on the basis of intent. What constitutes good intent? In our society, good intent encompasses the desire of good for other people, what Aristotle called "good will." If the effect of the communication on the audience would be to harm the audience's best interests, it would be morally wrong to design a message consciously to achieve that harmful effect no matter what techniques were employed. If the effect on the audience would be beneficial, it would be morally right to design a message consciously to achieve that benefit. If the proposed effect on the audience would neither harm nor help its members, the conscious preparation of a message to achieve that end would be amoral—neither ethical nor unethical, but neutral.

What this suggests, then, is that *the effect of a message cannot be used as the primary means of evaluating the ethical quality of an act of communication.* Furthermore, *the means of persuasion themselves are ethically neutral.* This is not to suggest that techniques of rhetorical communication cannot be used to evil ends; they certainly can. But as Aristotle observed:

> If it is urged that an abuse of the rhetorical faculty can work great mischief, the same charge can be brought against all good things (save virtue itself), and especially against the most useful things such as strength, health, wealth, and military skill. Rightly employed, they work the greatest blessing; and wrongly employed, they work the utmost harm.[2]

Ethical judgments in rhetorical communication should be based exclusively on the intent of the source toward the audience. If the source seeks to improve the well-being of the audience through the act of communication, he or she is committing a moral act. But the source who seeks to produce harm for the audience is guilty of an immoral act. If the intended effect upon the audience is neither to improve nor to harm their well-being, the source is committing an amoral act.

ETHICS AND ETHICAL PROOF

Throughout the history of rhetorical communication there have been those who have integrated their discussion of ethics with their discussion of ethos. (Recall the discussion in Chapter 1 of Quintilian's definition of rhetorical communication as "the art of a good man speaking well.") Ethics and ethos are both very important considerations for a total understanding of rhetorical communication. Considering them together, however, has led to considerable confusion. For example, ethos was one of Aristotle's three modes of proof.

The term *ethical proof* has been used to describe what Aristotle discussed under the heading of ethos. This is an unfortunate use of the term, because it obscures the true meaning of Aristotle's concept of ethos. Certainly if you are perceived by the audience to be a good person, your persuasiveness will be enhanced by your ethos. As noted in Chapter 5, however, there are many other elements that contribute to a source's ethos, including a source's competence on the topic, appearance, delivery, and use of supporting materials. The application of the term *ethical proof* to these elements is unfortunate. As you come across this term in readings about rhetorical communication, you should keep in mind that ethical proof has little to do with ethics. It is really ethos misnamed.

PERSUASION AND COERCION

In many cases a person desiring to influence the thoughts or actions of other people will have at her or his disposal the power to force the other people to do as he or she wishes. The availability of this force, or coercive power, presents a major ethical problem. It is not, however, a problem of rhetorical communication. Rather, it is a choice for the person to decide whether he or she wishes to be a rhetorical communicator. The use of force is not a technique of rhetorical communication. Rhetorical communication presupposes freedom of choice on the part of an audience to assent to, or dissent from, the view taken by the source or the action recommended by the source. *Whenever we exercise our coercive power over an audience to gain acceptance of an idea or to get the audience to act in a certain way, we are not indulging in rhetorical communication.*

Coercion is often thought to be an immoral act. If it always were, a person's choice regarding its use would be simple. One should never choose to be a coercive agent. However, coercion is not always evil. In some cases it is used to achieve a very desirable end. If a mob is coming up the street approaching someone's home, and a group of police officers stops it by pointing guns and saying, "Stop or we will shoot," this can only describe as "good coercion." In some cases, similarly, we must choose coercion over rhetorical communication on purely pragmatic grounds. Why do students take final examinations? Is it because they have been persuaded that this is a desirable thing for them to do? Hardly. They are coerced by the academic system in which they are enrolled. It might be possible to persuade them to take the exam, but this would be an excessively time-consuming, and probably unsuccessful, effort. Thus, the only expedient way to accomplish the necessary end is to exert coercive power.

Rhetorical communication and coercion are separate and distinct means of achieving what may be the same ends. Although we cannot universally condemn coercion on ethical grounds, rhetorical communication normally should be preferred to coercion. The exercise of coercion tends to reduce the later usefulness of the techniques of rhetorical communication. If you once coerce an individual, the person tends to lose respect for you and to replace that respect with fear. Thus, for purely pragmatic reasons, rhetorical communication is to be preferred over coercion in most cases.

AMORAL VERSUS MORAL APPROACHES TO THE ETHICS OF RHETORICAL COMMUNICATION

The view of the ethics of rhetorical techniques set forth here is an *amoral* one. Ethical evaluations in rhetorical communication must refer to the source rather than to the act of communication. The foundation for a source's ethical evaluation is his or her intent toward the audience; it is not the techniques used to accomplish the intent nor the effect that the source actually has. The same techniques may be employed by sources with vastly different intentions toward their audiences. Thus, an audience's meaningful ethical evaluations of a source must always apply to the intent of the source rather than to what he or she says or how it is said.

This basically amoral view of the ethics of rhetorical communication techniques is not universally accepted. Some people prefer to make ethical evaluations of the techniques used by a source rather than of the intent of the source. But even among people who do agree with my position, there is considerable variation in applying this view.

The amoral view leads to the conclusion that everyone should be allowed to speak and to be as fully trained in the art of rhetorical communication as possible; the moral view leads to the conclusion that only good people should be allowed to speak or to be fully trained in the art of rhetorical communication. Naturally, people holding the moral view reserve for *themselves* the right to determine who is a good person!

The Essence of Free Speech

Choosing a moral or an amoral view of the ethics of rhetorical techniques has a major effect upon how one views the desirability of free speech. The founders of the Constitution of the United States subscribed to the amoral view and decreed that every person should have the right to free speech. These men believed that if people had the opportunity to hear all sides of a question, they would, in most cases, draw correct conclusions. They were not unaware of all the factors that contribute to a decision a person makes, but they had faith in the basic rationality of human beings. Aristotle also took this position. When setting forth the values of rhetoric, Aristotle said that rhetoric is valuable, first because truth and justice are by nature more powerful than their opposites; so that, when decisions are not made as they should be, the speakers with the right on their side have only themselves to thank for the outcome. Their neglect of the art needs correction.[3]

This view of the rationality of human beings and of the potent persuasive force of truth and justice permits exercise of an amoral view of the ethics of rhetorical communication and, consequently, an acceptance of the concept of free speech. If we do not assume the basic rationality of humans, the moral view of the ethics of rhetorical communication may be more appropriate. If people are not basically rational, free speech may be dangerous; it must be controlled so that people will not be led to accept evil. Such control of free speech, of course, would necessitate having in control persons who know what is good and what is evil, and who are able to permit the advocacy of good, and to prohibit encouragement of evil. This type of control over free speech is the cornerstone of the governments of many countries but is forbidden by the Constitution of the United States.

The Advocate System

The advocate system is central to the American concept of justice. An important characteristic of this system is that every person is entitled to an effective spokesperson on his or her behalf in a court of law. Under the advocate system the techniques of rhetorical communication in a court of law are amoral. We do, of course, exercise some rules, such as those against perjury. But the basic concept is that, whether innocent or guilty of a charge, a person is entitled to effective defense on the part of a skilled rhetorical communicator. We believe that "truth and justice are by their nature more powerful than their opposites," and that if an innocent person is found guilty or a guilty person is found innocent the losing lawyer's "neglect of the art needs correction" (Aristotle, *Rhetoric*). While famous trials frequently test the strength of our belief in these principles, they have survived throughout the history of this nation.

Ghostwriting of Messages
for Rhetorical Communication

It is a common practice in both politics and business to employ a "ghostwriter"— a skilled communicator—to prepare a message for the source to present. Much has been written about the ethics of this practice. Many people hold that it is an unethical practice because it makes a source appear better than he or she really is. Actually, this practice is no more unethical than hiring a lawyer to represent one in a court of law. Both are amoral practices.

If one is unskilled in the art of rhetorical communication or must speak so regularly that there is no time to prepare one's own messages,

using a ghostwriter is almost essential. For example, a state governor who is seeking nomination for the presidency will be required to speak almost daily and in all parts of the country. A person cannot prepare all these speeches and still have time to run a state. Using the ghostwriter, then, is not only amoral, but in some cases essential.

The Totalitarian Ethic versus the Democratic Ethic

Totalitarian governments subscribe to the moral ethic of rhetorical communication. They reserve for themselves the right to determine what is a desirable end and what is a desirable means to that end. They systematically prohibit the exercise of communication for other ends or by other than approved means. Democratic governments subscribe to the amoral ethic of communication. They assume that the people should have the right to choose between what they consider right and wrong. They systematically encourage free speech and avoid proscribing either the end that may be sought or the means that may be employed.

An interesting "public-service" advertisement appeared on television occasionally for many years extolling the virtues of advertising itself. It said, in essence, that, in a totalitarian society the government chooses what is right for the individual, but in a democratic society, the individual chooses for herself or himself. Then the announcer asks, "Which country has advertising?" The point is well made. We may criticize advertising and find much of it employing techniques that we as individuals find reprehensible. But in a democratic society we are willing to tolerate it.

It would be easy to conclude, at this point, that totalitarian societies always prohibit free speech and that democratic societies always encourage free speech. Unfortunately, this is not wholly true. All societies restrict free speech. The main distinction between the totalitarian and the democratic society in their control of free speech is the means used. Totalitarian societies restrict free speech by law and coercion. Democratic societies restrict free speech primarily through social pressure. One who speaks for segregation in certain parts of the nation, for example, is not prohibited by law from doing so; one simply loses one's job! Such societal pressure can be just as effective in eliminating free speech as can a governmental edict. A person or group that exercises such societal pressure in order to eliminate free speech is employing the totalitarian ethic, although using a means different from that used by most totalitarian governments.

In some cases, a majority in a democratic society subscribe to the totalitarian ethic. The McCarthy era in the United States (the early 1950s) found the majority of people exercising societal pressure against free speech. During the Vietnam War there was much societal pressure against free speech. People opposed to the Vietnam War were branded by many as Communists. This effectively silenced many people who would have spoken against the war. But some of those who were against the war also exercised societal pressure against free speech. In some cases, their methods were almost as extreme as those to be found in a totalitarian society. They caused such disturbances at meetings where spokespersons for the government's position appeared that the speakers were unable to address the audience.

In the 1990s we saw a neo-McCarthyism arising on most college and university campuses in the form of demands for "political correctness" of speech both inside and outside the classroom. People who dared to question the policies used to establish "equal opportunity" or "affirmative action" that functionally discriminate against whites or males were loudly branded as racists or sexists and threatened with expulsion or termination, depending on their status as student or professor. In some places these threats actually were carried out. Those advocating such actions are employing the totalitarian ethic, for it is clear, at least in their solidly closed moral minds, they know what is right and the people who don't agree should be silenced and purged from the learning community. I have carefully "cleansed" this book to avoid such bigoted pressure, but I am quite sure some people can and will find something included here not to be politically correct. Even discussing this issue in a textbook is considered inappropriate by some extremists.

Each of us must make a personal choice. We have to decide whether we are going to subscribe to the totalitarian moral ethic or to the democratic amoral ethic. We should choose the democratic ethic. If we do, we must be constantly on guard against the totalitarian ethic, as exercised by ourselves as well as by other people. The only way to guarantee free speech for ourselves is to guarantee it for everyone.

ETHICAL OBLIGATIONS IN A FREE SOCIETY

The preceding discussion laid down very few guidelines for ethical practice with regard to rhetorical communication. This book takes an amoral view, holding that everything depends upon the intent of the source. The belief expressed in this chapter is that the techniques in themselves are amoral, placing judgment about the ethics of rhetorical communication squarely on the shoulders of the communicator. Each of us, then, must evaluate our own rhetorical communication on the basis of our intent toward our audience. This is our first ethical obligation in a free society.

There are four additional ethical obligations for a person in a free society: to speak, to speak well, not to speak, and to listen.

1. To speak. Each member of a free society has an obligation to speak. Whenever you sincerely believe that you know what is right, it is your ethical obligation to stand up for it. When you see injustice or wrong being perpetrated upon other individuals, it is your obligation to speak out against it. People will choose truth and justice only when these are offered to them. If only the opposite is being proposed, truth and justice cannot win. A free society demands that we speak out in favor of what we believe is true and right.

2. To speak well. Merely to speak in favor of what is right is not enough. We are obligated, as members of a free society, to use all our power to persuade, to see that truth and justice do win out over their opposites. There is no place in a free society for tokenism. The person who has had the opportunity to learn to speak well and to be an eloquent spokesperson for truth and justice, but has not developed the ability, has not lived up to her or his ethical obligation in a free society.

3. Not to speak. As important as it is to speak out when we believe that we know what is right, it is even more important that we do not speak when we are not reasonably sure we are right or when we are sure that we are wrong. In many cases silence is the most ethical act of communication. We must always be certain in our mind that what we advocate for acceptance by our audience is in its best interest. If we are not certain in our own mind that this is so, our ethical obligation is to remain silent.

4. To listen. Although a sizable portion of our learning comes from our experience, the overwhelming majority of our learning is based upon the speaking and writing of others. If we refuse to listen to, or to read, a wide variety of views on a question, we will most likely make less than intelligent decisions. As a result we may inadvertently believe that we know what is right and choose to speak out in favor of it, thus becoming unwitting exponents of evil. In large measure, therefore, our exercise of our ethical obligation to listen will determine how useful we shall be as members of society.

THE DIFFICULTY OF EXERCISING ETHICAL OBLIGATIONS IN A FREE SOCIETY

Exercising our ethical obligations in a free society is not easy. It is difficult at best and, in some cases, dangerous to our well-being. The person who fully lives up to these ethical obligations is a truly unique and praiseworthy individual. Consider the problems facing the individual who wishes to fulfill her or his ethical obligations in a free society.

1. To speak. Most of us fail to live up to this ethical obligation. In fact, so few people fully live up to it that those who do are quite conspicuous. President John F. Kennedy wrote a book, *Profiles in Courage,* about some of these people. It chronicles the difficulties faced by a number of people who did stand up and speak out, in the face of opposition, when they believed they were right. In some cases, if we speak out in favor of what we believe is right, we may jeopardize our livelihood and that of our families. It may prevent us from achieving a goal we have set for ourselves. Most of us regularly compromise our beliefs in order to protect ourselves. When we do this, we are failing in our ethical obligation in a free society.

2. To speak well. It is easy to speak. It is difficult to speak well. To be an effective spokesperson for what is right, you must learn the techniques of rhetorical communication. You have now almost completed this book, which gives you an introduction to those techniques. It still remains for you to make the effort to learn these techniques fully, practice them, and amass experience in utilizing them. But even after you have achieved the capability of an effective spokesperson, you still will not meet your ethical obligation in a free society unless you bring all these abilities to bear when you speak for what you believe is right. Anything less than this is a violation of your ethical obligation in a free society.

3. Not to speak. One of the most difficult obligations to meet is the obligation not to speak. If we are not certain that what we propose is in the best interest of our audience, we should refrain from speaking. However, our self-interest motivates us in many cases to speak anyhow. Often, our good is not consistent with the good of others. For example, the salesman who is marketing a $500 vacuum cleaner must sell it in order to make a living. Should he sell it to a family that has a monthly income of only $350? Is it in the best interest of such a family to purchase a $500 vacuum cleaner? Most of us probably would agree that it is not. However, it probably will not be difficult for the salesman to convince himself that it is in his client's best interest. If he does, he fails to live up to this ethical obligation in a free society.

4. To listen. Chapter 4 discussed many of the problems that confront a rhetorical communicator, including the problem of selective exposure. The text stated that it is natural for people to expose themselves to ideas that they already believe and to refrain from exposing themselves to conflicting ideas. There is, then, a natural psychological barrier to exercising the ethical obligation to listen. The person who wishes to live up to this ethical obligation must consciously attempt to overcome the tendency to expose herself or himself to communication selectively. The degree to which we allow selective exposure to control our listening is the degree to which we fail to meet this ethical obligation in a free society.

A FINAL WORD ON ETHICS

Taking an amoral view of the ethics of the techniques of rhetorical communication enables one to avoid specific condemnation of any individual technique. I have taken this view because I believe that it is the only one consistent with all of its implications for free speech in a democratic society. I have not meant to imply that I heartily approve of lying, distortion, misrepresentation, and so forth; I do not. I believe, however, that the art of rhetorical communication is a self-regulating art. The source who lies, distorts, and misrepresents the truth may succeed with audiences in the short term. I believe that in the long run, however, the source who makes a regular practice of such acts will be found out. The source's ethos will be lowered, and he or she will thereafter be an unsuccessful communicator. Whether the source of lies, distortions, and misrepresentations is a government or an individual, what has come to be called a *credibility gap* will eventually develop. When a credibility gap appears, the source is no longer effective with the audience. Although we should evaluate the ethics of a source only on the basis of her or his intent toward us as audience members, the primary means we rise to infer intent is the techniques the source employs. We may rightly infer that a person who regularly lies to us does not have our best interests at heart. We will naturally lower our evaluation of such a person, and we should in most instances.

In a totalitarian society, with its moral view of the ethics of rhetorical communication, the problems of choice for the individual are small; one simply does what one is told and nothing more. For you as an individual in a free society, however, the ethics of rhetorical communication present several very serious problems. You must determine on your own whether to speak out in favor of an idea or program. You must determine for yourself whether you will take the necessary time and effort to learn to be an effective rhetorical communicator and to practice this art. You will have to choose on your own whether your self-interest is more important than the interests of your audience. You will have to determine on your own whether you will expose yourself to conflicting views on a variety of questions. And you are left to determine independently whether your intent toward an audience is ethical or not. Exercising the ethical obligations of a free person in a free society is difficult. But who ever said that things that are of value come easily?

DISCUSSION QUESTIONS

1. Many people believe that the art of rhetorical communication is an amoral art. Do you agree? Why, or why not?

2. Do you agree with the intent-centered ethic of rhetorical communication presented in this chapter? Why, or why not?

3. Under what circumstances, if any, is coercion ethically superior to rhetorical communication?

4. Should an avowed racist be permitted to speak on a college campus? Why, or why not? At a high school? Why, or why not?

5. Should a professor at a university be permitted to express her or his opposition to affirmative action on the campus? In the classroom? Away from campus? In the community? Why, or why not?

6. If you were offered one dollar, would you write a speech for a person with whom you disagreed? Why, or why not? What if you were offered $10? $100? $1000?

7. Do we have any ethical obligations as rhetorical communicators in a free society in addition to those discussed in this chapter?

8. Read the speech by Charlton Heston in Appendix A. What implications do his comments have for ethical decisions?

NOTES

1. J. C. Nunnally and H. M. Bobrien, "Attitude Change in False Information," *Public Opinion Quarterly* 23 (1959): 260–67.
2. L. Cooper, trans., *The Rhetoric of Aristotle* (Englewood Cliffs, NJ: Prentice-Hall, 1960), p. 6.
3. Ibid.

SAMPLE SPEECHES

This appendix presents transcripts of six speeches. They have been selected to show a wide range of subject matter, political position, style, and general quality. Most of them were delivered from manuscript. Each speech illustrates characteristics of both effective and ineffective rhetorical communication. In total effect, the author would classify all of these speeches as good. How would you classify them?

Read and study these speeches with the theories discussed in the body of this book in mind. Evaluate them in terms of their probable (or actual) effect on the audiences to which they were addressed. Determine how, with your understanding of rhetorical communication, you could improve them. Evaluate the speeches on the basis of your ethical system. Determine how you would change them, if you would, in order to make them ethically more acceptable to you.

DECLARATION OF WAR ADDRESS*
FRANKLIN DELANO ROOSEVELT

Yesterday, December 7, 1941—a date which will live in infamy—the United States of America was suddenly and deliberately attacked by naval and air forces of the Empire of Japan.

The United States was at peace with that nation and, at the solicitation of Japan, was still in conversation with its government and its Emperor, looking toward the maintenance of peace in the Pacific. Indeed, one hour after Japanese air squadrons had commenced bombing in Oahu, the Japanese ambassador to the United States and his colleague delivered to the Secretary of State a formal reply to a recent American message. While this reply stated that it seemed useless to continue the existing diplomatic negotiations, it contained no threat or hint of war or armed attack.

*Delivered before a joint session of the United States Congress, December 8, 1941.

It will be recorded that the distance of Hawaii from Japan makes it obvious that the attack was deliberately planned many days or even weeks ago. During the intervening time the Japanese government has deliberately sought to deceive the United States by false statements and expressions of hope for continued peace.

The attack yesterday on the Hawaiian Islands has caused severe damage to American naval and military forces. Very many American lives have been lost. In addition American ships have been reported torpedoed on the high seas between San Francisco and Honolulu.

Yesterday the Japanese government also launched an attack against Malaya.

Last night Japanese forces attacked Hong Kong.
Last night Japanese forces attacked Guam.
Last night Japanese forces attacked the Philippine Islands.
Last night Japanese forces attacked Wake Island.
This morning the Japanese attacked Midway Island.

Japan has, therefore, undertaken a surprise offensive extending throughout the Pacific area. The facts of yesterday speak for themselves. The people of the United States have already formed their opinions and well understand the implications to the very life and safety of our nation.

As Commander-in-Chief of the Army and Navy, I have directed that all measures be taken for our defense.

Always we will remember the character of the onslaught against us.

No matter how long it may take us to overcome this premeditated invasion, the American people in their righteous might will win through to absolute victory.

I believe I interpret the will of the Congress and of the people when I assert that we will not only defend ourselves to the uttermost but will make very certain that this form of treachery shall never endanger us again.

Hostilities exist. There is no blinking at the fact that our people, our territory, and our interests are in grave danger.

With confidence in our armed forces—with the unbounding determination of our people—we will gain the inevitable triumph—so help us God.

I ask that the Congress declare that since the unprovoked and dastardly attack by Japan on Sunday, December 7th, a state of war has existed between the United States and the Japanese Empire.

INAUGURAL ADDRESS*
JOHN F. KENNEDY

My Fellow Citizens: We observe today not a victory of party but a celebration of freedom—symbolizing an end as well as a beginning—signifying renewal as well as change. For I have sworn before you and almighty God the same solemn oath our forebearers prescribed nearly a century and three-quarters ago.

The world is very different now. For man holds in his mortal hands the power to abolish all forms of human poverty and all forms of human life. And yet the same revolutionary beliefs for which our forbearers fought are still at issue around the globe—the belief that the rights of man come not from the generosity of the state but from the hand of God.

We dare not forget today that we are the heirs of that first revolution. Let the word go forth from this time and place, to friend and foe alike, that the torch has been passed to a new generation of Americans—born in this century, tempered by war, disciplined by a hard and bitter peace, proud of our ancient heritage—and unwilling to witness or permit the slow undoing of those human rights to which this nation has always been committed and to which we are committed today at home and around the world.

Let every nation know, whether it wishes us well or ill, that we shall pay any price, bear any burden, meet any hardship, support any friend, oppose any foe in order to assure the survival and success of liberty.

This much we pledge—and more.

To those old allies whose cultural and spiritual origins we share, we pledge the loyalty of faithful friends. United, there is little we cannot do in a host of cooperative ventures. Divided, there is little we can do—for we dare not meet a powerful challenge at odds and split asunder.

To those new states whom we welcome to the ranks of the free, we pledge our word that one form of colonial control shall not have passed away merely to be replaced by a far more iron tyranny. We shall not always expect to find them supporting our view. But we shall always hope to find them strongly supporting their own freedom—and to remember that, in the past, those who foolishly sought power by riding the back of the tiger ended up inside.

To those peoples in the huts and villages of half the globe struggling to break the bonds of mass misery, we pledge our best efforts to help them help themselves, for whatever period is required—not because the communists

*Delivered at the Presidential Inauguration Ceremony, January 20, 1961.

may be doing it, not because we seek their votes, but because it is right. If a free society cannot help the many who are poor, it cannot save the few who are rich.

To our sister republics south of our border, we offer a special pledge—to convert our good words into good deeds—in a new alliance for progress—to assist free men and free governments in casting off the chains of poverty. But this peaceful revolution of hope cannot become the prey of hostile powers. Let all our neighbors know that we shall join with them to oppose aggression or subversion anywhere in the Americas. And let every other power know that this Hemisphere intends to remain the master of its own house.

To that world assembly of sovereign states, the United Nations, our last best hope in an age where the instruments of war have far outpaced the instruments of peace, we renew our pledge of support—to prevent it from becoming merely a forum for inventive—to strengthen its shield of the new and the weak—and to enlarge the area in which its writ may run.

Finally, to those nations who would make themselves our adversary, we offer not a pledge but a request: that both sides begin anew the quest for peace before the dark powers of destruction unleashed by science engulf all humanity in planned or accidental self-destruction.

We dare not tempt them with weakness. For only when our arms are sufficient beyond doubt can we be certain beyond doubt that they will never be employed.

But neither can two great and powerful groups of nations take comfort from our present course—both sides overburdened by the cost of modern weapons, both rightly alarmed by the steady spread of the deadly atom, yet both racing to alter that uncertain balance of terror that stays the hand of mankind's final war.

So let us begin anew—remembering on both sides that civility is not a sign of weakness, and sincerity is always subject to proof. Let us never negotiate out of fear. But let us never fear to negotiate.

Let both sides explore what problems unite us instead of belaboring these problems which divide us.

Let both sides, for the first time, formulate serious and precise proposals for the inspection and control of arms—and bring the absolute power to destroy other nations under the absolute control of all nations.

Let both sides join to invoke the wonders of science instead of its terrors. Together let us explore the stars, conquer the deserts, eradicate disease, tap the ocean depths, and encourage the arts and commerce.

Let both sides unite to heed in all corners of the earth the command of Isaiah—to "undo the heavy burdens . . . [and] let the oppressed go free."

And if a beach-head of cooperation may push back the jungles of suspicion, let both sides join in creating a new endeavor, not a new balance of power, but a new world of law, where the strong are just and the weak secure and the peace preserved.

All this will not be finished in the first one hundred days. Nor will it be finished in the first one thousand days, nor in the life of this Administration, nor even perhaps in our lifetime on this planet. But let us begin.

In your hands, my fellow citizens, more than mine, will rest the final success or failure of our course. Since this country was founded, each generation of Americans has been summoned to give testimony to its national loyalty. The graves of young Americans who answered the call to service surround the globe.

Now the trumpet summons us again—not as a call to bear arms, tho arms we need—not as a call to battle, tho embattled we are—but a call to bear the burden of a long twilight struggle, year in and year out "rejoicing in hope, patient in tribulation"—a struggle against the common enemies of man: tyranny, poverty, disease, and war itself.

Can we forge against these enemies a grand and global alliance, North and South, East and West, that can assure a more fruitful life for all mankind? Will you join in that historic effort?

In the long history of the world, only a few generations have been granted the role of defending freedom in its hour of maximum danger. I do not shrink from this responsibility—I welcome it. I do not believe that any of us would exchange places with any other people or any other generation. The energy, the faith, and the devotion which we bring to this endeavor will light our country and all who serve it—and the glow from that fire can truly light the world.

And so, my fellow Americans: Ask not what your country can do for you—ask what you can do for your country.

Finally, whether you are citizens of America or citizens of the world, ask of us here the same high standards of strength and sacrifice which we ask of you. With a good conscience our only sure reward, with history the final judge of our deeds, let us go forth to lead the land we love, asking His blessing and His help, but knowing that here on earth God's work must truly be our own.

THE PROPOSED BASKETBALL RULE CHANGES*

How many of you watched some of the games played in the recent NCAA men's basketball play-offs? Did you enjoy the games? Do you think they could be better?

Several major coaches and athletic directors believe that the game of men's basketball can be substantially improved by changing some of the rules that apply to fouls near the end of the game. They have a proposal for rule changes which will be considered at the next convention of the NCAA.

*This speech was presented by a student in a public-speaking class who prefers to remain anonymous. It is printed with the student's permission.

It is too early to be sure whether the proposal will pass, but at least it will be considered. I am not certain whether I think the proposal is a good idea or not. Although I played on my high-school team, I have not played basketball at the college level. As a confirmed spectator, however, I think it is important for those of us who enjoy the game to know how it might change if the new proposal is adopted. My purpose this morning is to outline the proposed changes and indicate what effects they might have. I'll leave it to you to decide whether you like them or not.

To best understand the new rules that are proposed, we need first to understand the present rules. There are three rules that we must consider.

First, the present rule says that a player is awarded two free-throws when fouled in the act of shooting unless the basket is made. In that case, the basket counts and the player is awarded one free-throw.

Second, for the first six fouls on a team each half, no free-throws are awarded unless the player is fouled while shooting. The team fouled is awarded the ball out-of-bounds. For all non-shooting fouls after the sixth foul on a team, the fouled player is awarded one free-throw. If he makes that one, he is awarded a second free-throw. This is referred to as the "bonus" rule or the "one and one" rule.

Finally, anytime a referee judges that a player has been fouled intentionally, whether shooting or not, the fouled player is awarded two free-throws. If such an intentional foul is particularly serious, such as if one player punches another, the referee can also call a technical foul which gives the offended team one additional free-throw. The player who committed the foul can also be thrown out the game.

The new rules would apply only the last four minutes of the game. They are designed for only one purpose: to prevent excessive fouling near the end of the game when the score is close. Proponents of the changes argue that currently too many games end with a constant procession of players to the free-throw line and that the outcome of games has become overly dependent on a team's ability to shoot free-throws in comparison with other basketball skills. They also argue that officials are reluctant to call intentional fouls, even though they are fully aware that they are intentional, and the chance of injury to players is very high as a result.

There are two new rules that will be considered. First, all players fouled during the last four minutes of the game will be awarded two free-throws. Second, the team of the fouled player will be awarded the ball out-of-bounds after the free-throws have been shot.

The primary effect of these new rules would be to take away any possible advantage a team which is behind in the score could have for intentionally fouling the opposition. Presently, the team behind may foul in the hopes that the opponent will miss the free-throw and they can get the rebound.

Several years ago North Carolina State did this and succeeded in overcoming the University of Houston's lead and winning the national championship. Supporters of the rule changes argue that such a strategy should not be allowed. They suggest that no one should ever be allowed to win by breaking the rules. Opponents, on the other hand, argue that NC State did not break the rules, they simply used them to their advantage. The opponents argue that the game of men's basketball is more popular than ever before and that it does not need change. Further, they argue, with these new rules teams would be encouraged to stall the last four minutes if they are ahead; and, they say, nothing is worse to watch than "stall ball."

Frankly, I do not know who is right. I suppose using a time clock as is done in women's basketball could overcome the stalling problem, but whether the game would be better under the proposed rules than it is now is a matter for players, coaches, and fans to argue about for the next few months. I hope I have been able to help you understand what all that argument will be about.

REMARKS AT A CEREMONY COMMEMORATING THE 50TH ANNIVERSARY OF PEARL HARBOR*
GEORGE BUSH

Thank you, Captain Ross. Thank you, sir. To our Secretary of Defense and our Chairman of our Joint Chiefs; members of our Cabinet; distinguished Governors here; and so many Members of the United States Congress; Admiral Larson; members of our Armed Forces, then and now; family and friends of the *Arizona* and *Utah;* fellow veterans. Thank you very much for that introduction, Don, and thank you all for that welcome.

It was a bright Sunday morning. Thousands of troops slept soundly in their bunks. Some who were awake looked out and savored the still and tranquil harbor.

And on the stern of the U.S.S. *Nevada,* a brass band prepared to play "The Star Spangled Banner." On other ships, sailors readied for the 8 a.m. flag raising. Ray Emory, who was on the *Honolulu,* read the morning newspaper. Aboard *California,* yeoman Durell Connor wrapped Christmas presents. On the *West Virginia,* a machinist's mate looked at the photos just received from his wife. And they were of his 8-month-old son whom he had never seen.

---

*The President spoke at 8:10 a.m., December 7, 1991, from the U.S.S. *Arizona* Memorial at Pearl Harbor, Hawaii. He was introduced by Captain Donald K. Ross, retired U.S. Navy, a surviving, crewmember of the U.S.S. *Nevada* and Congressional Medal of Honor recipient. During his remarks, the President referred to Admiral Charles Larson, Commander in Chief, U.S. Pacific Command. Following his remarks, the President met with survivors of the Pearl Harbor attack.

On the mainland, people listened to the football games on the radio, turned to songs like the "Chattanooga Choo-Choo," comics like "Terry and the Pirates," movies like "Sergeant York." In New York, families went window-shopping. Out West, it was late morning, many families still at church.

At first, to the American sailors at Pearl, the hum of engines sounded routine, and why not? To them, the idea of war seemed palpable but remote. And then, in one horrible instant, they froze in disbelief. The abstract threat was suddenly real.

But these men did not panic. They raced to their stations, and some strapped pistols over pajamas, and fought and died. And what lived was the shock wave that soon swept across America, forever immortalizing December 7th, 1941. Ask anyone who endured that awful Sunday. Each felt like the writer who observed: "Life is never again as it was before anyone you love has died; never so innocent, never so gentle, never so pliant to your will."

Today we honor those who gave their lives at this place, half a century ago. Their names were Bertie and Gomez and Dougherty and Granger. And they came from Idaho and Mississippi, the sweeping farmland of Ohio. And they were of all races and colors, native-born and foreign-born. And most of all, of course, they were Americans.

Think of how it was for these heroes of the Harbor, men who were also husbands, fathers, brothers, sons. Imagine the chaos of guns and smoke, flaming water, and ghastly carnage. Two thousand, four hundred and three Americans gave their lives. But in this haunting place, they live forever in our memory, reminding us gently, selflessly, like chimes in the distant night.

Every 15 seconds a drop of oil still rises from the *Arizona* and drifts to the surface. As it spreads across the water, we recall the ancient poet: "In our sleep, pain that cannot forget falls drop by drop upon the heart, and in our own despair against our will comes wisdom through the awful grace of God." With each drop, it is as though God Himself were crying. He cries, as we do, for the living and the dead: men like Commander Duncan Curry, firing a .45 at an attacking plane as tears streamed down his face.

We remember machinist's mate Robert Scott, who ran the air compressors powering the guns aboard *California*. And when the compartment flooded, the crew evacuated; Scott refused. "This is my station," he said, "I'm going to stay as long as the guns are going." And nearby, aboard *New Orleans*, the cruiser, Chaplain Forgy assured his troops it was all right to miss church that day. His words became legend: "You can praise the Lord and pass the ammunition."

Captain Ross, right here, then a warrant officer or was it a chief, was awarded the Congressional Medal of Honor for his heroism aboard *Nevada* that day. I salute him, the other Congressional Medal winners with us today, wherever they may be also.

For the defenders of Pearl, heroism came as naturally as breath. They reacted instinctively by rushing to their posts. They knew as well that our Nation would be sustained by the nobility of its cause.

So did Americans of Japanese ancestry who came by the hundreds to give wounded Americans blood, and the thousands of their kinsmen all across America who took up arms for their country. Every American believed in the cause.

The men I speak of would be embarrassed to be called heroes. Instead, they would tell you, probably with defiance: "Foes can sink American ships, but not the American spirit. They may kill us, but never the ideals that made us proud to serve."

Talk to those who survived to fight another day. They would repeat the Navy hymn that Barbara and I sing every Sunday in the lovely little chapel up at Camp David: "Eternal Father, strong to save, Whose arm hath bound the restless wave . . . O hear us when we cry to Thee, For those in peril on the sea."

Back in 1942, June of '42, I remember how Henry Stimson, the Secretary of War, defined the American soldier, and how that soldier should be, and I quote: "Brave without being brutal, self-confident without boasting, being part of an irresistible might without losing faith in individual liberty."

The heroes of the Harbor engraved that passage on every heart and soul. They fought for a world of peace, not war, where children's dreams speak more loudly than the brashest tyrant's guns. Because of them, this memorial lives to pass its lessons from one generation to the next, lessons as clear as this Pacific sky.

One of Pearl Harbor's lessons is that together we could "summon lightness against the dark"; that was Dwight Eisenhower. Another, that when it comes to national defense, finishing second means finishing last.

World War II also taught us that isolationism is a bankrupt notion. The world does not stop at our water's edge. And perhaps above all, that real peace, real peace, the peace that lasts, means the triumph of freedom, not merely the absence of war.

And as we look down at—Barbara and I just did—at *Arizona's* sunken hull, tomb to more than 1,000 Americans, the beguiling calm comforts us, reminds us of the might of ideals that inspire boys to die as men. Everyone who aches at their sacrifice knows America must be forever vigilant. And Americans must always remember the brave and the innocent who gave their lives to keep us free.

Each Memorial Day, not far from this spot, the heroes of Pearl Harbor are honored. Two leis are placed upon each grave by Hawaiian Boy Scouts and Girl Scouts. We must never forget that it is for them, the future, that we must apply the lessons of the past.

In Pearl Harbor's wake, we won the war and, thus, the peace. In the cold war that followed, Americans also shed their blood, but we used other means as well. For nearly half a century, patience, foresight, personal diplomacy helped America stand fast and firm for democracy.

But we've never stood alone. Beside us stood nations committed to democracy and free markets and free expression and freedom of worship, nations that include our former enemies. Germany, Italy, and Japan. This year these same nations stood with us against aggression in the Persian Gulf. You know, the war in the Gulf was so different: different enemy, different circumstances, the outcome never in doubt. It was short; thank God our casualties mercifully few. But I ask you veterans of Pearl Harbor and all Americans who remember the unity of purpose that followed that momentous December day 50 years ago: Didn't we see that same strength of national spirit when we launched Desert Storm?

The answer is a resounding "yes." Once the war for Kuwait began, we pulled together. We were united, determined, and we were confident. And when it was over, we rejoiced in exactly the same way that we did in 1945—heads high, proud, and grateful. And what a feeling. Fifty years had passed, but, let me tell you, the American spirit is as young and fresh as ever.

This unity of purpose continues to inspire us in the cause of peace among nations. In their own way, amidst the bedlam and the anguish of that awful day, the men of Pearl Harbor served that noble cause, honored it. They knew the things worth living for but also worth dying for: Principle, decency, fidelity, honor.

And so, look behind you at battleship row—behind me, the gun turret still visible, and the flag flying proudly from a truly blessed shrine.

Look into your hearts and minds: You will see boys who this day became men and men who became heroes.

Look at the water here, clear and quiet, bidding us to sum up and remember. One day, in what now seems another lifetime, it wrapped its arms around the finest sons any nation could ever have, and it carried them to a better world.

May God bless them. And may God bless America, the most wondrous land on Earth.

REMARKS TO THE WORLD HEALTH ORGANIZATION FORUM ON WOMEN AND HEALTH SECURITY*
HILLARY RODHAM CLINTON

Thank you, Dr. Nakajima.

Dr. Nakajima, Dr. Sadik, Gertude Mongella, delegates to the Fourth U.N. Conference on Women, and guests from all corners of the world, I am honored to be here this morning among women and girls from everywhere.

I commend the World Health Organization for making women's health a top priority and for establishing the Global Commission on Women's Health.

*Delivered in Beijing, China, September 5, 1995.

I am proud that in the preparatory meetings for this Fourth World Conference on Women, the United States took the lead in highlighting the importance of a comprehensive approach to women's health. That approach builds on actions taken at previous women's conferences and the recent conferences at Cairo and Copenhagen, whose goals to promote the health and well-being of all people were endorsed by 180 nations.

Cairo was particularly significant as governmental and non-governmental participants worked together to craft a Program for Action which, among other things, calls for universal access to good quality reproductive health care services, including safe, effective, voluntary family planning; greater access to education and health care; more responsibility on the part of men in sexual and reproductive health and childbearing; and reduction of wasteful resource consumption.

Here at this conference, improving girls and women's health is a priority of the draft Platform for Action. It includes such goals as:

Access to universal primary health care for all people—a goal not yet achieved in many countries, including my own.

The promotion of breast feeding.

The provision of safe drinking water and sanitation.

Research in and attention to women's health issues, including: environmental hazards, prevention of HIV/AIDS and other sexually transmitted diseases, encouragement for adolescents to postpone sexual activity and childbearing, and discouragement of cultural traditions and customs that deny food and health care to girls and women.

Goals such as these illustrate a new commitment to the well-being of girls and women and a belief in their rights to live up to their own God-given potentials.

At long last, people and their governments everywhere are beginning to understand that investing in the health of women and girls is as important to the prosperity of nations as investing in the development of open markets and trade. The health of women and girls cannot be divorced from progress on other economic and social issues.

Scientists, doctors, nurses, community leaders and women themselves are working to improve and safeguard the health of women and families all over the world. If we join together as a global community, we can lift up the health and dignity of all women and their families in the remaining years of the 20th century and on into the next millennium.

Yet, for all the promise the future holds, we also know that many barriers lie in our way. For too long, women have been denied access to health care, education, economic opportunities, legal protection and human rights—all of which are used as building blocks for a healthy and productive life.

In too many places today, the health of women and families is compromised by inadequate, inaccessible, and unaffordable medical care; lack of sanitation; unsafe drinking water; poor nutrition; insufficient research and education about women's health issues; and coercive and abusive sexual practices.

In too many places, the status of women's health is a picture of human suffering and pain. The faces in that picture are of girls and women who, but for the grace of God or the accident of birth, could be us or one of our sisters, mothers, or daughters.

Today, at least fifteen percent of pregnant women suffer life threatening complications and more than one-half million women around the world die in childbirth. Most of these deaths could be prevented with basic primary, reproductive and emergency obstetric health care. In some places, there are 175,000 motherless children for every one million families. Many of those children don't survive. And of those who do, many are recruited into a life of exploitation on the streets of our world's cities, subjected daily to abuse, indignity, disease, and the specter of early death.

There must be a renewed commitment to improving maternal health. The WHO launched in 1987 a Safe Motherhood Initiative to halve maternal mortality by the year 2000. To reach that goal, more attention must be paid to emergency medical care as well as primary prenatal care. Providing emergency obstetric care is a relatively cheap way of saving lives—and along with family planning services is among the most cost-effective interventions in even the poorest of countries.

The commitment of the WHO and its Global Commission on Women's Health to make childbearing and childbirth a safe and healthy period of every woman's life deserves action on the part of every nation represented here.

One hundred million women cannot obtain or are not using family planning services because they are poor, uneducated, or lack access to care. Twenty million of these women will seek unsafe abortions—some will die, some will be disabled for life. A growing number of unwanted pregnancies are occurring among young women, barely beyond childhood themselves. As we know, when children have children, the chance of schooling, jobs, and good health is reduced for both parent and child. And our progress as a human family takes another step back.

The Cairo document recognizes "the basic right of all couples and individuals to decide freely and responsibly the number, spacing and timing of their children and to have the information and means to do so." Women should have the right to health care that will enable them to go safely through pregnancy and childbirth and provide them with the best chance of having a healthy infant.

Women and men must also have the right to make those most intimate of all decisions free of discrimination, coercion, and violence, particularly any coercive practices that force women into abortions or sterilizations.

On these issues, the U.S. supports the provisions in the Beijing Platform for Action that reaffirm consensus language that was agreed to at the Cairo Conference about a year ago. It declared that "in no case should abortion be promoted as a method of family planning." The Platform asks governments "to strengthen their commitment to women's health, to deal with the health impact of unsafe abortion as a major public health concern and to reduce the recourse to abortion through expanded and improved family planning services."

Violence against women remains a leading cause of death among girls and women between the ages of fourteen and forty-four—violence from ethnic and religious conflicts, crime in the streets and brutality in the home. For women who survive the violence, what often awaits them is a life of unrelenting physical and emotional pain that destroys their capacity for mothering, homemaking, or working and can lead to substance abuse, and even suicide.

Violence against girls and women goes beyond the beatings, rape, killings, and forced prostitution that arise from poverty, wars, and domestic conflicts. Every day, more than 5,000 young girls are forced to endure the brutal practice of genital mutilation. The procedure is painful and life-threatening. It is degrading. And it is a violation of the physical integrity of woman's body, leaving a lifetime of physical and emotional scars.

HIV, AIDS, and sexually transmitted diseases threaten more and more women—and experts predict that by the end of this decade more than half of the people in the world with HIV will be women. AIDS, which threatens whole families and regions, demands the strongest possible response. Governments and the international community must address head-on the growing number of women who are being infected.

More than 700,000 women worldwide face breast cancer each year—over 300,000 die of it. It's the leading cause of death for women in their prime in the developed world. In the time I speak to you today, twenty-five women around the world will die of breast cancer. In my own country, it is hard to find a family, an office, or a neighborhood that has not been touched by this disease. My mother-in-law struggled against breast cancer for four years before losing her battle.

Tobacco use is the number one preventable cause of death. Ninety percent of women who smoke began to smoke as adolescents—leading to high rates of heart disease, cancer, and chronic lung disease later in life.

As the WHO points out, we also need to recognize and effectively address the fact that women are far more likely to be exposed to work-related and environmental health hazards. Policies to alleviate and eliminate such health hazards associated with work in the home and in the workplace demand action.

Research also indicates that certain communicable diseases affect women in greater numbers. Tuberculosis, for example, is responsible for the

deaths of one million women each year and those in their early and reproductive years are most vulnerable . . .

When health care systems around the world don't work for women;
when our mothers, daughters, sisters, friends, and co-workers are denied
access to quality care because they are poor, do not have health insurance,
or simply because they are women, it is not just their health that is put at
risk. It is the health of their families and communities as well.

Like many nations, the United States brings to this conference a serious commitment to improving women's health. We bring with us a series of
initiatives which represent the first steps to carrying out this Conference's
Platform for Action.

We are continuing to work for health care reform to ensure that every
citizen has access to affordable, quality care.

We are proposing a comprehensive and coordinated plan to reduce
smoking by children and adolescents by 50 percent.

We are working to address the many factors that contribute to teenage
pregnancy, our most serious social problem, by encouraging abstinence and
personal responsibility on the part of young men and women; improving
access to health care and family planning services; and supporting health
education in our schools.

We are pursuing a public policy agenda on HIV/AIDS that is specific to
women, adolescents, and children.

We are continuing to fund and conduct contraceptive research and
development.

We are addressing the health needs of women through initiatives such as:

- The National Action Plan on Breast Cancer—a public, private partner-
ship working with all agencies of government, the media, scientific
organizations, advocacy groups, and industry to advance breast health
and eradicate breast cancer as a threat to the lives of American
women.
- An Expansion of the National Breast and Cervical Cancer Early Detection Program—which will ensure that women who need regular
screening and detection services have access to them, and that those
services meet quality standards.
- The inclusion of women in clinical trials for research and testing or
drugs or other interventions that probe specific differences between
men and women in patterns of disease and reactions to therapy.
- The special health care needs of older women will be addressed
through educational campaigns about osteoporosis, cancer, and other
diseases.
- And the U.S. is conducting the largest clinical research study ever undertaken to examine the major causes of death, disability, and frailty in post-
menopausal women.

Women's health security must be a priority of all people and governments working together. Without good health, a woman's God-given potential can never be realized. And without healthy women, the world's potential can never be realized.

So let us join together to ensure that every little boy and girl that comes into our world is healthy and wanted; that every young woman has the education and economic opportunity to live a healthy life; and that every woman has access to the health care she needs throughout her life to fulfill her potential in her family, her work, and her community.

If we care about the futures of our daughters, our sons, and the generations that will follow them, we can do nothing less.

Thank you for the work you do every day to bring better health to the women, children, and families of this world.

Thank you for helping governments and citizens around the world understand that we cannot talk about equality and social development without also talking about health care.

Most of all, thank you for being part of this historic and vital discussion, which holds so much promise for our future.

WINNING THE CULTURAL WAR*
CHARLTON HESTON

I remember my son when he was five, explaining to his kindergarten class what his father did for a living. "My Daddy," he said, "pretends to be people."

There have been quite a few of them. Prophets from the Old and New Testaments, a couple of Christian saints, generals of various nationalities and different centuries, several kings, three American presidents, a French cardinal and two geniuses, including Michelangelo. If you want the ceiling re-painted I'll do my best. There always seems to be a lot of different fellows up here. I'm never sure which one of them gets to talk. Right now, I guess I'm the guy.

As I pondered our visit tonight it struck me: If my Creator gave me the gift to connect you with the hearts and minds of those great men, then I want to use that same gift now to re-connect you with your own sense of liberty . . . your own freedom of thought . . . your own compass for what is right.

Dedicating the memorial at Gettysburg, Abraham Lincoln said of America, "We are now engaged in a great Civil War, testing whether this nation or any nation so conceived and so dedicated can long endure."

Those words are true again. I believe that we are again engaged in a great civil war, a cultural war that's about to hijack your birthright to think

*Presented before the Harvard Law School Forum, February 16, 1999.

and say what resides in your heart. I fear you no longer trust the pulsing lifeblood of liberty inside you . . . the stuff that made this country rise from wilderness into the miracle that it is.

Let me back up. About a year ago I became president of the National Rifle Association, which protects the right to keep and bear arms. I ran for office, I was elected, and now I serve . . . I serve as a moving target for the media who've called me everything from "ridiculous" and "duped" to a "brain-injured, senile, crazy old man." I know . . . I'm pretty old . . . but I sure Lord ain't senile.

As I have stood in the crosshairs of those who target Second Amendment freedoms, I've realized that firearms are not the only issue. No, it's much, much bigger than that.

I've come to understand that a cultural war is raging across our land, in which, with Orwellian fervor, certain acceptable thoughts and speech are mandated.

For example, I marched for civil rights with Dr. King in 1963—long before Hollywood found it fashionable. But when I told an audience last year that white pride is just as valid as black pride or red pride or anyone else's pride, they called me a racist.

I've worked with brilliantly talented homosexuals all my life. But when I told an audience that gay rights should extend no further than your rights or my rights, I was called a homophobe.

I served in World War II against the Axis powers. But during a speech, when I drew an analogy between singling out innocent Jews and singling out innocent gun owners, I was called an anti-Semite.

Everyone I know, knows I would never raise a closed fist against my country. But when I asked an audience to oppose this cultural persecution, I was compared to Timothy McVeigh.

From *Time* magazine to friends and colleagues, they're essentially saying, "Chuck, how dare you speak your mind. You are using language not authorized for public consumption!"

But I am not afraid. If Americans believed in political correctness, we'd still be King George's boys—subjects bound to the British crown.

In his book, "The End of Sanity," Martin Gross writes that "blatantly irrational behavior is rapidly being established as the norm in almost every area of human endeavor. There seem to be new customs, new rules, new anti-intellectual theories regularly foisted on us from every direction. Underneath, the nation is roiling. Americans know something without a name is undermining the nation, turning the mind mushy when it comes to separating truth from falsehood and right from wrong. And they don't like it."

Let me read a few examples. At Antioch College in Ohio, young men seeking intimacy with a coed must get verbal permission at each step of the process from kissing to petting to final copulation . . . all clearly spelled out in a printed college directive.

In New Jersey—despite the death of several patients nationwide who had been infected by dentists who had concealed their AIDS—the state commissioner announced that health providers who are HIV-positive need not . . . need not . . . tell their patients that they are infected.

At William and Mary, students tried to change the name of the school team "The Tribe" because it was supposedly insulting to local Indians, only to learn that authentic Virginia chiefs truly like the name.

In San Francisco, city fathers passed an ordinance protecting the rights of transvestites to cross-dress on the job, and for transsexuals to have separate toilet facilities while undergoing sex change surgery.

In New York City, kids who don't speak a word of Spanish have been placed in bilingual classes to learn their three R's in Spanish solely because their last names sound Hispanic.

At the University of Pennsylvania, in a state where thousands died at Gettysburg opposing slavery, the president of that college officially set up segregated dormitory space for black students.

Yeah, I know . . . that's out of bounds now. Dr. King said "Negroes." Jimmy Baldwin and most of us on the March said "black." But it's a no-no now. For me, hyphenated identities are awkward . . . particularly "Native-American." I'm a Native American, for God's sake. I also happen to be a blood-initiated brother of the Miniconjou Sioux. On my wife's side, my grandson is a thirteenth generation native American . . . with a capital letter on "American."

Finally, just last month . . . David Howard, head of the Washington D.C. Office of Public Advocate, used the word "niggardly" while talking to colleagues about budgetary matters. Of course, "niggardly" means stingy or scanty. But within days Howard was forced to publicly apologize and resign.

As columnist Tony Snow wrote: "David Howard got fired because some people in public employ were morons who (a) didn't know the meaning of niggardly, (b) didn't know how to use a dictionary to discover the meaning, and (c) actually demanded that he apologize for their ignorance."

What does all of this mean? It means that telling us what to think has evolved into telling us what to say, so telling us what to do can't be far behind.

Before you claim to be a champion of free thought, tell me: Why did political correctness originate on America's campuses? And why do you continue to tolerate it? Why do you, who're supposed to debate ideas, surrender to their suppression?

Let's be honest. Who here thinks your professors can say what they really believe?

It scares me to death, and should scare you too, that the superstition of political correctness rules the halls of reason.

You are the best and the brightest. You, here in the fertile cradle of American academia, here in the castle of learning on the Charles River, you are the cream. But I submit that you, and your counterparts across the land, are the most socially conformed and politically silenced generation since Concord Bridge.

And as long as you validate that . . . and abide it . . . you are-by your grandfathers' standards-cowards.

Here's another example. Right now at more than one major university, Second Amendment scholars and researchers are being told to shut up about their findings or they'll lose their jobs. Why? Because their research findings would undermine big-city mayor's pending lawsuits that seek to extort hundreds of millions of dollars from firearm manufacturers.

I don't care what you think about guns. But if you are not shocked at that, I am shocked at you. Who will guard the raw material of unfettered ideas, if not you? Who will defend the core value of academia, if you supposed soldiers of free thought and expression lay down your arms and plead, "Don't shoot me."

If you talk about race, it does not make you a racist. If you see distinctions between the genders, it does not make you a sexist. If you think critically about a denomination, it does not make you anti-religion. If you accept but don't celebrate homosexuality, it does not make you a homophobe.

Don't let America's universities continue to serve as incubators for this rampant epidemic of new McCarthyism.

But what can you do? How can anyone prevail against such pervasive social subjugation?

The answer's been here all along. I learned it 36 years ago, on the steps of the Lincoln Memorial in Washington D.C., standing with Dr. Martin Luther King and two hundred thousand people.

You simply . . . disobey. Peaceably, yes. Respectfully, of course. Nonviolently, absolutely. But when told how to think or what to say or how to behave, we don't. We disobey social protocol that stifles and stigmatizes personal freedom.

I learned the awesome power of disobedience from Dr. King . . . who learned it from Gandhi, and Thoreau, and Jesus, and every other great man who led those in the right against those with the might.

Disobedience is in our DNA. We feel innate kinship with that disobedient spirit that tossed tea into Boston Harbor, that sent Thoreau to jail, that refused to sit in the back of the bus, that protested a war in Vietnam.

In that same spirit, I am asking you to disavow cultural correctness with massive disobedience of rogue authority, social directives and onerous law that weaken personal freedom.

But be careful . . . it hurts. Disobedience demands that you put yourself at risk. Dr. King stood on lots of balconies.

You must be willing to be humiliated . . . to endure the modern-day equivalent of the police dogs at Montgomery and the water cannons at Selma.

You must be willing to experience discomfort. I'm not complaining, but my own decades of social activism have taken their toll on me. Let me tell you a story.

A few years back I heard about a rapper named Ice-T who was selling a CD called "Cop Killer" celebrating ambushing and murdering police officers. It was being marketed by none other than Time/Warner, the biggest entertainment conglomerate in the world.

Police across the country were outraged. Rightfully so-at least one had been murdered. But Time/Warner was stonewalling because the CD was a cash cow for them, and the media were tiptoeing around it because the rapper was black. I heard Time/Warner had a stockholders meeting scheduled in Beverly Hills. I owned some shares at the time, so I decided to attend.

What I did there was against the advice of my family and colleagues. I asked for the floor. To a hushed room of a thousand average American stockholders, I simply read the full lyrics of "Cop Killer"-every vicious, vulgar, instructional word.

"I GOT MY 12 GAUGE SAWED OFF
I GOT MY HEADLIGHTS TURNED OFF
I'M ABOUT TO BUST SOME SHOTS OFF
I'M ABOUT TO DUST SOME COPS OFF . . ."

It got worse, a lot worse. I won't read the rest of it to you. But trust me, the room was a sea of shocked, frozen, blanched faces. The Time/Warner executives squirmed in their chairs and stared at their shoes. They hated me for that.

Then I delivered another volley of sick lyric brimming with racist filth, where Ice-T fantasizes about sodomizing two 12-year old nieces of Al and Tipper Gore.

"SHE PUSHED HER BUTT AGAINST MY . . . ."

Well, I won't do to you here what I did to them. Let's just say I left the room in echoing silence. When I read the lyrics to the waiting press corps, one of them said "We can't print that." "I know," I replied, "but Time/Warner's selling it."

Two months later, Time/Warner terminated Ice-T's contract. I'll never be offered another film by Warners, or get a good review from Time magazine. But disobedience means you must be willing to act, not just talk.

When a mugger sues his elderly victim for defending herself . . . jam the switchboard of the district attorney's office.

When your university is pressured to lower standards until 80% of the students graduate with honors . . . choke the halls of the board of regents.

When an 8-year-old boy pecks a girl's cheek on the playground and gets hauled into court for sexual harassment . . . march on that school and block its doorways.

When someone you elected is seduced by political power and betrays you . . . petition them, oust them, banish them.

When Time magazine's cover portrays millennium nuts as deranged, crazy Christians holding a cross as it did last month . . . boycott their magazine and the products it advertises.

So that this nation may long endure, I urge you to follow in the hallowed footsteps of the great disobediences of history that freed exiles, founded religions, defeated tyrants, and yes, in the hands of an aroused rabble in arms and a few great men, by God's grace, built this country.

If Dr. King were here, I think he would agree.

Thank you.

AUTHOR INDEX

■ ■ ■ ■ ■ ▬▬▬▬▬▬▬▬▬▬▬▬▬▬▬▬▬▬▬▬▬▬▬▬▬▬▬▬

SUBJECT INDEX

altruism, 80
amorality, 8–9
analogy, 114–116, 182
apportioning, 215
argument, 104–126, 190–194
arranging, 215–223
attention, 236–240
attitude, 63–82
  behavior and, 64
  beliefs and, 67–69
  change, retention of, 77–79
  characteristics of, 66–67
  consistency and change, 73–79
  defined, 64
  formation of, 69–71
  nature of, 63–67
  opinion and, 66
  persistence of, 71–73
audience adaptation, 8
audience analysis, 63, 166–169,
  194–195

behavior alteration messages, 246–248
bodily action, 281–283
boomerang effect, 76

canons of rhetoric, 24
caring. *See* goodwill
causation, 111
channel, 22–23, 169–172
chronemics, 132–134
claim, 104–105, 108–109
classification, 116–118
co-cultures, 145
coercion, 296–297
communibiology, 37, 52–53, 60
communication
  accidental, 21, 30
  defined, 20–21
  expressive, 21, 30–31
  intentional, 30
  interpersonal, 28–30

misconceptions, 31–35
models, 22–30
rhetorical, 21–22, 30–31
communication apprehension, 38–44
  defined, 40
  types, 40–44
communication breakdown, 34–35
communications, 20
competence, 85–86
concept-centered communication,
  95–96
conclusions, 262–268
consistency theories, 73–77
context, 146
control, 19
conversational quality, 275–276
credibility. *See* ethos
cultural sensitivity, 143–144
culture, 142–159
  defined, 144
culture shock, 152–153

data, 104–106, 119–123
decoding, 25–28
deduction, 116–118
deliberative speaking, 7
delivery, 91–92, 269–287
  effects of, 270–273
  elements of, 278–285
  nature of, 273
  nervousness and, 276
derived ethos, 83, 91–95
disposition, 214–231
  invention and, 224–225
distance, 131–132
diversity, 142–159

elocution, 13
encoding, 24–25
enculturation, 145–146
enthymeme, 104
epideictic speaking, 7

chapters
2, 3, 9, 10, 11, 12, 13